GOVERNMENT EDUCATION AND EXAMINATIONS IN SUNG CHINA

Government Education and Examinations in Sung China

Thomas H.C. Lee

The Chinese University Press
Hong Kong

St. Martin's Press
New York

For information, write:
St. Martin's Press, Inc., 175 Fifth Avenue, New York, NY 10010
Printed in Hong Kong
First published in the United States of America in 1985
ISBN 0-312-34131-8

Library of Congress Cataloging in Publication Data

Lee, Thomas H. C.
    Government Education and Examinations in Sung China, 960-1278

    Bibliography: p.
    Includes index.
    1. Education—China—History.   2. Civil Service—China—
Examinations—History.   3. China—History—Sung dynasty, 960-
1279.   I. Title.
LA1131.L32   1985   379.51   85-14169
ISBN 0-312-34131-8

Contents

TABLES

CHARTS

Preface

In 1978, when I first started to write this book, I had a total of thirteen parts in mind, covering three major aspects of Sung education: the organizational, the social and the intellectual. Before I hardly finished the research for the organizational aspect, I had realized that the materials for that aspect alone were enough for me to write an independent book. What is presented here is thus a partial fulfilment of my hope of a comprehensive study of Sung education.

Any one who attempts to study Sung education will immediately find that it was intertwinely related to the practice of the civil service examinations by the Sung government, in that an increasingly larger number of non-aristocratic elite children were able to enter the officialdom, thereby enjoying the largest share of the society's rewards of prestige and privileges. This is a new and significant phenomenon, and in fact was to help determine the course of development of the Chinese society in later dynasties. To me, therefore, the central concerns of a study of Sung education have to be to delineate how the examinations affected the organization of Sung's state education, how the society at large viewed the purpose of that education and how it prepared its young members for the examinations under such circumstances. It is only because of an understanding of such concerns of theirs that we come to grip with the anxiety exhibited by so many Sung intellectuals over the relapse of the moral ideal of education and how this anxiety led them to groping for an alternative, which resulted in the rise of the Neo-Confucian academies.

The history of government education is, however, significant in its own right. As I delved further into the Southern Sung sources, which, incidentally, are more scattered and hence less systematic, I became convinced that many institutional developments in the field of education in later dynasties also had origins in the Sung. In a rather peculiar way, the experiments undertaken by late Northern Sung reformers, though unsuccessful, did impress later educationalists, and some of them transmitted at least the conceptual framework of those experiments to later generations. We know a lot about Ming and Ch'ing education and civil service examinations; it is about time that we trace their imaginative, if then considered radical, origins to the Sung.

The book naturally is more than just a simple presentation of the themes I outlined above. If this book should appear to be covering too many things, it is because I find the experiences of Sung state education so immensely interesting and resourceful, that I could hardly refrain myself from occasional indulgence in some sort of pedantic exercise. Still, detailed summaries of researches, which may sometimes seem boring or pretentious, have to be reported, especially when they are studied for the first time.

In the process of putting the findings together for presentation, I found that it is fairly useful to cite individual stories to illustrate my arguments. These experiences are often rather unique and may not fit satisfactorily in a narrative that deals primarily with generalizations. However, unique experiences often reveal the most genuine of the human quality. I am sure that my readers will share the view that history is only made more meaningful when it allows human dimension in its varigated forms to be intimately appreciated.

I began my study of Sung education when I had the good fortune of working with the late Arthur F. Wright. I can never forget the days when we would sit by his backyard at the Connecticut shore overlooking Long Island Sound and talked about the education of a time and people so incredibly remote to us. But maturity has made it increasingly evident that these people were actually not as removed as they once seemed. If what is presented in this book as a result has differed somewhat from the dissertation I wrote under his direction, it only serves to show how his opinions were indeed ever so trustworthy and enlightening.

I have also profited from the insightful suggestions given to me over the years in direct conversations, correspondences or notes written to comment my manuscripts by a number of people; some of them have to be mentioned here: Wm. Theodore de Bary, Ying-shih Yü, Jonathan D. Spence, Nathan Sivin, Conrad Shirokauer, Shiba Yoshinobu, Arthur Wolf, Chi-yun Chen, John Chaffee, Ming-shih Kao, Shu-hsien Liu, James Lee, Chun-chieh Huang, Keng-wang Yen, Han-sheng Chuan and David Faure. If the interpretations in this book still do not measure up to their criticisms, it is entirely because of my obstinancy and I am solely responsible for all the errors, mistakes and shortcomings.

In the course of my researches, I received grants and awards from Harvard-Yenching Institution, the Institute of Chinese Studies of The Chinese University and Yale-China Association. To all of them, I owe my sincere thanks. Individuals involved in making the awards available, including Tien-yi Li, Te-k'un Cheng, Ching-ho Ch'en and Ambrose Y. King have to be mentioned here. Thomas Wu, a personal friend, should also be specially mentioned for his financial contribution. Without the encouragement and support of these individuals, this book would never have been completed.

Thanks are also due to the libraries of Yale, Stanford (Hoover Institution), Harvard-Yenching, Toyo Bunko and The Chinese University of Hong Kong. Their librarians have proven to be most helpful. Many of the articles not readily available here at The Chinese University libraries have been reproduced for me often from Japan by the library's staff. I am most grateful for their service.

And finally, a note of thanks to my immediate family is in order. I regret that this procedure may seem so conventional, even though the statement is most deeply felt. I have taken too long a time to finish this book. In between, Jonathan has been born and is now starting his formal education; Jennifer has also grown beyond the stage when she would come to stand in front of my chronically messy desk, asking: "Daddy, are you writing another book?" As for the sacrifices my wife has endured, I only hope that they could be compensated by the book's being published. To the sacrifices, indeed, my readers as well as this author are placed in her debt. To Nina, thus, I dedicate this book.

November 26, 1984   THOMAS H. C. LEE

Major Abbreviations

Abbreviations are used mainly in the notes, but many appear occasionally in the text and are thus listed here. Old-style Chinese books with independent pagination for each chapter (*chüan*) are noted as, for example, 16/3b, meaning the second part of the third leaf of chapter 16. Those printed with modern pagination are usually noted as, for example, 167:3394, meaning chapter 167, page 3394 of the entire pagination. Modern books are only noted by their pages. Journal articles are noted, in addition to the journal's name and pagination, volume and issue numbers, by, for example, 16/3, which means number 3 of volume 16.

AS/BIHP	Academia Sinica, *Bulletin of the Institute of History and Philology* (Chung-yang yen-chiu yüan, *Li-shih yü-yen yen-chiu so chi-k'an*).
CYYL	Li Hsin-ch'uan, *Chien-yen i-lai hsi-nien yao-lu.*
HCP	Li T'ao, *Hsü Tzu-chih t'ung-chien ch'ang-pien.*
HJAS	*Harvard Journal of Asiatic Studies.*
HTC	Pi Yüan, *Hsü Tzu-chih t'ung-chien.*
HTS	Ou-yang Hsiu, *Hsin T'ang-shu.*
JAS	*Journal of Asian Studies.*
JICS/CUHK	*Journal of the Institute of Chinese Studies, The Chinese University of Hong Kong.*
Kang-yao	Li Chih, *Huang Sung shih-ch'ao kang-yao.*
KHTS	*Kuo-hsüeh chi-pen ts'ung-shu.*
SHY	Hsü Sung (comp.), *Sung hui-yao chi-kao.*
SKCS	*Ssu-k'u ch'üan-shu.*
SPPY	*Ssu-pu pei-yao.*
SPTK	*Ssu-pu ts'ung-k'an.*
SS	T'o-t'o, *Sung-shih.*
SSYCC	Sung-shih yen-chiu hui (ed.), *Sung-shih yen-chiu chi.*
TSCC	*Ts'ung-shu chi-ch'eng.*
WHTK	Ma Tuan-lin, *Wen-hsien t'ung-k'ao.*

Part I
Introduction

It was spring, in the third year of the Ch'ien-te era (965) of the Emperor T'ai-tsu. The Sung had just conquered the State of Shu (in present Szechwan). Among the war spoils was a bronze mirrow with an inscription stating that it was cast in "the fourth year of Ch'ien-te." Puzzled by the strange coincidence in the era name, the Emperor turned to his ministers for an explanation. Tou I (914–966), then the Minister of Rites, pointed out that the conquered Shu state had used the era name before the Sung emperor adopted it. Emperor T'ai-tsu was impressed and commented that it was indeed important to appoint *"tu-shu jen"* (literally, "persons who read books") to be ministers.[1]

This was probably the first time that the phrase, *"tu-shu jen,"* was used.[2] There is a whole complement of symbolic implications in the comment, because the Sung has left the legacy of being a dynasty that awarded civil officials with preferential treatment and that civil officials, themselves generally scholars, were the most influential political force in the government. Indeed, the Sung was probably the first Chinese dynasty to staff its civil bureaucracy with so many officials recruited through the civil service examinations.

Steady progress in informal education was also evident in Sung society. Economic success made it possible to extend educational opportunities to a wider range of the population. Sung educationalists also were quick in proposing ways for transmitting official ideology to the mass polution. As a result, to understand many of the important educational practices found in later dynasties, it is always necessary to go back to study the Sung.

In the following pages, I shall summarize the main components of education, as conception as well as institution, in traditional China and discuss their relations with Sung education as a whole. I shall then give a brief account of my understanding of the salient features of Sung educational activities. In Chapter Three I shall take up the definition of education and discuss, within the context of that definition, the strength and limitation of source materials, and the significance and possibilities of a good historical study of the subject. While this book itself centers only on the study of the government's education practices and how these were

---

[1] T'o-t'o, *Sung-shih* (Peking: Chung-hua, 1977) (*SS* hereafter), 3:50. See also Pi Yüan, *Hsü Tzu-chih t'ung-chien* (Peking: Chung-hua, 1957) (*HTC* hereafter), 173:4705 for a reference to this term as late as 1250.

[2] Araki Toshikazu, *Sōdai kakyo seido kenkyū* (Kyoto: Dōhōsha, 1969) (*Kakyo* hereafter), 5.

related to the civil service, I consider that a comprehensive, if general, discussion at the outset is meaningful, if we wish to understand the full significance of state education during this formative era of early modern Chinese government education.

CHAPTER 1
Education before the Sung

A. Education and Meritocratic Ideals

For more than two millennia, the single most important intellectual force that helped to shape Chinese educational ideals and practices was Confucianism. It has always been the source for inspiration in ethical teachings; it has also been the origin of various social philosophies.

Two important principles of Confucian social thought have had the most pervasive influence on Chinese perception of a good, that is, harmonious and ordered, society: society is necessarily hierarchical, and the award of privileges should be by merit. These principles made their appearance as early as the seventh and sixth centuries B.C., when hereditary privileges started to decline. While social structure continued to be hierarchical, it became imperative to propose a general theory on how to recruit social leaders,[3] in response to the need for talented leaders in an increasingly complex society. Confucius no doubt was the first thinker to present a clear formula on which a merit-based social hierarchy could be constructed. For Confucius, those who were awarded social privilege and honor should also be morally superior. His formula consisted of four interrelated idea:

1. The government should educate everyone without class or racial distinction; all men are born with equal potential for goodness.[4]
2. The emphasis of education should be on ethical rectitude. It is possible to achieve moral perfection through education.[5]

[3] Huang Chün-chieh, *Ch'un-ch'iu Chan-kuo shih-tai shang-hsien cheng-chih te li-lun yü shih-chi (Shang-hsien cheng-chih* hereafter) (Taipei: Wen-hsüeh, 1977), 43–78.

[4] Donald Munro, *The Concept of Man in Early China (The Concept of Man* hereafter) (Stanford: Stanford University Press, 1969), 1–22.

[5] Confucius does allow that the wise of the highest class (*shang-chih*) and the stupid of the lowest class (*hsia-yü*) could not be transformed (see *Analects,* XVII, 3). Chu Hsi agrees that there are indeed irredeemable people who could not be educated. Generally, however, all people can be taught to achieve moral rectitude. For a collection of various commentaries on the *Analects,* see Ch'ien Ti-chih, *Lun-yü Han Sung chi-chieh* (Taipei: Chung-hua, 1980). See also James Legge's note on this passage in his translation (Hong Kong: Hong Kong University Press, 1960), Vol. I, 318.

3. Morally superior people should be selected for service in the government; they are the leaders of society.[6]
4. Chinese society should remain hierarchical, with the ruling class
composed mainly of the selected few who meet the moral qualifications.[7]

These principles imply that a socity, in order to keep stable, should give
the highest social rewards, including privilege, prestige and wealth, to the
talented few to whom the government and society entrust leadership.[8]

Education was not clearly assigned any place in the principles discussed
above. However, Confucian thinking on education stressed equality in man's
natural endowment for learning, especially learning good behavior.[9] The
result was an emphasis on the equal chance for every individual to be
selected, as long as he learned to behave according to the Confucian code.
This egalitarian approach gave education a new significance in that the
education of an individual became a means of his possible advancement
on the social ladder.

The relationship between a meritocratic principle stressing an equal
potential for goodness and a hierarchical principle affirming the necessity
for unequal distribution of social rewards did not immediately become
accepted by Chinese people. Mo-tzu (468–376 B.C.), for one, proposed
an egalitarian society in which the educated (*hsien*) were to be chosen to
bear social responsibilities.[10] In the long run, however, the Confucian

---

[6] Donald Munro, *The Concept of Man*, 84–116.

[7] Kung-chuan Hsiao, *A History of Chinese Political Thought*, tr. by F. W. Mote
(Princeton: Princeton University Press, 1979), Vol. I, 377–378; Donald Munro, *The
Concept of Man*, 112–116.

[8] There is not enough space in the text to discuss the specific historical circumstances
in which Confucius worked out his social ideas. Without sufficiently delineating the
context, it is easy enough to accuse Confucius of being conservative, standing in
defense of the *status quo*. In an agrarian society, such as China during Confucius' time,
where the state had grown to such a size that it demanded an elaborate bureaucracy,
and yet was comparatively backward in communication, the only way to run an effective
government was to rely on a small segment of social leaders for political and social
control. To bind these selected few to the government, a disproportionately great
amount of social rewards, especially in the form of wealth, privilege and honor, had
to be awarded to them. For the sake of stability, social inequality therefore became
inevitable. This had been Confucius' dilemma, and his proposal for unequal treatment
of different social groups seems to have succeeded in grounding the traditional Chinese
society on a relatively stable base for many hundreds of years. For a discussion on
social inequality in an agrarian society, see Gehard Lenski, *Power and Privilege* (New
York: McGraw-Hill, 1966), 295–296; for a discussion of Confucius' idea about social
equality, see Donald Munro, *The Concept of Man*, 12–14, 47–49, and passim.

[9] Munro, *The Concept of Man*, 51–58, where he names this as an "evaluating mind."

[10] Huang Chün-chieh, *Shang-hsien cheng-chih*, 100–105.

doctrine of differential treatment of people, advocating the necessity of social stratification carried the day.[11]

Mencius (372—289 B.C.) further elaborated this Confucian social ideal. While Confucius singled out moral rectitude as the virtue of the ruling class, Mencius added a more socially defined qualification: the ruling elite should be those who labor with their mind, in contrast to those who labor with their hands.[12] Mencius then argued forcefully that the innate goodness of an individual could be cultivated and that education—cultivation of the innate goodness—should become a definite part of social advancement.[13] This obviously was a clearly articulated philosophy of education; education now was looked upon as a means for social advancement.

Mencius' contemporary and intellectual opponent, Hsün-tzu (313—238 B.C.), on the other hand, believed that men were born evil, and that only education was capable of helping to correct one's bad nature.[14] He thus shared with Mencius a profound conviction that education was essential for any individual's moral perfection, as well as for his advancement into the ruling class. Hsün-tzu went further, arguing that a social hierarchy, for

[11] Mo-tzu and his followers obviously believed that it was through a pragmatic network of love and mutual profit that division of labor and social class was maintained. The utilitarian assumption that love comes from an individual's calculation for profit must necessarily lead to the conclusion that love should not imply differentiated treatments of people according to social and family relations. Instead, only undifferentiated love could guarante a maximum prospect for profit. This idea lacked a comprehensive theory for the exercise of authority; especially, when authority had to be exercised within a social and political hierarchy. Mo-tzu answered the difficulty by resorting to the will of heaven. But, evidently, this could not satisfy the need then for a well integrated society based on the bureaucratic distribution of responsibility and authority. On this point, see *ibid.*, 105. Philosophically, Mo-tzu also failed to appreciate, as Mencius later obviously did, the important aspect of love as a subjective feeling which, when applied to different people, was by nature discriminative. This point is raised by Kung-chuan Hsiao in his *History of Chinese Political Thought*, Vol. I, 234. Hsiao also shows the similarity between Mo-tzu's utilitarian philosophy and that of Jeremy Bentham.

[12] *Mencius*, IIIA, 4.

[13] Mencius regards innate goodness as natural to men and that evil originates from underdevelopment of that goodness. Self-cultivation is therefore not to "violate human nature." See *Mencius*, VIA, 1—6. See also VIIA, 4: "When in one's conduct one *vigorously exercises* altruism, humanity is not far to seek, but right by one." For more studies on Mencius' conception of human nature, see D. C. Lau, "Theories of Human Nature in *Mencius* and *Shyuntzyy*," in *Bulletin of School of Oriental and African Studies*, No. 15, Pt. 3 (1953), 541—565.

[14] Kanaya Osamu argues that Hsün-tzu, in most parts of his work, uses "human nature" in a neutral sense, and hence does not differ fundamentally in terms of educational thinking from Mencius and, thus, Confucius. See Kanaya Osamu, *Junshi* (Tokyo: Iwanami, 1962).

all of its inherent inequality, was necessary in a society that had become secularized:[15]

> When the benevolent man is in control, the farmers by their strength will be experts at the fields; the merchants by their knowledge of values will be experts at using wealth; all kinds of artisans by their skill will be experts at using tools; none of those above the grade of Officer and Prefect, up to the Duke and Marquis will fail to fulfill the duties of their office according to benevolence, generosity, wisdom and power—then this will be called the ultimate equity.

This quotation reflects the unprecedented change that Chinese society had undergone in Hsün-tzu's time, creating a social reality that made even Confucian theories looked moribund. Realist espousal for social transformation seemed inevitable, and the Legalists (*Fa-chia*) who came into being about the time when China was going through the Warring States Period (483–221 B.C.) seemed to be capable of proposing some solution.[16] Without an expectation of the moral perfectibility of the individual, the legalists chose to approach the problem of constructing a well-ordered society by proposing the establishment of a rigid but efficient bureaucracy. Amid an increasingly complicated but hierarchically structured society, this bureaucracy would effect adequate cohesion and control. The basic Confucian tenet of dividing society into the ruling and the ruled classes was maintained, but the Legalists also added a new theory of social and political control which was carefully worked out by prominent thinkers in the fourth and third centuries B.C.[17]

In actual educational thinking, however, the Legalists made no meaningful contribution, except that the meritocratic principle continued to be the fundamental tenet for selection. Since the idea that goodness could be taught continued, Legalist contribution only reinforced the belief in the basic Confucian teachings.

[15] Cited from Ping-ti Ho, *The Ladder of Success in Imperial China* (*The Ladder* hereafter) (New York: Columbia University Press, 1962), 8. Please note the important comment Ho makes in the note on p. 320, where he explains why he translates *"chih-p'ing"* as "ultimate equity" but not "ultimate equality" or "ultimate equableness." But I cannot see the significance of such a distinction. See Ch. 8, note 31.

[16] Kung-chuan Hsiao, *A History of Chinese Political Thought*, Vol. I, 386–381. See also H. G. Creel, *Shen Pu-hai* (Chicago: Univeristy of Chicago Press, 1974), 135–162, esp. 156–158 for Creel's suggestion that *fa-chia* should not be translated as "Legalist" school. For Chinese works, see Ch'en Ch'i-yu, *Han Fei tzu chi-chih* (Hong Kong: Chung-hua, 1974), 4–10; Huang Chün-chieh, *Shang-hsien cheng-chih*, 125–144; and Yang Shu-fan, "Han Fei," in Wang Shou-nan (ed.), *Chung-kuo li-tai ssu-hsiang chia* (Taipei: Shang-wu, 1977), Vol. II, 721–801 (2/1–79).

[17] See Arthur Waley, *Three Ways of Thought in Ancient China* (Garden City, N.Y.: Doubleday Anchor Books, 1956), 151–188. Note that Waley called the Legalists realists. See also note 16 above.

By the end of the third century, it had become evident that meritocratic principles associated with the strong belief that human nature was malleable and could be changed for the good, had become the established doctrine in a society which was constructed according to a hierarchical demarcation between the privileged few and the ruled. The complex of ideas surrounding the principle of selection according to educated goodness gave justification to the rise of official education as well as the much known, admired, often condemned, but seldom challenged, civil service examination system.

B. Classical Education

Formal education probably existed as early as the Shang dynasty (roughly 1850–1100 B.C.).[18] Institutionalized schooling then was most likely available only to the upper class, the aristocrats. With the rise of meritocratic ideas, formal education started to become available also to the commoners, resulting in the creation of a brilliant age of Chinese philosophy in a time of great social change. The unification that followed saw the systematic establishment of government schools; the Han dynasty (206 B.C.–A.D. 220) was particularly keen on maintaining a system of schools supported by the government.[19]

Almost from the beginning, education consisted of the study of the classics. Those more readily available works including the celebrated five, *Book of Documents* (*Shu-ching*), *Book of Poetry* (*Shih-ching*), *Book of Change* (*I-ching*), *Record of Rites* (*Li-chi*) and the *Spring and Autumn Annals* (*Ch'un-ch'iu*), became canonized during Han times. Students learned the works by heart and were convinced that these works, containing ideas derived from a variety of disparate strands of thinking, could be referred to for solving political and moral problems.[20]

The study of the classics remained the center of formal education. Even though classical learning appeared to be in a decline during the T'ang (618–907) when literary studies—poetry (*shih*) and writings in the style

[18] Yang K'uan, "Wo-kuo ku-tai ta-hsüeh te t'e-tien chi ch'i ch'i-yüan," in his *Ku-shih hsin-t'an* (Peking: Chung-hua, 1965), 197–217.

[19] For a discussion of the Han school system, see Ch'en Tung-yüan, *Chung-kuo chiao-yü shih* (*Chiao-yü shih* hereafter) (Taipei: Shang-wu, 1976), 44–107; Howard Galt, *A History of Chinese Educational Institutions* (London: A. Probsthain, 1951), 197–269; and T'ang Ch'eng-pin, "Han-tai chiao-yü chih-tu yen-chiu," in *Kuo-li Cheng-chih ta-hsüeh hsüeh-pao*, Vol. 20 (1969), 153–176.

[20] There is still no satisfactory history of classical learning. For a brief overview, see P'i Hsi-jui, *Ching-hsüeh li-shih, Kuo-hsüeh chi-pen ts'ung-shu* (*KHTS* hereafter) edition.

of *p'ien-wen*—gained prominence, the general history of Chinese formal education can be said to be a history of repeated efforts to inculcate the classical values into generations of Chinese pupils.

There is no need to try to summarize the history of the development of classical studies here. Nonetheless, a brief discussion on classical learning as a practice of formal education is necessary. First of all, before government schools became widespread, powerful or wealthy families often hired classical scholars to teach their children. In a society where the poor could not reasonably hope for even rudimentary literary training, knowledge deemed useful by the ruling class was only too naturally monopolized by the few leading erudites. Classical learning was a privilege and generally was the sole possession of the wealthy or aristocratic families.[21] The rise of the civil service examination system made it possible for more people to dare aspire to education. Even so, classical learning in general continued to be the center of educational activities.

Secondly, the tradition of classical education was marked by repeated efforts to establish or maintain the orthodoxy of a reliable text and by continual attempts to redefine the heritage. Engraving the sanctioned texts on stone tablets became the symbol of a good government,[22] but even more important was the persistent attempts by individual scholars to compile new commentaries on the classics.[23] The esteemed position of the classics lended such weight to scholars that disputes over the legitimacy of a certain school of interpretation often had serious political ramifications.[24]

Finally, in terms of actual teaching and study of the classics, it is important to note that classics as such were taught to a child almost

---

[21] For a brief discussion of private education for aristocratic children, see Ch'ien Mu, "Lüeh-lun Wei, Chin, Nan-pei ch'ao shih-tai hsüeh-shu wen-hua yü tang-shih men-ti chih kuan-hsi," in his *Chung-kuo hsüeh-shu ssu-hsiang shih lun-ts'ung*, Vol. III (Taipei: Tung-ta, 1977), 134–199. See also my "Chiang-chang i-feng: ssu-jen chiang-hsüeh te ch'uan-t'ung" ("Ssu-jen chiang-hsüeh" hereafter), in Liu Tai (ed.), *Chung-kuo wen-hua hsin-lun*, Vol. II (Taipei: Lien-ching, 1981), 343–410.

[22] See Ma Heng, *Fan-chiang chai chin-shih ts'ung-kao* (Peking: Hsin-hua, 1977), 199–260 for some studies on this problem; see especially, 211–224. See also Ch'en Tung-yüan, *Chiao-yü shih*, 108–117.

[23] For a comprehensive bibliography of known commentaries on the classics, see Chu I-tsun, *Ching-i k'ao*, 8 vols., *SPPY* ed.; there are also extensive bibliographies on individual classics such as the *Analects*, etc.

[24] See, for example, the repurcussions, which resulted from the early T'ang attempt to enforce a standard set of commentaries, discussed in Kao Ming-shih, "T'ang-tai kung-chü tui ju-hsüeh yen-chiu te ying-hsiang," in *Kuo-li pien-i kuan kuan-k'an*, Vol. 2, No. 1 (1973), 61–94.

immediately after the child had become barely literate. The easier classics, such as Confucius' *Analects* (*Lun-yü*, which was canonized much later than the five classics mentioned above, but had always been treated as an equally valuable work) were introduced for recitation sometimes when a pupil had only barely finished his primers.[25] The impression these classics made on the children must have been enormous. Students began to learn commentaries only after they were generally familiar with the classics themselves.[26] Even so, because certain commentaries received official sanction, and were made the basis of standard examination answers towards the end of the T'ang, they also exerted consistent and often permanent influence on a student's world view; his knowledge of nature and the universe, as much as his ethical convictions, often came from certain interpretations put forth by commentators. The classics and their commentaries alike occupied such an important place in the formation of the personality and knowledge of Chinese children that it is impossible to comprehend Chinese education without properly understanding the Chinese tradition of classical learning.

C. The Civil Service Examination System

The civil service examination system served as a mechanism for the practice and transmission of both the meritocratic principle and the values created by classical learning. Without the examination system, not only would the meritocratic principle have become difficult to practice, but the tradition of classical learning would also have become difficult to sustain. The recruitment of the talented into governmental service had begun in the Warring States Period, but the first instance of institutions designed for systematic selection of the qualified appeared in the second century B.C., under the Han government. Besides setting up an Imperial University (*T'ai-hsüeh*) which sons of ranking officials entered for formal education, the Han emperors also ordered recruitment of virtuous subjects for service in the government.[27] This system, evolving into a permanent, if gradually

[25] Many T'ang and Sung records show that the *Analects* was among the first books (including the *Classic of Filial Piety*) taken up by a little child just finishing reciting the standard primers. For the T'ang, see Kao Ming-shih, "T'ang-tai te ssu-hsüeh chiao-yü" ("Ssu-hsüeh" hereafter), in *Kuo-li T'ai-wan ta-hsüeh wen shih che hsüeh-pao*, No. 20 (1971), 219–289.

[26] *Ibid.*

[27] Franklin Houn, "The Civil Recruitment System of the Han Dynasty," in *Ch'ing-hua hsüeh-pao*, Vol. 1 (1956), 138–164. See also Teng Ssu-yü, *Chung-kuo k'ao-shih chih-tu shih* (Taipei: Hsüeh-sheng, 1967), 17–49.

ceremonial, institution, was called *"ch'a-chü"* system. The idea continued to serve as a basis for selecting officials throughout the Period of Disunion (220–589), although Chinese society had in reality reverted to an aristocratic selection system and had largely abandoned meritocratic ideal.[28]

No serious attempt was made to restore the *ch'a-chü* method in its original sense until China was reunited under the Sui (589–617), which introduced a rudimentary written examination system, evidently designed to carry out the ideal as embodied in the *ch'a-chü* system.[29] The examination system grew to complexity in T'ang times when questions on current national affairs and policy-making matters were introduced. This type of test, called the *chin-shih* (*belles lettre*) test, was looked upon by the T'ang people as more prestigious than those which only examined classical knowledge in terms of memorization of texts.[30]

By the eighth century, the influence of the examination system had become obvious. A new group of generally young and talented officials who obtained their status from the examinations, especially of the *chin-shih* type, became a force in the court.[31] The aristocrats, who had been on the decline for various other reasons,[32] were now confronted with fierce competition by the new members of the officialdom. Eventually new people successfully replaced the old aristocrats and became the mainstay of China's ruling class.

[28] The *chiu-p'in chung-cheng* system widely practiced during the Period of Disunion deviated significantly from the meritocratic principle. See David Johnson, *The Medieval Chinese Oligarchy* (Boulder: Westview, 1977), 19–27; Miyazaki Ichisada, *Kyūhin kannin hō no kenkyū* (Tokyo: Dōhōsha, 1977).

[29] See Ch'en Tung-yüan, *Chiao-yü shih*, 163–165, for a discussion on this matter.

[30] A false impression held by many people is that the main content of the *chin-shih* tests was poetry. This is not entirely correct. Throughout the T'ang, the policy discussion questions (*ts'e*) had always been the main portion of the tests, while poetic writings, introduced as late as 754, constituted only a minor part of the test on the *chin-shih* subject. See notes 6 and 7 of Ch. 6. See also Lo Lung-chih, *Chin-shih k'o yü T'ang-tai te wen-hsüeh yü she-hui* (Taipei: T'ai-wan ta-hsüeh, 1971).

[31] Howard Wechsler, "Factionalism in Early T'ang Government," in Arthur F. Wright and Denis C. Twitchett (eds.), *Perspectives on the T'ang* (New Haven: Yale University Press, 1973), 87–120. See also Wechsler, "T'ai-tsung the Consolidator," in Denis C. Twitchett (ed.), *Cambridge History of China*, Vol. 3, Pt. I (Cambridge: Cambridge University Press, 1979), 188–231. See especially 200–202.

[32] This is not the place to discuss the various theories held by leading T'ang experts on when and how the traditional "aristocrats" (oligarchic families) declined. My personal inclination is to agree with Twitchett who holds that "they survived remarkably well" and that "the ever-accelerating process of radical change . . . was, by the end of the tenth century, to have swept the last remnants of the old aristocratic order into final oblivion." See his "The Composition of the T'ang Ruling Class," in *Perspectives on the T'ang*, 47–86, see esp. 86.

The *chin-shih* degree-holders generally had bright career prospects in the government, certainly much brighter than those of holders of other degrees. Therefore, during the Sung, the *chin-shih* test ultimately overshadowed other tests, resulting in the reduction of tests to only this one. But in the process, the importance of classical learning was reintroduced: candidates were often expected to display their classical knowledge even when answering questions not testing directly their classical learning. Discussions on the system of Sung civil service examinations in this book will bear this out.

The civil service examinations as a whole not only embodied the entrenched Chinese belief in the meritocratic principle, they also theoretically provided a chance for commoners to ascend in a society where there were few alternate routes to obtaining honor and privilege. The system continued to be the most respected social institution for recruitment in China well into the twentieth century) It also helped to sustain an economic class of "gentry" by awarding some of its members the honorable status of degree-holders.[33] This last fact will become evident when we probe into the impact the examination system exerted on Sung society. The last, but not the least, consequence of the examination system was the delicate symbiosis this system was able to achieve to nurture and sustain the strength of classical learning. In such a peculiar manner, and for the reasons mentioned above, the civil service examination system had succeeded in becoming the most important social institution in imperial China.

D. The Tradition of Private Education

The great irony in the development of Confucian educational ideals in imperial China was the "officialization" of Confucian ideology.[34] Indeed, despite the fact that Confucius has been in the past two thousand years

---

[33] For a brief discussion on the origin of the so-called "gentry" class in the Sung, see Brian McKnight, *Village and Bureaucracy in Southern Sung China* (Chicago: Chicago University Press, 1971), 197–185. For that of the Ming and Ch'ing, see Ping-ti Ho, *The Ladder*, 34–40; Chung-li Chang, *The Chinese Gentry* (Seattle: University of Washington Press, 1955), 3–32; Kung-chuan Hsiao, *Rural China, Imperial Control in the Nineteenth Century* (Seattle: University of Washington Press, 1960), 574; and others, such as Wolfram Eberhard, *Rulers and Conquerors* (Leiden: E. J. Brill, 1965), 42–47 for his interesting and important study of an earlier phase of yet another kind of "gentry." See also Denis C. Twitchett, "A Critique of Some Recent Studies of Modern Chinese Social-Economic History," in *Transactions of the International Conference of Orientalists in Japan,* Vol. X (1965), 28–41.

[34] See my "Ssu-jen chiang-hsüeh."

hailed as the fountain head of all officially sanctioned ideologies, he started out, and remained throughout his life, a private teacher.[35] Private education in China has therefore never been neglected, although it was under constant pressure from the government which relentlessly sought to control any type of unofficial educational gatherings, once these gatherings grew in strength. The prviate school was where major new ideas were born and tested. When new ideas became popular and widespread, the government became interested in manipulating the situation and, if possible, eventually taking over the new thinking and making it official. The process was not always smooth; pressures to stamp out heresies were often more in evidence than any attention paid to comprehend the significance of a new idea. The history of classical learning gives ample witness to this, but the decision in the second century by Emperor Wu-ti of the Han to make Confucianism the officially sanctioned ideology is a clasical example.

The earliest private educational centers were often organized by classical scholars. After all, only classical learning appeared to have had the form of systematic scholarship. This was very much a result of Han government's decision to require potential officials to study the five specific classics.[36] Towards the end of the Former Han, a good number of classical tutors, retired officials as well as peripatetic scholars, were teaching in a private capacity and would draw hundreds or even thousands of students. This method of private instruction became even more popular in the Later Han.[37] Private education throughout the period was marked by the following characteristics:

1. Nearly all accomplished scholars had their own groups of disciples; even those in government service could manage to attract private followers who spent a period of time studying with them.
2. Private schools appeared to be located more often in isolated places rather than in urban areas, although the records we possess do not appear to emphasize this fact.
3. Students were always perfectly willing to travel great distances to seek acceptance by a renowned scholar. Stories are plentiful depicting the painstaking efforts made by disciples in order to be accepted by

[35] The best biography of Confucius in English remains H. G. Creel, *Confucius and the Chinese Way* (New York: Harper & Row, 1960).

[36] The term, "Five classics," originated from the fact that *po-shih* teaching officials were appointed by Emperor Wu-ti of the Han in 132 B.C. to teach the so-called "Five classics." See p. 9 above.

[37] Information is scattered in Pan Ku's *Han-shu* (Peking: Chung-hua, 1962) and Fan Yeh's *Hou-Han shu* (Peking: Chung-hua, 1965). Hou Wai-lu lists them in his *Chung-kuo ssu-hsiang t'ung-shih* (Peking: Jen-min, 1957), Vol. II, 350–354.

a distinguished teacher.

4. The development of classical scholarship was so much affected by these educational gatherings that famous teachers often were identified with certain distinct schools of learning, as if they were themselves the incarnation of the scholarship. Teachers, not the school itself, were the center of attention and intellectual continuity.[38]

Naturally, in a time when education was expensive, the success of these informal gatherings depended much on the support of wealthy or powerful families, a fact that would become even more obvious when Chinese society adopted the *chiu-p'in chung-cheng* method and became aristocratic in the third century. During the Period of Disunion, one could hardly distinguish between a school supported by the government and a private educational organization, except in institutional terms: whereas governmental schools were publicly financed, private schools were generally supported by private families. There was very little difference between the two in terms of content of education which at the time had been shifted to emphasizing proper rites and social norms.[39] The classics on rites received more attention than before and were widely studied.

A couple of new elements in the tradition of Chinese private education started to emerge at this period. First, largely because of Buddhist influence, methods for instruction became more systematic, and students, like Buddhist monks, were now given more strenuous training; meanwhile, monasteries or temples would also accept Confucian scholars where the latter were free to propagate Confucian, and not only Buddhist, teachings. Another important influence from Buddhist practice was that of *vihara*, which started to penetrate into the Chinese conception of schooling so much so that teachers were now looking for quiet and tranquil environments for schools, mountain areas being the most popular.[40] One can hardly refrain from mentioning the delightful story about Monk Hui-yüan's retiring to Mount Lu. The small mountain hut sheltered the famous monk for thirty years, and Hui-yüan never went beyond a little Hu (tiger) stream when seeing off his visitors. The legend growing from this story has inspired many a painter who perpetuated it in famous paintings,[41] and must have had engaging fascination over Chinese private teachers who freely imitated Hui-

---

[38] See my "Ssu-jen chiang-hsüeh."

[39] Hu Mei-ch'i, *Chung-kuo chiao-yü shih* (*Chiao-yü shih* hereafter) (Taipei: San-min, 1978), 212.

[40] See my "Ssu-jen chiang-hsüeh."

[41] Hui-chiao, *Kao-seng chuan*, Hai-shan hsien-kuan ed. (Taipei: Kuang-wen, 1971), 5/5b−6a.

yüan by building their schools in *shan-lin* (mountain and forest) lands.[42] This new dimension would continue throughout Chinese history, with generations of teachers or students choosing to retreat to scenic mountains for private study.[43]

Towards the end of the Period of Disunion, the creation of a civil service examination system started to gradually affect the content and practice of private education. But it was the decline of the aristocratic society that ultimately gave a new form to it. The traditional large group of disciples following an accomplished classical scholar was replaced by a small number of students studying on their own, and the teacher-disciple relationship appeared to last a shorter time than before. In the earlier part of the T'ang, mainly because of the successful government educational system, private education was not particularly active. But towards the end of the ninth century, and especially during the tenth century, the decline of central governmental power led more and more students to believe that studying on their own in *shan-lin* areas was more meaningful. Nearly all the scenic mountains saw gatherings of young people, building their own huts and preparing for the civil service examinations. Sometimes a student might stay in such an environment for as long as ten years. It was said that as a result, some mountains became so famous that no candidate in the area could afford not to pay homage to them.[44]

During the T'ang, private education continued to receive influence from Buddhism, especially in elementary education and in the *vihara* ideal. Monasteries customarily organized elementary schools to teach not merely Buddhist texts, but also traditional Confucian classics. Many students also elected to utilize the tranquil Buddhist temples and monasteries, and took up lodging in them to concentrate on their studies. Some wealthy temples could even afford to provide financial aid to needy students. One can hardly deny that the Buddhist practice of discipline and the ideal of *vihara* training greatly influenced Chinese private education.[45]

The last phase of Chinese private education is definitely that of the *shu-yüan*, academies. A *shu-yüan* included nearly all the basic features of

---

[42] Mount Lu has been persistently loved by both Buddhists and Confucianists. The first comprehensive work on it dated back to the Sung, by Ch'en Shun-yü (?–1074) who compiled a *Lu-shan chih* (Gazetteer of Lu-shan) which is still extant.

[43] By way of an interjection, it is worthwhile noting that mountains seem to have been preferred over rivers or seas. Chinese people did not sail out of sight of land until the thirteenth century.

[44] The tradition continued well into the Sung. See p. 139.

[45] The best articles dealing with T'ang private education are: Kao Ming-shih, "Ssu-hsüeh"; and Yen Keng-wang, "T'ang-jen hsi-yeh shan-lin ssu-yüan chih feng-shang,"

traditional private education, but also added some important new features. *Shu-yüan,* as an ideal continues to flourish even today. Accordingly, a student of the history of Chinese education should not lose sight of its importance.

One interesting feature made up the most important part of China's tradition of private education. In an historical society where education was aimed at public office and centered in the study of officially sanctioned classics, it was, to say the least, difficult for schools privately founded to become completely distinguishable, academically, from those organized and supported by the government. The educated Chinese has always striven to seek for greater moral and intellectual independence.[46] Yet, since knowledge was for service and Chinese history indicated that once an idea did prevail the government would lose no time in controlling it, this hardly left any room for genuine independence. The private was always part of the public. In this sense, China's private educational tradition was not all that private. From this one can see how difficult it has been for private education to have stood out on its own and become one of the most remarkable achievements in China's educational history.

---

in his *T'ang-shih yen-chiu lun-ts'ung* (Hong Kong: Hsin-ya yen-chiu-so, 1969), 367–424. For Buddhist influences, see my "Ssu-jen chiang-hsüeh"; Ch'en Tung-yüan, "Ch'an-lin te hsüeh-hsiao chih-tu," in *Min-to tsa-chih,* Vol. 6, No. 3 (1925); Kenneth K. S. Chen, *The Chinese Transformation of Buddhism* (Princeton: Princeton University Press, 1973), 240–255; and Thomas H. C. Lee, "Chu Hsi, the Academies and the Tradition of Private *Chiang-hsüeh,"* in *Chinese Studies,* 2/1 (1984), 301–330.

[46] For a comprehensive study of the intellectuals in ancient China, see Yü Ying-shih, *Chung-kuo chih-shih chieh-ts'eng shih-lun* (Taipei: Lien-ching, 1970). See also Frederick Wakeman, "The Price of Autonomy: Intellectuals in Ming and Ch'ing China," in *Daedalus* (Spring, 1972), 35–70.

CHAPTER 2
Sung Education in Chinese History

In 1973, Professor Robert Brumbaugh of Yale published a book on educational philosophy which opens with an eloquent preface on the desire for going back to the basics of Greek educational ideals. Living on the island of Ikaria, surrounded by the sea and the continent on which Socrates once walked, talked and speculated with his disciples, the author could not help being overwhelmed. Then, in a sober reflection on what was happening on a continent with which he was unfamiliar but towards which he was very sympathetic, the author commented:[1]

> We remember that undramatic island atmosphere, in this last week of February, 1972, when the reports coming out of the President's visit to China are of a once great university—Peking—brought to its knees as a three-year technical school with classes from eight till six. . . . So this book is, strangely, dedicated to Ikaria and to its people with affection: to its resonance for the birth of Western civilization and the educational ideal, without which civilization and Oriental despotism are indistinguishable.

Professor Brumbaugh was referring to the revolutionary turmoil that had been sweeping across China just a couple of years before. Among the revolutionary measures was the closing of higher educational institutions, converting them into technical and political training schools. New "universities" were to admit only those who had peasant or working class backgrounds. Teachers no longer graded the progress of students; instead, it was students who elected among themselves the best for promotion to upper classes. This last measure was particularly strange, but for one who valued the great traditions of human civilization, it was not simply strange. It was a grave human tragedy.

However, for a Sung historian, this may not seem all that strange. In 1086, commissioned to draft a report on how to reorganize the Imperial University, Ch'eng I (1033–1107) recommended that students should elect the better ones from among themselves for promotion to the upper class.[2]

---

[1] Robert Brumbaugh and Nathaniel M. Lawrence, *Philosophical Themes in Modern Education* (Boston: Houghton Mifflin, 1973), viii.
[2] Ch'eng I, *I-ch'uan i-shu*, in *Erh-Ch'eng ch'üan-shu*, SPPY ed., ch. 3.

This specific recommendation of Ch'eng I's, radical as it was, did not receive support from his contemporaries. But his philosophy quickly became widely studied and was one of the sources of Neo-Confucian ideology which was to dominate Chinese thinking over the following centuries. The re-appearance of such ideas furnishes us with a telling example of the tenacity of Chinese tradition. Sung education brought forth not a few insights and ideas which have survived even the changes after 1949.

There are five important features in Sung education: the rise in the importance of the civil service examinations; the opening up of a large number of local schools and the government's willingness to invest in these institutions; the rise of Neo-Confucianism and its eventual victory in the struggle to define Chinese educational ideals; the rise of academies (shu-yüan); and, finally, the widespread use of printing presses and their influence on mass education.

A. The Rise in Importance of the Civil Service Examinations

By Sung times, the civil service examinations had become the established machinery for recruiting civil officials. The mechanism was useful in two significant ways. First of all, the system provided an image of impartial recruitment for the commoners who sought to compete with the aristocrats for a position in officialdom. By the tenth century, the traditional aristo-crats, who used to enjoy national reputation and influence, had largely declined and their power had diminished.[3] Secondly, as a result, it became necessary and also possible for rulers to have some degree of freedom to recruit for service from among the commoners, as well as from the elite.

The Sung government, from the beginning, reinstated the civil service examinations. In the first two decades, the government did not seem to have a consistent policy as to the purpose of the system. It also lacked understanding of how the examinations could affect the structure of Chinese society. Soon, however, the government developed two ideas about what the system should achieve. First, the system should succeed in safeguarding a certain degree of impartiality by opening up chances for entering officialdom to a wider range of commoners. Secondly, the system should also achieve a degree of equal distribution of chances for success among candidates coming from different districts.

The idea of impartiality (kung),[4] when enforced, hampered the ideal

[3] See Ch. 1, note 32.
[4] See Ch. 8, section A.

of observing the moral performance of examination candidates. The emphasis on the need to observe an individual's moral uprightness was, of course, fundamental to the examination system from the earliest days of the system. But once it became open to more people, the need to keep it open and impartial became increasingly imperative. How then could an examiner reasonably hope to judge a candidate's moral uprightness without being somewhat subjective? The issue grew serious, at least during the Northern Sung period (960–1126).

To achieve a more or less equitable distribution of successful candidates from different districts was a difficult task, too, making impartiality particularly difficult. A device, the quota measure, was introduced and eventually developed into a permanent system. Under the quota system, the backward areas usually were given more generous quotas of successful candidates for the primary local tests, who would then compete in the secondary, departmental test which determined who should actually qualify for the degree. The quota system was enormously significant, and caused frequent debates on the division of quota areas. The system also ensured that the government had a more complicated task than merely safeguarding an open, if limited, route to social upward mobility. Eventually, the quota system became partially instrumental in constructing a new social order.

The most significant consequence of the civil service examination system was the creation of a new social structure in which degree-holders became part of the ruling elite.[5] The numbers of degree-holders at any given time during and after the Sung had always been miniscule, constituting, for example, in the early twelfth century, only about 0.005% of the total population; the social inequality was thus enormous. This small fraction of people and their immediate family members naturally enjoyed disproportionate social prestige. Their influence in local and national affairs was tremendous. The examination system, which set out to be an impartial social mechanism, actually served to enhance the hierarchical nature of traditional Chinese society.

Furthermore, because the system awarded an enormously great share of honor and privilege to a small number of qualified members of the Chinese society, it quickly became a useful instrument for imperial control over degree-holders, most of whom now constituted the mainstay of the civil service. Their knowledge, basically that of the classics and applicable merely to the examinations, was virtually useless outside of officialdom. The reward for their knowledge, on the other hand, was

[5] See Ch. 1, note 33.

handsome and attractive. The ruler could have found no easier way to control this handful of civil officials.[6]

Likewise, once the system lost its original purpose of recruiting only the morally superior people, and was transformed into a social institution, the ideal of investigating the moral behavior of a candidate quickly declined. The assumption that knowledge of the classics was equal to the potential to do good now received universal acceptance. The result was for the system to become increasingly a machine that could only test candidates' classical knowledge. The Chinese government quickly lost sight of the ancient ideal of recommending morally superior people for service. Worse than this was the stress on the prevention of corruption in the examination halls, under the pressure for impartiality. The exaggerated concern for the avoidance of corruption became so overwhelming that the basic purpose of the examination system became blurred. Ultimately, the examination system grew into a stupefying institution which was to haunt generations of Chinese students.

The most decisive transition in the history of Chinese civil service examinations came during the Sung dynasty.

B. The Formation of State Educational System

The Chinese government had long taken part in the establishment and maintenance of schools at the local level before the Sung. But the Sung government's experimentation in local education was perhaps of the greatest scale and importance in Chinese history. The major parts of the Sung government's effort in local education remained largely unchanged throughout the late imperial period until the introduction of the modern Western system in this century.

There were virtually no officially supported local schools in the early Sung. Beginning in the ninth century, with the decline of the T'ang central government, education at the local level was very much neglected. More and more students went to private schools, which were usually maintained and sponsored by Buddhist monasteries or wealthy social leaders. Many of these schools were found in isolated mountain areas.[7]

This situation continued throughout the tenth century. In the early eleventh century, some local officials started to build and finance local schools. These new schools, which increased rapidly in the mid-eleventh

---

[6] Frederick Wakeman, "The Price of Autonomy: Intellectuals in Ming and Ch'ing China."

[7] Yen Keng-wang, "T'ang-jen hsi-yeh shan-lin ssu-yüan chih feng-shang."

century, shared the following main features: a set of officially printed and endowed classics, some classrooms, a temple of Confucius and, most importantly, a piece of land, normally about five to ten *ch'ing* (approximately 70 to 140 acres). The increase of such schools indicated the widened educational opportunities; it also reinforced the importance of classical learning in governmental education. The endowment of land was particularly significant because the practice became a permanent feature of Chinese local education. Local schools henceforth were generally self-sufficient, each deriving its revenue from the income of the rentals of its own land.

Local education received even greater attention in the late eleventh century and early twelfth century, during the reform movements of Wang An-shih (1021–1086) and Ts'ai Ching. Besides continuing the main features mentioned above, the reformers also sought to further widen educational opportunities at the local level. Specifically, the reformers hoped to incorporate civil service recruitment into the local educational process, so that, ultimately, the selection could be based on the scholarly progress of students within schools and the existing civil service examination system, which was then not directly related to the schooling of individual candidates, could be abolished. To show their determination, reformers legislated aid to students and frequently increased budgets for local schools. All students received support for meals and dormitory accommodation, and there was also a significant increase in the number of local school students during the Ts'ai Ching period of power.

Efforts to reform education weakened and fell apart after Ts'ai Ching left the government. Still, the idea that the examination system should have a definite relationship with the schools continued. Ironically, this idea had a detrimental effect on the development of government schools in later dynasties: when government local schools became exclusively a part of the examination system, they admitted only those who had already been awarded some preliminary qualification and had become eligible to sit for the examinations. These students of government local schools, like their counterparts in Sung times, held special privileges such as exemption from certain labor services, and enjoyed aid towards their living expenses. Such treatment distinguished them as a special status group. When state-run local schools evolved into this kind of examination-oriented offices, they ceased to assume active instructional activities, and their number consequently did not grow in response to the increase in the number of students. Rather, actual teaching was assumed by local private schools, which were often called academies, and often also run by local government offices, though without the orthodox position enjoyed by *the* school for qualified examination candidates.

The contribution of the Sung to government local education is therefore mixed. On the one hand, the Sung created the pattern of a state's local education for later dynasties to imitate, of which the school field system obviously was the most important resultant. On the other hand, the evolution of local government schools into institutions basically for qualified examination candidates resulted in ambiguity as to the purpose of local schools. Registration in government schools became a part of the examination qualification, and such schools assumed few teaching functions. Instead, it was other forms of local education, chiefly sponsored by clan or community organizations, which took up the responsibility of actual teaching and moral discipline.

C. Neo-Confucian Thought and Its Impact

The most significant change on the intellectual side of Sung education was the rise of Neo-Confucian thought. Originally a scholarly preserve of a coterie of speculative thinkers, the school of thought developed into a powerful intellectual movement touching on virtually every aspect of social, political and economic theory, as well as metaphysical speculation. The leading theoreticians included the Ch'eng brothers: Ch'eng Hao (1032–1085) and Ch'eng I, Chou Tun-i (1017–1073), Chang Tsai (1020–1077) and, above all, Chu Hsi (1130–1200) and Lu Hsiang-shan (1139–1193).

Their influence, won after a series of intellectual debates and quarrels, began to appear towards the end of the Southern Sung and culminated when the Mongol Yüan dynasty ordered that Chu Hsi's interpretations of the classics be made standard for the civil service examinations.

The first consequence of the rise of Neo-Confucianism is the proliferation of a new vocabulary. This included terms such as "principle" (*li*), "material force" (*ch'i*), "sincerity" (*ch'eng*), "quietude" (*ching*), "investigation of things" (*ko-wu*) and others.[8] These concepts reflect the Neo-Confucian

---

[8]Wm. Theodore de Bary (ed.), *Sources of Chinese Tradition* (New York: Columbia University Press, 1960), 455–502; idem, "A Reappraisal of Neo-Confucianism," in Arthur F. Wright (ed.), *Studies in Chinese Thought* (Chicago: Chicago University Press, 1953), 81–111; A. C. Graham, *Two Chinese Philosophers* (London: Lund Humpheries, 1958); and Wing-tsit Chan (ed.), *A Source Book in Chinese Philosophy* (Princeton: Princeton University Press, 1963) are all useful. The translation of the terms is that of Chan. I have found Ch'ien Mu, *Chu-tzu hsüeh t'i-kang* (Taipei: San-min, 1971); idem, *Sung Ming li-hsüeh k'ai-shu* (Taipei: Chung-hua wen-hua shih-yeh ch'u-pan wei-yüan hui, 1956); Shimada Kenji, *Shushigaku to Yōmeigaku* (Tokyo: Iwanami, 1967); and Fumoto Yasutaka, *Hoku Sō ni okeru jugaku no tenkai* (Tokyo: Shoseki Ryūtsūsho, 1968) also useful.

speculation on the nature and moral rectitude of an individual. Apart from its concern with metaphysics, the Neo-Confucian movement endeavored to define anew the Confucian moral man; "sincerity," "quietude" and later "mind" (*hsin*) and "human nature" (*hsing*) were ideas constantly mentioned in relation to a perfect person. Generations of Chinese pupils were taught to grapple with these concepts in their process of *Bildung*. Although not always comprehending the subtle meanings of the vocabulary, they faithfully worked to transmit the surface meanings of the big words.

The second consequence of Neo-Confucian influence on Chinese education was the widespread use of a large number of Neo-Confucian works and commentaries on the classics. Chu Hsi's commentaries on the *Four Books* became the most widely studied work by examination candidates well into this present century, and is still taught in Taiwan as an integral part of its high school curriculum. Other Neo-Confucian works, such as Chang Tsai's *Hsi-ming* (The Western Inscription),[9] Chou Tun-i's *T'ung-shu* (Penetrating the *Book of Changes*),[10] the works of the Ch'eng brothers, especially the *I-shu* (Survived Works),[11] and above all the *Chin-ssu lu* (Reflections on Things at Hand) edited by Chu Hsi and Lü Tsu-ch'ien (1137–1181),[12] have been studied and recited by generations of Chinese students. Their influence can scarcely be exaggerated.

In terms of the education of children, the Neo-Confucian influence was less visible at the beginning. They did not succeed in compiling a sufficiently "Neo-Confucian" primary text to replace the conventional primers, of which the *Thousand Characters Essay* (*Ch'ien-tzu wen*) and the *Hundred Surnames* (*Pai-chia hsing*) were the most popular. Towards the end of the Sung, however, the *San-tzu ching* (Three-character Classic), which reflects much Neo-Confucian ideology, began to circulate widely. The text served as one of the three most important primers in late imperial China, when its influence was tremendous.

The third consequence of Neo-Confucian influence on Chinese education was the concern for popular education. Chu Hsi proposed and established community schools which quickly replaced government schools and took up the actual instruction at local level; their importance in propagating Neo-Confucian thought was no less than that of the academies (*shu-yüan*),

---

[9] Chang Tsai, *Chang Tsai chi* (Peking: Chung-hua, 1978).

[10] Chou Tun-i, *Chou-tzu ch'üan-shu, Wan-yu wen-k'u* ed. (Shanghai: Shang-wu, 1937).

[11] See note 2 above.

[12] Chu Hsi and Lü Tsu-ch'ien (eds.), *Chin-ssu lu, SPPY* ed. is a collection of commentaries, as well as the text itself, and was compiled by Chiang Yung (1681–1762). The work is available in an excellent translation by Wing-tsit Chan, *Reflections on Things at Hand* (New York: Columbia University Press, 1967).

which were also the brain-children of Chu Hsi. In the broader area of social education and ideological control, Neo-Confucians also made significant contributions. The immensely important *hsiang-yüeh* lecture system was first proposed in the eleventh century and received enthusiastic endorsement and elaboration by Chu Hsi.[13] Similarly, the *hsiang-yin-chiu* ceremony, which had, over a period, declined into virtual oblivion, was revived and given new significance by Neo-Confucians.[14] But the main contribution of Neo-Confucianism to ideological control was not chiefly institutional; it was its philosophical reflections on the purpose, and potentials for abuse, of monarchical power. For Neo-Confucian political thinkers, the state was the single most decisive institution to exert shaping influence on the education and ideological consistency of the populace. A Neo-Confucian thinker sees a tension between the state's search for ideological control and comformity and the ultimate goal of an individual's moral cultivation. And yet, they considered that a good Chinese intellectual, defined especially in Neo-Confucian terms, was to, not intensify, but reduce the tension, and effect a harmonious coordination between the two. However, the state, especially after the Ming dynasty, often chose to exploit this stress for harmony, and tried constantly to mobilize all available social institutions, such as schools, clan organizations and even guilds, to enhance the ideological unity, which could be essential to a stable empire. As a result, imperial ideology was constantly adumbrated to the commoners through these channels. This development was quite unforeseeable when early Neo-Confucian thinkers articulated their ideas. Therefore, the paradox of the Neo-Confucian approach to the education of the Chinese individual was vitiated by their premise that the ruler, if properly guided, should be trusted as the most effective source of moral influence. The development, needles to say, affected Chinese education for many hundreds of years.

D. The Rise of the Academies

The last but most important influence Neo-Confucians exerted on Chinese education was the ideal and practice of the academies.

Shu-yüan (academies) as a term appeared as early as the eighth century. By the late T'ang, advanced private schools appeared *en masse* all over China,

---

[13] Liu Chen, "Sung-tai te hsüeh-kuei han hsiang-yüeh," in Sung-shih yen-chiu hui (ed.), *Sung-shih yen-chiu chi* (*SSYCC* hereafter), Vol. I (1958), 367–392. See also Wm. Theodore de Bary, *The Liberal Tradition in China* (Hong Kong: The Chinese University Press, 1983), 32–34.

[14] See later in Ch. 5, especially notes 18, 23 and 24.

especially in isolated mountain areas. Some of these schools conducted teaching, but most of them were not more than very simple and private places where students prepared for the civil service examinations. Many of these private study-areas were called *shu-yüan*.[15] The existence of *shu-yüan* continued into the Sung. Primarily private and clearly lacking permanence and institutional strength, these gatherings were quickly replaced by schools funded by the government.

Official local education had declined after the twelfth century and had ceased to play an active role in instruction. Seeing that officially sponsored education had failed to conform to the general Confucian ideal of education, Chu Hsi decided to revive the tradition of private education, with a hope that the *shu-yüan* could assume the responsibility of Confucian education. The decision was to have immense consequences for Chinese education.

First of all, as a result of Chu Hsi's efforts, the *shu-yüan* became a permanent feature of Chinese education, taking up the major responsibility of local education. By the end of the Southern Sung, the establishment of academies had become a common feature in local education. Many late Sung statesmen and scholars received their initial education in academies.

Secondly, the organization within schools also developed a permanent pattern. Initially modelled upon Sung local government schools, the academies had roughly the similar personnel arrangement as local schools. Academies also sought official endowment of public land, the rental from which provided the major part of the academies' income. But academies generally maintained a much more coherent and better structured curriculum than local government schools; they also carried out actual instruction and discipline and eventually became the center of formal education in imperial China. During Ming and Ch'ing China, in nearly every county, a *shu-yüan* and a government school usually coexisted. Whereas the latter was by and large a part of the examination system, the former appears to have conducted more day-to-day instruction and intellectual activities.

Since Neo-Confucian thinkers stressed the importance of library collections, nearly every academy had a small collection of books. A good number of academies also established printing presses and took an active part in the publishing business. The combination of book collecting and book publishing created a possibility for the academy to become not merely an educational center, but also a center of social and intellectual activities. Much in the same manner that the *she-hsüeh* and *tsung-hsüeh*

---

[15] See Sheng Lang-hsi, *Chung-kuo shu-yüan chih-tu* (Taipei: Hua-shih, 1977), 8–14; see also Yen Keng-wang, "T'ang-jen hsi-yeh shan-lin ssu-yüan chih feng-shang" for more references.

became an integral part of community life, academies also became an indispensable part of local development and control. The resulting rise in the importance of academies in local affairs, while not clear in the Sung, was definitely evident in Ming and Ch'ing times.

Finally and most importantly, academies were most instrumental in the propagation of Neo-Confucian thinking. The texts used in the academies were Neo-Confucian; the theories of teaching practiced in the academies were also unmistakably Neo-Confucian. An academy could be regarded as not fulfilling its purpose if it failed to instill Neo-Confucian moral values into its students. To understand the Neo-Confucian educational program properly, apart from observing its influence on mass education, one must look into the function and operation of the academies.

E. The Widespread Use of Printing Skills and the Progress in Mass Education

Further contributing to the progress in the education of commoners was the mass utilization of printing skills in the century during which the Sung dynasty was founded. Its impact on China's popular education was perhaps scarcely less than that of Neo-Confucianism. The idea of duplicating written materials by seals or by engraving stones for later rubbing was by no means new in China. But the truly significant breakthrough in the history of "printing" in China came in the tenth century when wooden blocks started to be used. With them, it became economically feasible to distribute books by "printing" in large numbers. The Sung therefore benefited from the invention of block printing, a skill remarkably convenient and economical, which marked an important turning point in Chinese history.

The widespread use of printing technology had both positive and negative effects on Chinese society. First of all, it definitely created an unprecedented opportunity for Chinese people to have access to books,[16] resulting in an increase in the number of students who could take part in the civil service examinations. The rise in importance of the civil service examinations was as much a result of the general increase in the opportunities for education as a result of encouragement on the part of Sung rulers.

The second effect of the use of printing presses was the rise in literacy.[17]

[16] A very rough estimate by Weng T'ung-wen shows that the price of books was cut to a tenth. See his "Yin-shua shu tui-yü shu-chi ch'eng-pen te ying-hsiang," in *Ch'ing-hua hsüeh-pao,* Vol. 6, Nos. 1 & 2 (1967), 35–43.

[17] In a joint research project, "The Changing Significance of Popular Literacy in Chinese History, 960–1937," supported by the Institute of Chinese Studies of The

The rate of literacy is a difficult social phenomenon to measure, but all indications suggest that there was an increase in literacy rate in the Sung. The effects of the increase were reflected in the following developments. First of all, Sung society saw the emergence of story-telling as a profession, which was responsible for the appearance of early novels. The rise of this profession, however, was doubtlessly a result of both a wealthy society which created a leisured class and an increasingly literate society which provided both story-tellers and an audience.[18] Secondly, there was a rapid increase in all kinds of publications, including literary collections, encyclopedias, and most notably, the "moral books" (*shan-shu*). The last category of books was aimed at the populace at large. The rapid growth in book publication reflected an important social reality: the increased demand for books by a larger readership. Thirdly, though the increase in literacy was by no means sudden or extraordinarily spectacular, it did pose problems for ideological control. Many important ideological control measures were invented or revived in the Sung, chiefly because there was a need to re-evaluate the significance and impact of widespread literacy. In a sense, then, increased literacy added a new dimension to the Chinese conception of education, and a rather complicated dimension at that.

Thirdly, the invention and the widespread use of printing technology most certainly led to a serious change in Chinese intellectual attitudes. More people were reading and becoming aware of the possible diversity of ideas. The result probably was the appearance of a number of people who, because of the chance to become literate, espoused extreme or even radical ideas. During the Sung, especially the Northern Sung, the emergence of such a new group of people advocating a wide range of reforming ideas must partially have been a result of easier access to printed materials. At least, it is probably fair to say that the unprecedented magnitude of Sung reform movements and their opposition owed a lot to the fact that an increased number of people were literate enough to become involved in the debates. The change in reading habits and the influx of ancient ideas, now popularized and inevitably modified by story-tellers in marketplaces, resulted in a different way of looking at nature

---

Chinese University of Hong Kong, the researchers now believe that the changing rate of literacy was generally a result of social change. This would mean that the invention of the printing press could only have an indirect influence on the rise of literacy which was a result of general societal change.

[18] Jaroslav Průšek has written many articles dealing with this issue. His conclusions remind one of the opinions found in Ian Watt's *The Rise of the Novel* (Berkeley: University of California Press, 1967), especially in his second chapter: "The Reading Public and the Rise of the Novel," 35–59.

and society. Chinese society was rapidly becoming secularized in the Sung, taxing the time and energy of the traditionalists who fought vigorously to forestall this trend.

Printing technology had an enormous influence on Chinese society. Although the speed and magnitude of the impact were not comparable to that of the Gutenburg Revolution,[19] its importance should not be minimized. It not only created in Sung society various radicalized reforming groups, but also helped to shape the examination system and sustained it as a useful social institution. Its ultimate consequence was to broaden the reading public, a consequence that created new dimensions in China's social problems.[20]

[19] Evelyn S. Rawski: *Literacy and Popular Education in Ch'ing China* (Ann Arbor: University of Michigan Press, 1979), 140−154.
[20] See Ch. 3, section B.

CHAPTER 3

The Study of Sung Education: Problems and Purposes

In his important article discussing the present state of Chinese historiography,[1] Professor Yü Ying-shih of Yale University argues that the present task for a Chinese historian is to search for the unique features of Chinese civilization. Yü Ying-shih does not rule out the necessity and possibility of comparative history, but points out the danger in forced analogy. For him, comparisons, more often than not, serve to make differences even more evident, and, paradoxically, uniqueness even more distinct.[2]

The same may be said of the study of Sung education. Sung China is remote from the China we know in the twentieth century, and its educational practices, for all of their intrinsic interest and values, have been very much abandoned or even forgotten. Such education was not only uniquely Chinese, but also uniquely Sung, and the continuation of the Sung system we detect in later dynasties serves only to demonstrate the particular historical setting and circumstance in which the Sung institutions and ideas developed. It is thus important to place Sung educational achievement in its unique historical context. Then, we can hope to understand the system and clarify some of the myths which surround these systems.

In this chapter, I hope to provide a general introduction to the historical sources that have so far determined our understanding of Sung education. I shall try to analyze the circumstances in which these sources were compiled, in hope of finding out the historiographical devices and ideas behind those materials. I shall then discuss the late nineteenth-century efforts to publish some of the important first-hand sources, which had by then been more or less forgotten and little, if at all, studied. With the publication of these works, we are now in a much better position to comprehend the attempts by reformers in the early twelfth century to transform the Sung educational

---

[1] Yü Ying-shih, "Chung-kuo shih-hsüeh te hsien chieh-tuan: fan-sheng yü chan-wang," in *Shih-hsüeh p'ing-lun*, No. 1 (1979), 1–24; tr. by Thomas H. C. Lee and Chü-chieh Huang as "The Study of Chinese History: Retrospect and Prospect," in *Renditions*, No. 15 (1981), 7–26.

[2] A point very much shared by Benjamin Schwartz, although Schwartz approaches it differently. See Schwartz, "Area Studies as a Critical Discipline," in *Journal of Asian Studies* (*JAS* hereafter), Vol. 40, No. 1 (1981), 15–26.

system. These efforts, though eventually abandoned, left their mark on later educational practices. I shall also try to discuss some of the possibilities in widening the definition and significance of educational history, by listing my concerns in the last section.

A. Some Reflections on the Past Histories of Sung Education

Our knowledge of government education in Sung China was largely shaped by works generally compiled after the fall of the Sung. Two of them stand out: the standard *Sung History* (*Sung-shih*)[3] and the *Comprehensive Study of Decuments* (*Wen-hsien t'ung-k'ao*)[4] compiled by Ma Tuan-lin (1254–?), who actually lived through the end of the Sung. A third work, the *Sung Yüan hsüeh-an* (Studies on Various Intellectual Schools in Sung and Yüan Times), though much later, should also be considered a standard work. Since these books, as well as many others, were completed after Neo-Confucianism was firmly established as the ruling school of thought; their interpretation of Sung history in general, and Sung education in particular, was inevitably tinged with Neo-Confucian predilections. It is therefore necessary to start with Neo-Confucian historiography.

First, Neo-Confucian historiography displays a generally cautious or unfavorable attitude towards reform ideas and politics. While the first reform movement in 1044 led by Fan Chung-yen, Han Ch'i, and others received general approval, subsequent reforms led by Wang An-shih, Lü Hui-ch'ing, Chang Tun and above all, Ts'ai Ching have come down in Neo-Confucian, and hence, traditional, Chinese historiography as the worst examples of opportunitism; reform (*pien-fa*) as a political idea was often looked down upon with absolute disdain.[5] The educational programs undertaken by reformers were not specifically condemned, but they were seldom

[3] For a study of the history of compilation of *SS*, See Chin Yü-fu, *Chung-kuo shih-hsüeh shih* (*Shih-hsüeh shih* hereafter) (Shanghai: Shang-wu, 1957), 106–111; Chao I, *Nieh-erh shih cha-chi* (Taipei: Shih-chieh, 1958), 23:304–309. See also Sudō Yoshiyuki, *Sōdai shi kenkyū* (Tokyo: Tōyō Bunko, 1969), 513–622, for three detailed studies of the sources and compilation of *SS*.

[4] Pai Shou-i, "Ma Tuan-lin te shih-hsüeh ssu-hsiang," in Wu Tse (ed.), *Chung-kuo shih-hsüeh shih lun-chi* (Shanghai: Jen-min, 1980), Vol. II, 353–398; Chin Yü-fu, *Shih-hsüeh shih*, 196–199. See also note 17 below.

[5] For a general introduction to Chinese historiography, see Arthur F. Wright, "Historiography: Chinese," in *International Encyclopedia of Social Sciences* (New York: Macmillan, 1968), Vol. 6, 400–407. See also Chin Yü-fu, *Shih-hsüeh shih*; Wu Tse, *Ching-kuo shih-hsüeh shih lun-chi*, 2 vols, Tu Wei-yun et al. (eds.), *Chung-kuo shih-hsüeh shih lun-wen hsüan-chi*, 3 vols. (Taipei: Hua-shih, 1976–1980); and W. G. Beasley and E. G. Pulleyblank (eds.), *Historians of China and Japan* (Oxford: Oxford University Press, 1961).

mentioned. One good example is probably the first modern work on the history of education (*chiao-yü*) in China. Written by Kano Ryōchi in the late nineteenth century, possibly under the influence of Fukuzawa Yukichi (1834–1901), the author states:[6]

> There were only two scholars [during the Sung] who made it to the position of prime minister. They were Wang An-shih and Ssu-ma Kuang. An-shih, however, was egoistic and self-centered. He proposed to change the law [of the land] and caused great disturbances for the common people. He defended his wrongdoings by referring to the way of sage kings, using it to cheat the world. The result was trouble for the nation. As for the *New Commentaries*, they were actually the work of his son, Fang. It was but one private school of interpretation and offers nothing worthy of our attention.

The picture presented here by a historian under the influence of traditional historiography has remained very much unchanged even into the twentieth century. In the particular case of Wang An-shih, despite the efforts of Ts'ai Shang-hsiang and Liang Ch'i-ch'ao,[7] his historical status remains dubious at best, not to mention that of people like Ts'ai Ching, mentioned above, and Han T'e-chou (1151–1202) or Chia Ssu-tao (1213–1275).[8]

Secondly, there existed a strong predilection towards private education, especially the academies (*shu-yüan*). As already mentioned above, the traditional Chinese intellectuals had worked within a very constraining political culture to create a tradition of private instruction, and Neo-Confucians under the leadership of Chu Hsi had sought not merely to regenerate this important tradition, but also to use academies to train students who would eventually become the bearers of their teaching. By the end of the Southern Sung, it had become obvious that Neo-Confucianism had well established itself as the dominant ideology. Subsequent historical works, including the *Sung-shih*, very naturally interpreted the Neo-Confucian success as a result of the superior quality of educational programs in private academies. The picture perpetuated by traditional Chinese historians depicting the

---

[6] Kano Ryōchi *Shina kyōgaku shi ryaku*, translated into Chinese as *Chih-na chiao-yü shih-lüeh* (Shanghai: Shang-wu, 1889), 3/4b.

[7] Ts'ai Shang-hsiang, *Wang Ching-kung nien-p'u k'ao-lüeh* (Shanghai: Jen-min, 1974); Liang Ch'i-ch'ao, *Wang Ching-kung* (Taipei: Chung-hua, 1956), now available in Liang's collected works (various editions) and Liang et al., *Chung-kuo liu-ta cheng-chih chia* (Taipei: Cheng-chung, 1963), 5/1–208.

[8] At least two articles attempt to rewrite the biography of Han T'e-chou. One is by Ch'en Teng-yüan, "Han P'ing-yüan chuan," in *Chin-ling hsüeh-pao*, Vol. 4, No. 2 (1934), 89–142. The other is by Li Chia-chü, "Shih-lun kuan-yü Han T'e-chou p'ing-chia te jo-kan wen-t'i," in *Chung-kuo shih yen-chiu*, 1981/2, 146–161. For a recent work on Chia Ssu-tao, see Herbert Franke, "Chia Ssu-tao (1213–1275): A 'Bad Last Minister'?" in Arthur F. Wright and Denis C. Twitchett (eds.), *Confucian Personalities* (Stanford: Standford University Press, 1962), 217–234.

rapid decline of government education in the Southern Sung was in part a consequence of the attention paid almost exclusively to the activities of the academies. In general, however, it seems that while there was not much innovation in the government's educational system, schools founded by the government continued to increase steadily throughout the Southern Sung. Also, while most people were silent about their education in those schools,[9] there is no hard evidence that they had severely deteriorated. Indeed, one may even say that there was a tendency for academies to become even more controlled by local governments, and hence hardly distinguishable from official schools. The Neo-Confucian predilection for academies is nevertheless justified, because the thirteenth century was doubtlessly the century of academies. The situation was such that it became, in practice, difficult even for the most capable historian of the Sung to be aware of the steady development in the government's educational system.[10]

Thirdly, Neo-Confucian philosophical premises affected biographical writings. They stressed an individual's moral aptitude, as seen in their attention to such matters as social customs or education. While Chinese biographies continued to make an individual's political career their central concern, there was a visible rise in emphasis on an individual's commitment to moral affairs, rather than on his purely institutional activities. Indeed, beginning with the Ch'eng brothers, the Neo-Confucians had become doubtful of the use of institutional changes for social betterment. While one should refrain from saying that Neo-Confucian philosophy was idealist, it is not wrong to suggest that there was indeed a profound conviction on the part of Neo-Confucians that a better society could only be created if moral transformation could be effected by individual members of the society. External factors such as changes in social structure, material conditions and educational institutions were only secondary in the process; Neo-Confucians believe that a search for a return to the ideal society as found in antiquity, through external means, would always be futile if carried out without moral rectitude.[11]

The practical result of this philosophical conviction was a stress on an

---

[9] See Ch. 7, note 3.

[10] Some attempts by Emperor Li-tsung to reinvigorate local government education are generally not discussed in regular educational histories. For this, see Ch. 9, section C.

[11] Chu Hsi himself has this point clearly stated. See his *Chu-tzu yü-lei*, 1473 reprint of 1270 edition (Taipei: Cheng-chung, 1962), 108/2a: "In general, any law (institution, here referring to feudalism) whatever has its own intrinsic defects. There is no law that does not have defects. The essential thing is to have the right person." Or, *ibid.*, 9a: "To change all the defects in our institutions is rather easy. But problems of our society stem mainly from people: if every person pursues his own private desire, how are we to change our society?"

individual as a moral agent capable of achieving the ideal of a perfect human being. Academies were the institutional answer by Chu Hsi and his disciples to the need for a ground on which moral cultivation, in terms of example-giving and intimate instruction, could be carried out. Neo-Confucian teachers relegated the regulations concerning how academies should be managed to a secondary position in their minds. It was the content of the education and the intense attempts by individuals to arrive at a state of perfection, such as absolute sincerity, which were worthy of full attention. Consequently, Neo-Confucians were especially concerned with whether the faithful should engage themselves in moral cultivation or educational efforts. They were also careful to take down their master's sayings concerning how to improve an individual's search for moral success. In short, Neo-Confucians always had a penchant for both the ideal and practice of educating the mind of the moral individual.

The effect of this concern for individual education was immediately obvious. The biographies of important thinkers of the Southern Sung are full of stories of their efforts to transmit ethical teaching and education to their families, neighborhood, or the districts in which they served.[12] Records of these overshadow those for institutional measures as found in most Northern Sung sources. The result is that we know generally a great deal about the political (and educational) institutions of the Northern Sung, but always face difficulties in describing them for the Southern Sung. Any discussion of Sung education thus cannot avoid probing into the depths of the Sung thinkers' minds to find out how they conceived of moral eduation.

A good work on which to start this kind of search is the *Sung Yüan hsüeh-an*. Although this is only a Ch'ing compilation, it definitely is a result of the new approach to scholarship conceived by Sung Neo-Confucians.[13] If one is willing to be less exact, then one may as well consider this intellectual historical work as the first educational history ever, a history that could receive full approval from Neo-Confucian disciples. This work no doubt is a good source for pedagogical information on leading Neo-Confucian thinkers; it also provides a very balanced presentation of scholarly activities in Sung China. One example is a series of important articles on geography of scholarship by Ho Yu-sen published in the 1950s, essentially

---

[12]To give just a few examples, *SS*, 416:12480, 450:13258, 456:13402; Li Hsin-ch'uan, *Chien-yen i-lai hsi-nien yao-lu* (*CYYL* hereafter), 150:2412; and Chu Hsi, *Hui-an hsien-sheng Chu Wen-kung wen-chi* (*Wen-chi* hereafter), 92:1623.

[13]Juan Chih-sheng, "Hsüeh-an t'i-ts'ai yüan-liu ch'u-t'an," in Tu Wei-yün et al. (eds.), *Chung-kuo shih-hsüeh shih lun-wen hsüan-chi*, Vol. I, 574–596.

based on this *hsüeh-an*.[14]

If *Sung Yüan hsüeh-an* can be considered a standard Neo-Confucian reference work on Sung education, then *Sung-shih* provides us with its general historical and institutional background. The *Sung Yüan hsüeh-an* compiled by ardent Neo-Confucians in the best tradition of the Neo-Confucian concern for moral rectitude, is well known.[15] The standard *Sung-shih*, compiled in haste during the Yüan rule, however, cannot be readily regarded as a representative Neo-Confucian work, although the history of its compilation clearly reflected the influence of Neo-Confucian concerns.[16] The *Wen-hsien t'ung-k'ao* is slightly different and, despite its collection of documents already abridged or even edited, it nevertheless shows interesting signs of being a work less affected by the dominant contemporary ideology.[17] It is one of the most important primary works to start with for a study of Sung educational institutions. The work records quite faithfully what did happen in Sung China. In general, however, one feels some dissatisfaction because of the book's brevity. The information provided is largely institutional, and the documents are highly cryptic. It is thus extremely difficult to sort out from the limited amount of information the complex historical process in which these institutional measures were formulated and practiced.[18] The use of Ma's *Wen-hsien t'ung-k'ao* should therefore be supplemented by that of the *Sung-shih*, which provides a massive volume of information obviously copied from a number of Sung works, composed primarily of governmental archival documents. These materials were then edited, though only crudely, to fit the framework of a formal standard history.

From the discussion above, it is obvious that Neo-Confucian influences permeated all of the three leading historical works. Indeed, by the end of the thirteenth century, intellectuals had already arrived at some concensus about the interpretation of nearly every aspect of Sung history, and the concensus by and large did reflect the Neo-Confucian dominance; this dominance was so powerful that it led some historians to reedit their works, which might originally have been just drafts based on a loose compilation

[14] Ho Yu-sen, "Liang-Sung hsüeh-feng chih ti-li fen-pu" and "Yüan-tai hsüeh-shu chih ti-li fen-pu," in *Hsin-ya hsüeh-pao*, Vols. 1 and 2 (1955, 1956).

[15] See note 13.

[16] See note 3.

[17] See Hok-lam Chan, " 'Comprehensiveness' (*T'ung*) and 'Change' (*Pien*) in Ma Tuan-lin's Historical Thought," in Hok-lam Chan and Wm. Theodore de Bary (eds.), *Yüan Thought* (New York: Columbia University Press, 1982), 27–88.

[18] A lot of information covered by *WHTK* is now superseded by sources found in *Hsü Tzu-chih t'ung-chien ch'ang-pien* (*HCP* hereafter), *Sung hui-yao chi-kao* (see note 22 below) and private collected works.

of official documents. This is evident in Li T'ao's famous *Hsü Tzu-chih t'ung-chien ch'ang-pien* (Drafted Continuation to the Comprehensive Mirror for Aid in Government), by far the most comprehensive chronicle of the Northern Sung history.[19] The chapters that deal with the reform periods, however, are lost, and other chapters which had anything to do with the reform ideas have been deleted. The loss of these chapters does great damage to our understanding of the policies pursued by the reformers, and the restoration in the late Ch'ing by Huang I-chou only partially succeeded in shedding some light on the reform movements.[20] Other fragments of information found in various contemporary works, such as Li Hsin-ch'uan's *Chien-yen i-lai ch'ao-yeh tsa-chi* (Summaries of Various Governmental Policies since the Chien-yen Era), Wang Ch'eng's *Tung-tu shih-lüeh* (An outline History of the Eastern Capital), and Wang Ying-lin's *Yü-hai* (Sea of Jade) fit easily under the distinct contour of the Neo-Confucian edifice of consensus.

The irony is that by the fifteenth century, even Li T'ao's extensive *Drafted Continuation to the Comprehensive Mirror* (*Hsü ch'ang-pien* hereafter) had ceased to be circulated, much less published. Some of the materials which had belonged to those chapters edited out of the work, but somehow preserved in another reference work based on Li's original book, naturally also disappeared.[21] From the fifteenth century to almost the end of the nineteenth century, one could say that as a result there had not been one single significant piece of historical study of Sung education that could provide any new glimpses into what occurred during the days when the reformers were experimenting with their educational ideas.

The situation changed after the rise of Ch'ing interest in historical criticism and in the restoration of lost historical texts. The rediscovery of Li's entire

[19] See Sudō Yoshiyuki, "Nan-Sō no Ri Dō to *Shiji tsugan chōhen* no seiritsu," in his *Sōdai shi kenkyū*, 469–512. See also Yang Chia-lo, "*Hsü Tzu-chih t'ung-chien ch'ang-pien* hsin-ting-pen hsü," in *HCP*, Vol. I, 1–17; *idem*, "chi-lüeh," in *HCP*, Vol. I, 1/1a–2/2b. See also Yves Hervouet (ed.), *A Sung Bibliography* (Hong Kong: The Chinese University Press, 1979), 72–75.

[20] The chapters restored, called *Shih-pu* (*HCPSP* hereafter), are for hsitories from the fourth month of 1067 (Chih-p'ing 4th year) to the third month of 1068 (Hsi-ning first), the seventh month of 1093 (Yüan-yu 8th) to the third month of 1097 (Shao-sheng 4th), and the second month of 1100 (Yüan-fu 3rd) to the end of the Northern Sung dynasty. They are inserted in between chapters 209 and 210, 484 and 485, and after 520.

[21] This is Yang Chung-liang's *Hsü Tzu-chih t'ung-chien ch'ang-pien chi-shih pen-mo* (*Chi-shih pen-mo* hereafter) which had not been widely circulated until it was published in 1893 in Canton, by Kuang-ya shu-chü as part of its *Chi-shih pen-mo hui-k'o ts'ung-shu*. See Chao T'ieh-han, "*Hsü Tzu-chih t'ung-chien ch'ang-pien chi-shih pen-mo* t'i-tuan," in *Chi-shih pen-mo*, Vol. I, 1–5.

book from the early Ming encyclopedia, the *Yung-lo ta-tien* (The Grand Dictionary of the Yung-lo Era) and its subsequent publication in 1881 marks one very important turning-point not only in the study of Sung education, but in that of the Sung history as a whole. The work was published together with those missing chapters now restored by Huang I-chou. Sung scholars thus had now a comprehensive work to arrive at a more detailed and balanced understanding of Sung education.

Another important work also started to receive attention at about the same time as the publication of Li's *Hsü ch'ang-pien*. This was a collection of Sung Court documents, called the *Sung hui-yao* (Compendium of Important Sung Official Documents). The work is almost entirely unedited, and is an even looser compilation of official documents than Li T'ao's *Hsü ch'ang-pien*, the majority of the documents being memorials submitted to the emperors. Though incomplete, the work was voluminous enough to provide a large amount of new information that has hitherto been unknown to historians. Moreover, its very nature makes it all the more attractive as a reliable firsthand source. The *Sung hui-yao* was made available to a wide reading public in 1937 when photo-copied and issued by the National Pei-p'ing Library (in present Peking). The data on economic history has so far attracted the most attention. Scholars are only beginning to use the materials in this encyclopedic work for educational history.[22]

The information found in these two important works,[23] rich as it is, may not compel us to radically change the traditional viewpoint concerning Sung education. In any case, there has not been any study on Sung education that has systematically used the sources found in these two works or compendiums.[24] Indeed, not until Terada Gō published his *Sōdai kyōiku shi gaisetsu* (A General Survey on Sung Education) were the materials of the *Hsü ch'ang-pien* used significantly.[25]

---

[22] For a study of the restoration, transmission and publication of Hsü Sung's *Sung hui-yao chi-kao* (Peking: Chung-hua, 1966, a reprint of the 1936 Pei-p'ing t'u-shu kuan edition) (*SHY* hereafter), see T'ang Chung, *Sung hui-yao yen-chiu* (Shanghai: Shang-wu, 1932). See also Yves Hervouet (ed.), *A Sung Bibliography*, 177–178.

[23] Huang I-chou's *HCPSP* relied on Yang Chung-liang's *Chi-shih pen-mo* heavily, because it so happened that the latter preserves a lot of information missing from the present *HCP*.

[24] See my "Sung-tai chiao-yü shih yen-chiu te chi-ko wen-t'i," in my *Sung-tai chiao-yü san-lun* (*San-lun* hereafter) (Taipei: Tung-sheng, 1979), 97–128. John Chaffee's "Education and Examinations in Sung Society," as well as my "Education in Northern Sung China," are probably the first English works to make systematic use of sources related to education found in the *SHY* and *HCP*.

[25] Terada Gō, *Sōdai kyōiku shi gaisetsu* (*Kyōiku shi* hereafter) (Tokyo: Hakubunsha, 1965). See my review essay in *San-lun*, 97–128.

Scholarly articles dealing with Sung education and examinations since Terada's time have used these two works more systematically and intelligently. The studies by Chin Chung-shu on the Sung examination system,[26] published in the 1960s and 1970s, and the excellent work on the same subject by Araki Toshikazu[27] have also benefitted from the information found in both the *Sung hui-yao* and *Hsü ch'ang-pien*. The same unfortunately cannot be said of educational histories. Here is one example: for all of its comprehensiveness and usefulness, Wang Chien-ch'iu's work on the Sung Imperial University (*t'ai-hsüeh*) published in 1965, made use of only part of the immediately available sources in the *Sung hui-yao*. The materials he did cite were used only to supplement the main line of narrative.[28] In general, because of the rather incoherent way the *Sung hui-yao* was compiled, its data is difficult to use effectively, to say the least.

Today, any work that hopes to be credited as a reliable study on Sung education cannot afford to bypass these two important collections of sources. Indeed, we are just beginning to find studies which make use of them, and it is necessary for us to bring together their findings in order to achieve a new and perhaps more definitive understanding of the educational legacy of Sung China.

In summary, our knowledge of Sung education has so far been shaped by the three major compilations mentioned above, each of a general, institutional and intellectual historical nature. Interpretations offered by these works are by and large Neo-Confucian. However, with the rediscovery, careful re-editing and publication of Li T'ao's *Hsü ch'ang-pien* and the massive, if miscellaneous, *Sung hui-yao*, we are at the critical point of being able to write a more objective and comprehensive history of Sung education, although I do not consider that they will offer any radically different interpretations.

B. The Study of Sung Education: Historiographical Possibilities

A successful study of Sung educational history will first have to answer

---

[26] Chin Chung-shu, "Pei-Sung k'o-chü chih-tu yen-chiu" ("Pei-Sung k'o-chü" hereafter), in *Hsin-ya hsüeh-pao*, Vol. 6 (1964), No. 1, 205–281, No. 2, 163–242; *idem*, "Pei-Sung k'o-chü chih-tu yen-chiu hsü" ("Pei Sung k'o-chü hsü" hereafter), in *Kuo-li Ch'eng-kung ta-hsüeh li-shih hsüeh-pao*, Vols. 5 and 6 (1978 and 1979), 135–243 and 87–186.

[27] Araki Toshikazu, *Kakyo*. See my review essay in *San-lun*, 97–128.

[28] For Wang's failure to use *SHY* materials to clarify the admission method of the Southern Sung University, see my *San-lun*, 116–124. See also pp. 97–128 for a review essay on the works of Wang, Terada and Araki.

two questions: was there an educational ideal and practice that we could define to be uniquely Sung and how did that education affect the latter periods of Chinese history? It is important to point out that there was indeed one central concern in the education offered by the government during the Sung and this was to search for a reliable institution to practice the Confucian ideal of meritocratic selection. Government education in the Sung dynasty was consequently intertwined with the practice of civil service examinations. It is supremely important to study the nature of the civil service examinations if one wishes to understand the purpose, as well as the success or failure, of government education.

In relation to the search for a viable institution, one sees the academies as yet another alternative. Clearly, as we shall see later in this book, the examinations provided too few positions to satisfy all the people who received education one way or the other. Academies naturally did not create enough challenge to the society for it to open up more positions for those people educated in the Confucian curriculum. But at least they provided a mental or psychological alternative to studying for entrance to officialdom.

However, systematic government policies on education and on the civil service examinations are easier to study and describe than private education in the academies. There have already been a number of excellent studies on the history of the civil service examinations in the Ming and Ch'ing periods, and the current scholarly consensus remains that they were rather open. Among the successful candidates at the examinations, a good proportion came from among the commoners.[29] More recent studies on the family background and the preparation of the candidates for the examinations, however, suggest that powerful lineages in the provinces often had a tremendous physical ability to perpetuate themselves, and that they were able to sustain the family luck by producing successful candidates and hence, officials in the government, for generations.[30] This newly discovered fact may not necessarily contradict the conventional viewpoint, but it seems that a Sung educational historian should not be blind to a variety of angles from which to look at the examinations. Did the examinations open up enough positions for a large number of commoners to move up into officialdom? If not, then the tremendous fluidity within the bureaucracy in terms of turnover rate of officials must have a significance beyond what we may call "open" competition.[31] What kind of social mobility did the civil service examinations create? How much mobility among the successful candidates

[29] Ping-ti Ho, *The Ladder*.

[30] Hilary J. Beattie, *Land and Lineage in China* (Cambridge: Cambridge University Press, 1979).

[31] See later in Ch. 8.

was there during the Sung? Above all, how was the Sung civil service examinations system different from that of the later periods? The last question has to be answered if we wish to make comparisons between the importance of the examination system during the Sung and that during the subsequent dynasties.

The civil service examinations certainly had a tremendous influence on the development of education in Sung China. But education itself also progressed significantly. There is much information on the founding and finance of schools, but in terms of information on the life in local schools, we hardly possess any systematically collected materials. Fortunately, Sung historians wrote down a large amount of information on life in the higher educational institutions, and this information has also been constantly studied.[32] However, traditional frameworks and historiographical concerns dominated the selection and presentation of sources. For example, in the West, town-gown relationship dominated the narratives on medieval universities, but Chinese historians were primarily concerned with the patriotic deeds of students of government's higher educational institutions.[33] It is thus challenging enough for a modern historian to present the concerns of students, especially those of the *T'ai-hsüeh*, as revealed to him by his data, without, at the same time, sacrificing the modern man's interest in such matters as town-gown relations. I consider it an important task to try to strike a balance between those two historiographical concerns, at least in the area of life in schools.

Even within the area of planned educational activities, modern interests in education have gone beyond simply understanding schools as pedagogical institutions where moral or intellectual values are taught to children. What was the social composition of the student body? How did schools finance themselves and their students? The sociology of education has grown into a major field, with research studies appearing in a multitude of monographs. Some books are even devoted entirely to school buildings.[34] A modern

[32] See notes for Ch. 7, sections B and C.

[33] See, for Western examples, works by Hastings Rashdall, Charles Haskins and Lynn Thorndyke, etc.

[34] I am limiting myself to historical studies only. There is a growing awareness among educational historians of the importance of school buildings in teaching. The philosophy espousing the idea of having children live at school, rather than at home, rose in Renaissance times. We have since seen more stress on the importance of environment in general, and school setting or building in special, as opposed to home than before. For a Renaissance statement, see Petrus Paulus Vergerius, *De Ingenuis Moribus*, in William H. Woodward (ed.), *Vittorino de Feltre and Other Humanist Educators* (New York: Teachers' College, Columbia University, 1963), 93–118. See, especially, 101.

educational historian therefore cannot afford to ignore these issues.[35] While it is true that materials normally determine the way questions are raised and even the method of studying the questions, it is no less true that a knowledge of methods derived from works dealing with a comparable topic could help a historian to look for materials hitherto thought to be irrelevant.

Institutional change is a good example, and a discussion of the issue is relevant to the second question raised at the beginning of this section. How did official schools in China after the Sung gradually evolve into non-instructional institutions, simply to become places where local scholars registered as primary degree candidates. A careful study of Sung education should show that the Sung school system created an incentive for examination aspirants to compete for a place in local schools. They could then be recommended to the University, whose graduates were better prepared for further departmental tests. At any rate, they enjoyed a better chance to take the examination because of the more generous quota the University enjoyed. This Sung method of reserving University positons and, hence, better chances for success in the civil service examinations for distinguished local school graduates were largely maintained in Ming and Ch'ing practices.

Similarly, it seems that nobody has yet asked the question how *chü-jen* as a status, enjoying official-like treatment in the Ming and Ch'ing, actually started.[36] This is mainly because, traditionally, Chinese educational historians were never trained to treat the candidates and officials as a special group possessing some special traits which may perhaps be called "class phenomenon."[37] Thanks largely to modern historians of China who study the so-called "gentry" of late Imperial China, we are now better able to conceive of them as a political and economic group possessing the basic distinction of a class.[38] Similarly, we are also in a better position in historiographical terms to sort through all kinds of sources to study the political

---

[35] See *Education Index* (New York: The H. W. Wilson Co.) for the tens of thousands of titles that poured out each year on all aspects of education, and these do not even include regular books or monographs.

[36] See John Chaffee's "Education and Examinations in Sung Society" for an excellent study on the status of *chü-jen* in Sung China, and I have based my discussion on this subject on his study. See Ch. 6, section D and Ch. 8, section A.

[37] The excellent institutional histories of *T'ung-tien*, *T'ung-chih* and *WHTK* have not developed adequate theoretical framework to reveal the kind of characteristics of a class of "gentry." None of them had ever said something similar to this: "At the very heart of the bureaucracy this spiritualism turns into a crass materialism, the materialism of passive obedience, of trust in authority, the mechanism of an ossified and formalistic behavior, of fixed principles, conceptions and traditions...." (Karl Marx, *Critique of Hegel's "Philosophy of Right"*, ed. by Joseph O'Malley [Cambridge: Cambridge University Press, 1970], 47.)

[38] See Ch. 1, note 33.

and financial aspects of this group of people including both *chü-jen* and regular bureaucrats. A careful study of these matters should enable us to know better how the *chü-jen*, who in Sung times were only successful candidates from primary, prefectural examinations, should in Ming and Ch'ing times become a visible group with power and social prestige in local affairs.[39]

The educational historian is interested in more than institutions and their evolution. Modern conceptions of educational history have clearly moved away from centering on institutionalized actions to such matters as the social significance of education or political development of students. I believe that many questions that are being raised by educational historians of other civilizations ought also to be posed to Chinese historical sources. The following are just some examples. The study of literacy has by now grown into a vast field, and discoveries in theoretical, not to mention statistical or sociological, terms, are quickly deluging even the most diligent student.[40] We are now lucky that the first book ever dealing with popular literacy in Chinese history has come out, and has received a generally enthusiastic review.[41] It appears that a Sung historian should also attempt to look into this problem and describe for us the picture of popular literacy and commoners' education.[42]

Or, for another example, the recent interest in the problem of the concepts of "childhood" should also be equally attractive. We have at our disposal a good number of Sung paintings, some of which could supplement our knowledge, derived from various books, of how the Sung period perceived a child and how they thought about his education.[43] A knowledge

---

[39] I have left out any lengthy discussion on academies, neither have I discussed how they affected later educational practices. The reason is that the main concern of this book is the relationship between government education and the examinations, and how the relationship affected Chinese society in the Sung and later dynasties. For the present purpose, it is adequate to point out that the academies provided the best available solution to the central problem of Sung education.

[40] And I am limiting myself only to works of historians.

[41] Rawski, *Education and Popular Literacy in Ch'ing China*. See my review (in Chinese) in *Shih-hsüeh p'ing-lun*, No. 3 (1981), 242–245.

[42] A group of historians from the Chinese University are currently conducting an investigation into the historical significance of popular literacy in China, covering a period from 960 to 1937. Preliminary results were presented to the annual conference of the Association of Asian Studies, 1982, at Chicago. See Ch. 2, note 17.

[43] Despite severe criticisms by authors like Lloyd deMause, Philippes Aries' *Centuries of Childhood*, translated by Robert Baldick (New York: Alfred A. Knopf, 1962), remains an excellent work. See my "The Discovery of Childhood: Children and Education in Sung China," in Sigrid Paul, *Kultur—Begriff und Wort in China und Japan* (Berlin: Dietrich Reimer Verlag, 1984), 159–202.

of this may help us to understand the different policies pursued during the Sung concerning the so-called "Children's examinations" (*t'ung-tzu shih*), or the significance of the many new primers.

Similarly, the impact of printing technology on education is equally worthy of study. Some Japanese authors have studied the legal or diplomatic aspects of control of the printing press.[44] The magnitude of the impact which the widespread use of the printing press made on Sung education has not been systematically studied, at least not in a manner like that of Elizabeth Eisenstein.[45] The study of this issue has to be centered in, among many things, the special ideographic nature of the Chinese language, as this might have made it doubly difficult for the printing press to have an impact similar in kind to that which the Gutenberg machine had on European civilization.[46]

The modern concern for mass education leads one to pay attention to popular readers. Primers, literacy books and the like have scarcely been studied hitherto. Indeed, not until the discoveries in Tun-huang came to light did we realize that the *Miscellaneous Notes* (*Tsa-ch'ao*) and *The Family Instruction of T'ai-kung* (*T'ai-kung chia-chiao*) were so popular in the T'ang and Sung times.[47] The first modern historian to deal specifically with popular reading texts in Sung China is Ch'en Tung-yüan, whose contribution to the study of Chinese educational history stands out as one of the best.[48] The study of Sung education therefore should include a discussion of the various standard primers and other popular readers.

There is much more that can be said about possibilities, now that we have this new spectrum of methodological insights. But it is necessary to return to some of the truly fundamental issues. To give just one example, educa-

---

[44] Niida Noboru and Miyazaki Ichisada, for examples.

[45] *The Printing Press as an Agent of Change*, 2 vols. (Cambridge: Cambridge University Press, 1979).

[46] This is related to the problem of literacy education. K. Gough argues, largely taking examples from writings of Joseph Needham, to show that the ideographic feature of the Chinese writing system did not make it specially difficult for the Chinese to acquire adequate basic literacy. Whether the argument is correct or not depends on a thorough examination of the vocabulary range of basic primers in contrast to that of popular reading materials. For Kathleen Gough's opinion, see Jack Goody (ed.), *Literacy in Traditional Societies* (Cambridge: Cambridge University Press, 1968), 69–84.

[47] Naba Toshisada, "Tō shōhon *Zōshō* kō," in his *Tōdai shakai bunka shi kenkyū* (Tokyo: Sōbunka, 1974), 197–268. See also Wang Ch'ung-min, *Tun-huang ku-chi hsü-lu* (Peking: Chung-hua, 1979), 215–224.

[48] Ch'en, *Chiao-yü shih*. The book contains some relatively revisionist interpretations, but is not ideological.

tional theories should very naturally occupy a great, if not necessarily central, position in any history of education. The Sung was undoubtedly one of the most philosophically brilliant ages, and a student of the history of education in the Sung cannot afford to shy away from attempting to comprehend the development in educational thinking in Sung China.[49] Our knowledge of Sung educational thinking, as mentioned before, will have to come primarily from works compiled by Neo-Confucians, and we would naturally assume that there were preferential concerns in their records. But because of this, there exist opportunities to be critical, as was Liang Ch'i-ch'ao, who in the early twentieth century wrote the famous but controversial *Wang Ching-kung.*[50] On the other hand, the revisionist works, published after 1949, serve more to highlight the viscissitudes of political struggles in contemporary China rather than provide any signficant or rational rethinking. They cannot be of much help.[51] In any case, since most of the significant contributions to educational theories were made by Neo-Confucians, and since Neo-Confucians had the greatest influence on our understanding of Sung education, a reliable and balanced account of the Sung ideal and theories about education and pedagogy will be perhaps the most challenging part of a book on Sung education.

Thus, it is obvious that the field of Sung education has ample possibilities for exploration, and there are many questions one could take up. Not all the questions raised above can be answered satisfactorily, and there is no point in pretending that all of them have answers. But with the help of modern scholarship in educational history, it seems that the time has come to produce a more comprehensive and reliable study.[52]

---

[49] *Sung Yüan chiao-hsüeh ssu-hsiang* by Wang Yün-wu (Taipei: Shang-wu, 1971) is disappointing. Regular surveys such as Ch'en Tung-yüan's *chiao-yü shih* contain treatments on educational thinking, but the *Chung-kuo chiao-yü shih* by Hu Mei-ch'i has been especially useful. Ku Shu-sen's *Chung-kuo ku-tai chiao-yü chia yü-lu lei-li* (Shanghai: Chiao-yü, 1983) is also useful.

[50] Liang Ch'i-ch'ao, *Wang Ching-kung.*

[51] The 1961 anthology, *Chung-kuo ku-tai chiao-yü shih tzu-liao*, edited by Meng Hsiang-tseng et al. (Peking: Jen-min chiao-yü, 1982 reprint) has one part devoted to quotations from educational thinkers. The selections are, by and large, balanced, and editors have refrained from quoting ideologically controversial modern or Communist interpretations. But it remains mainly an anthology.

[52] For a more detailed thinking on the historiographical possibilities, see my *San-lun*, 1–22. See also John Talbott, "Education in Intellectual and Social History," in Felix Gilbert and Stephen R. Graubard (eds.), *Historical Studies Today* (New York: W. W. Norton & Co., 1972), 193–201; and Gillian Sutherland, "The Study of the History of Education," in *History*, 54 (1969), 49–59.

C. The Purpose of This Book

From the discussion above, one sees that an educational history of the Sung should include sections on planned, institutional activities, especially on those of government schools. It should also have sections on private education, touching on the development of academies and educational theories. Naturally, if the book could also deal with such informal aspects of education as literacy or conceptions of childhood, it would be ideal. When education is defined in its broadest possible sense, it could very well mean socialization and the transmission of scientific ideas. Similarly, the use of printed materials is one form of communication, and therefore could also be discussed along with its influence on educational practices.[53] In short, a history of Sung education should at least cover two main areas: government education and how it was influenced by the civil service examinations, and private education, including the academies and the formation and transmission of the cultural values of Chinese society. It is my intention to limit myself in this book to a general discussion of the first area.

As has already been mentioned, the civil service examination system grew into a more or less permanent form in Sung times. It became the most important machinery for the recruitment of officials and, hence, the most important channel for a commoner to move up the ladder of Chinese society. The development had many implications for educational practices. Unless we have a clear understanding of the operation and significance of the civil service examination, as well as the entire recruitment activity of the Sung government, we can never hope to have any meaningful understanding of Sung education. I hope to include a discussion of the system as it was and how it worked during the Sung as a part of Sung government education. This will include considerations of the examination subjects, the procedure of the examinations, and above all, the ideas related to how the examinations could be both impartial and equal in the distribution of successful candidates. I shall also discuss the psychological dilemma of examination candidates. Furthermore, I shall also try to examine the social significance of the institution. Obviously, the examination system had a tremendous impact on the structure of Chinese society. I hope to delineate how Chinese society changed in response to the changing composition of the upper elite in society. On the other hand, the government, seeing that the examination system was growing into an important social, as well as political, institution, naturally had to devise measures to insure that the geographical distribution of

---

[53] The subtitle of Elizabeth Eisenstein's *The Printing Press as an Agent of Change* is "Communications and Cutlural Transformations in Early Modern Europe."

potential officials be equitable, that the system was not corrupted, and above all, that the government could exercise full control over this machinery for upward social mobility. In a sense, these issues are not directly related to education. But, because the system was such an important social institution, an analysis of how it operated in Sung society will assist us to better understand the psychology of Sung students.

Furthermore, there was an intricate relationship between the ideal of the examinations and that of education. Since the earliest days, the Chinese had constantly regarded education as cultivation of *shih*,[54] or for that matter, the preparation of potential officials. It has, therefore, always been true that the method of examining and selecting potential officials was closely related to education. The ideal of the examination was to recruit only the morally acceptable candidates.[55] As a result, if the examination system as an institution failed to take in only the morally qualified candidates, then one could conclude that the system had not achieved its designated goal. The Sung people were constantly worried about the probability of their ever succeeding in this moralistic mission. Anxiety over such matters had many implications for education in government schools. The Sung saw the first comprehensive attempt to replace the examinations by a hierarchical school system, so that the best could be selected from within schools for governmental service. This effort at mass education in the early twelfth century failed, however. It is important to look into the achievements and problems of this program. The examinations system, on the other hand, survived the reform; it is equally important to assign a reason for its survival.

The Sung also created the local school system for late Imperial China.[56] Many of the government schools which were still thriving in the early twentieth century could trace their beginnings to the Sung. How did the Sung create a system that could last for such a long time, and how did these schools evolve into an even closer part of the institution of examinations? One important item is the quota system. The Sung started to reserve special quotas of successful candidates for local school graduates. Eventually candidates of the civil service examinations were allowed to be admitted to local government schools for registration purposes as a recognized step in the degree structure. The train of this development started in the Sung. I will try to make clear how the Sung contributed to it. Similarly, special privileges awarded to students also helped to create a situation in which local govern-

---

[54]"*Yang-shih chiao-yü*," coined by Ch'en Tung-yüan, literally meaning "education for preparing students for offices," or "cultivation of bureaucrats," in his *Chiao-yü shih*, 3–5.

[55]See above, Ch. 1, section A.

[56]See above, Ch. 2, section B.

ment school graduates became distinguished from commoners. When this development was combined with the development that schools became a recognized stage in the degree structure of the examinations, the encroachment of the examinations on Chinese institutionalized education (especially that administered by the government) was complete. The "officialization" process, which was particularly visible in the private educational tradition, also occurred in government schools.

In dealing with government education at the local level, it is necessary to provide a general survey of the organization and finance of schools, the composition of the student body and, above all, the appointment and examination of teaching personnel. The last point is important because the Sung created the first office of Educational Intendant. It is necessary to look into the historical background and the significance of this office. A clear understanding of the involvement of the government in those areas will enable us to better understand why the relationship between recruitment and education became so close, even at local levels.

Higher education was even more intertwined with the preparation of students going into government service. The higher educational institutions serviced primarily aristocratic students during the T'ang, who normally went into service by hereditary right. By Sung times, however, this started to change. The government found out, as early as the second decade of the dynasty, that the facilities were more useful for all those who were preparing for the civil service examinations.[57] The consequence was for more and more commoners to seek admission to them (especially the Directorate). This was an important change, and needs attention and clarification. Secondly, the distinction between the two branches of higher educational institutions, namely, the School of the Directorate of Education and the Imperial University, was very clear in the T'ang. Did this distinction gradually disappear because of the influences of examinations on government education in general? Thirdly, in institutional terms, how did the University evolve into becoming practically a part of the examination degree structure?

In order to answer these problems, one would have to study the relationship between the *T'ai-hsüeh* (Imperial University) and the *Kuo-tzu hsüeh* (The School of the Directorate of Education). A study of this relationship will help us to clarify the process by which the higher educational institutions during the Sung gradually evolved into schools chiefly for preparing students of commoner background for the civil service examinations. A study of the admission methods of the University will help us to understand how even the people admitted to study in the University were essentially similar

[57]*SS*, 165:3909–3910; *SHY*, "Ch'ung-ju" section (cj hereafter), 1/29b.

to those who, in any case, would take the examinations. Finally, when these questions are answered, we shall be in a better position to go back to the fundamental question concerning the relations between the examinations and the practice of education in Sung and late Imperial China.

Generally speaking, the Sung government by and large had abandoned the rather complex system of higher education of the T'ang. Except for brief periods in the early twelfth century, the Sung did not systematically supervise the professional training within the Directorate. The government seemed undecided as to whether the training of technical officers such as painters, calligraphers, mathematicians, astronomers and even legal experts should be trusted to the Directorate of Education or to relevant governmental agencies. This will be discussed in the part on higher education, which will also include discussions on such general topics as the organization, finance and development of the University and other schools under the Directorate.

This is a book about more than the effects of examinations on educational practices. I have, therefore, included one chapter on life in the government schools of Sung China, and it deals primarily with extracurricular activities. I cannot deny that the involvement of University students in national politics has so far drawn the most attention,[58] but it seems to me that since the book is primarily about education, it should devote to this topic only a section in the chapter on school life. I shall try also to present a more neutral interpretation of the political activities of Sung students. I have full sympathy with their social and political concerns, though their actions were often as much a result of inflammation or unscruplous convictions as of careful and rational deliberation.

There are many more items which were directly related to government education. I have decided to leave them out for the time being, to avoid confusion. One example is the elementary school system. I hope to discuss it in another volume dealing with private education. Local government schools also ran technical training programs, especially that of medicine. This has also been left out, as these programs are not very directly related to the concerns of this book.

---

[58] Making up nearly half of Wang Chien-ch'iu's *Sung-tai t'ai-hsüeh yü t'ai-hsüeh sheng* (*Sung-tai t'ai-hsüeh* hereafter) (Taipei: Chung-kuo hsüeh-shu chu-tso chiang-chu ch'u-pan wei-yuan hui, 1965).

Part II
Government Education and Examinations in Sung China

"On the day of *ping-tzu,* we performed the following divination: children are going to school, will they meet rain when they come back?"[1] recorded a piece of Shang dynasty (c. 1766—1122 B.C.) oracle bone, suggesting that organized education was perhaps already in existence as early as the second millennium B.C.

Since then, the Chinese government has always regarded education as an important responsibility. Almost without exception, the first edicts of a new dynasty included one concerned with education. In Ch'en Tung-yüan's characterization, the purpose of government education in traditional China was one of "cultivation of bureaucrats" (*yang-shih*).[2] The government considered its supreme duty to be educating and training qualified young men to take up service in the government.

In addition to the training of young men for government service, the imperial Chinese government also considered it a fundamental duty to administer low-level, elmentary education, a task which they generally supported with varying degrees of enthusiasm.

The Sung was no exception. In terms of size and sophistication, it succeeded in running some convincingly well-organized government educational institutions. The salient features of Sung government schools were, first, the unsuccessful but important proposal to make students' performance in schools a more important criterion for admission to governmental service than mere success in the civil service examinations. The result was a series of reform attempts, eventually unsuccessful, during the late eleventh and early twelfth centuries to require actual attendance and residence at schools. Secondly, the civil service examination was elevated to become the single most important recruiting machinery at the expense of formally organized school education. The result of this development was for the Chinese people to regard performance in the examinations as the single most important goal of education. It also led to the ultimate decline of officially established schools, at least in terms of educational quality. Thirdly, most of the techniques and procedures of the civil service examination system were developed and perfected in the Sung, and would become standardized in later dynasties. Lastly, the advance of political activism manifested itself in large scale student movements. This would have a far-reaching impact on Sung politics.

---

[1] Quoted from Yang K'uan, "Chung-kuo ku-tai te ta-hsüeh" ("Ku-tai ta-hsüeh" hereafter), in *Ku-shih hsin-t'an* (Hong Kong: Kuo-hua, 1976), 197.
[2] Ch'en Tung-yüan, *Chiao-yü shih,* 3—5.

CHAPTER 4

Higher Education

Briefly speaking, Sung higher education mainly provided preparatory education for the sons of ranking officials or for young men with a commoner background to qualify for the civil service examination degrees. The government supervised and financed the Directorate of Education (*Kuo-tzu chien*), which consisted in turn of schools teaching general subjects and other special training schools, offering instruction on such matters as law, mathematics, painting, medicine and calligraphy.

A. Historical Background

Though it has often been argued that "universities" existed as early as Chou times (c. 1122–221 B.C.),[3] the first reliable evidence of an organized institution of higher education was the founding of the *T'ai-hsüeh* (translated as "Imperial University" hereafter) in the second century B.C.[4] The Han government established the Imperial University to admit young men of good family background to the study of classical learning, and its graduates were guaranteed a position in the officialdom. Virtually every dynasty continued this system. However, as it developed, the university expanded into two branches, because of the increase in the number of students. The university proper continued to admit all eligible students, but a new branch, the *Kuo-tzu* ("national youth") school, was set up to admit only the sons

---

[3] Yang K'uan, "Ku-tai ta-hsüeh"; Ch'en P'an, "Ch'un-ch'iu shih-tai te chiao-yü," in *Bulletin of the Institute of History and Philology, Academia Sinica (AS/BIHP* hereafter), 45 (1974), 731–812. Here Ch'en states that "higher educational facilities" existed as early as the Western Chou (1122–771 B.C.). But note that H. G. Creel, in his *The Origins of Chinese Statecraft* (Chicago and London: University of Chicago Press, 1970), 409, states: "What we can definitely say on the basis of the Western Chou sources is that there was a concept of the royal service and a concept of education at more than one level, and that in at least one case one officer was educated by the king to prepare him for the royal service. There was also a royal school of archery, at which various officers studied. They may have studied other subjects, there or elsewhere. As to that we can only speculate."

[4] Pan Ku, *Han-shu* (Peking: Chung-hua, 1962), 6:171–172; 88:3593–3594.

of aristocrats. This change occurred in A.D. 276,[5] and remained a standard practice throughout the entire Period of Disunion (220–589), until the founding of the Sui dynasty (581–618).

Higher education changed somewhat during the Sui, when the School of National Youth (*Kuo-tzu hsüeh*) began to supersede and overshadow the Imperial University which was briefly suspended (601–605). But the most significant development was the creation of the Directorate of Education (literally, Directorate of National Youth, *Kuo-tzu chien*) to coordinate these two schools and to supervise other special institutions such as Schools of Mathematics and Calligraphy.[6] This new system is significant because it clearly marked the growing importance of higher education as an independent institution, which now was no longer loosely controlled under the supervision of other bureaus.[7]

When the T'ang overthrew the Sui in 618, they based their education on the Sui framework. But in contrast to the previous two levels, the T'ang created a three-level distinction among students of official higher education, and set up a new special School of Law (see Table 1); the result was that the Directorate of Education during the T'ang had direct control of seven schools, educating elite students to prepare for either general or special official services. Salaried officials made up the main body of the teaching staff in these T'ang institutions. The imperial government also provided the revenue for these schools.

The T'ang system of higher education was therefore highly centralized and well organized. It was quite satisfactory as an educational instrument designed to train eligible young men for official service. The system, however, had to compete with the rise in importance of the civil service examinations from which an increasing number of students could enter officialdom without official higher education. This group of successful candidates quickly took up positions in the bureaucracy, and became a major new political force. They started to present a challenge to the power of the traditional aristocrats, who obtained their offices through hereditary means. The same phenomenon also

[5] Fang Hsüan-ling, *Chin-shu* (Peking: Chung-hua, 1974), 3:66; 24:736 (where the date is put down as 278); Shen Yüeh, *Sung-shu* (Peking: Chung-hua, 1974), 24:356. See also Yang Chi-jen, *San-kuo liang-Chin hsüeh-hsiao yü hsüan-shih chih-tu* (Taipei: Cheng-chung, 1968), 66; and Kao Ming-shih, "T'ang-tai hsüeh-chih chih yüan-yüan chi ch'i yen-pien," in *Kuo-li T'ai-wan ta-hsüeh li-shih hsüeh-hsi hsüeh-pao*, 4 (1977) ("T'ang-tai hsüeh-chih" hereafter), 195–219, esp. 196–197.

[6] Wei Cheng *et al., Sui-shu* (Peking: Chung-hua, 1973), 23:777 and 793. Other special schools, such as the School of Medicine, also existed outside the control of the Directorate.

[7] Tu Yu, *T'ung-tien, Wan-yu wen-k'u* ed. (Shanghai: Shang-wu, 1935), 27:159–162; Kao Ming-shih, "T'ang-tai hsüeh-chih," 196.

TABLE 1
The T'ang Organization of the Directorate of Education*

Name of school	Admission qualifications	Age limits (Chinese *sui*)	Years of study	Number of students
School of the Directorate	Sons or male descendents of high-ranking officials	14–19	9	315
Imperial University	Sons or male descendents of middle-ranked officials	14–19	9	515
School of Four Gates	1. Sons or male descendents of low-ranked officials	14–19	9	560
	2. Intelligent sons of commoners	14–19	9	800
School of Law	As for School of Four Gates	18–25	6	55
School of Calligraphy	As above	14–19	9	33
School of Mathematics	As above	14–19	9	32
Kuang-wen School	Students of the Directorate School who specialized in the *chin-shih* subject			70

*Based on Kao Ming-shih, "T'ang-tai te kuan-hsüeh hsing-cheng," in *Ta-lu tsa-chih*, 37/11 & 12 (1968), 39–53.

influenced the practice of the official educational system.

The trend in the Sung was that more and more young men from commoner's background aspired for officially sponsored higher education. Ultimately, the majority of them chose to win official positions through the examinations, rather than merely going through the Imperial University, since a graduating degree did not exempt them from the examinations. Also, fewer and fewer students were actually graduating from the Directorate schools.[8] The Sung therefore saw a steady erosion in importance of these higher educational institutions; and yet, the students could still enjoy certain privileges and some degree of prestige by being admitted to the Imperial University. These students asserted a lot of influences on national politics throughout the Sung dynasty.

B. The Directorate of Education

The Directorate of Education supervised and coordinated the higher educational institutions. Established in 962,[9] two years after the dynasty was founded, the Directorate began as a government agency of little importance, in charge of instructing the young men of higher officials' families. It took about seventy years to grow into a full-fledged bureau which not only defined the distinction between the administrative Directorate and the academic Directorate School (in 994),[10] but also formally recognized the Imperial University as an integral part of the government's higher educational system.[11]

The responsibilities of the Directorate included:

1. In the first few decades, it organized the teaching of the so-called "national youth," which consisted of all aspiring students regardless of their family background. The institution was not yet fully developed, and though it theoretically only admitted sons or male descendents of ranking officials, it appears that it actually accepted all applicants. Besides organizing instruction within the institute itself, the Directorate did not take charge

---

[8] The number of students enrolled in the Directorate schools peaked in the early twelfth century, but declined thereafter. The largest number of students during the Southern Sung was never more than a half of the largest number achieved in the Northern Sung. See Table 3 for the number of students in various years.

[9] SS, 431:12816; SHY, "Chih-kuan" section (ck hereafter), 28/la and "Ch'ung-ju" section (cj hereafter), 1/29a.

[10] For the discussion of this distinction, see section D of this chapter. As for the distinction mentioned here, see HCP, 35/9b.

[11] For a discussion of the evolution of the University, see next section.

of any of the other major activities which it later would take on.[12]

2. By the 1040s, the Imperial University was established under the Directorate to formally admit students whose qualifications did not permit them to enroll in the Directorate School, which now restricted admission only to qualified students coming from families of officials of the seventh rank and up. This meant that the Directorate became an institution at once coordinating and supervising both the Directorate School and the Imperial University.[13]

3. By 1078, after the reorganization of the central government, the Directorate played a much more important role in the nation's system of education. It began to take charge of the following general and special schools: the Directorate School, the Imperial University, the Military School (*Wu-hsüeh*), the School of Law (*Lü-hsüeh*), the Elementary School (of the capital, *Hsiao-hsüeh*),[14] the *Pi-yung* School (1102–1121),[15] and, intermittently, the special Schools of Calligraphy, Mathematics, Painting and Medicine.[16]

4. Throughout most of the Sung dynasty, the Directorate operated a printing office. In addition to supervising government's education system in the capital area, the faculty members of the Directorate were also engaged in the compilation and collation of the classics which the Directorate's printing office printed and distributed. Many famous Sung editions, now still extant and appreciated by collectors, are products of the printing office managed by the Directorate. During the height of Wang An-shih's reforms, the Directorate issued the notorious commentaries on the *Book of Documents* (*Shang-shu*), the *Book of Poetry* (*Shih-ching*), and the *Rites of the Chou* (*Chou-li*), all edited by the reformers.[17] The printing office's activities were far-ranging: besides the classics and standard histories, the Directorate also published reference books for preparing for the civil

---

[12] *SS*, 165:3909–3910. The number of students set by the government was 70 when the Directorate was first founded, but the government soon found it hard to fill this number of students and therefore ordered in 975 the admission to the Directorate of examination aspirants in the capital region who previously would not be qualified for admission. This kind of students presumably made up the majority of the student body of the Directorate School until the University was formally established in 1044.

[13] See note 10.

[14] The readers are reminded here that the Directorate during the T'ang did not run the capital's elementary schools.

[15] A special branch of the Imperial University. See next section.

[16] For more on these schools see section H.

[17] *HCPSP*, 11/6b, 12/3b, 12/19a and passim. See also Yang Chung-liang, *Chi-shih pen-mo*, ch. 74. A special office was set up within the Directorate to take charge of the compilation works.

CHART 1

The System of Schools in the Sung

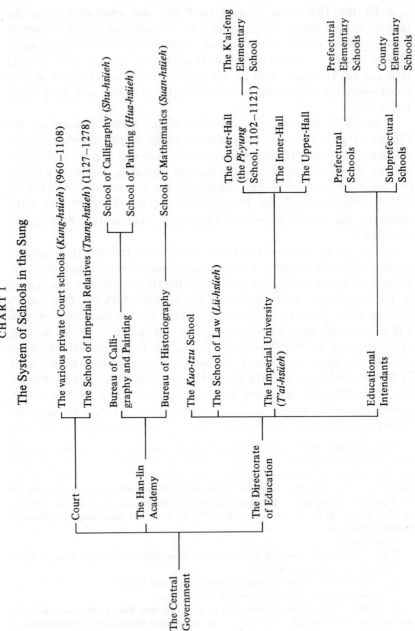

service examinations (such as Pai Chü-i's *Liu-t'ieh*), agricultural tracts (such as Chia Ssu-hsieh's *Ch'i-min yao-shu*),[18] legal texts,[19] and even obscure medical works such as "Prescriptions by a Matchless Physician to Cure All Diseases" (*Shen-i p'u-chiu fang*).[20] The printing office had no role in education, but was under the supervision of the Directorate which controlled its revenue and expenditure.[21]

Besides the responsibilities listed above, the Directorate became directly involved in a number of other activities in connection with related government offices, notably the Ministry of Rites (*Li-pu*).[22] Members of the teaching staff in the Directorate were often consulted by high officials about problems such as appropriate rites or ceremonies; a famous professor of the Imperial University in the 1050s, Hu Yüan (993–1059), for example, first became known in the 1030s because of his opinions on the precise pitch of official music.[23] The importance of the Directorate in relation with these ceremonial matters became even more visible after 1080 when the Director of the Directorate was promoted to a higher rank in the official bureaucracy and thereby could be involved more directly in advisory responsibilities. In general, however, the Directorate was not an influential organ in the central government. In 1069, when Emperor Shen-tsung (r. 1068–1084) ordered a comprehensive review of education and the examinations, heads of "the two Drafting Offices (i.e., Drafting Offices of the Secretariat and the Han-lin Academy), the two Departments (i.e., the Chancellery Department and the Secretariat Department), the Censorate, the Finance Commission, the three Institutes (the Hung-wen Institute, the Institute of History, and the Chi-hsien Library)"[24] were all required to submit recommendations. The head of the Directorate, however, is conspicuously missing from this list. However, in terms of indirect influence, the Directorate actually played a very significant role in that it helped to propagate the officially accepted versions of the classics. Thus the Directorate asserted an intellectual power which could be felt by almost every student. As early as 988, the Associate Supervisor of the Directorate was put in charge of printing the official

[18] *SHY*, ck, 28/2b–3a.
[19] *SHY*, ck, 28/14b–15a.
[20] *HCP*, 507/8b.
[21] *SHY*, ck, 28/5a; *SS*, 431:12798–12799.
[22] Under which the Directorate eventually was placed. See *SS*, 165:3915.
[23] *SS*, 84:3055–3056. For complete information on the discussion on the official music, see Yang Chung-liang, *Chi-shih pen-mo*, ch. 31, the entire chapter. Hu Yüan, then a successful candidate of the prefectural examination, was recommended by Fan Chung-yen to take part in the debate in 1036 in the Sung Court. Later he became a prefectural school preceptor and subsequently a professor at the University, recommended by Ou-yang Hsiu.
[24] *HCPSP*, 4/26a.

Commentaries of the Five Classics (*Wu-ching cheng-i*) compiled by K'ung Ying-ta (574–648). The entire printing project, including a detailed collation, lasted for more than ten years. Classics printed by the Directorate were of course treated with respect and confidence and they were often given as imperial gifts to local schools. Similarly, the new commentaries on the three major classics, mentioned above, compiled by the reformers in the 1070s were not only printed and published by the printing press of the Directorate, but the compilers were also members of the Directorate. Their influence, very naturally, was enormous.

The importance of the Directorate as an official organ was in no way comparable to the power it enjoyed in directing Sung intellectual life. The bureau after all was designed to provide educational direction and leadership and, in a peculiar way, it could be said to have quite successfully fulfilled its designated function, at least before the rise of Neo-Confucianism.

C. The Imperial University

The Imperial University, during the T'ang period, as mentioned above, was designed to admit students from the families of lower ranking officials. In 962, when the Directorate was opened, it was in theory also to admit only qualified ranking officials' sons, but as it turned out, a great number of students of lower family qualification also sought admission. Without specifically regulating how the Directorate should cope with this request for admission from otherwise unqualified young men, the government simply decided to accept all of them without questioning their credentials. After all, the total number of students who actually showed up for registration did not seem to exceed the quota set for the Directorate. In 975 the Directorate memorialized the emperor by saying that students registered in the Directorate did not exceed the quota of seventy and therefore recommended that examination candidates in the capital area who wished to utilize the facilities be permitted to fill the quota of the student-body.[25]

By 1040, it became apparent that this new group of students was endangering the chances of qualified students being admitted to the Directorate. In 1042, accordingly, *Ssu-men hsüeh* (School of Four Gates) was established, presumably to allow students without family background to qualify for the Directorate. Two years later, during a comprehensive reform, the Imperial University formally proclaimed its "independence."[26]

[25] *SS*, 157:3658.
[26] *SS*, 157:3659; *WHTK*, 42:395–401; *HCP*, 148/14a.

The Imperial University therefore replaced the newly founded School of Four Gates.[27] The independence meant that University students were to be treated differently from Directorate students in terms of faculty members made available to them, in terms of their status in the civil service examinations, what privileges to be accorded to them, and in terms of stipend or meal allowances. The University's independence also meant a separate revenue and likewise a separate budget.[28] This can be said to be the proper beginning of the Sung Imperial University.

The University was purely a teaching institution, organizing educational activities for advanced students who, after graduation, could be exempted from taking the primary level of the civil service examinations and sit in the Departmental examinations directly.[29] Throughout the Sung, the *T'ai-hsüeh* continued to serve this educational function and produced a good number of distinguished graduates.

After the reform of 1044, the independence of University was abolished, and the Directorate took over both management and instruction.[30] Nevertheless, increased numbers of students of all backgrounds continued to register for study, thanks to two prominent teachers, Hu Yüan and Sun Fu (992–1057), who laid down the fundamentals of the teaching and fought for the right of an independent curriculum.[31] They also carefully perpetuated the ideal of political reform. Their students included important reformers in the 1070s, Wang An-shih among the most notable. Thus, higher education, despite the loss of an independent University branch,

[27] Although the position of "Teaching Assistant in the [School of] Four Gates" continued to exist as late as 1058, there is no indication that the School was in existence. The title was honorary. See *HCP*, 187/13b–14a. See also *HCP*, 184/6a for the existence of this title prior to the founding of the *Ssu-men* school.

[28] On the finance of the Directorate and the University, see section G.

[29] For an explanation on "departmental examinations," see Ch. 6, section B. Directorate School students presumably enjoyed the same privilege.

[30] The building assigned to the University in 1044 was returned to its original use in 1045 and the University was forced to move to a smaller compound—a military barrack, but the teaching continued. See Wang Chien-ch'iu, *Sung-tai t'ai-hsüeh*, 9–10.

[31] Hu Yüan, before joining the University, was already an established teacher in his native Hu-chou (present Wu-hsing, Chekiang). However, he was invited by Ou-yang Hsiu and his associates to take up a professorial position only in 1052, but not during the 1044 reform, as is commonly held. See Huang Tsung-hsi, *Sung Yüan hsüeh-an, Ssu-pu pei-yao* (*SPPY* hereafter) ed. (Taipei: Chung-hua, 1965), 1/1a–5a; see also Wm. Theodore de Bary, "A Reappraisal of Neo-Confucianism." Sun Fu, on the other hand, had been very close to the reformers and joined the University as soon as it was founded, together with the maverick Shih Chieh (1005–1045). He was forced to leave the University after the reform failed, but managed to return in 1055 and stayed until his death.

continued to progress after the reform failed.[32] The number of students increased from fewer than 100 to 450, and then to 600 in 1058, the year Hu died,[33] and finally the school had to borrow more army barracks for classrooms.[34] This growth continued until well into the 1060s and up to the eve of Wang An-shih's reform (1068), when the total student population of the open and hereditary categories together reached 1,200.[35] This growth, in both quantitative and qualitative terms, characterized the first phase of reformers' efforts to improve higher education.

Wang An-shih's reform, which lasted until 1086, marked the second stage of the development of the University. The University's independent status was reaffirmed, and separate financing was obtained from the Directorate. Wang An-shih introduced a tripartite class system (Three-Hall System, *San-she*) into the University, which apparently required students to go through the classes before they could qualify for any special exemptionary status in the civil service examinations.[36] Wang, however, was preoccupied with other reform measures, and could not devote adequate time to educational reform. Except for supervising the compilation and publication of the *New Commentaries to the Rites of the Chou, the Book of History and the Book of Poetry* (*San-ching hsin-i*) which came out in 1075,[37] most of the restructuring of the University occurred after Wang resigned from his Chief Councillor's post and retired to Chiang-ning (present Nanking, Chiang-su) in 1077. Li Ting (1028–1087) and Chang Tsao were the chief advocates. Ts'ai Ching who later was to become the leading reformer of the early twelfth century was then a fledgling official whom Li recruited to help in the planning. The detailed plan was sent to the Emperor in early 1080, containing the following measures:[38]

1. Expansion of the University's campus, to include eighty buildings, accomodating a total of 2,400 students; of these, 100 were to be upper-hall students, 300 inner-hall students and 2,000 outer-hall students.

---

[32] The University lost its independence and accordingly its revenue. See section G.

[33] *HCP*, 170/16b; *SHY*, cj, 1/30ab; *SHY*, ck, 28/4b; *HCP*, 187/8b. See also my *San-lun*, 97–128.

[34] Wang Chien-ch'iu, *Sung-tai t'ai-hsüeh*, 10.

[35] *SHY*, ck, 28/4b; cj, 1/30ab.

[36] The details of Wang's policy on the University are discussed in Ch. 9, section A. A lot of his follower's policies have been, however, mistaken as those of Wang's. In general, it is safe to assume that measures adopted by Wang's followers bore out Wang's basic beliefs. See my *San-lun*, 129–157.

[37] *HCP*, 265/4a. The commentaries were sent to the printing press of the Directorate in the same month (sixth month), see *HCP*, 265/8b.

[38] *HCP*, 301/8ab; *SHY*, ck, 28/9b. See also my *San-lun*, 149–150.

2. Strict annual and monthly tests were to be instituted for grading students' achievements and for recommendation for promotions.
3. The appointment of the best graduates from the upper-hall directly into government service.

The last point, as will be shown later, was the essence of the educational reform.[39] However, throughout the entire period when this plan was carried out (1080–1086), only one graduate was actually appointed to office directly after completion of studies at the University.[40]

The reforms were suspended immediately after Emperor Shen-tsung died. Anti-reformers seized the opportunity to recommend their own version of higher education. The responsibility of drafting a program was entrusted to Ch'eng I, the famous philosopher.[41] Interestingly, Ch'eng's recommendation, submitted in the sixth month of 1086, touched only on minor issues. It suggested that Wang An-shih's *Commentaries* be treated only as equal to commentaries compiled by others, and that all nine classics should be taught at the University. The value of promoting upper-hall graduates directly into government service was questioned, although he did not suggest suspending the measure. In general, it is obvious that Ch'eng I did not recommend any drastic reversal of the system enacted by the reformers. Therefore, his rather long report shows that anti-reformers differed little from the reformers in their conception of higher education. Nevertheless, it contains enough material for us to gain a fairly clear picture of the position the University occupied in young students' minds. From his report we see that the University was attracting a great number. of students, so that "two students have to share one bed, and it becomes unbearable in the summer months; they are forced to take turns sleeping away from the dormitories."[42] Ch'eng I recommended further expansion of the University's facilities. Except for a small and temporary increase in government appropriations for administrative expenses,[43] however, there is no indication that either the revenue or the facilities expanded substantially.

The climax of the Sung government's reform efforts in education was reached later, in 1102, now led by Ts'ai Ching. Among the various reforms, it was the University which was most clearly affected. In spite of his con-

---

[39] See Ch. 5, section D and Ch. 9, section B.
[40] See Ch'eng I, *I-ch'uan i-shu*, in *Erh-Ch'eng ch'üan-shu*, Ch. 3. See also Wang Ying-lin, *Yü-hai* (Taipei: Hua-lien, 1964; reprint of Yüan edition), 112/33b.
[41] *HCP*, 378/1a; see also *ibid.*
[42] See note 40.
[43] See my *San-lun*, 73–96.

troversial political career, Ts'ai Ching without a doubt was the most important source of reform ideas affecting the Sung educational apparatus especially in terms of recruiting a national elite for the civil service. Some of his recommendations became permanent features in later Chinese educational practice.

The center of Ts'ai's reform was the practice of a kind of "universal education," establishing schools in virtually every sub-prefecture and promoting the better graduates from these local schools to study in the Imperial University. According to the plan, the government could then recruit from the best graduates of the University to staff the bureaucracy. Unlike Wang An-shih, Ts'ai Ching appointed University graduates to official posts in large numbers, and he also undertook, rather prematurely, attempts to abolish the civil service examinations. In the end, the examination system remained the primary avenue for entrance into the civil service.[44]

To accomodate the possible increase in students recommended by local government schools, Ts'ai Ching ordered the outer-hall of the University detached and moved to an independent location.[45] The new site and buildings were planned and designed by a famous architect, Li Chieh (d. 1111) and called *Pi-yung* (a preparatory school), a fancy allusion taken from the *Book of Poetry*, meaning a secluded environment ideal for moral cultivation.[46] The head of the *Pi-yung* school was called *Ta ssu-ch'eng* (the grand formator), again a name full of classical overtones (taken from the *Record of Rites*), whose rank was to be higher than that held by the Director (*Chi-chiu*, lit. libationer, also from the *Record of Rites*) of Education. After completing at least one year's study, the *Pi-yung* students would then move on to the inner-hall of the University.

The number of University and *Pi-yung* students increased steadily during the years when Ts'ai Ching was in power (1102–1106, 1107–1109, 1112–1120, 1124–1125) and reached a high point of 3,800 students in 1104.[47] This was undoubtedly one of the most outstanding periods in the history of Chinese higher education. The unprecedented efforts to expand higher and local education marked the only time in Chinese history that the validity of the civil service examination system, which was rapidly becoming

[44] Chin Chung-shu, "Pei-Sung k'o-chü," No. 2, 221–229.

[45] *SHY*, ck, 28/15a; *SS*, 157:3662–3663; *Chiu-ch'ao pien-nien pei-yao, SKCS* ed. (1977), 26/48b–49a.

[46] For some studies of this term and its ceremonial function, see Yang Che-ming, "Ming-t'ang chien-chu lüeh-k'ao," in *Chung-kuo chien-chu*, Vol. 3, No. 2 (1935), 57–60, and Henri Maspero, "Le *Ming-t'ang* et la crise religieuse chinoise avant les Han," in *Mélanges chinoises et bouddhiques*, No. 8 (1948–1951), 1–71.

[47] *SS*, 157:3663.

an immensely important social, as well as political institution, was brought into question. The collapse of Ts'ai Ching's reform reflected his failure to appreciate the difficulty of introducing a mass educational program into a society which was not ready for it.[48] Ts'ai Ching's difficulties in the matter of his personal conduct and moral integrity also did not help. By the time he left the government, it had become obvious that the University expansion had lost its momentum and ceased to function as an alternative to the examination system. The number of students had decreased, partly because of the turmoil which accompanied dynastic decay, but also as a result of the loss of dynamism within the University itself.[49] Despite all of this, the University continued to attract students for various reasons. Also, Ts'ai Ching's reform of promoting students from local prefectural schools to the University continued in the Southern Sung, and evolved into the system of school-examinations that the Ming and Ch'ing were to use. Therefore, however short-lived and perhaps ill-conceived, it is impossible to dismiss the contribution which Ts'ai Ching had made to Chinese higher education.

The Imperial University continued to be a popular center of advanced intellectual activities. Graduates of the University were usually exempted from the prefectural screening, so that it easily became a much coveted place among the ever increasing examination candidates. However, the size of the student population as well as institutional innovations had diminished substantially. The University began as a temporary gathering in 1127 when the exiled government moved to the South and admitted only a handful of students,[50] but eventually it received a semi-permanent site in 1142, when the political situation stabilized.[51] And as time went on, more and more students competed for admission. As a result, the policy on admissions became an unexpectedly serious matter.[52] The popularity of the University was also evident in the fact that outside scholars were participating in University activities; many of them were candidates who had failed to be admitted to the University or in the civil service examinations. The appearance of unregistered "wandering scholars" (*yü-shih*) on the University campus and in other schools in the capital area

---

[48] More on this, see Ch. 8, section B.

[49] The number of students was reduced to 600 just on the eve of the Jurchen invasion. See Hsü Meng-hsin, *San-ch'ao pei-meng hui-pien* (Taipei: Wen-hai, 1962 reprint), 99.

[50] Thirty-six students followed the government to the new capital. See *SS*, 157:3669.

[51] *Ibid.;* see also *SS*, 30:556.

[52] For a detailed study of Southern Sung admission methods, see my *San-lun*, 116–124. See also Table 4 in section E.

created administrative problems, and must have made it doubly difficult to maintain discipline within the campuses.[53] In terms of the size of the student body, as well as in terms of the students' educational purpose, however, the Imperial University in the Southern Sung obviously could not be compared to its predecessor in the Northern Sung. The largest group of University students, during the early thirteenth century, amounted to only 1,636, less than a half of the number reached during Ts'ai Ching's reform.

But the most notable feature of life in the University was the intensified political awareness among University students, an awareness which made many of them to eventually become directly involved in political activities, including openly criticizing high officials in the court, boycotting classes, and other sometimes questionable activities.[54] Because of its proximity to the center of power, young men of the elite found the University's setting favorable not merely for study, but also for acquiring political connections. The situation became so alarming that the notorious Chief Councillor of Emperor Li-tsung (r. 1225–1264), Chia Ssu-tao, had to plant student-spys in the University.[55]

Finally, the Southern Sung University preserved the tripartite class system and actually made effective use of it, so that more structured teaching could take place. Although some opposed the rigidity in grading students' academic aptitudes, the class system seemed to stand up to criticisms well, as least on paper.[56] In reality, a reliable tripartite class system depended on constant examinations within the University. During the Southern Sung, however, there is evidence that many outer-hall students did not take any examination for as long as five years. Political movements, as well as other gentlemen's activities took priority over serious learning. The situation deteriorated even further towards the end of the dynasty.[57] This may indicate that the University probably served much more successfully its social than its academic functions.

---

[53] Wang Chien-ch'iu, *Sung-tai t'ai-hsüeh*, 31–34, 263, 306. These pages discuss how University students cut classes apparently induced to do so by unregistered students.

[54] More on the political activities of the University students in Chapter 7.

[55] Chou Mi, *Kuei-hsin tsa-chih*, pieh-chi, shang, *Hsüeh-chin t'ao-yüan* ed. (1805), 26b. See my "Life in the Schools of Sung China," in *JAS*, 37 (1977), 45–60.

[56] Such as Chu Hsi who suggested that the tripartite system, which was founded on strict examinations within the school, was "to encourage students to strive for profits and to satisfy their selfishness, to create ambivalence and shamelessness" and "could by no means achieve the ideal of education and of cultivating talented people." See his *Wen-chi*, 69:1273–1277.

[57] Wang Chien-ch'iu, *Sung-tai t'ai-hsüeh*, 60–78.

The University met for the last time in 1275, just a few months before the Mongols seized Lin-an, the capital. Emperor Kung-ti (r. 1274–1276) decreed: "The destiny of the nation is suffering multiple hardships; people have deserted the area along the (Yangtze) River. It is therefore appropriate that students who still stay in the three schools (the Directorate School, the Imperial University and the School of Imperial Relatives) and are considering leaving be permitted to do so according to their wishes."[58] Thus ended the much loved, often controversial, but always influential University. Some students stayed anyway, and were given special official appointments. The Mongols arrived next spring, captured Kung-ti, his family, and household servants and maids. Among other captives forced to travel to the Mongol Court were several hundred students of the three capital schools.[59]

D. The Relation between the Two Higher Educational Institutions

In 1058, one year before Hu Yüan's death, Li Kou, a leading University professor memorialized the throne:[60]

> If we hope that the Directorate and the Imperial University will not interfere with each other, and that there is no ritual responsibility between the two (i.e., no hierarchical relations), then it is most appropriate to imitate the T'ang system. In the T'ang dynasty, the Directorate, the Imperial University, the School of Four Gates, the School of Law, the School of Calligraphy, the School of Mathematics and the Kuang-wen School were all under the Directorate, and the University was one of these seven schools. Their relationship with the Directorate was like that of the Ministry of War or the Ministry of Personnel and the Department of Ministries. It is evident that [these two ministries] did not interfere with each other. . . . I humbly recommend that the Directorate be abolished now that the teaching responsibility has been trusted to the Imperial University.

The memorial is a notable example of scholarly ambiguity. The author appeared to be defending the different function of the Imperial University from that of the Directorate school, by citing T'ang practice to support his argument. And yet, throughout the memorial, Li did not distinguish clearly between the Directorate as such and the Directorate School which was open to ranking officials' sons; this distinction, as described above,

---

[58] Anonymous author, *Sung-chi san-ch'ao cheng-yao,* Po-ku chai ed., now included in *Ts'ung-shu chi-ch'eng* (*TSCC* hereafter) ed. (Shanghai: Shang-wu, 1935–1937), 5:57.

[59] *Ibid.,* 5:62–63.

[60] Li Kou, *Chih-chiang Li hsien-sheng wen-chi, SPTK* ed., 29:221–222 (*Wen-chi* hereafter).

was very clear in the T'ang school system.[61] As a result, this memorial includes such a strange sentence as, "in the T'ang dynasty, the Directorate . . . [was] under the Directorate," both Directorates in the original being *"Kuo-tzu chien."* The confusion stemmed from the Sung practice of calling both the Directorate as such and the Directorate school by the same name, sometimes, *Kuo-tzu chien,* sometimes *Kuo-tzu hsüeh.*[62] Obviously, the first "Directorate" in Li Kou's essay referred to the Directorate School, while the second referred to the administrative office as such. Once this is made clear, then the author's point becomes clear: he was arguing that the Directorate and the teaching of the elite students from ranking officials' families should be separated from the instruction offered by the Imperial University.

This memorial, as mentioned above, was written in 1058, when the University had been deprived of not only its independent budget, but also its physical plant. In this situation, Li Kou's purpose became more obvious. It described the uneasy relationship between the Directorate and the University that existed throughout the Sung dynasty. This tension had two sources. On the one hand, the legacy of the Directorate, and the school named after it, suggested an aristocratic orientation and purpose of education. From the view point of new officials coming from a commoner background, this was unacceptable. On the other hand, from the beginning, the Directorate seemed to have been controlled by conservative scholars, who perpetuated a fundamentally moribund classical learning, consisting largely of the study of T'ang commentaries. The relatively liberal scholarly climate, which made it possible to study the classics in new ways, had not yet reached the Directorate. As a result, an undercurrent of both intellectual and social tension must have existed even in the early days of the Directorate.

In the early 1040s, the tension erupted when a group of bureaucrats led by Fan Chung-yen (989–1052), Ou-yang Hsiu (1007–1072) and Han Ch'i (1008–1075), seized the opportunity to demand an independent University. They managed to oust the supervisor and the associate-supervisor,

---

[61] See Kao Ming-shih's article on the T'ang school system cited in note 5 above.

[62] When the Sung first founded the Directorate in 962, it probably was only a very simple gathering of students without the completeness of the T'ang system. The Directorate was in charge of some teaching as well as probably a little administrative responsibility. There was consequently no need to make the distinction between the Directorate *per se* and the school it ran for students. The entire thing was called the Directorate (*chien*) of Education. See *SHY,* ck, 28/20b, and *SS,* 431:12816. The name was then changed into *Kuo-tzu hsueh* in 989, and then reverted back to *Kuo-tzu chien* in 994. See *HCP,* 30/11b, 35/9b. The T'ang distinction between the administrative Directorate and the teaching institution did not exist for the Sung.

Chia Ch'ang-ch'ao (998–1056) and T'ien K'uang (1005–1063), both northerners of strong official family backgrounds.[63] New people to join the newly independent University, including Sun Fu, Shih Chieh and Li Kou, were all from poor family backgrounds, and none of them claimed official status for their fathers or grandfathers.[64] Moreover, all of them were very young. In the words of T'ien K'uang, these were "men of light ages."[65] The situation reflected the nature of the larger reform happening at the same time, also led by Fan and Han, which touched upon virtually every aspect of Chinese government. There is no doubt that bureaucrats who came primarily from the south and from families without previous official appointments now had grown into a political force of sufficient influence to directly confront the more conservative officials, usually from the north. These northerners often had generations of family members before them in government service.[66] The new southern bureaucrats were by and large in favor of political reforms, and sometimes succeeded in convincing the more reluctant northern officials to join them; Han Ch'i was a remarkable example of a converted northerner.[67] The correlation between geographical origin and liberalism, therefore, was not as clear as I present it here, but there is little doubt that most of those who demanded more open higher education were southerners.

The need for a more liberal platform to propagate new scholarship also explained why demands for a separate higher educational institution arose in the 1040s. Early eleventh-century intellectual leaders such as Nieh Ch'ung-i, Hsing Ping (932–1010), Sun Shih, Ts'ui Sung, Kung Wei and a number of others who served in the Directorate all appeared to be generally conservative, and introduced no new or stimulating interpretations.[68] One famous episode concerning a certain Wang Tan (957–1017) says that he chose

---

[63] For Chia, see *SS*, 285:9613. For T'ien, see *SS*, 292:9778.

[64] See *SS*, 432 for biographies of all three.

[65] T'ien K'uang, *Ju-lin kung-i, TSCC* ed., 9–10.

[66] For a discussion of this issue concerning the conflict between the northerners and the southerners, see, among other articles, Miyazaki Ichisada, *Ajia shi kenkyū*, Vol. I (Kyoto: Nakamura Press, 1962), 228–292. See especially 249–251. Ch'ien Mu has made this argument, too, in his *Kuo-shih ta-kang* (Taipei: Shang-wu, 1960), Vol. II, 414–420.

[67] Interestingly, the Han family, which originated in the North, achieved political eminence in Han Ch'i's father's time, and continued to be influential over several generations throughout the Sung, had generally worked with those advocating changes. One of Han Ch'i's grandsons was Han T'e-chou, and another grandson was in charge of the famous "public field method" created by Chia Shih-tao. The family tradition of education should make a very interesting case study.

[68] See *SS*, 431:12792–12825.

to fail an examination candidate because the candidate introduced a new way of interpreting a certain word, whereas another candidate who made a mistake in rhyming was passed.[69] This anecdote has often been cited as evidence of early Sung conservatism.

An exciting intellectual atmosphere started to emerge after the nation's reunification in 989. Experimentation in new literary styles introduced by Liu K'ai (947–1000), Wang Yü-ch'eng (954–1001) and later Shih Chieh went hand in hand with attempts by Mei Yao-ch'en (1002–1060) and Ou-yang Hsiu to experiment with new poetic forms. Classical learning, above all, progressed along an equally liberated direction. Sun Fu's *Ch'un-ch'iu tsun-wang fa-wei* (An Exploration into the Subtle Meanings of the *Ch'un-ch'iu* Theory of Elevating the King) not only continued the tradition started in the late T'ang of interpreting the classic itself without referring to the traditional three standard commentaries (which themselves were also given canonical status), it also contained many new and unorthodox ideas.[70] Li Kou's classical scholarship clearly illustrates the trend; his utilitarianism presaged a whole generation of pragmatic thinkers, and led him to strongly criticize Mencius, who stressed the superiority of moral sincerity over utility. Li Kou even publicly promoted the *Rites of the Chou* as a model for the Chinese government.[71] Last, and not least, an important figure in propagating new and liberal interpretations of the classics was Ou-yang Hsiu whose notorious "Questions by a Little Child on the *Book of Changes*" (*I t'ung-tzu wen*), "On the *Spring and Autumn Annals*" (*Lun Ch'un-ch'iu*) and "The Original Meaning of the *Book of Poetry*" (*Shih pen-i*) have constantly been regarded as the first milestones of Sung critical scholarship.[72] All told, it is evident that a much freer attitude towards classical learning was on the rise at the time when the University was becoming independent; it goes without saying that the first people to staff

---

[69] *SS*, 282:9550. See also Su Ch'e, *Lung-ch'uan pieh-chih*, Han-fen lou ed. (Shanghai: Shang-wu, 1933). The episode is also recorded in *WHTK*, 30:286. The person passed was Li Ti, whose biography is in *SS*, 431:10171–10175. It is interesting to note that he was to become the father-in-law of the liberal classical scholar, Sun Fu.

[70] For a recent study of Sun's classical scholarship, see Mou Jun-sun, "Liang-Sung Ch'un-ch'iu hsüeh chih chu-liu," in *SSYCC*, Vol. III (1966), 103–123.

[71] Li's writing on *Chou-li*, called "On That the *Chou-li* Could Lead to a Great Harmonious [Government]" ("*Chou-li* chih t'ai-p'ing lun"), predated Wang An-shih's own commentary on and enthusiasm for this canon, and most likely influenced Wang. On Li Kou, see Hsiao Kung-ch'üan, *Chung-kuo cheng-chih ssu-hsiang shih*, 452–456. See also Shan-yuan Hsieh, *The Life and Thought of Li Kou, 1009–1059* (San Francisco: Chinese Materials Center, 1979).

[72] Sanaka Sō, "Sōgaku ni tsukeru iwayuru hihanteki kenkyū no tansaku ni tsuite," *Shigaku zasshi*, 54/10 (1944). See also James T. C. Liu, *Ou-yang Hsiu* (Stanford: Stanford University Press, 1967).

the University were indeed those who had long been fighting for this attitude.[73]

The combined influence of the two factors, social and intellectual, made it possible to create an educational institution which, by implication, stood for open and popular instruction as well as encouraging change and reform. Both positions contrasted strongly with the more conventional pedagogical ideals which had dominated the Directorate School. The independence of the Imperial University as a branch equal to the Directorate School under the Directorate *per se* should be understood in this perspective. And subsequently, to understand the vissicitudes of the Imperial University, one has to always refer them to the political climate of each period concerned. In general, it can be said that those who stood for reform would support the independence of the University, while those who resisted change took the opposite stand.

When the Imperial University became independent in 1044, it not only enjoyed a separate faculty, but also received a separate revenue and budget. Students from the families of ranking officials naturally continued to be registered at the Directorate School, had their own teaching faculty and derived their support independently of the University. The University admitted those who did not qualify for the Directorate School, and had a faculty evidently superior to that of the Directorate School. They also received living subsidies from the revenue set aside for the University.[74] In addition to these differences, each institution also had its own buildings, though in the same general compound. These differences, begun in 1044, established the distinction between these two schools. During Wang An-shih's reform, the number of University students increased rapidly, while the number of Directorate School students remained fundamentally the same. The same was also true during Ts'ai Ching's reforms. At one point, the desire for an independent University became such a symbolic issue that whenever Ts'ai was in power, the University was given an independent status with its own faculty, and then, whenever he left the scene, its independence was again abolished. Nonetheless, throughout the changes, the quota of Directorate School students apparently remained at the officially prescribed number of 200.[75]

The demand for an independent University ebbed quickly in the early

---

[73] See P'i Hsi-jui, *Ching-hsüeh li-shih*, 221–230.

[74] For a more detailed discussion of the revenue and expenses of these two schools, see section G.

[75] For the numbers of University and Directorate School students, see Table 3. See also Table 2 for the different periods of the University's independence as reflected by its having its own professors distinct from those of the Directorate School.

Southern Sung. In any event, those meaningless reversals in the University's status during the last thirty years of the Northern Sung had made it evident that they were nothing more than symbols of the determination of both the reformers and their opponents, and no significance could actually be attached to these outward manifestations of change. Intermittent changes still occurred in the University's status throughout the Southern Sung, most notably in the faculty titles. Sometimes, a part of the faculty members were designated as "Faculty (such as professors, rectors, associate rectors, etc.) of the University," to be distinguished from the "Faculty of the Directorate (National Youth)." This seems to indicate that there were two types of faculty, each teaching its own students. But in other times, all faculty members would be called the "Faculty of the University," presumably teaching students of both branches together under the control of the Directorate. Why this should be so was never clearly spelled out and perhaps will forever elude us.[76] Besides this rather minor difference, however, the distinction between the University and the Directorate School was minimal; in most cases, when the *T'ai-hsüeh* was mentioned, it also meant the Directorate School.

While there were no practical differences between the bureaucracies and faculties of the two branches of higher education, some difference in the composition of the student bodies between the two might have developed. Above all, the elitist nature of the Directorate School remained. However, students of both schools shared a number of privileges, such as exemption from labor service,[77] and had largely the same social status and prestige. After the fall of the Sung, the formal distinction ceased to exist; the Directorate's student body consisted of those specially aspiring for a position in officialdom; they could be sons of high officials, who otherwise enjoyed *yin* protection privilege, in that they could enter service because of their fathers' official status, unsuccessful candidates from the departmental examinations (metropolitan examinations in later dynasties), or students recommended by local schools to register for civil service examinations. The distinction which had existed previously in the Sung had all but disappeared.[78]

In recapitulation, then, one finds that the ambiguities in Li Kou's memorial were not without significance. The search for the identify of

---

[76] See Table 2.

[77] See Ch. 6, section D.

[78] For a discussion on later Directorates, see Ch'en Tung-yüan, *Chiao-yü shih,* 303–309, 356–361, 413–414. To better understand the development of later Directorates, one has to remember Ts'ai Ching's reform ideas which were continued in later practices, despite his own personal failure. A brief discussion is found in section E and Table 4.

TABLE 2
Personnel Changes in the Directorate and the University*

Major policitical events	Year	University			Directorate School			
		Professor	Rector	Assoc. Rector	Professor	Rector	Assoc. Rector	Librarian
	Early Sung				3	1	1	
	1043				4			
reform	?				0(?)	0(?)	0(?)	1(?)
	1071	8	2	2				
	1079	10	5	10				
	1080	10	5	5				0
anti-reform	1086	6†		5	6†			
reform	1099	10						
Ts'ai Ching in power	1107	6(?)	2(?)	2(?)	4	2	2	1
	1108	5			5			
anti-reform	1110	10	3	2	0	0	0	
Ts'ai Ching in power	1119	7‡	3	3	5	2	2	1
anti-reform	1121	10	5	5	0	0	0	
	1133	2						
	1143	3	1	1	1	1	1	
	1156		2	2		2	2	
	1159		1	1		1	1	
	1161							
	1162	2						0
	1163	2	1	1	0	0	0	
	1166		2		1	1	1	
	1168			2				
	1169							
	1171	3	1	1	1	1	1	1

*Sources are found primarily in *SHY*, ck, 28 passim. If no new number appears, it is assumed that the number had not changed from the one above. Other numbers are either found in original sources or derived from them.

†The two new professors were responsible for instruction on the *Ch'un-ch'iu* classic.

‡Two new professors were added to teach Taoist works. The posts were discontinued in 1121.

the University not only reflected the rise of bureaucrats of commoner background, coming primarily from the south, and their political importance, but also the increasingly liberal intellectual atmosphere which strongly influenced nearly every aspect of scholarly activity, as well as the educational policy of the government. For a while, the University seemed to be the hot-bed of reform ideas,[79] and, at least during the Northern Sung, continued to be the center of new ideas. However, as education became more open, as more students sought to receive higher education, and, above all, as the civil service examinations became even more important, these perceptions dissolved. In the end, the distinction disappeared completely, and even the nominal difference in terms of students' qualifications also lost its significance; this development completed the last chapter of medieval Chinese aristocratic society and its education.

E. Composition of the Student Body

Further discussion of the students' qualifications in the two higher educational institutions is needed here. The Directorate students consisted mainly of the sons or male descendents of officials of the seventh rank and up, whereas the students of the University were primarily those coming from families of lower-ranked officials and commoners.[80] However, even from the beginning it became clear that more students were interested in passing the civil service examinations than actually studying in the Directorate. In the words of Wang Chu, who recommended the restoration of the School of Four Gates in 1042, "When the examination year comes, the Directorate School is flooded with more than a thousand students, . . . and then when the examination is over, they all disappear, and teachers find nothing to do except sit in their chairs."[81] The generally relaxed, or even contemptuous attitude of the students registered in the Directorate

---

[79] Particularly during the aftermath of the 1044 reform, when both Hu Yüan and Sun Fu were in charge of the University. Not only did they attract an unexpectedly large number of students, including the students of the Directorate School (because all faculty members officially belonged only to the Directorate), but were also vividly and warmly remembered as great teachers. See note 31 above and section F, and Wang Chien-ch'iu, *Sung-tai t'ai-hsüeh*, 124–138.

[80] Compared with the T'ang system, it is evident that the Sung system was simpler, because the latter had abolished the Ssu-men School which came into existence only very briefly in 1042–1044. The fact that students who qualified for the Directorate School included those who previously, during the T'ang, would qualify only for the University, reflected the fact that fewer students competed for admission to the Directorate School.

[81] *SHY*, cj, 1/29a.

was the reason why the supervisor recommended in 975 taking in students in the capital area who were preparing for the civil service examinations but were not qualified for admission to the Directorate School.[82] Thus, even before the University was formally established, the Directorate was already admitting students who theoretically could not use its facilities.[83] The independence of the University in 1044 therefore marked only the retroactive adoption of the policy of admitting a wider range of students. This practice was maintained throughout the entire Sung dynasty. In fact, after 1098, even the distinction in qualification between the Directorate School and the University was all but abolished. A decree issued in that year permitted any student whose father was a "rank official" to study in the University.[84] In theory, there had been distinctions between the qualifications of Directorate School and those of University students from almost the beginning of the dynasty; however, this distinction was never as clear as was originally intended.

Admission of students from a commoner background grew substantially after the introduction of the famous "Three-Hall System [for Local Schools]" in 1097 by Chang Tun (1035–1101) which was brought into wide practice by Ts'ai Ching after 1102.[85] The method marked the most important change, one that fundamentally altered the composition of the students in the Directorate Schools. Under this method, students were directly recruited from among distinguished graduates of prefectural or even county schools for admission to the Directorate Schools (usually the Imperial University). In order to carry out this method, local schools were divided into three classes (also called "Three Halls"), which provided a graduated promotion system, from which talented students could be recommended to the University.

After 1102, the system, now modified by Ts'ai Ching, only admitted graduates from prefectural schools to the University, while graduates from county schools had to attend the prefectural schools first. Recommendation for admission took place once every three years. In order to accommodate

---

[82] See note 12; see also *SHY,* cj, 1/29a.

[83] Apparently, these students were then classified according to their respective family backgrounds into different categories: the *Kuo-tzu* students, the *T'ai-hsüeh* students and the *Kuang-wen* students, presumably entitling them to different treatments, although it is conceivable that they received the same kind of instruction (provided instruction did exist). The distinction here is implied in the memorial submitted by Wang Chu in 1042, now found in *SHY,* cj, 1/29a. Ou-yang Hsiu was a *Kuang-wen* student in 1029.

[84] *SHY,* ck, 28/13a.

[85] *HCP,* 518/20a. More on this in Ch. 5.

TABLE 3

Numbers of Students in the Directorate School and in the Imperial University[1]

Year	Directorate School	The Imperial University			Total[2]	Sources
		Upper-Hall	Inner-Hall	Outer-Hall		
Early Sung	indefinite	—	—	—	—	SS, 157:3657.
975	70	—	—	—	—	Ibid.
1044	—	—	200	—	—	See note 3.
1051[3]	—	—	100	—	—	HCP, 170/16b.
1058[4]	450	—	—	—	—	SHY, ck, 28/4b; HCP, 197/8b.
1058	600	—	—	—	—	Ibid.
1068	900	100	200	100	—	SHY, ck, 28/4b; SHY, cj, 1/30ab.
1071	—	100	200	no limit	—	SHY, ck, 28/7b.
1072	—	—	200	700	—	YH, 112/4a.
1074	—	—	—	—	more than 1,000	HCP, 253/11b.
1079	—	100	300	2,000	—	SHY, ck, 28/9b.
1080	200	—	—	—	—	HCP, 304/11a.
1092	—	100	300	2,000	—	HCP, 474/5b.
1093	—	—	—	2,175	—	HCP, 482/10a–11b.
1102	—	100	300	3,000	—	SHY, ck, 28/15a.
1104	—	200	600	3,000	—	SS, 157:3663.
1127	—	—	—	—	600	Ibid.
1129	36	—	—	—	—	SS, 157:3669.
1142	—	—	—	—	300	SHY, cj, 1/32a.
1143	80	—	—	—	—	CYYL, 149/2b.
1143	—	30	100	570	700	SS, 157:3669; CYYL, 153/4b.
1145	—	—	—	—	900	SHY, cj, 1/36a; CYYL, 154/9b.
1146	—	—	—	1,000	—	CYYL, 155/1ab.

Table 3 (cont.)

Year	Directorate School	The Imperial University			Total	Sources
		Upper-Hall	Inner-Hall	Outer-Hall		
1146	—	30	100	700	—	*YH*, 112/4a.
1146	—	—	—	—	916	*Ibid.*
1148	—	—	—	—	1,000	SS, 30:564.
1156	—	—	—	—	1,000	*WHTK*, 42:399.
1156[5]	—	—	—	—	more than 2,000	*CYYL*, 172/2a.
1156[6]	—	—	—	—	1,000	*CYYL*, 173/8a.
1159	—	—	—	—	533	*CYYL*, 183/11ab.
1199	—	—	—	1,400	—	SS, 157:3671.
1206	—	—	120	—	—	SS, 38:739.
1205–1207[7]	—	30	206	1,400	1,636	See note 7.
1209	—	40	—	—	—	SS, 39:753.

Notes:

1 Since most of the numbers are rounded numbers, they should be interpreted as quotas, or, possibly, numbers reported by the Directorate in applying for financial support. Judging from the figures of 1093 and 1146, it appears that registered students were as many as reported; but in other times, the actual number of students attending schools was far smaller than the reported figure, see, for example, notes 5 and 6.

2 This means the total of Imperial University students, but since these two schools were in fact inseparable in the Southern Sung, the figures cited as total after 1145 might have included the Directorate School students.

3 *SHY*, cj, 1/30ab puts the date vaguely as between 1041–1048, I am following here the record in Ch'en Pang-chan, *Sung-shih chi-shih pen-mo* (Peking: Chung-hua, 1977), 38:370.

4 For the interpretation of the sources on which I based my estimate of the numbers of students in the Directorate School in 1058 and 1068, see my *San-lun*, 105–107.

5 The quota was set at 2,000, as reported in the source, which says, however, that only 300 actually were attending the school.

6 The source says that not more than one fifth of the students showed up.

7 Wu Tzu-mu, *Meng-liang lu* (Peking: Chung-hua, 1957), 142. This source coincides with the one appearing in *Hsien-ch'un Lin-an chih*. For detail, see Wang Chien-ch'iu, *Sung-tai t'ai-hsüeh*, 111–112.

students coming from local schools, the University built a *Pi-yung* School outside the south gate of the capital, as already briefly mentioned.[86]

Thus, the institution of the "Three-Hall System [for Local Schools] " made it obligatory for the nation's highest educational institutions to admit nearly all capable students, regardless of their background. A new category of students was thus created.

The method of directly promoting local school graduates to the University continued until 1121, when Ts'ai Ching was forced out of power and never to really regain it. In theory, the practice was discarded. During the early Southern Sung, however, graduates from local schools continued to come to the University. The number of applicants was apparently very large, and the government therefore decided in 1153 to exercise some control over how many applicants each prefecture could nominate. These students took the entrance examination to the University along with successful candidates of prefectural examinations who did not pass the secondary, departmental examinations in the capital. This policy, however, was abandoned in 1163 when the government decided that only a certain number of examination candidates could be recommended to enter the University. No local school graduates were to be eligible for direct entry into the University. This was in effect equal to abolishing the "Three-Hall System [for Local Schools] ." The decision might have been prompted by the fact that the number of the unsuccessful candidates (of the departmental examinations) was so large and their needs so much more pressing that the government had to accommodate them in the University first. Indeed, according to one account, in 1175 their number reached as many as 16,000.[87]

The subsequent changes revolved around whether the University should simply accept unsuccessful candidates of the departmental examinations or whether it should also take in distinguished local school graduates. Generally speaking, the University admitted applicants from both categories (see Table 4), and except for the 1163 admission, all applicants had to pass entrance examination. This admission policy was generally called as *"hun-pu"* (mixed admission).

Thus, it could be said that in the first part of the Southern Sung, another new category of University students had made their appearance. They consisted of mainly local school graduates, but also successful candidates of prefectural examinations who did not pass the departmental screening.

---

[86]*HCPSP*, 20/6a–7a; *SHY*, cj, 2/7b–9a. A translation of the decree is in Appendix D.
[87]*SHY*, cj, 1/41a. Compare this figure with the actual numbers of students in the University and the Directorate School in Table 3.

The admission method was revised in 1177, when it was decided that the University should only admit unsuccessful candidates of the civil service examinations. Those who passed the prefectural tests but failed the departmental ones could sit for the University's entrance examination. In addition to these, three per cent (changed to six per cent in 1183, but reverting back to three per cent again in 1223) of those who failed in the primary, prefectural examinations were also eligible to sit for the entrance examination.[88] This exclusive method was called *"tai-pu"* (waiting for admission) which apparently was used for the most part during the remaining decades of the dynasty, with perhaps only one exception during the years between 1196 and 1223 when the University used the *hun-pu* method to admit students. The final change, as far as the source is concerned, came

TABLE 4

Admission Methods of the University in the Southern Sung

1127:	Examination: graduates from local schools and successful candidates of prefectural examinations. (strict *hun-pu*)
1153:	Examination: graduates from local schools recommended by respective schools according to given quotas and successful candidates of prefectural examinations. (modified *hun-pu*)
1163:	Recommendation: unsuccessful candidates of the departmental examinations. Number for each region: 10%–20% of the quota of candidates from that region permitted to take the departmental examination that year. (modified *hun-pu*)
1165:	Examination: same as 1153.
1166:	Examination: all successful candidates of prefectural examinations. (modified *hun-pu*)
1170:	Examination: same as 1127–1152.
1175:	Examination: same as 1153 (except that quotas were different).
1177:	Examination: successful candidates of prefectural examinations, but unsuccessful candidates of departmental examinations, and 3% of unsuccessful candidates of prefectural examinations. (*tai-pu*)
1183:	Examination: same as above, except that the 3% was changed to 6%.
1196(?):	Examination: *hun-pu*, similar to that of 1153?
1223:	Examination: same as 1177.
1250:	Examination: half of the new students should be graduates of local schools. (modified *hun-pu*)

[88] *SS*, 157:3670–3671; *SHY*, cj, 1/38a–49b.

in 1250 when the government decreed that half of the new students should be local prefectural school graduates.[89]

For all these changes, the Sung government did not succeed in checking the growth and problem of "wandering scholars." Also, the evolution of the admission methods leads one to see that the University was increasingly becoming a part of the civil service examinations, taking in primarily examination candidates. When local schools could send their graduates to study in the University and eventually obtain the qualification through the University to sit for the departmental examinations, then these schools, as well as the University, naturally became parts of the civil service examination system. This is precisely what we see in Ming and Ch'ing China.[90]

Another category of University students came into being during Ts'ai Ching's reforms. In 1106, it was decreed that "people who are filially pious, kind to brothers, considerate to relatives, respectful to one's wife's family, sincere, nice to the unfortunate, loyal and harmonious, are known for being distinguished in these virtues and are respected in their native districts . . . could be admitted into the University without examination."[91] This method, called the "Eight Virtues (pa-hsing) Method" gave many people a chance to enter the University without either examination or previous education, as long as the local officials recommended them as morally qualified.

Because of its lack of reliable selection criteria, the pa-hsing method quickly resulted in abuses and corruption. It also created chances for otherwise unqualified students to occupy the majority of positions. In 1113, it had become apparent that some measure of controlling the admission of "virtuous" students had to be enacted.[92] The measure eventually adopted was to require "virtuous" candidates to undergo tighter scrutiny and to compete on equal ground with graduates recommended by local prefectural schools.[93] In any case, the pa-hsing system did not develop into a permanent

[89] The discussion above on the admission methods is based on the sources cited in note 88 and my San-lun, 116–124, where a more detailed treatment is in order. One additional piece of information which was not included in the sources above is found in Pi Yüan, Hsü Tzu-chih t'ung-chien (Peking: Chung-hua, 1957), 173:4707, pertaining to the decision in 1250 to reserve half of the number of places for local school graduates.

[90] The evolution of admission methods clearly reflected the importance of the civil service examinations. Eventually, the University, and similarly the Directorate School, admitted only those who already had the qualification to take the departmental (metropolitan in Ming and Ch'ing times) examinations. The train of changes was set in motion in the Southern Sung.

[91] SS, 157:3657–3670; WHTK, 46:429–434.

[92] HCPSP, 32:1–15.

[93] HCPSP, 35:1–11; for a more detailed discussion, see Wang Chien-ch'iu, Sung-tai t'ai-hsüeh, 34–43.

feature of the University system. There is very little information on individuals who were admitted as virtuous students.

Finally, it is necessary to mention that there were a number of foreign students in the Sung Directorate School and University. Most foreign students came from Korea and therefore were seen only during the Northern Sung. After the fall of north China to the Jurchens, the Chinese Imperial University ceased to have Korean students.[94] Compared to the T'ang Directorate, the number of foreign students studying in the nation's most prestigeous educational institutions decreased greatly during the Sung.[95]

From the discussion above, it is evident that the two branches of Sung higher education had for the most part two different categories of students. The Directorate School throughout the Sung probably admitted only students of ranking official families and was therefore an exclusive institution. The number of its students remained small when contrasted with the number of University students. The University was obviously a more active educational organization and its admission methods correspondingly varied from time to time. In theory and in reality, the University was open to a wider range of students and therefore asserted an influence which reached a greater number of people than the Directorate School.[96]

F. Teaching Faculty and Staff

The teaching members in the Directorate of Education consisted of salaried officials for whom positions in educational institutions were merely stages in their official career. It is difficult to say that this had any advantage, but it is equally hard to say that therefore there were disadvantages such as a lack of professionalism. As a matter of fact, by Sung times the Chinese bureaucracy had developed a certain sophistication which demanded a clear division of expertise, such that some officials, by dint of their financial ability, would be appointed to positions in the area of finance.[97] Likewise, those with a natural inclination for or personal interest in education would be appointed to positions more related to education and scholarship.[98]

---

[94] See, e.g., *HCP*, 343/11a; *SS*, 487:14035–14056.

[95] For a discussion on T'ang foreign students, see Yen Keng-wang, "Hsin-lo liu-T'ang hsüeh-sheng yü seng-t'u," in his *T'ang-shih yen-chiu lun-ts'ung*, 425–481.

[96] A discussion on the family background of University students is in Ch. 10, section A.

[97] Robert Hartwell, "Financial Expertise, Examinations, and the Formulation of Economic Policy in Northern Sung China," *JAS*, 30 (1971), 281–314.

[98] Thomas H. C. Lee, "Life in the Schools of Sung China."

Many of these officials at one point or another would serve in the Directorate School or the University as professors. From there they would then move on to other positions normally related to historiographical, tutorial or advisory capacities. It seems then that we can conclude that there was not necessarily any lack of either devotion or professionalism among the University teachers.

Suprisingly, the supervisor (*chu-p'an,* or *chi-chiu* [director] after 1080) of the Directorate was merely a middle-rank official in the governmental hierarchy. Nevertheless, his responsibility was to supervise the entire operation of the Directorate and therefore he can properly be regarded as the highest official in charge of educational matters. The supervisor was assisted by a deputy (associate supervisor, called *p'an-chien* before 1080 and changed to *ssu-yeh* [vice-director] after 1080) whose terms of responsibility were not differentiated from those of the supervisor.[99]

The backbone of the Directorate and University education were the professors (*chih-chiang,* etc. before 1080 and *po-shih* afterwards) who were in charge of actual instruction. Their number varied from as few as three (throughout most of the Southern Sung) to more than twenty during the height of Ts'ai Ching's reforms. The job description for professors in the *Sung History* is terse: "a professor is in charge of lecturing on [his] specialized work of the classics, examining [the students] and correcting their essays, and instructing them on moral principles, ways (*tao*) [of life] and skills."[100] In reality, professors seemed to provide more scholarly instruction than attending to the prescribed job of teaching students how to tell right from wrong. Indeed, at one time, professors were even banned from meeting students outside class hours. Under such conditions, it is difficult to imagine how they could possibly teach their students such matters as "moral principles and ways of life."[101]

Other staff members included rectors (*hsüeh-cheng*), and associate-rectors (*hsüeh-lu*), both in charge of assisting professors in their instruction and of watching over students' manners and behavior. Assistant rectors (*chih-shih hsüeh-cheng*) and assistant associate-rectors (*chih-shih hsüeh-lu*) were the deputies of the officers from whom they derived the names of their own offices. There were also a number of demonstrators (*hsüeh-yü*), deans of dormitories (*chai-chang*), and dormitory demonstrators (*chai-yü*), responsible for other matters related to students' daily life other than academic affairs. The administrative part of the organization consisted

---

[99] *SS,* 165:3909–3910.
[100] *SS,* 165:3911. *Chih-chiang* literally means auxiliary lecturer.
[101] *Ibid.*

of a secretary (*ch'eng*) and an accountant (*chu-pu*), both in charge of the finances of the Directorate. Other Directorate personnel included librarians (*shu-k'u kuan*), guards, and the like.[102]

The organizing principle of the Directorate reflected unmistakably the over-riding concern for moral education. Professors were looked upon as men who passed on ethical lessons as well as knowledge of the classics. Rectors and their associates and assistants were specifically appointed to keep watch on the discipline of students, most of them already in their late teens or twenties. It also gave the superiors of the Directorate the power to manage the Directorate not merely as a teaching institution, but also a "school" in a broad sense. The Directorate schools had a set of regulations along with a penalty scheme, and enforced discipline within the campus. The government often found itself involved in unexpected disputes with the Directorate over how to mete out appropriate punishments to students who entangled themselves in law suits. Thus, like the universities of medieval Europe, the Directorate officials sometimes were forced to side with students and come to their defense in occasional town-gown imbroglios. The tightly intertwined pattern of life created by the nature of the institution had the unexpected result of giving birth to a clan-like structure, capable of mobilizing itself into a potentially destructive political force when circumstances warranted.[103]

In general, one must be cautious in estimating the amount of direct influence the directors or professors could exercise on the government. As previously noted, the directors could easily be left out of important educational discussions while other ranking officials were ordered to submit their opinions.[104] Capable supervisors or directors could naturally see to it that their own educational policy passed with official sanction, and even encouragement, as in the case of Li Ting who won the court's approval of a comprehensive plan for reorganizing the University during his tenure as the director between 1071 and 1075.[105] But Li's case was exceptional; more often than not, the directors were hampered by their own low position and encountered repeated frustrations within the government.[106]

The last question is how much "master-disciple" relationship existed

---

[102] *SS*, 165:3909–3915.

[103] A brief discussion on town-gown issues is in Ch. 7. The possibility for the Directorate schools to be a potential political force is also discussed there.

[104] See above, note 24.

[105] See my *San-lun*, 141.

[106] This is easily seen in the case of Kao K'ang. See his biography in *SS*, 433:12857–12858.

TABLE 5

Titles and Salary Scale of the Directorate Officials[1]

Title		Rank	Pay[2]										
Before 1080	After 1080		Regular Salary[4]					Office Fee					
								N. Sung			S. Sung		
			A	B	C	D	E	X	Y	Z	X	Y	Z
Supervisor	Director	4B	45	25	3	1	50	35	32	30	35	32	30
Associate Supervisor	Vice-Director	6A	25	15	—	1	30	32	30	28	32	30	28
Secretary	same	8A	12	5	—	—	15	22	20	—	22	20	—
Auxiliary-Lecturer	Professor[3]	8A	20	5	—	—	30	20	18	16	20	18	16
Accountant	same	8B	5	5	—	—	15	20	18	—	18	16	—
Rector	same	9A						18	17	16	18	17	16
Associate Rector	same	9A						18	17	16	18	17	16
Demonstrator	same	9A						18	17	16	18	17	16
---	Professor[5]	8B						20	18	16	20	18	16

Explanations:
A: salary in cash (liao-ch'ien); unit is string (kuan).
B: raw silk (chüan), given in spring and winter; unit is p'i.
C: cultured silk (ling), given in spring and winter; unit is p'i.
D: hemp cloth (lo), given in spring; unit is p'i.
E: cotton (mien), given in winter; unit is liang.
X: "commission" (hsing or ch'üan).
Y: "custodial" (shou).
Z: "probatory" (shih).

Notes:
1 For definition of X, Y, Z and "Rank," see Edward Kracke, Jr., Translation of Sung Civil Service Titles (Paris, 1957).
2 There were also other benefits, given according to one's rank.
3 Professor of the Directorate (kuo-tzu po-shih).
4 Regular salaries for rectors, assistants, prefectural school rectors and the professors of the Imperial University varied from time to time. There were no set salaries.
5 Professor of the Imperial University (t'ai-hsüeh po-shih).
6 See SS, 168:4014–4017, 171:4101–4114.

in the University, which itself was a government bureau. It appears that there were not many meaningful associations in the University between teachers and students. The truth is that most faculty members and directors were in the Directorate for very short length of time—as a rule, most Sung officials were in their positions for less than three years[107]—too short for meaningful relations to develop. Also, University students were generally committed to the institute with a very clearly defined goal in life, that is, to pass the civil service examinations. These conditions were certainly not conducive to the development of genuine and permanent relationship between teachers and students. Nonetheless, since the system was at least on the theoretical level designed as a scholarly community (similar to a medieval "nation"), associations did also rise between teachers and their students. At least two teachers were held in fond memory by their students. Hu Yüan, whom we mentioned earlier was one. The legacy of Hu, aside from his enthusiasm and willingness to assist students,[108] lay in his giving equal emphasis to both classical learning and the application of it to practical affairs. A strong trend of pragmatism, distinct in the Northern Sung, continued during the Southern Sung, thanks to the initial influence of Hu Yüan.[109] During the Southern Sung, when Neo-Confucian thinkers became skeptical of the effectiveness of government education, fewer and fewer students of Neo-Confucian conviction registered in the University. Still, there were a number of outstanding Neo-Confucian scholars who became widely respected in the University. Lü Tsu-ch'ien (1137–1181) was among the most famous. An intellectual compatriot of Chu Hsi, Lü was known for the books and treatises he wrote to propagate and popularize Neo-Confucian doctrines. He was also a successful teacher in the Directorate, widely respected by his students. Discussions on the Neo-Confucian contribution to Sung higher education, however, necessarily demand separate treatment.[110]

In conclusion, one sees that some of the teachers did come down in history as true educators with distinguished careers in the profession, and

---

[107]Brian McKnight, "Administrators of Hangchow under the Northern Sung: A Case Study," in *Harvard Journal of Asiatic Studies* (*HJAS* hereafter), Vol. 30 (1970), 185–211.

[108]Many episodes about his fond relations with students have come down to us; among them, the most vivid one to me, is his recommendation that the University be allowed to light the lamps after dark on its campus. The use of fire was banned in K'ai-feng during the Sung. See Ch. 7, section B.

[109]See Hsiao Kung-ch'üan, *Chung-kuo cheng-chih ssu-hsiang shih*, 461–469.

[110]See *SS*, 434:12872–12874. Other famous teachers included Kao K'ang; see *SS*, 433:12857–12858.

it is therefore dangerous to underestimate the potential for genuine and meaningful relations developing between teachers and their students. Nonetheless, the very fact that these teachers were in the first place salaried bureaucrats suggests that it was natural for teachers in the Directorate schools to evaluate their association with the institutions in political, rather than in educational, terms.

G. The Finance of the Directorate Schools

The government was responsible for nearly all the expenses of the Directorate schools. These expenses could be divided into three major categories: first, the salaries for faculty and staff members who were regular ranked officials; second, the subsidies to students in the form of meals and living allowances; and thirdly, the miscellaneous expenses, including regular maintenance fees, wages paid to workers, various kinds of administrative expenses and money needed to run a printing office.[111] The first category of expenses was managed directly by the government, and was not a part of the Directorate's responsibility. The second category evidently was the most important part of the Directorate's financial responsibility and is relatively well documented. We know very little about the third category of the Directorate's expenses which was no doubt very involved, especially as it was related to a wide range of expenditures which continually varied in their importance. We do know, however, that the government had an appropriation for the Directorate's administrative fee in its annual budget, called "kung-shih ch'ien" (public-use fee) which was actually given to all important bureaus for exactly the purpose its name suggests.[112] In 1078, the amount of "public-use fee" given to the Directorate was 700 strings, which was increased to 1,000 a few years later.[113] These figures are indicative of the general trend. The printing office of the Directorate, on the other hand, was probably self-sufficient. In 1066, according to the report of the Directorate, the financial balance of the printing office, after meeting its expenses, yielded a surplus, which the Directorate recommended be returned to the government treasury.[114] In any case, the management of the printing office, though under the direct control of the Directorate,

---

[111] The most extensive collection of sources about the finances of Sung Directorate schools is found in *SHY,* ck, 28. For a detailed discussion on this subject for the Northern Sung period, see my *San-lun,* 73–96.

[112] *HCP,* 296/9b.

[113] *HCP,* 302/9b.

[114] *SHY,* ck, 28/5b.

was quite separate from that of the schools, and therefore needs not concern us here.

The most important part of the Directorate's expenses was the students' meal allowances, which normally consumed about three quarters of the total revenue of the Directorate.[115] The Directorate relied primarily on the rents collected from its land appropriated by the government to meet these expenses. It supplemented the rents with the government's annual appropriations which were made in various amounts according to the needs. The Directorate also collected fees from candidates who took the University's entrance examinations. These fees eventually found their way into the general revenue of the Directorate, and may very well have been used to meet students' expenses.[116]

The Directorate owned different lands of various sizes at different times. However, it appears that the income from these lands made up less than half of the total income of the Directorate; during most of the reform periods, when the University was expanding, the government steadily increased its annual grants to the Directorate and it was these grants which constituted the largest portion of the Directorate's revenue. The amount of this annual grant reached 35,000 strings in 1104, when the number of students in the Directorate was 4,000 (200 attending the Directorate School and 3,800 the University).[117] In contrast, the income from the rents collected from the school land, according to my estimate, was only about 13,700 strings.[118]

The money collected from the registration fees of candidates was 2,000 cash (2 strings) per person.[119] This source of income could have been very large, especially during the Southern Sung, when candidates competed to be admitted to the University. If the practice of collecting a registration fee was indeed continued in the later part of the twelfth century, when there were 16,000 candidates,[120] the registration fee could have been a very significant addition to the revenue.

The amount for meal allowances seems to have been generous and by and large enough to meet the minimum daily needs. In 1086, when the price of rice was at its lowest, the monthly allowance for an upper- or inner-

---

[115] See note 111.
[116] I did not include income from this source in my estimates of the Directorate income in the discussion of my *San-lun*, 73–96.
[117] See Table 2.
[118] See note 111.
[119] *SHY*, ck, 28/5ab.
[120] See note 87 above.

hall student was 900 cash.[121] According to the estimate of Kinugawa, an adult during the Sung could live on a minimum of three *sheng* (roughly 406 cubic inches) of rice or its equivalent a day.[122] This would mean a monthly allowance of about 0.9 *tan* of rice just to survive. 900 cash during the 1080s would buy about 1.71 *tan* of rice. The allowance cannot be regarded as exceptionally generous.[123] On the other hand, the government made a substantial commitment by putting aside enough money to subsidize *all* students taking up higher education.[124]

From the brief discussion above, one gets the impression that the government's financial support to higher education, whether in the form of outright grants, or land, or regular budgetary allocations, was adequate, or even generous. This is applicable to both Directorate schools—the School as such and the University. In the early years of the University, especially right after the failure of the 1044 reform, the University suffered a financial setback, namely, the loss of the land allocated to it when it became independent, and a smaller allowance for the meal subsidy to students than what the Directorate School offered. However, this situation lasted only for about twenty years.[125] No further unequal treatment seems to have occurred, at least in the area of finance.

Before turning to another subject, I wish to point out that the discussion above has centered largely on the Northern Sung. This is mainly because there is insufficient source material for us to look into the financial situation during the later centuries. Nonetheless, it appears that the Southern Sung Directorate Schools relied heavily on the income from its land and properties. It is interesting to note that there are no records showing that the Southern Sung government ever made any special grant in cash form to the University. On the other hand, we do know that when the Southern Sung government reconvened the Directorate Schools, a piece of landed property with the buildings on it that formerly belonged to the renowned general, Yüeh Fei (1103–1141), was turned over to the Directorate. There is no record of

---

[121] See note 111.

[122] Kinugawa Tsuyoshi, "Kanryō to kanhō," in *Tōhō gakuhō*, No. 42 (1973), 177–208.

[123] According to the estimate made by P'eng Hsin-wei, an average Northern Sung laborer's monthly wage was just about enough to buy 339 *sheng* of rice. See his *Chung-kuo huo-pi shih* (Shanghai: Jen-min, 1965), 468–469.

[124] We shall come back to the issue of the financial burden of the Chinese government in running its official education during the later eleventh and early twelfth century in the next chapter.

[125] See note 111.

the size of this property,[126] but one imagines that it was significant. The Southern Sung government also made it a regular policy to turn over unclaimed lands to schools.[127] A piece of land confiscated in 1143 in Lin-an, the Southern Sung capital, was then capable of generating an income of at least 33,600 strings per year. This was more than enough to support a Directorate of 300 students.[128]

In short, the Sung government showed a tendency to encourage the Directorate to rely for its income on rents collected from its own landed property.[129] When this source of income was not enough to cover the expenses, the government generally intervened by allocating special annual grants. This was particularly true during the Northern Sung. After the loss of north China, however, the size of the University was reduced, and as a result it could more easily raise adequate money from its own lands. The government seemed to have ceased to make regular budgetary allowances as a consequence. In any event, since the land technically belonged to the government, the revenue was still of official origin.

H. Technical Schools under the Directorate

In his marvelous survey of Chinese mathematics and astronomy, in volume three of *Science and Civilisation in China*, Joseph Needham cites as his front page quotation the following:

> Probably another reason why many Europeans consider the Chinese such barbarians is on account of the support they give to their Astronomers—people regarded by our cultivated Western mortals as completely useless. Yet there they rank with Heads of Departments and Secretaries of State. What frightful barbarism!

This quotation is significant for Needham, but its irony overstates his case, because, while astronomers were by no means "regarded . . . as completely useless" in imperial China, they never "ranked with Heads of Departments and Secretaries of State." This was particularly true during the Sung, when at least in the area of mathematics (which was closely

---

[126] But see *SHY,* "Fang-yü" section, 4/25ab for some idea of the size of other parts of his estate.

[127] See Ch. 5, section E.

[128] *CYYL,* 89/14a; *SHY,* cj, 1/34b.

[129] For example, in 1077, when the government gave a piece of unclaimed land to the Directorate, the condition was that the government would reduce the grant *pro rata* with the amount of income generated from this piece of land. See *HCP,* 280/12b and 282/17a.

related to astronomy), "the greatest mathematical minds were now mostly wandering plebeians or minor officials."[130] Indeed, the reason that China did not live up to its putative "frightful barbarism" was precisely because in imperial China, as in Europe before the nineteenth century, astronomers and other technical personnel were held to be largely, if not completely, useless or unimportant.

There were times when Chinese governments tried to institutionalize the education of at least some bureaucrat-technicians, so that their training could be coordinated and related to education in a wider spectrum. The Sui dynasty placed the training of mathematicians (but not astronomers) and calligraphers (scribes) under the Directorate of Education. But the general practice was to relegate the responsibility of training to the respective governmental agencies. This caused a certain degree of confusion which lasted through the T'ang, when the training of astronomers continued to be entrusted to the Astronomical Observatory (*Ssu-t'ien t'ai*) (also given various other names)[131] while the training of mathematicians was taken away from that office and became part of the Directorate's duty. Similarly, during the T'ang, while different imperial academies and the Imperial Library (*Mi-shu sheng*) had their own apprenticeship programs, the Directorate nonetheless maintained a School of Calligraphy (*Shu-hsüeh*) which presumably offered the same kind of training. Moreover, the *Chiu T'ang-shu* says that the educational method used by these academies and the Library to train the scribes was modeled on that of the Directorate.[132] It is hard to understand why the arrangement should be so; worse, both the Schools of Mathematics and Calligraphy briefly reverted to the Bureau of Astronomy and the Imperial Library during the late seventh century.

The confusing state of T'ang programs of special technical training probably reflected some uncertainty about the significance of professionalized knowledge in general, and about the position of technical personnel in particular. But the early Sung policy was to let respective official agencies conduct their own training programs and institute examinations to recruit technical bureaucrats. Not until Fan Chung-yen's reform in 1044 did the policy of placing special training or selection programs under the Directorate take shape, and medicine was the first to become a part of the responsibility of the Directorate.[133] Since the reform failed in one year, the change was

[130] Joseph Needham, *Science and Civilisation in China*, Vol. III, (Cambridge: Cambridge University Press, 1962), 42.

[131] Ou-yang Hsiu, *Hsin T'ang-shu* (Peking: Chung-hua, 1975) (*HTS* hereafter), 47:1215–1216.

[132] Liu Hsü, *Chiu T'ang-shu* (Peking: Chung-hua, 1975), 43:1848, 44:1909.

[133] *SHY*, ck, 22/35ab.

abandoned; nevertheless, the idea seemed to have gathered enough momentum so that the Bureau of Medicine could continue to function relatively well under the *T'ai-ch'ang ssu* (Court of Imperial Sacrifices) and by late 1050s had more than one hundred students.[134]

Among Wang An-shih's reforms, the institution of the School of Law was the most important in the area of technical education.[135] He also enacted legislation to require all candidates in the civil service examinations to pass questions on legal codes.[136] These moves revealed his particular concern with the law, but they also reflected reformers' determination to place the recruitment and training of professional personnel under the general educational system. Whether this was a good practice is of course another matter.[137] Thus, by the time of Wang's reform in 1068, one sees some indication of willingness on the part of the Sung government to strengthen the training of legal and medical personnel.[138] Most governmental agencies of course continued to manage their own training programs, but Wang An-shih and his followers were determined to centralize the training of special technical bureaucrats in the hands of the Directorate, though in reality he only succeeded in instituting a new School of Law.

The general founding of special schools came in 1104. Some schools, such as the School of Medicine, could naturally be established on an already existing base, but other schools had to start from scratch. Only the School of Law was an integrated part of the Directorate and continued thus through the reforms of the 1070s.[139] New schools included those of Calligraphy, Mathematics, and Painting, as well as those of Medicine and Law.[140]

Since these special schools were the brain children of Ts'ai Ching, it is conceivable that their chance of extended existence as branches of the Directorate was very limited, related as they were to Ts'ai's political fortunes.

---

[134] *SHY*, ck, 22/36ab.

[135] *SHY*, ck, 22/35ab. See also *HCP*, 244/2ab.

[136] *HCP*, 246/8b, 266/8ab.

[137] There was probably a certain advantage in doing so, because students in the Directorate and the Military School (*Wu-hsüeh*) were made available to medical students for examination and treatment. Students' performance in treating their more esteemed compatriots was used to decide who should be promoted. See *SS*, 164:3885–3886; *SHY*, ck, 22/37a.

[138] The Bureau of Medicine was made independent in 1079. *SHY*, ck, 22/37b.

[139] It is pertinent to point out here that while other technical officers were generally looked down upon during the Sung, and their career prospects were generally poor, the legal bureaucrats were normally ranked as officials of regular service and therefore were distinct from other technical officers.

[140] *SHY*, cj, 3/1a.

In the twenty years that followed, there were several changes which directly affected the status of these schools, and these changes were in turn related to the rise and fall of Ts'ai; almost without an exception, whenever he was in power, the special schools were placed under the Directorate, and relegated to different agencies whenever he lost imperial favor.[141]

In the Southern Sung these special schools came to be managed by relevant governmental offices, such as the School of Painting by the Bureau of Painting (*T'u-hua chü*) of the Han-lin Academy and the like.[142] Clearly, technical education continued, as the government relied on the technical officers to provide services the generalists could not provide. The only difference is that these training programs were no longer managed by the Directorate, and therefore do not concern us here.

Besides the obvious interest of reformers such as Wang An-shih in strengthening the exercise of law and justice, the personal fondness of Emperor Hui-tsung (r. 1101–1126) for painting and calligraphy accounted for the independence of the special schools mentioned above. But the most significant development was the establishment of a School of Mathematics.

The special significance of the School of Mathematics founded by the reformers probably lay in that the School was named *Suan-hsüeh*, and not *T'ien-wen hsüeh* (School of Astronomy).[143] Mathematicians had traditionally been employed by astronomy bureaus, and since astronomy agencies had traditionally been in charge of the more dubious responsibilities such as divination and fortune-telling, mathematics inevitably wore a cloak of pseudo-scientific colors. The decision on the part of the Sung government to establish a school with a much more clearly defined name implies most likely a genuine understanding of the need for people capable of non-astronomical computation.

The School was officially opened in 1104, though preparations started as early as the late 1070s.[144] The number of students was to be two hundred and ten, and the progression of training modeled on that of the University, in that monthly and annual examinations were held to select students for

---

[141] See Chart 2. There is no need to attach too much significance to these bureaucratic changes.

[142] Not to be confused with the Han-lin Commission (*ssu*). The Han-lin Commission was also in charge of the monarch's entertainment and daily provisions. See *SS*, 157:3687, 164:3892.

[143] On at least one occasion, the name of the School of Mathematics appeared in a memorial submitted to the throne as "School of Astronomy and Mathematics," suggesting the close association made by contemporaries between the training of astronomers and the School of Mathematics. *SHY*, cj, 3/3b.

[144] *SHY*, cj, 3/2ab.

promotion. Distinguished graduates from the upper-hall (*shang-she*) would be appointed directly to official posts.[145] The last measure was of some importance, because it suggested that the government was ready to give mathematicians an opportunity to enter official service similar to that of graduates of the Imperial University.[146]

The content of the education reflected the need to produce a specialist with a generalist's concerns. In addition to the regular mathematical texts they studied, students also had to specialize in at least one "minor classic."[147] The mainstay of the training, nevertheless, remained similar to that for the astronomical students before 1104. All students of the new School continued to study the three main branches of astronomical knowledge, namely, calender making and mathematics (*li-suan*), general astronomy (*t'ien-wen*) and the so-called "three formulas" (*san-shih*),[148] but they also were required to study more strictly mathematical works (*fa-suan*, methodical arithmetic)[149]—the famous *Mathematical Canons*

---

[145] *WHTK*, 42:397. A detailed record on the organization of the School of Mathematics is found in an anonymous *Suan-hsüeh yüan-liu*, quoted by Li Yen, "T'ang, Sung, Yüan, Ming shu-hsüeh chiao-yü chih-tu" ("Shu-hsüeh chiao-yü" hereafter), in his *Chung-suan shih lun-ts'ung*, Vol. IV (Peking: K'o-hsüeh, 1955), 258–260. Takikawa Masajirō has written an article to discuss this work: "Sōhan *Sangaku genryū* ni tsuite," in his *Shina hosei shi kenkyū* (Tokyo: Yūhikaku, 1940).

[146] Regular graduates from the civil service examinations were generally appointed to posts equal to lower eighth rank (see note 29 of Ch. 6). Graduates from the School of Mathematics were normally appointed to the following three positions: *T'ung-shih lang, Teng-shih lang*, or *Chiang-shih lang*, which were equal to subprefects, general executive inspectors, or other staff members in subprefectural offices; see *SS*, 169:4054. An equally significant change lay in their being appointed to civil service offices, and not to military service posts, as they had been before the School was placed under the Directorate.

[147] The "major classics" were *Poetry, Record of Rites, Rites of the Chou*, and *Tso's Commentary*. The "minor classics" were *Documents, Changes, Kung-yang's Commentary, Ku-liang's Commentary*, and *Book of Rites*. See *SS*, 155:3620, 157:3687; *SHY*, cj, 3/6b–7a.

[148] The first two branches are self-evident, but the "three formulas" need some explanation. It probably was one para-scientific aspect of traditional Chinese knowledge of the heavens, consisting of, according to one theory, six-*jen* (*liu-jen*), hidden-*chia* (*tun-chia*) and the supreme-*i* (*t'ai-i*), *jen, chia* and *i* each being the ninth, first and second of the ten "heavenly" cyclic numbers (*t'ien-kan*). These obviously were mixtures of divination, astrology, geomancy, and other quasi-scientific knowledges.

[149] The term, *fa-suan*, which I translate as "methodical arithmetic" might be the systematic study of standard mathematical texts, e.g., the *Ten Mathematical Canons*. See *SHY*, cj, 3/4a, and Nathan Sivin, "Review on Lam Lay Young: *A Critical Study of the Yang Hui Suan Fa*," in *Bulletin of Sung-Yüan Studies*, No. 16 (1981), 91–94 where, in 93, Sivin also refers to this term and translates it also into "methodical arithmetic."

(*Suan-ching shih-shu*) compiled and annotated in the eighth century, but revised and printed in 1084.[150] A passage found in the appendix of a contemporary mathematical manual best catches the flavor of the operation of the training program:[151]

> The grading of the questions shall be based on two kinds of answers: "comprehensive" and "passable." Two "passable" answers are equal to one "comprehensive" answer. [A student whose answers] are distinguished in having made "comprehensive answers" to at least three questions on the meaning of texts, and on actual mathematical exercises shall pass. Those taking the test in the subject of calendar (*li-suan*) will be examined on their knowledge of calendar computation, be required to deduce [both] the positions dawns and dusks occupy in the heavenly lodges (*hsiu*), and the times and degrees of solar and lunar eclipses that occurred during the preceding season. Those taking the test in the subject of "three formulas" shall answer questions on [both] the [circulation of] *yin* and *yang,* and the prediction of the weather for the next three days. Those taking the test in the subject of "general astronomy" will be required to forecast the good and evil omens according to the *fen-yeh* theory of field allocation, for the coming month or season. All "comprehensive" answers must be in accord with the content of ancient [canonical] works.

The School lasted until the third month of 1110, when it was closed, apparently because Ts'ai Ching had fallen. Students were transferred to the Bureau of the Grand Astronomer. Three years later, when Ts'ai was again in power, the School was revived and some more detailed regulations on examinations within the School and the appointment of graduates were issued.[152] The revived School continued until 1120, when it was again closed, again because of the fall of Ts'ai Ching.

[150] The *Ten Mathematical Canons* was compiled and annotated by Li Shun-feng (late 7th century), a famous T'ang mathematician, in 656, to be the standard mathematics textbook for the Academy of Mathematics (*Suan-kuan*) founded by Emperor Kao-tsung in the same year. The work contains the most important mathematical treatises in Chinese history. Though the academy lasted for only seven years, the textbook continued to be studied and was the standard text on which candidates in the mathematics subject of the civil service examinations were examined. By the late eleventh century, one of the ten books was lost. A new and revised (with supplements) edition was printed in 1084. Presumably students of the School of Mathematics were to study this newly printed standard work. See Needham, *Science and Civilisation,* Vol. III, 38−48, and Ch'ien Pao-ts'ung (collator), *Suan-ching shih-shu,* 2 vols. (Peking: Chung-hua, 1963).

[151] From anonymous author, *Suan-hsüeh yüan-liu,* quoted in Li Yen, "Shu-hsüeh chiao-yü," 258−260.

[152] *SHY,* cj, 3/5b, 6a−7b. Li Yen, "Shu-hsüeh chiao-yü," 263−267. During the first period of the School's existence, a detailed order on how sacrifices should be conducted to commemorate past mathematicians was issued. A total of seventy pre-Sung astronomers and mathematicians were chosen to have sacrifices paid to them.

Since the School had only a very short existence, it did not succeed in creating any significant transformation in the training of mathematical and astronomical personnel, much less any significant impact on the development of mathematics and astronomy in China.[153] It would be grossly misleading to attribute much significance to this School; indeed, the study of it serves mainly as a demonstration of the reformers' perception of special training. We shall see this more clearly as we consider other special schools.

The School of Medicine was, in contrast to the School of Mathematics, better organized and had been well institutionalized even before Wang An-shih and his followers ordered its reform. However, it became a part of the Directorate much later, in 1103, when Ts'ai Ching was in power. A total of three hundred students were divided into three classes, modeled on the Three-hall system of the University; the outer-hall would have two hundred students, the inner-hall sixty, and the upper-hall forty. The method of examinations within the School was also similar to that of the University. An unusually detailed regulation covering the major aspects of the educational content, the evaluation of students' achievements and their intern practices was issued and provides us with a very clear picture of how the School operated.[154] It is worthwhile summarizing the major points of this document.[155]

First of all, students in the School of Medicine were expected to study three major branches of medical knowledge, with each branch covering at least three different courses. Four leading historical treatises on medicine were required of all students no matter in what areas. These were: the *Su-wen* (Plain Questions [and Answers on the Yellow Emperor's Inner Classic]), the *Nan-ching* (Difficult Questions and Answers [on the Yellow Emperor's Inner Classic]), the *Ping-yüan* ([Mr. Ch'ao's Systematic Treatise on] Diseases and Their Origins) and the *Pu Pen-ts'ao* (A Supplement

---

[153] Significant developments in mathematics, of course, were made during the Sung, and it cannot be denied that there were also important breakthroughs in the area of scientific astronomy. Nonetheless, it appears that in mathematics, most of the now famous practitioners, including Yang Hui, Li Chih and Chu Shih-chieh were mainly self-taught and that few of them benefited from attending this special school.

[154] Joseph Needham and Lu Gwei-djen, "China and the Origin of Qualifying Examinations in Medicine," in idem (eds.), *Clerks and Craftsmen in China and the West* (Cambridge: Cambridge University Press, 1970), 379–395. A very useful work which preserves examination questions of the School and the Bureau of Medicine is *T'ai-i chü chu-k'o ch'eng-wen ko, SKCS* ed. (Taipei: Shang-wu, 1975), which Needham knew of but did not see when he wrote the article mentioned above, is now available. The work gives us a fairly good impression of how examinations were conducted then.

[155] *SHY*, cj, 3/12ab.

to the *Materia Medica*).[156]

Second, examination questions included three forms: written elucidation questions, elucidation of meanings of medical texts, and therapeutic recommendations on hypothetical cases.[157] In reality, the School clearly regarded good performance in the third form of questions as the most important, and students who did well in hypothetical diagnosis of diseases regularly received priority in promotion.

Third, distinguished graduates from the School would receive appointments in the area of medical offices ranging from posts in the Court to assignments in the provinces. Subsequent regulations issued in 1111 and 1113 show that local medical officers had also been placed under the control of Educational Intendants (*t'i-chü hsüeh-shih*), clearly indicating that the reformers were determined to include all examinations—civil service examinations and other special examinations to recruit technical officers—under the control of the Directorate and a newly established office of Educational Intendants.[158]

The last and not least important point concerning the operation of the School has to do with the advantage of the School's being under the control of the Directorate. Students from the University, Military School, and other special schools were made available for medical students to examine and treat. This actually had been a long established practice in official Sung medical training programs, but with the structural change in medical education, the method was further strengthened.[159]

The School of Medicine was discontinued in 1110, but revived in 1113. In 1117, it was taken out of the Directorate and placed directly under the control of the Ministry of Rites (*Li-pu*), but was soon closed down in 1120, again evidently because of the fall of Ts'ai Ching (see Chart 2 on p. 102).[160]

---

[156] See Table 1 in my "Technical Officers, Legal Bureaucrats and Special Training Schools in Sung China," to be published in *Ch'ing-hua hsüeh-pao* ("Technical Officers" hereafter).

[157] The *T'ai-i chü chu-k'o ch'eng-wen ko* (see n. 154), instead, gives six different forms of questions: *mo-i, mai-i* (knowledge of pulses), *ta-i* (exposition on the secrecy of the cosmos and the origins of human organs), *lun-fang* (methods employed by the ancients to manufacture medicine), *chia-ling* (treatment of diseases) and *yun-ch'i* (theories on the consonances between the human body and the *yin-yang* circulation in each year).

[158] *SHY*, cj, 3/14b. For a discussion on the "Educational Intendant," see Ch. 5, section C.

[159] See note 137.

[160] The discussion on the School of Medicine above was also based on a useful article by Miyashita Saburō, "Sō, Gen no iryō," in Yabuuchi Kiyoshi, *Sō Gen jidai no kagaku gijutsu shi* (Kyoto: Kyoto Daigaku Jimbun Kagaku Kenkyujō, 1967), 123–170, besides the sources and references cited in the notes above.

The School of Painting, which, according to Suzuki Kei, was as much a brain child of the Emperor Hui-tsung as of Ts'ai Ching, and which was established to propagate the Emperor's own theories of art, was equally short-lived.[161] I doubt if the School was ever so much a product of artistic interest as it was an instrument of political reform.[162] There is, however, very little information about how the school actually functioned; we do know that Emperor Hui-tsung's personal predilection for combining poetry with painting was instilled into the School's educational philosophy.[163] Candidates were tested on their skills in rendering poems, especially those about landscapes, into actual paintings.[164] This resulted in sophisticated and refined artistic activity, a legacy which was only remotely echoed by lesser painters in the Southern Sung, who, although they continued to receive training by the Han-lin Bureau of Painting, had lost both the stimulus of imperial interest like that of Hui-tsung's, and the drive for real creation. On the other hand, reaction to the Bureau's preoccupation with technical precision led ironically to the rise of the famous "literati painting," which was practiced by amateur literati-scholars who consciously differentiated themselves from the official painters.

The reformers attempted to impose rigid principles of examination and the so-called "Three halls" on the organization of the School of Painting.[165] In this respect, the rationale and overt purpose of the School was not dissimilar to those of other schools discussed above, in that the reformers sought to regularize the training of the painters, whose art would not ordinarily be thought amenable to such regimentation. The most we can say is that the School did not become significant enough to greatly influence a remarkable period of accomplishment in Chinese cultural history, though

---

[161] Suzuki Kei, "Gagaku o chūshin to shita Kisō Gain no kaikaku to intai sansuiga yōshiki no seiritsu," in *Tōyō Bunka Kenkyūjo shūyō*, No. 38 (1965), 145–184. It is to be noted that court painters previously were recruited and trained by the Bureau of Painting (*T'u-hua chü*) under the Han-lin Academy. See my "Technical Offices."

[162] I believe that there existed a tension between the newly established School of Painting and the Bureau of Painting under the Han-lin Academy. Unfortunately there is not enough evidence to substantiate this. For more on this, see my "Technical Officers."

[163] There still is no useful and substantial treatment of Hui-tsung and his ideas about art.

[164] See Suzuki Kei, "Gagaku o chūshin" (see n. 161 above), 172–177.

[165] Very ironically interpreted by A. G. Wenley: "So we may suppose that while necessarily submitting to the emperor's whims in regard to the honors bestowed on painters for their painting alone, the really patriotic men of the court managed to keep the art officially as a minor branch of the government . . . ." See his "A Note on the So-called Sung Academy of Painting," in *HJAS*, Vol. 6 (1941), 269–272. The quotation is from 272. For the reformers' arguments, see *SHY*, cj, 3/1a.

it may have contributed to it.

The School of Calligraphy is the least known institution in Sung higher education. The School was very similar to the School of Painting and what has been said of the latter probably holds true of the former as well. The cultural splendor of the early twelfth century also included the achievement of those calligraphers appointed as professors in the School of Calligraphy, which, along with the long-established Bureau of Calligraphy, left a legacy warmly remembered and transmitted by later practitioners of the art.[166]

Finally, we must discuss the School of Law, also founded by reformers, which had gone through much the same vicissitudes as the other special schools, although there were significant differences between it and other special schools. The School was founded during Wang An-shih's reform, and faithfully reflected the concern about and stress on the importance of law. Among the measures taken by Wang An-shih to strengthen government's use of law was the requirement that *chin-shih* candidates answer questions on legal codes, and the continuation of the *ming-fa* degree, while other degrees of the civil service examinations were abolished.[167] The School of Law should therefore also be understood as another measure taken by Wang An-shih to promote legalism, or better, the systematic use of law and institutional reform.[168] The School was formally opened in 1073.[169]

One important fact distinguished the School of Law from other special schools: it admitted only ranked officials or degree-holders from the civil service examinations. The content of education was divided into two main courses: legal codes (*lu*) and statutes (*ling*) and their meanings, and legal cases. Since the school only admitted officials or degree-holders, one can easily imagine that the career prospects for graduates were very bright or

---

[166]There is, as far as I can ascertain, not one single article that deals specially with the School of Calligraphy. The basic information on this School as an institution is in *SHY*, cj, 3/1a–2a. Most other works on the history of Chinese calligraphy dwell on the life and artistic accomplishment of famous calligraphers or on calligraphy as an art, but not on the education of calligraphers.

[167]Hsü Tao-lin, "Sung-tai te fa-lü k'ao-shih," in his *Chung-kuo fa-chih shih lun-chi* (Taipei: Chih-wen, 1975), 188–229.

[168]The first explicit accusation of Wang An-shih as a "student of *hsing-ming* or Kuan-Shang" was made by Ch'en Huan and Yang Shih, and has since been accepted by later Chinese interpreters of Wang's reform and thinking. See Chu Hsi, *Wen-chi*, 70:1283–1286. Wang's label as a legalist (*fa-chia*) had an unexpected turn in the early 1970s in China during the campaign against Confucianism, in that legalism all of a sudden was considered a progressive way of thinking. For a study of Wang that more or less reflects this new trend, see Teng Kuang-ming, *Wang An-shih* (Peking: Jen-min, 1975).

[169]*SS*, 157:3673; *WHTK*, 42:397.

no officials would have wanted to study in this school. While reformers were in power, the School functioned without difficulty, drawing aspiring lowly ranked officials and affording them a less strenuous promotion opportunity. But this practice was itself flawed, a fact only temporarily concealed by the reformers' enthusiasm, and the cracks were to be revealed as soon as the reformers left the scene.

Except for the period of Yüan-yu (1086—1094) during which the meal subsidy was discontinued for law students, the School did not seem to encounter many obstacles, and apparently continued to operate until the fall of the Northern Sung (1126). In this respect also, the School of Law differed from other special schools, and this indicates that in the mind of Sung bureaucrats, the knowledge of law probably had a much higher priority than the knowledge of, say, painting, calligraphy, astronomy or even medicine. Still, be that as it may, the School was not revived after the government moved to the South, and the education or training of legal bureaucrats was again without a permanent institution.[170] The School remained an integrated part of the legacy created by late Northern Sung reformers.[171]

I. Recapitulation

The important feature of Sung society, namely, the decline of the aristocrats and the new opportunities for commoners, was reflected in the development of the nation's higher education. During the T'ang, the Imperial University had been only one of the seven schools under the Directorate, and by and large only admitted sons of lowly ranked government officials. The sons of ranking officials were admitted to the Directorate School. Moreover, during the T'ang, commoners were admitted only to the School of Four Gates. These arrangements changed drastically in the Sung. By the middle of the eleventh century, not only had the School of Four Gates ceased to exist, but the distinction between the Directorate School and the Imperial University had also become blurred. The University was obviously admitting students of commoners origins.

The development went hand in hand with the rising importance of the civil service examinations, with which the government recruited distinguished

---

[170]The discussion above of the School of Law is based largely on the sources in *SHY*, cj, 3/7b—11b.
[171]A useful collection of information on the Schools discussed above, providing independent information from that of *SHY*, on which I rely primarily for this study, is in Yang Chung-liang, *Chi-shih pen-mo*, 135/7a—11b.

CHART 2

Special Training Schools in Early Twelfth-century China

Year	Month	Major political events	Schools of			
			Medicine	Mathematics	Painting	Calligraphy
1100		anti-reformers in power				
1102	7	Ts'ai Ching in power				
1103	9		established			
1104				established	established	established
1106	2	anti-reform				
	4		abolished	abolished	abolished	abolished
	11			restored		
1107	1	Ts'ai Ching in power	restored			
	3				restored	restored
1109	6	anti-reform				
1110	3	Ts'ai Ching in power	abolished	abolished	abolished	abolished
1112	5	Ts'ai Ching in power				
1113	3			restored		
	4		restored			
1120	6	anti-reform				
1124	7		abolished	abolished		
	12	Ts'ai Ching in power				

Source: See notes 4, 33, 53, 70, 71 and 82. See also *HCPSP*, 22/11a, 24/6a–7a, 26/7ab, 26/22b, 27/3a, 27/4b, 29/7a, 32/2b, 32/3b–4a, 41/10ab.

candidates on an impartial basis, and which commoners relied upon for upward social mobility. This was first seen in the early twelfth century, when the Sung government, under the leadership of Ts'ai Ching, sought to promote University graduates directly into government service, showing that the University played much the same role as the civil service examinations. The development in the Southern Sung showed the fact even more clearly: the University, admitting unsucceesful candidates from the civil service examinations, served as a *de facto* station on the journey through the examinations system.

From what has been mentioned above, it is safe to conclude that Sung higher education can only be understood in the context of its relationship with the Sung government's recruitment machinery. The result of this relationship, among others, was the opening up of higher educational opportunities to a larger social spectrum of Sung students.

The Directorate of Education, which coordinated not only the Directorate School and the University, but also the nation's education, evidently was not an especially powerful government organ. Rather, it asserted its influence through informal channels, the compilation and publication of the officially sanctioned versions of the classics being the most important.

Because of the relatively low position the Directorate occupied in the Sung government, the teachers can be considered as merely salaried functionaries with special interests in scholarship and teaching. Nevertheless, there was no lack of devoted University professors.

Finally, in the early twelfth century, the Directorate of Education administered a few technical schools. The lives of these schools within the Directorate were short and were only significant as part of government's over-all training programs. In terms of education, their existence served to highlight the attempts by Ts'ai Ching and other reformers to replace the examinations with a more systematic training process, attempts which failed.

I have not discussed the quality of higher education in the Sung. Neither have I mentioned the social composition of Sung University students. It suffices, nonetheless, to say that while the Directorate had control over the issuance of officially sanctioned classics, it did not succeed in creating an atmosphere in the University conducive to intellectual creativeness and imagination. It remained for the Neo-Confucians to work out new ways of looking at the universe, society and history.[172] As for the social composition of University students, it is also sufficient, for the time being, to point out that almost half of them were commoners.[173]

---

[172] I hope to be able to pick up this issue in another volume.
[173] See Ch. 10, section A.

CHAPTER 5

Local Schools

The Sung government organized its educational system at the local level to answer the needs of pupils who aspired to a degree in the civil service examinations. The system was generally divided into two levels, prefectural schools and subprefectural, or county, schools. A rough estimate indicates that by the end of the Southern Sung, there were at least 588 local schools run by the government, 72 of which were prefectural and 516 of which were county schools.[1]

A. Historical Background

The argument which claims that there was already in existence, before the Ch'in unification, an educational system, organized by the government, other than that for aristocrats in state capitals, is difficult to substantiate.[2] The evidence does show that Han rulers were aware of the importance of setting up offices at the local level which would take responsibility for education, defined in a broad sense of overseeing the subjects' moral behavior while giving instructions on the classics. Some of these schools had as many as several hundred to one thousand students. Towards the end of the Han, schools were ordered to be built in counties with more than five hundred households.[3]

The practice was carried on throughout the Period of Disunion, apparently without significant modification, although records seem to indicate that some teaching officials were given very distinguished treatment. Of course

[1] This is based on John Chaffee's estimation. It is most likely that the total number should be more than this. See John Chaffee, "Education and Examinations in Sung Society," 304.

[2] Confucius has traditionally been regarded as the first teacher to bring education to the commoners. He was a great practitioner of private education, but did not succeed during his life-time in making education available to commoners in state-run institutions. For a study of pre-Ch'in education, see Ch'en P'an, "Ch'un-ch'iu shih-tai te chiao-yü."

[3] Yen Keng-wang, *Chung-kuo ti-fang hsing-cheng chih-tu shih*, Part I (Taipei: Chung-yang yen-chiu yüan Li-shih yü-yen yen-chiu so, 1961), 245–251.

we do possess much more detailed information about the actual organization of these local schools.[4] In general, initiatives had come basically from local officials, and it was only on rare occasions that the central government would issue directives encouraging the establishment of schools, most of which were only open to sons of aristocrats.[5] At the same time, the distinction between schools sponsored by local officials and schools privately managed by teachers was probably very slight. While in theory private schools were founded upon the presumption of receiving no financial assistance from officially originated revenue,[6] in practice, private teachers often turned to official authorities for helps. Another matter worth mentioning here is that while we have little information as to how students were supported and what their social status was, sources do suggest that many students were sons of officials or aristocrats. They probably supported themselves. In any case, obtaining a position in an official local school would mean acquiring certain privilege and could very well lead to feelings of jealousy on the part of those who were not qualified for local schools; the latter might then seek to enter the schools by cheating.[7] Schools founded by local officials and financed with their own salaries or by revenue raised privately by them could of course admit students otherwise deemed inadmissable by government educational institutions. These schools were therefore considered to be private schools, too.

By the end of the Period of Disunion, local educational organizations sponsored by the state had evolved into a rather complete system, as detailed regulations concerning acceptable numbers of different teachers and students, as well as suitable qualifications for the setting up of schools were cleary articulated. The T'ang government was able to issue directives the very year when it was established, as to how local schools should be built. During the T'ang, local schools usually included three branches: the classics, medicine and Taoist studies (ch'ung-hsüan), each with its own quota of students and teachers. Two kinds of teaching staff were appointed to local

---

[4] Yang Chi-jen, Hsüan-shih chih-tu, 28–40, 50–64, 79–83.

[5] Ibid.

[6] In other words, at a time when education for service was confined largely to hereditary aristocratic familes, education, official as well as private, was for aristocratic children, and the distinction between an official school and a private one is very hard to discern. See my "Ssu-jen chiang-hsüeh."

[7] For some discussion on the ch'a-chü system and school organization during the Period of Disunion, see Yen Keng-wang, Chung-kuo ti-fang hsing-cheng chih-tu shih, Part II (Taipei: Chung-yang yen-chiu yüan Li-shih yü-yen yen-chiu so, 1963), 351–371, 653–670. See also Yang Chi-jen, Hsüan-shih chih-tu, esp. 70–72, where Yang refers to the fact that the Director of the Eastern Chin (317–420) Directorate of Education pointed out the failure to enforce qualification of entering students.

schools: professors (*po-shih*) and teaching assistants (*chu-chiao*). Students from families of both elite and commoners were accepted, and were given subsidies towards their living expenses.[8]

By the end of the T'ang, local education had fallen into virtual discontinuation, mainly because the government was not able to keep up the supervision or support of such a complex system of education. The common practice was for local officials to utilize Confucian temples for makeshift schools where rudimentary instruction continued. For those who could afford to search for better teachers and more ideal places to study, mountain resorts or monasteries became attractive and quickly rose in prominence replacing the traditionally more rigidly controlled schools, sponsored by the government. The idea that it was the government's responsibility to set up schools at local level nonetheless remained, and as soon as the government found itself financially strong enough, it immediately turned to establishing schools in the prefectural or even subprefectural seats. This came only in the early part of the eleventh century, after nearly three hundred years of turmoil and wars, when local education, and to a less extent, higher education in the capital, were turned over to private hands.[9]

B. The Organization and Content of Local Education

Measures promulgated by the government in the early eleventh century included encouraging local officials to establish schools, which were to replace the temple schools that previously served as makeshift educational gatherings during the early days of the dynasty.[10] New schools often received a set of officially printed classics and received support either from regular budgetary appropriations from local governmental offices or even from the personal income of the prefects or governors.[11] By the 1030s, the speed with which new schools were established by the government or officials had increased to such an unprecedented degree, that the government decided to allocate pieces of land to these new schools, ranging from five to ten *ch'ing* (c. 75 to 150 modern acres).[12]

The most significant development in local education, however, came in the early twelfth century during the reform of Ts'ai Ching, when im-

---

[8]Kao Ming-shih, "T'ang-tai hsüeh-chih," 215–217; Taga Akigoro, *Tōdai kyōiku shi no kenkyū* (Tokyo: Fumaidō, 1953), 51–56.

[9]See note 45 in Ch. 1.

[10]See Anonymous author, *Sung ta-chao-ling chi* (Peking: Chung-hua, 1962), 590. See also *SS*, 157:3658–3659.

[11]See section D below.

[12]*Ibid.*

portant measures such as the further endowment of landed property, a strengthening in the recruitment of teachers, and above all, the promotion of graduates from local prefectural schools to the University were instituted. It was reported that nationwide, the total number of students reached as many as two hundred thousand. This was definitely the highest point of government management of local education, and a rare achievement in the area of education in the history of Imperial China.

Governmental education at local level during the Southern Sung was definitely less impressive when compared to the height of the early twelfth century. The educational system nonetheless remained active, although it was overshadowed by the newly developed academies towards the end of the dynasty.[13] Local education took on a mature shape during the Southern Sung, and its relationship with the civil service examinations gradually evolved into what was observable in Ming and Ch'ing local school systems.[14] In the following, I hope to discuss a few aspects of the organization of government local schools during the Sung.

To best understand why State's local education should eventually become so intertwined with the practice of the civil service examinations, one should start with how education and schools were defined traditionally. Indeed, schools during the Sung were looked upon as performing a variety of functions, only one of which was the transmission of "knowledge" as defined by the study of the classics. Local schools included in their functions such a wide range of affairs as the printing of books, the management of libraries, the administration of various Confucian ceremonies, rituals and the like, as well as conducting actual teaching.[15]

A good number of prefectural schools ran printing presses and managed to make money from selling books. For example, Chiang-ning (present Nan-ching, Kiangsu) Prefectural School undertook the printing of books in the 1130s when Yeh Meng-te, a famous bibliophile, was its prefect. By the end of the Southern Sung, the school had a collection of over twenty-thousand wood-blocks for sixty-eight titles.[16] In general, printing facilities were found only in prefectural schools because they were better organized

[13] For an interpretation of the relatively inactive local government education, see Ch. 10, section C.

[14] Most local gazetteers clearly trace their local schools back to the Sung and rarely beyond. For example, of the 69 prefectural and county schools recorded in Ch'en Shou-ch'i's *Fu-chien t'ung-chih* (1871 ed., reprinted by Taipei: Hua-wen, 1968), 50 were founded during the Sung and 15 after the Sung, and only 4 were founded before the Sung.

[15] So far, reliable accounts of Sung local education remain general works. Terada Gō's *Kyōiku shi* is most useful for local education.

[16] Chou Ying-ho, *Ching-ting Chien-k'ang chih*, *SKCS* ed., 33/1a–25a.

and had better equipment. However, county schools were also in the business of printing books. Most of the titles that we know of that were printed in prefectural or county schools were serious works, often written by authors of the district. But popular works also appeared in the list of publications.[17]

Local schools were generally also in charge of such ceremonial functions as maintaining Confucian temples, where sacrifices would be offerred to famous Confucian disciples and scholars, and practicing *hsiang-yin-chiu* rituals, which became increasingly important during the Southern Sung. Other occasional assignments included giving instructions about books dealing with legal codes, official decrees and works of moral teaching, which were distributed by the central government.[18] In 1114, local schools were even ordered to be in charge of giving instructions on archery.[19]

A few more words must be devoted to the ceremonial aspects of Sung local education before we turn to the discussion of the formal aspects of the educational process. Confucian temples were the center of all schools, and in reality, a great number of early Sung schools evolved out of temples.[20] *Shih-tien* ceremonies were held twice a year, in the spring and the fall, during which time special staff members were appointed to manage the affairs.[21] Confucius' title became increasingly elevated, and after the rise of Neo-Confucianism, he had virtually become the undisputed source of all teachings with authority.[22] *Hsiang-yin-chiu* ceremony was a relatively important part of local education. This ritual, the community libation ceremony, was as old as Confucianism itself and was already a part of local educational responsibility at least in Sui times.[23] The ceremony then fell into oblivion and was replaced by a *lu-ming* (dear wail) ceremony during the T'ang. The *lu-ming* ceremony was continued until 1113 when Emperor Hui-tsung ordered the restoration of the *hsiang-yin-chiu* ceremony. Several reviews

[17]Yeh Te-hui, *Shu-lin ch'ing-hua* (Peking: Ku-chi, 1957), 42–88. See also note 16 above.

[18]*SHY*, cj, 2/13ab.

[19]*SHY*, cj, 2/25a.

[20]Information on this is found in *HCP*, pasim. See Terada Gō, *Kyōiku shi*, 21–31.

[21]See note 43 below.

[22]Ch'in Hui-t'ien, *Wu-li t'ung-k'ao*, Chiang-su shu-chü ed. (1880) (Taipei: Hsin-hsing, 1970), Ch. 118; *SS*, 105:2547–2555. The sacrifice paid to Confucius was elevated from "middle sacrifice" (*chung-ssu*) to "upper sacrifice" (*ta-ssu*) in 1137 or 1140. See *SS*, 105:2554 and *SHY*, li, 16/1a. An honorary title given to Confucius was decreed in 1008, in the name of "the primeval sage" (*hsüan-sheng*), and changed into "the ultimate sage" (*chih-sheng*) in the following year. See *SS*, 105:2548. The *shih-tien* sacrifice made to Confucius every spring and autumn in prefectures and counties remained that of "middle sacrifice" after 1140.

[23]Ch'in Hui-t'ien, *Wu-li t'ung-k'ao*, 168/2a. The use of this ceremony in imperial universities was earlier than this.

and revisions as to how the schools should perform it properly were ordered in the thirteenth and fourteenth centuries resulting in its becoming an important ceremony. The ritual was normally celebrated in the year when prefectures were recommending their successful candidates to take the departmental examinations in the capital, and therefore was generally performed once every three years during the Southern Sung. Archery was a traditional part of the ceremony, and remained so, even though the archery contest was not much more than a mere formality throughout the dynasty. Special funds were put aside for the purpose.[24]

The ceremonial responsibilities should never be forgotten, if one wishes to understand Sung local education properly. Since education in modern times has largely excluded these concerns, we are therefore more prone to thinking in terms of education as merely a process of transmitting knowledge. Ceremonies for moral purposes were such an important part of Sung education, that when we look into what actually was taught in Sung schools, we cannot overlook the moralistic overtones of that education. But bookish learning, as long as it was related to moral concern, remained important: the study of the Confucian canons made up the basic element of Sung local education, although poetry was also an integrated part of the curriculum.

First of all, there is very little information about how actual instruction was carried out in Sung local schools. It is quite obvious that the curriculum was designed to prepare students for the civil service examinations, so much so that despite the fact that standard Confucian canons made up the core of their readings, emphasis was given to only those classics which were examined in the civil service examinations. The study of the classics often centered around certain commentaries which were adopted as the standard for the examinations. For example, in the early years of the dynasty, the commentaries which were adopted were generally the standard ones issued by the T'ang government in the seventh century. The "Nine Classics" printed in the late tenth century by the Directorate of Education and distributed to schools were these T'ang versions. By the mid-eleventh century, a rather liberal intellectual spirit gradually permeated classical learning, creating a good variety of new interpretations. Further changes included the attempts made by Wang An-shih to enforce the study of those commentaries compiled by his group of reformers,[25] and the appearance of new kinds of com-

---

[24]*Ibid.*, 168/8a–13a. See also *SHY*, li, 46/1a–5b; *SS*, 114:2720–2722; *CYYL*, 148/12b. For other references to the *hsiang-yin-chiu* ceremonies, see *CYYL*, 156/2ab, 160/10ab, 172/15a. It is interesting to note that Wang An-shih disliked the ceremony and ordered the abolition of it during his reform. Ssu-ma Kuang then revived it. See Ch'in Hui-t'ien, *Wu-li t'ung-k'ao*, 118/10a.

[25] See above, Ch. 4, note 37.

mentaries prepared by Neo-Confucianists, notably those by Chu Hsi.[26] Any changes in the trend of classical interpretation eventually led to changes in educational content.

Towards the middle of the thirteenth century, the rise of Neo-Confucianism started to make its impact felt in local schools, and important Neo-Confucian works, including the famous *Reflections on Things at Hand* (*Chin-ssu lu* compiled by Lü Tsu-ch'ien and Chu Hsi), Chu Hsi's own *Elementary Learning* (*Hsiao-hsüeh*), Chang Tsai's *Western Inscription* (*Hsi-ming*) and Chou Tun-i's *Penetrating the Book of Changes* (*T'ung-shu*) as well as various commentaries on the classics compiled by Chu Hsi and others were widely taught in local schools.[27]

The second point is that local schools almost without exception administered elementary schools within their premises. Serious teaching activities probably did take place in these elementary schools.[28] A number of new primers appeared and circulated widely there. The single purpose of these primers was the teaching of Chinese characters, for the most important goal had traditionally been the teaching of some degree of literacy, which would enable pupils to tackle the basic Confucian canons. The more widely used primers included the *Meng-ch'iu* (Ignorance and Inquiry), the *Pai-chia hsing* (Hundred Surnames), the *Ch'ien-tzu wen* (Thousand-characters Essay), and towards the end of the dynasty, the *San-tzu ching* (Three-characters Classic). Other primers included the *Shih-ch'i shih meng-ch'iu* (Ignorance and Inquiry in the Seventeen Histories), *T'ai-kung chia-chiao* (Family Instructions by the Grand Old Man), and so forth.[29] Besides basic literacy and classical learnings, students in local schools also learned to compose *shih* and *tz'u* poems, *fu* proses, as well as other essays required in the civil service examinations.[30]

Finally, local schools in general maintained a small library. The local school

---

[26] Liu Po-chi, *Sung-tai cheng-chiao shih* (Taipei: Chung-hua, 1971), Vol. II, 1168–1191.

[27] See, for examples, *SS*, 409:12331, 400:12148, or, for that purpose, the school instructions of 1249, found in Juan Yüan, *Liang-Che chin-shih chih, Shih-k'o shih-liao ts'ung-shu* ed. (Taipei: I-wen, 1967), 12/16a-17b, which, according to the postscript of the inscription, were based on the school regulations composed by Chu Hsi. There are many more examples.

[28] I have purposely left out a discussion of elementary schools and hope to take them up elsewhere. For a primary study of the subject, see Edward A. Kracke, "The Expansion of Educational Opportunity in the Reign of Hui-tsung of the Sung and Its Implication," in *Sung Studies Newsletter*, No. 13 (1977), 6–30.

[29] Ch'en Tung-yüan, *Chiao-yü shih*, 311–317.

[30] *Ibid.*, see also Weng Yen-chen, "Ku-tai erh-t'ung tu-wu," in *T'u-shu-kuan hsüeh chi-k'an*, Vol. 10, No. 1 (1936), 91–146.

libraries serviced teachers and students primarily, but gradually, they appeared to have been open also to outside readers. Some schools held impressively large collections of books; the Academy of Ying-t'ien Prefecture of the early Sung which evolved into the Prefectural School in 1036 reportedly had as many as several thousand volumes.[31] The Wu-yüan County School, on the other hand, possessed more than fourteen hundred volumes, which was quite impressive for a county institution.[32] In general, most collections were meager and some leading schools, such as the Prefectural School of Hangchow in the capital, did not even possess a library.[33]

C. Teachers

Teachers in local government schools of traditional China were normally

---

[31] *WHTK*, 46:431. See also *HCP*, 71/9a where the collection of books is said to be "more than one thousand volumes" and *SHY*, cj, 2/2a where the number is put down as about "1500 volumes." See also Liu Chih's *Chung-su chi, SKCS* ed., 9/23a–24b, where Liu reported that the prefectural school in Jun-chou had 2700 volumes of books in 1092.

[32] Chu Hsi, *Wen-chi*, 78:1432.

[33] Kung Chia (comp.), *Hang-chou fu-chih*, 1896 ed. (Taipei: Ch'eng-wen, 1974), 14/28ab. See the following for a moving account of the discovery by Chu Hsi of a small library in a county school:

"The County School of T'ung-an had a box of books which had never been cataloged, and clerks in care of them have passed them on over generations without examining them. I have recently discovered the books, finding that they are badly damaged and are full of loose pages, so much so that it is nearly impossible to restore the pagination order. Nevertheless, I do find that at the end of each book there is a mark stating that these were collected by a county magistrate whose last name was Lin; the marks also bear his official titles: . . . After checking with the records found in the inscriptions on the walls of the county office and of the school, I was able to ascertain the magistrate's name: Tu, whose style name was Tao-yüan. He was the magistrate in the fourth year of Chih-p'ing (1067) and was responsible for renovating the school in the second year of his term, being the first year of the Hsi-ning era (1068). The books were collected in that *Wu-shen* year, that is to say, eighty-eight years ago, now being the twenty-fifth year of the Shao-hsing era (1055). This is not long ago, and yet, because of the negligence of the school teachers and because of the hazards and thefts, the books which remain are miserably few. Moreover, the books left were stacked away along with mice, bugs and dust in this broken box. Noboby seems even to know of its existence. How pitiful this is!

"I have looked through the books to pick out those which are still legible and have been able only to restore six books, totalling 191 volumes. I then circulated an order among the county people and was able to recall an additional two books in 36 volumes. . . ." (Chu Hsi, *Wen-chi*, 75:1380.)

See a further account about how he was able to raise enough money to bolster the collection to 985 volumes, in *Wen-chi*, 77:1415.

paid officials, serving amid their official careers in positions they might not necessarily take pleasure and interest in.[34] But there were significant institutional and conceptual innovations during the Sung with respect to the function and value of a teacher. First of all, the Sung instituted various examinations to recruit teachers for local schools. These examinations presumably would have resulted in improving the quality of teachers. Secondly, a new office, that of Educational Intendant, was created in the Sung to supervise local education. This office was to become an integral part of the Chinese educational system, and served during the Ming and Ch'ing as an institutional link between the civil service examinations and the schools which registered and occasionally gave instruction to perspective examination candidates. Thirdly, with the rise of Neo-Confucian educational thinking, the meaning of the role of a teacher acquired a new dimension in that the classical ideal of a teacher found concrete grounds for realization. I shall concentrate on discussing the first two innovations and leave out the third for the moment.

It is necessary first to understand the hierarchy of teaching staff within local schools. Very simply stated, the local prefectural schools were administered by a preceptor (*chiao-shou*), who was the mainstay of all educational responsibilities, while county schools were normally governed under the administration of a "school master" (*hsüeh-chang*). But this rather oversimplified generalization fails to bring out the relatively complex structure of local school personnel, which matured and emerged in the early twelfth century. The personnel of a relatively large prefectural school could easily number in the tens, including a couple of preceptors, a school master (*hsüeh-chang*), a school demonstrator (*hsüeh-yü*), a school assistant (*chih-hsüeh*), a dormitory dean (*chai-chang*), a dormitory demonstrator (*chai-yü*), and in prefectures which had elementary schools, an elementary school instructor (*hsiao-hsüeh chiao-yü*), and an elementary school master (*hsiao-chang*).[35] But of course these were not the only persons mentioned in various sources in relation to Sung prefectural schools. Other "offices"

---

[34] This is of course a very simplified generalization. I have in Ch. 1, section D pointed out that "officialization" was a very common phenomenon in the history of Chinese education. I wish to make a corollary to this point by saying that the Chinese conception of local administration, at least beginning with the Han, had been understood as including "education." In this sense, some local officials were teachers. For a study of Han local administration, see Yen Keng-wang, *Chung-kuo ti-fang hsing-cheng chih-tu shih*, Part I, esp. 252–256.

[35] Though these postions appear frequently in Sung works, it is very difficult to ascertain their respective responsibilities. See Kao Ssu-sun, *San-lu*, 1870 ed. (Taipei: Ch'eng-wen, 1970), 1/14a.

included those of assistant (*chu-chiao*),[36] rector (*hsüeh-cheng*),[37] associate rector (*hsüeh-lu*),[38] "impeacher" (*chiu-t'an*),[39] treasurer (*ssu-chi*[40] or *ssu-k'u*[41]), "literatus" (*wen-hsüeh*),[42] and others.[43] All but the preceptor were outside of regular service, meaning that they were only clerks, and were distinct from the so-called *liu-nei* officials who were in regular service and acquired their official positions via regular recruitment.[44] In fact, many of these clerks were themselves students in the schools.[45] As a result, preceptors became the single most important persons in prefectural schools, and had to take up the responsibility of "instructing and guiding students according to the classical lessons and moral principles, taking charge of teaching and examining [their progress], and correcting those whose behavoir does not agree with the regulations."[46] They occupied the central place in local education, and were consequently given special office halls erected on school sites.[47]

County schools often possessed a variety of clerks, bearing names largely similar to those found in prefectural schools. Instructors (*chiao-yü*) were the counterpart of preceptors, though it was the school masters (*hsüeh-chang*) who held the administrative authority. Ideally, instructors should come

[36] This appears to have been an honorary position, often used to place the descendants of distinguished officials who could not benefit from the *yin* privileges, as in *HCP*, 120/12b, 139/6b, 140/12a, and *SS*, 456:13390. Assistants sometimes also were in charge of actual instruction. See *SHY*, cj, 2/2a.

[37] A rector in the Imperial University ranked only second to the professors, and was in charge of assisting professors in actual teaching. Prefectural school rectors presumably also assisted preceptors in instruction.

[38] Presumably, the associate rectors were in charge of assisting the rectors.

[39] The office means, literally, "correct and impeach." For this term, see Juan Yüan, *Liang-Che chin-shih chih*, 12/16b–17a, 13/2a.

[40] *Ibid.*

[41] *Ibid.*

[42] Presumably a fellow-like position, to award commoners for their patriotic actions, such as in *CYYL*, 91/8a, or to descendants of distinguished officials of the previous T'ang dynasty, as in *HCP*, 62/4b.

[43] Such temporary posts as *chang-i* (ceremony master), in charge of the *shih-tien* rituals, and the *ssu-cheng* (also ceremony master), in charge of the *hsiang-yin-chiu* rituals. See *SHY*, cj, 2/39b–40a.

[44] For the distinction, see Edward A. Kracke, *Civil Service in Early Sung China, 960–1067* (*Civil Service* hereafter), 41–50.

[45] See Juan Yüan, *Liang-Che chin-shih chih*, 12/14b, 12/16a, 12/34a. See also Anonymous author, *Chiang-su chin-shih chih*, *Shih-k'o shih-liao ts'ung-shu* ed., 15/3b–4a.

[46] *SS*, 167:3976.

[47] Chu Hsi, *Wen-chi*, 77:1416; Chang Chung-ch'i, *Hu-pei chin-shih chih*, *shih-k'o shih-liao ts'ung-shu* ed., 11/41b; Yeh Shih, *Shui-hsin chi*, *SPPY* ed., 10/9ab.

from among officials in regular service, but more often they were chosen from commoner-scholars, who again might well be examination candidates themselves.[48]

The completed conception of a school staff as outlined above emerged only in the twelfth century. The development of a more or less complete staff hierarchy during the Sung involved two major experiments which I mentioned in the beginning of this section. The first had to do with the examination of teachers, which itself grew out of an increased concern with the qualification of teaching personnel on a local level. In the first decades of the dynasty as the government did not take upon itself the responsibility of actually managing schools, a unified standard of teaching qualifications naturally did not exist. By the early eleventh century, more and more prefectures (or even counties) increased local education resources by renovating and remodelling Confucian temples into schools. Local leaders then asked the government's permission for officially printed, and by implication, sanctioned, classics. In turn, the government became involved in regularizing national educational practices, one of which was determining the qualifications of instructors. A memorial submitted by a famous *Ch'un-ch'iu* scholar Liu Ch'ang (1019–1068) recommended that prefects should recruit from among their associates or subordinates those who could teach to be the "teaching officials" (*chiao-kuan*) and appoint them to a four-year term.[49] This memorial, submitted in the 1030s, set the tone as to how teachers should be recruited.

By 1062, according to a memo written by Ssu-ma Kuang, there was already a rather complete set of regulations governing the qualification of local teachers. This included rules such as that a qualified "teaching official" should possess a degree either in the *belles lettres* (*chin-shih*) subject or in that of the Nine Classics (*chiu-ching*), and that he should be under forty years old. In general, these people would come from the prefectural (or county) staff,[50] and serve for a three-year term. Preceptor (*chiao-shou*), as an official title, also began to be used at about this time.[51]

[48] See, for example, *SHY*, cj, 2/22a. For a more detailed discussion on the personnel in local schools, see my "Sung-tai ti-fang hsüeh-hsiao chih-shih k'ao," in *Shih-hsüeh p'ing-lun*, Vol. 8 (1984), 223–241.

[49] Liu Ch'ang, *Kung-shih chi*, *TSCC* ed., 31:387–388, 33:405–406. Liu's memorial refers to the established practice of appointing only people of more than forty years old to preceptorship.

[50] *SHY*, cj, 2/2ab.

[51] Persons responsible for actual teaching in early Sung local schools were variably called *po-shih* (literally, erudite, which was a T'ang post), *chiang-shu*, *shuo-shu* (both lit. lecturer, ceased to be used apparently after the late eleventh century), and *chiang-shou* (lit. also lecturer, also ceased to exist after the late eleventh century). See Juan

Sweeping changes occurred in 1071 when Wang An-shih specially appointed a total of fifty-three "teaching officials" to key localities in northern
China proper, in the following five circuits: Ching-tung, Shan-hsi, Ho-tung,
Ho-pei and Ching-hsi. This measure appeared to reflect the attention paid
by reformers to local education, and suggested that preceptors in these
circuits were different from the conventional teaching officials.[52] It is
not known if Wang An-shih had singled out these five circuits for the first
experiment, in the hope that his own version of preceptors could eventually
be applied nationwide. However, the policy as such was significant enough,
and indeed in fewer than five years, now under the initiative of Li Ting,[53]
a close associate of Wang An-shih, a recruiting examination for teachers
was instituted. The Bureau of Drafting Officials (She-jen yüan) administered
the recruiting examination and each candidate had to pass the test of five
ta-i (exposition on the meanings) questions on one specific classic selected
by the candidate.[54] The examination was applied to the prefectures where
preceptors were directly appointed by the Court; other prefectures not
entitled to Court-appointed preceptors continued to appoint their own
preceptors, nominated by the circuits' fiscal intendants (chuan-yün shih),
or by prefects and their associates.[55] Meanwhile, county schools had also
become more widespread and the county magistrates (subprefects) were
in charge of nominating instructors from among native scholars.[56] The
competition to become preceptors appeared to be rather keen. A report
in 1112 says that, in 1083, the rate of successful candidates was one in
fifteen.[57]

The examination method was introduced by reformers and was accordingly abolished in 1086 when anti-reformers came back to power. The new
policy was for ranking officials in the Court to nominate preceptors.[58]

Yüan, Liang-Che chin-shih chih, 12/15b—17b; Wang Ch'ang, Chin-shih ts'ui-pien, Sao-
yeh shan-fang ed. (1919), 132/5a, 134/7a; SHY, cj, 2/2a.

[52] WHTK, 46:432.

[53] HCP, 267/2b; SS, 329:10601—10603.

[54] Ibid.

[55] HCP, 294/6b—7a, 229/8b, 344/3b, 356/5b and SHY, cj, 2/5a. The appointment
was made stricter in 1083 when the Court ordered that nominees should be approved
by the Directorate of Education. SHY, cj, 2/5b.

[56] Their "official" title was still not fixed, but probably they were consistently
called "chiang-shu" (lit. lecturer, as distinct from preceptor). See note 52 above, HCP,
294/6b—7a, and Fan Chung-yen, Fan Wen-cheng kung chi (Wen-cheng chi hereafter),
KHTS ed., 18:137 where a preceptor was called, in 1027, "chiang-shu."

[57] SHY, ck, 28/19b.

[58] What actually occurred was that anti-reformers first enacted in the second (leap)
month of 1086, the law that ranking Court officials should recommend teaching officials

This led to a surplus of nominees, and some measures were taken subsequently to maintain their quality. These measures included establishing provisions which stipulated that teaching officials must be over thirty years old, must have passed the civil service examinations in the *chin-shih* subject,[59] and have held the degree for more than four years.[60]

Further developments are summarized in Table 6. The main points are:

a. The examination system was employed throughout the dynasty except for the periods 960–1075 (when there was no systematic policy on recruitment), 1086–1094, 1100, 1110 and 1135–1142.

b. Distinguished successful candidates from the civil service examinations and outstanding graduates from the University normally were given priority in the selection procedure, and were at one time even exempted from actually sitting for the examinations.

c. The content of the examinations invariably included the exposition of the classics (*ta-i*); the classic (or classics) to be tested was either selected by the candidates or designated by the examiners. After 1145, candidates were also required to compose poems as a part of the test.

d. Those districts which did not receive Court-appointed preceptors normally could appoint their own preceptors from among the native *chin-shih* degree-holders. In case that these were not available, local holders of "facilitated degrees" or (in sequence of priority) respected scholars, would then be called upon to perform the duty.

The account above was applicable to preceptors at the local level,[61] whereas the instructors in county schools continued to come pri-

---

and then ordered in the seventh month that since there was an over-supply of recommended teaching officials, there was accordingly no need for the examination which subsequently was abolished. See *HCP*, 370/9b, 382/1ab.

[59] The subject of *chin-shih* had become the only subject tested in the civil service examinations since 1075 (see later in Ch. 6), but during the reaction of the anti-reformers (1086–1094), new methods of recruitment such as that of the "Ten Categories" (*shih-k'o*) and of those "well versed in classical learning and morally outstanding" (*ching-ming hsing-hsiu*) were introduced as supplementary routes for the ascent to officialdom.

[60] *SHY*, hc, 28/25ab, 31/18b. When the selection test of the subject in "being well versed in the classical learning and morally outstanding" was established, in 1086, successful candidates in this test were made eligible also for taking the examination to become teaching officials. See *HCP*, 370/9b; *SHY*, ck, 28/11b. See Ch. 9, section B, too.

[61] The examinations were primarily for preceptors. But on some occasions, the better candidates from these examinations could be appointed to be rectors (*hsüeh-cheng*) or associate rectors (*hsüeh-yü*) in the University. See *SS*, 165:3914.

marily from native scholars. By the late eleventh or early twelfth century, they had been customarily called *"chiao-yü."*[62] In general, the sequence of priority in appointing local officials or native scholars was similar to that of appointing preceptors in areas without Court-appointed ones.

The significance of special examinations for the recruitment of teaching officials did not lie in the technique or the content of the examinations *per se;* rather, it lay in the desire of the government to strengthen the quality of reliable teaching staff of local schools through a strict selection process. With schools in nearly every prefecture (and eventually every county), it is conceivable that the government saw it as its own responsibility that teachers be carefully scrutinized before they actually assumed their teaching posts. The concern also reflected Wang An-shih's personal predilection for a controlled and unified ideology. It appears that the care given to the examination as such had lapsed towards the end of the twelfth century, without actually disappearing altogether, but the policy that teaching officials, especially the preceptors, should be selected and appointed by the Court had by then been well established. In later dynasties, schools at both prefectural and county levels received an assigned quota not merely of preceptors, but also of the majority of other types of staff members subordinate to the preceptors.[63]

The newly created "Office of Educational Intendant" (*t'i-chü hsüeh-shih ssu*) was related to the method of examination of teachers.[64] The post eventually became a permanent feature in the Chinese educational system and therefore is of special importance commanding our attention. As has already been mentioned,[65] in the beginning local government education was generally trusted to prefects and their subordinates who chose teachers to conduct the actual teaching. The increase in the number of schools, students and other miscellaneous duties necessitated the appointment of special personnel to supervise and coordinate them. The government first

---

[62]For *chiao-yü*, see note 48 above. The information seems to suggest that *chiao-yü* was also in charge of the administration of county schools. In general, it appears that it was *hsüeh-chang* who was mainly responsible for daily adminstration.

[63]See various gazetteers for information about this. For example, Li Ming-huan et al., *Su-chou fu-chih*, 1883 ed. (Taipei: Ch'eng-wen, 1970), 26/14a, 41b and Wu Hsiu-chih et al., *Wu-hsien chih*, 1933 ed. (Taipei: Ch'eng-wen, 1970), 26b/20b.

[64]*"T'i-chü"* is one of the many names designating the "commission" type of appointment. While the Chinese government had constantly regarded education as part of the responsibilities of local officials, the Sung was the first dynasty to feel the real need of appointing a special person to be in charge of *hsüeh-shih* (school affairs). In a sense, the terms of reference had to be more limited and precise than those for, for example, *san-lao* (three elders) of the Han.

[65]*SS*, 167:3976.

relied on Circuit Fiscal Intendants to perform the work. They were assigned these tasks partly because their job required them to make annual trips to the prefectures within the circuit to supervise various financial matters. This situation continued throughout a good part of the eleventh century.[66] However, as time went on, the burden of coordinating educational affairs simply went beyond what the peripatetic approach could handle. In a sense, the vigorous approach undertaken by Wang An-shih in appointing fifty-three teaching officials was perhaps a part of the awareness that specially appointed people, mostly the preceptors, might better take up the job of directing local school affairs. This, however, did not solve the whole problem.[67] Consequently, towards the later eleventh century, suggestions that a special coordinator be appointed to take care of school matters at the local level appeared. This person was to come from circuit offices, while prefects or subprefects would be held actually responsible for the direct administration of educational matters. No new title was created,[68] but finally, in 1103, the office was formally inaugurated.[69] Its responsibility was "to maintain order in prefectural and county schools within the circuit, to tour the circuit once a year and investigate the good or bad performances of teachers, and the diligence or laziness of students."[70]

As this occurred during Ts'ai Ching's reform period, the use of Educational Intendants was regarded as a part of the reform efforts. Nevertheless, since the post was also created as a result of a real need, it did not suffer the kind of fate professional schools suffered. On the contrary, intendants seem to have been very active until their office was temporarily abolished in 1121.[71]

The post was revived in 1143. However, for reasons unclear to me, the government in 1146 again reverted to the 1099 or post-1121 method in that the local officials were now required to "take care of" (*kuan-kan*) the coordinating responsibility, while someone from the circuit's office

[66]See, for examples, Wang Ch'ang, *Chin-shih ts'ui-pien*, 132/22a, 134/25a for various commission types of appointment and note 105 below.

[67]Although the majority of these fifty-three prefectures fell within the more developed areas, I believe the practice did not have much influence on Sung education in general.

[68]*SHY*, cj, 2/7a. For an even more detailed account, see Han Yüan-chi, *Nan-chien chia-i kao*, *SKCS* ed., 9/1a–2a.

[69]*SHY*, cj, 2/10a. Tilemann Grimm's "Inauguration of *T'i-chü hsüeh-shih ssu* (Education Intendants) during the Northern Sung Dynasty," *Études Song*, Vol. 1 (1976), 259–274, is only slightly useful.

[70]*SS*, 167:3971.

[71]*Ibid.*; *SHY*, cj, 2/30b.

TABLE 6

Changing Regulations on the Appointment and Examinations of Teaching Officials

Year	Exam./Recom.	Regulations on the qualifications (a) in areas with Court-appointed preceptors	(b) in areas without Court-appointed preceptors	Content of the examinations	Other related events	Sources
1075	exam.	The Bureau of Drafting Officials to administer.		Five exposition questions (ta-i) on the classic elected by the candidate.	Reformers in power.	HCP, 267/2b.
1078			Local officials to nominate respected scholars who had passed the prefectural civil service examinations.			HCP, 294/6b–7a.
1079			Same as above, but to be screened by the Directorate of Education first.			
1084			Same as above, except that the responsibility of recommendation now fell on Fiscal Intendants.			HCP, 299/8a, 350/5b; SHY, cj, 2/6a.
1086	recom.	(1) Ranking Court officials to nominate. (2) Nominees should be over 30, and hold a chin-shih degree for at least 4 years.			Anti-reform period.	HCP, 382/1ab, 429/8ab.
1094		Same as above, but holders of a degree in ching-ming hsing-hsiu subject also eligible.				SHY, cj, 2/6b, ck, 28/12a.
1095	combined	(1) Ranking Court officials to nominate one each year. (2) Must be over 30.	Native scholars holding a chin-shih degree, specializing in the classical learning.	One exposition question on each of the two classics elected by the candidate.	Reformers in power.	SHY, hsüan-chü (hc hereafter), 28/25ab, 31/18b, cj, 2/6b–7a.

Year		Description	Source
1098		(3) Distinguished successful candidates from the civil service examinations and outstanding University graduates could be appointed directly to posts. (4) Other nominees to take the examination administered by the Ministery of Personnel (*Li-pu*). (5) Two exams. each year. Specialization in poetic writing not allowed. 3 exposition questions on each of the 4 classics elected. Soon changed to 3 classics, also to be elected.	*HCP*, 497/18b–19a, 500/1b; *SHY*, cj. 2/7a.
1100	recom.?	Anti-reform period.	
1101	exam.	Same as above, except that the examination would be given once each year. Ts'ai Ching in power.	*SHY*, ck. 28/14b–15a.
1103		Educational Intendants first appointed.	*SS*, 167: 3971.
1106		Numbers of preceptors reduced: and only for 100 and more students.	*SHY*, cj. 2/11a.
1110	recom.	(1) Nominees to be natives. (2) Nominees should have attended the University or the *Pi-yung* School, or taken the civil service examinations. 2 preceptors for 500 and more students; one for 50 and more; none if fewer than 50.	*HCPSP*, 29/18b.

TABLE 6: Changing Regulations on the Appointment and Examinations of Teaching Officials (*cont.*)

Year	Exam./Recom.	Regulations on the qualifications		Content of the examinations	Other related events	Sources
		(a) in areas with Court-appointed preceptors	(b) in areas without Court-appointed preceptors			
1111	exam.	Similar to that of 1075, except that the Ministry of Personnel to administer the examination.				*SHY*, cj, 2/16b.
1112	exam.	Same as above, but graduates from the University could be appointed directly.				*SHY*, ck, 28/19b.
1113	exam.	Same as above, but *Pi-yung* graduates also to be appointed directly.				*SHY*, cj, 2/19b, 20ab.
1118	exam.	(1) Same as 1075 qualifications, but only distinguished successful candidates from the civil service examinations and outstanding graduates from the University could register for the examination. (2) University graduates, after passing the examination, to serve in prefectural or county offices for one term, before being assigned to teaching posts.		5 exposition questions on one classic.		*SHY*, ck, 28/21b.
1128				Test on composing *shih* poem and *fu* rhyme prose added.		*CYYL*, 17/4b.
1129					Office of "Teaching officials" abolished.	*CYYL*, 24/9b.

Year	Type	Description	Source
1132		Office of "Teaching officials" restored.	*CYYL*, 53/2a.
1133		Holders of "facilitated degree," however distinguished, to be excluded from being appointed directly to teaching posts.	*SHY*, cj, 2/33a.
1135	recom.		*CYYL*, 84/12a; *SHY*, cj, 2/33a.
1138		No prefecture to have more than 2 preceptors.	*SHY*, cj, 2/34a.
1142	exam.		*CYYL*, 145/9b.
1143		Composition of *shih* and *fu* eliminated.	*SHY*, cj, 2/35ab.
1145		*Ta-i* question (from 2 of 6 classics randomly chosen by examiners) and poetic writing both examined.	*CYYL*, 154/a; *SHY*, cj, 2/37a.
1146		To appoint in sequence of priority, (1) a ranked official, (2) a "facilitated degree" holder, or (3) a respected scholar, from among the natives.	*SHY*, cj, 2/37b.

was designated to "supervise" (*t'i-chü*).[72]

Thus, the post, either filled by a specially appointed person or held concurrently by an official from the local government's office, continued to function. It was continued by the Mongols and evolved into the *t'i-hsüeh ssu* office of the Ming dynasty.[73]

The practical purpose of the post best explains the continuity of it throughout the later dynasties. There is very little doubt that the post was created so as to facilitate the selection of students under the scheme of the "Local Three-Hall System." This is most evident in the famous memorial submitted by Ts'ai Ching in 1102.[74] A reading of the memorial shows that Ts'ai had wanted to have Circuit Intendants to "*t'i-chü*" educational matters in relation to the selection of the best school graduates for promotion and for eventual office. The presence of a need to have tighter control of education for examination purposes is unmistakably evident. The evolution was such that the educational intendants were increasingly trusted with the responsibility of determining the qualifications of local students for enrollment in local government schools. As this selection process was actually a part of the civil service examinations in Ming and Ch'ing China, the continuity of the post can thus be understood in this light.

D. Students in Local Schools

There is very little information as to how students were recruited into local schools, and still less on their family background. What is presented in the following is only a very tentative discussion and questions relating to the social composition of students in local schools probably will continue to elude scholars for some time to come. Estimates in the early twelfth century

---

[72]*CYYL*, 150/3b and 155/7b, but the most original source for this is found in Han Yüan-chi, *Nan-chien chia-i kao*, 9/1a–2b, which reveals a situation slightly more complicated than what I describe here: the Ts'ai Ching method would formally award a specially designated title of "*kuan-kan*," if the intendant was from the office of a prefect or subprefect, of "*t'i-chü*" if he held the rank of *T'ai-chung tai-fu* and above, but no special title if he was a military officer. After 1121, apparently, the duties of educational intendants were made an obligatory responsibility of a prefect or subprefect, except for the short period between 1143 and 1146 when Ts'ai's method was briefly restored.

[73]Tilemann Grimm, "Ming Educational Intendants," in Charles O. Hucker (ed.), *Chinese Government in Ming Times: Seven Studies* (New York: Columbia University Press, 1969), 129–148.

[74]Translated in Appendix E.

do show that there were as many as two hundred thousand students supported by the government who were studying in government's local schools.[75] This would amount to one student in every two hundred and twenty or thirty registered Chinese people. This may not be a particularly impressive record, but is comparable to English achievement in the sixteenth century.[76] Since there were so many Chinese adolescents going to schools, it would be extremely difficult to dismiss the educational institutions as *merely* centers where wealthy and powerful local scions spent their time to evade labor duties, even if some cursory evidences apparently suggest that this might be the case.[77]

Related to the number of students was the question of students' age. Local schools presumably admitted those who were serious in preparing to take the civil service examinations and hence would be admitting relatively mature young men. One source indicates that men became eligible for going to local schools when they turned fifteen years (*sui*) old.[78] However, local schools almost without exception also maintained elementary schools, which would admit boys at a much younger age, normally those of seven to the early teens.[79]

Students were admitted after they were examined.[80] But the little information we have about the entrance examinations suggests that they were nominal, and what actually mattered was whether a student could

[75] See later in this section, especially Table 7.

[76] See note 42 of p. 163 of my "Education in Northern Sung China" where I quote S. J. Curtis, *History of Education in Great Britain* (London: University Tutorial Press, 1948), 54, for comparison. See also my *San-lun*, 64.

[77] See section E, especially notes 112 and 113. See also *WHTK*, 46:433.

[78] See, for example, Tu Ch'un-sheng, *Yüeh-chung chin-shih chi, Shih-k'o shih-liao ts'ung-shu* ed., 7/4b where it states that children of eight years old were permitted to enter the elementary school and those of fifteen the school proper. See also Lü Ssu-mien, *Yen-shih hsü-cha* (Shanghai: Jen-min, 1958), 136–138 for a discussion on the entrance ages of children in the Period of Disunion. See also *SS*, 447:13194, 387:11876 for concrete examples. During the Southern Sung, it was not uncommon for local government schools to have students of forty or fifty years old. See Liang K'o-chia, *San-shan chih, SKCS* ed., 40/3a. *SHY*, cj, 2/26a, on the other hand, states that students seeking to enter the prefectural school could be admitted, provided that they fulfilled moral requirements and were fifteen or below.

[79] *Ibid.*; see also *SHY*, cj, 2/9a (ten years old), and 2/27b (eight years old). See also Wang Ch'ang, *Chin-shih ts'ui-pien*, 134/24b, where the age fifteen appears to be an important dividing line between students studying at the Yung-hsing (present Hsian) military prefectural school and those studying at its elementary school, during the 1050s.

[80] Chao Sheng, *Ch'ao-yeh lei-yao, TSCC* ed., 2:21–24.

be eligible for the government's subsidy towards meals.[81]

The few references to residence requirements are the ones pertaining to the reform of Ts'ai Ching. These regulations demanded that students be in residence variously for a quarter of a year (1114), half a year (1104), a year (1104), or for a three-year period (1106 and 1115).[82] During Ts'ai's reform and during most of the Southern Sung, a certain number of local school students, after having graduated from prefectural schools, could be chosen to study in the University either by recommendation or by taking another entrance examination.[83] It is thus reasonable to assume that a three-year residency was the common pattern as the University then was normally admitting students only in examimation years. Students aspiring to be admitted to the University would very likely stay for the required length of time.

There is no doubt that local boys made up the main body of students. However, this became practical only after every prefecture, or eventually every county, had its own school. In other words, it appears that it was only towards the end of the Northern Sung that it became feasible to admit only students from the local district. The issue is interesting, if not necessarily significant: since local school students could be exempted from labor services,[84] it might be necessary for school administrators, or, for that matter, local officials to do their best to ward off intruders from outside, so that they could hand out favors to local people. Nevertheless, we do not possess evidence suggesting that situations like this did commonly occur. Similarly, when prefectural school students became eligible for promotion to the University, it is also conceivable that outside students would meet specially stringent scrutiny for admission, probably to such an extent that eventually each prefecture had to have its own school. After the "Local Three-Hall System" was introduced in 1101 by which distinguished local school graduates were admitted directly to the Imperial University, it can be inferred that each prefecture had to have its own school.

After having graduated from local schools, students generally aspired to pass the civil service examinations so as to go into service. During the

---

[81]*Ibid.*, which indicates that students, once admitted, had to pass a second test to compete for support. It appears whenever the number of a quota of students is mentioned, it meant the number of students supported. See Liang K'o-chia, *San-shan chih*, 12/3b–4b.

[82]*SHY*, cj, 2/22b–23a; *WHTK*, 46:433; *HCPSP*, 23/5a. County schools also imposed a three-year residence requirement on students, and if at the end of the residence a student could not qualify for prefectural schools, he would be dissmissed. See *SHY*, cj, 2/28b.

[83]More on this is in a later part of this section. See also Table 4.

[84]See notes 93, 94 and 95.

first two decades of the twelfth century, a comprehensive educational reform was launched under the direction of Ts'ai Ching, which we have already touched upon in various parts of this book. The part of the reform that was related to local education was the so-called "Local Three-Hall System." Modelled on the "Three-Hall System" of the University, distinguished graduates from local schools could be admitted to the University without taking any entrance examination and thence be admitted to officialdom. The idea had been openly discussed since the 1070s, and was enacted in 1099 by Chang Tun, but there is no evidence that it was actually put into practice. Instead, it was after Ts'ai Ching rose to power that he ordered the program to be carried out with vigor and enthusiasm.[85]

In reality, local schools, including those of prefectures and counties, had only two classes, the outer and the inner halls. Students of the outer halls were addressed as "*hsüan-shih*" (lit. selected scholars), and called themselves "outer-hall students." Students of the inner hall were to be addressed as "*chün-shih*" (distinguished scholars), but called themselves "inner-hall students." Graduates qualifying for admission to the *Pi-yung* school were addressed as "*kung-shih*" (tribute scholars) and would call themselves by the same name.[86]

The "Local Three-Hall System" was discontinued after 1121 when Ts'ai Ching left office. However, the idea of the system was maintained during the Southern Sung, when graduates of local schools were intermittently tested after a certain period of school residence in order to go on to the University according to a quota set aside specially for them. At times during the Southern Sung, graduates of local schools would be admitted to the departmental examinations in the capital under a special quota.[87]

One final point about local school students is their official status and privileges. Theoretically, all students were supported by the school with subsidies towards meals. They were also put up in school dormitories.[88] In practice, because of the limitation of school budgets, some students were not accorded this treatment.[89]

---

[85] See my *San-lun*, 60–63, 152–154.

[86] *HCPSP*, 32/2b. But see note 92.

[87] See Table 4: "Admission Methods of the University in the Southern Sung." By 1161, there were still suggestions to revive the "Local Three-Hall System"; See *CYYL*, 189/8a. For the information about a special quota for graduates of local schools, see *CYYL*, 152/3a.

[88] Some interesting anecdotes about life in school dormitories have come down to us. For a layout of a Sung local school, see, for example, Chiao Hung, *Ching-hsüeh chih*, Ming ed. (Taipei: Kuo-feng, 1965). See also Tu Ch'un-sheng, *Yüeh-chung chin-shih chi*, 7/12a.

[89] Chao Sheng reports that the actual numbers of students were different from

Other supports given to students included such miscellaneous expenses as money for lamp oil and charcoal,[90] revenue put aside especially to help occasional but urgent needs such as expenses a student might need for a wedding, burial of their relatives and the like,[91] and money to supply students with copies of books printed at the school.[92]

As for the status of students in terms of exemption from labor service, the only regulation we know of was issued in 1116:[93]

> Students of prefectural and county schools who have passed the entrance examination and/or are studying in the outer-hall shall be exempted from performing the labor services in person. Those who are in the inner hall shall be exempted from hiring replacements (for themselves). Upper-hall students would be treated according to the regulations applicable to "official households."

This is quite an exceptional regulation, because the awarding of "official household" status was not a frequent privilege, and was not even accorded to officials possessing no formal rank.[94] It is therefore possible that this regulation might have been discontinued in 1121 when the "Local Three-Hall System" was suspended.

Local school students probably were not given any labor service exemptions during the Southern Sung, as there is no direct evidence of this policy taking effect. One nonetheless imagines that a certain form of understanding must have existed so that no complaints would have arisen, because during most of the Southern Sung, graduates from local schools were treated as equal to those having passed the local civil service examinations, and ought to have shared the priviledges of the latter group which included exemptions from the *ting* (male adult) tax and from hiring replacements for corvee labor service.[95] In other words, it would appear very likely that certain

---

those given meal and dormitory support. See his *Ch'ao-yeh lei-yao*, 2:21 See also note 80 above.

[90] Chou Ying-ho, *Ching-ting Chien-k'ang chih*, 29/4b–5a. This particular piece of information is about a Ming-tao Academy, but should no doubt be applicable to regular government local schools.

[91] Information on this is found in various local gazetteers.

[92] Mei Ying-fa, *K'ai-ch'ing Ssu-ming hsü-chih*, *Sung Yüan K'ai-ch'ing liu-chih* ed., 1/6ab.

[93] *HCPSP*, 25/3b–4a. This seems to suggest that there were not merely two classes, but three classes in the local schools. For a more detailed discussion on this decree, see John Chaffee, "Education and Examinations in Sung Society," 117, note 2.

[94] For information on the status of the "official household," see Hsieh Shen-fu, *Ch'ing-yüan t'iao-fa shih-li*, Sung ed. (Tokyo: Koten kenkyūkai, 1968), 48:453. See also Wang Tseng-yü, "Sung-ch'ao chieh-chi chieh-kou k'ai-shu," in *She-hui k'o-hsüeh chan-hsien*, 1979/4, 128–136.

[95] In 1133, the government decreed that all prefectural successful candidates should

official or social privileges were awarded to graduates of local schools during the Southern Sung period.

To sum up the discussion concerning the admission method and the social status conferred upon local school students, we can observe that there was a tendency to award increasingly privileged position to local students, or at least, local graduates. The development resulted in a reduction in the opportunity for the local schools, and thus, the number of students, to grow and expand. The Ch'ing system, whereby registration in the local schools was equal to being granted degree status, shows a natural evolution from the Ming, and hence, Sung practice. Both Ming and Ch'ing methods originated from the Sung, during which local school students, for the first time, were either formally given an exemption from services or were awarded certain privileges.[96]

E. Finance

"The [Wen-chou (present Yung-chia, Chekiang)] county school has a piece of land of five *ch'ing*; the income from this piece of land is about enough to support one hundred students," reported Lin Chi-chung in 1147.[97] This is a rather interesting piece of evidence. When the Sung government started to appropriate land to local schools in the early 1030s, the decision as to the size of the land was between five and ten *ch'ing*, and since Wen-chou was located in a rather fertile area, it is reasonable to assume, therefore, that it was the government's desire that an average local school should be able to support roughly about one hundred, if not more, people.

---

be exempted from both *ting* tax and corvee labor service. The provision was revised in 1137 when it was decided that they should continue to be exempted from *ting* tax but should hire replacements for labor and corvee services. In cases where the *te-chieh jen* was the only male adult in the family, then he could also be exempted from corvee service. See my "The Social Significance of the Quota System in Sung Civil Service Examinations," *JICS/CUHK*, Vol. 13 (1982), 287–318; see also *SHY*, shih-huo (sh thereafter), 12/8b, 14/27a, 14/30ab, and *CYYL*, 64/7b, 160/3b–4b, and next Chapter.

[96] Local school students in early Ming China were exempted from corvee service. See Wu Han, "Ming-ch'ao te hsüeh-hsiao," in his *Tu-shih cha-chi* (Peking: San-lien, 1961), 317–341. See especially 338.

[97] Lin Chi-chung, *Chu-hsüan tsa-chu*, *SKCS* ed., 6/16b–18b. A similar report shows that in Hu-chou (present Wu-hsing, Chekiang), a piece of land of seven *ch'ing* was capable of providing each of its hundred students with 250 cash per month in 1056–1063. See Chao T'ieh-han, "Sung-tai te chou-hsüeh," in *SSYCC*, Vol. 2, 343–363. 250 cash per month was barely adequate to cover meal expenses at this period.

There is a wealth of information about the management of school land in Sung China. The following is only a very general summary of what we know,[98] even though there is no doubt that the creation of a school land system was the one single most important contribution to Chinese education made by the Sung people. The idea originated with the action of a single individual, the famous classicist, Sun Shih (962–1033), who decided to use the income from his personal official land to support the temple school in Yen-chou (in present Shan-tung) in 1022.[99] His action was soon followed by the government's decision in 1024 to endow the Mao-shan Academy with a piece of land.[100] Thereafter, the endowment of official land became standard and every new school received some land when it was founded.[101]

School lands made up the mainstay of most school properties, but local schools also received other forms of subsidy, such as direct appropriation of money from local governments. The majority of local government met the school needs with income from miscellaneous sources, such as surpluses from the management of public granaries,[102] sales of official documents, books, or forms,[103] and the like.

The control and management of school land in particular and school finance in general was, in the early eleventh century, largely in the hands of prefectural or county officials. Obviously, the central government ceased to supervise or take care of local school funding after the land was handed out and it became entirely the responsibility of local officials to see to it that these schools continued to function. By the late eleventh century, thanks to the heightened interest of the reformers, a more systematic control of school finance started to emerge. In 1074, the Directorate of Education recommended that those prefectures which already had Court-appointed

[98] For a very detailed discussion on these materials, see Fukuzawa Yokurō, "Sō Gen jidai shū ken gakusan kō," in *Fukuoka Gakugei Daigaku kiyō*, No. 8 (1958), 27–42, and No. 9 (1959), 27–36.

[99] *SHY*, cj, 2/2a.

[100] *SHY*, cj, 2/41a.

[101] A decree in 1071 made it standard for government schools to receive lands. See *HCP*, 221/5a.

[102] The first instance of using the so-called "*t'ou-tzu ch'ien*" to support local education was by Fan Yung in 1038 in Yung-hsing Military Commandary (present Hsi-an). See Wang Ch'ang, *Chin-shih ts'ui-pien*, 126/8a–9a. The use of granary money to support local schools was very common. See *SHY*, cj, 2/16b, 2/19a, and Lu Tseng-hsiang, *Pa-ch'iung shih chin-shih pu-cheng*, Wu-hsing Hsi-ku lou ed. (Taipei: Wen-hai, 1967), 119/18a (where the manager of a public granary was responsible for school finance). See also note 119 for a moving account of appropriating money from public granaries to support local schools.

[103] *SHY*, sh, 35/1a; Su Shih, *Tung-p'o tsou-i*, in *Tung-p'o ch'i-chi*, SPPY ed., 6/1a–2a.

preceptors (see Table 6) should also take charge of the financial matters of all schools, including county schools and academies (which presumably were by then also supported by local governments), within the prefectural district.[104]

Further measures concerning the control of local school finance were isssued during the early twelfth century reform. These included letting Fiscal Intendants manage financial matters for local schools.[105] After the office of Educational Intendants was established, the responsibility was then transferred to the Intendants. The practice of unified financing was continued in the early Southern Sung until 1143 when individual local government offices apparently resumed the responsibility of taking care of the school financing for their own districts.[106]

During the early twelfth century Sung local education reached its height, and the financial situation was equally impressive. At this time, the government decided to exempt school lands from paying the summer and autumn taxes (the "Two taxes").[107] This is also the time when a special person was appointed to each school to be in charge of accounting and supervision of expenditures.[108] We find that a surplus existed for the first time, and that the central government had to instruct the Educational Intendants to invest the capital in other profit-taking activities.[109] Finally, this is also the time that the government took the initiative to investigate and interfere with the arbitrary invasion and abuse of school lands by powerful local families.[110] It is therefore important to remember that local educational achievement, in financial terms, had without question reached its zenith in the early twelfth century. The statistics in Table 7 shed some light on its full dimensions.[111]

Since school land constituted the mainbody of school property, the management of the land either by the school or by the local government created many serious problems. The first question to be raised is perhaps

[104]*HCP*, 252/22b. The Director was Ch'ang Chih (1019–1077), a respected if incompetent educator supported by Wang An-shih. See my *San-lun*, 134–143 for a discussion of his role in Wang's educational reform.

[105]*SHY*, cj, 2/16b; *HCPSP*, 21/10b.

[106]*CYYL*, 15/11b, 150/8b; *SHY*, cj, 2/36a.

[107]*SHY*, cj, 2/19. This was enacted in 1112.

[108]Called *k'u-tzu* which literally meant "the ware-house runner," this was to become a permanent position in Sung schools. *SHY*, cj, 2/13a. The date was 1108.

[109]*SHY*, cj, 2/19a.

[110]*Ibid.*, 2/14b.

[111]*HCPSP*, 24/16a; Ko Sheng-chung, *Tan-yang chi, Ch'ang-chou hsien-che i-shu* ed. (1896), 1/3a. A more detailed analysis of these two sets of statistics is in Ch. 8, section A.

TABLE 7

Educational Statistics, 1104 and 1108

	1104	1108
Number of students	over 210,000	167,622
Number of buildings	90,020	95,298
Expenditure:		
cash (strings)	3,400,000	2,678,787
rice (*tan*)	550,000	337,944
Income from school lands:		
cash (strings)	?	3,058,872
rice (*tan*)	?	640,291
Properties held by schools:		
land (*ch'ing*)	?	105,990
buildings	?	155,454

the extent to which the proper management of school land was given a high priority in the minds of local officials. My answer is that, except for the early twelfth century, it probably had a relatively low priority. However, local officials appear to have by and large managed the properties efficiently for most of them were profitable enough to meet the needs of a steadily growing number of students. There is no doubt that officials and locally powerful elite-families, the so-called "families of style and potential" (*hsing-shih hu*), were more concerned with the aggrandizement and proper management of their own lands, which received legal and illegal protection, rather than with the management of school lands. In their selfish pursuits, they did not exclude school land from either being forcefully occupied,[112] or leased so that they could sublease the lands to other poorer tenants.[113] Lands legally exempted from taxes included not only school land and other official lands (including lands allocated to officials as part of their emolument, the so-called *chih-t'ien*), but also lands controlled and owned by Buddhist temples and monasteries. Disputes between local schools and Buddhist establishments over all kinds of land issues appear

[112] See note 109 above. See also *CYYL*, 162/17ab; *SHY*, cj, 2/38b. For a very detailed account of abuse of school land by a powerful local landlord, see Anonymous author: *Chiang-su chin-shih chih*, 15/52a–55a. Also, a report of 1243 indicates that only half of the total rental income for Wu-hsi County school was actually collected. *Ibid.*, 17/20b, 37b.

[113] For a study of this phenomenon, see Ch'i Hsia, "Sung-tai hsüeh-t'ien chih chung feng-chien tsu-tien kuan-hsi te fa-chan," in *She-hui k'o-hsüeh chan-hsien*, 1979/3, 147–153.

all over Sung records, and indicate that in the eyes of local officials, Buddhist institutions had at least as much power as government schools in such contests as to who should be given priority to use irrigation water and facilities. Not infrequently, Buddhist temples or monasteries gained the upper hand in the litigations.[114] Although it is generally known that Buddhism had substantially declined as an organized religion during Sung times, Buddhist estates still figured very prominently on the local scene,[115] and could even occasionally afford to offer some support to local school.[116]

On the other hand, local officials ensured that at least minimal support was given to schools, and throughout the Southern Sung, local schools were maintained without much financial difficulty. The government did not, of course, have an unlimited supply of land and had to resort to other means to meet the demands when a new school was founded or when an old school had to be expanded. Heirless lands or lands confiscated for various reasons from commoners were often made available to schools. Both types of land had been awarded since at least the early twelfth century, but the second became increasingly important, and by the mid-thirteenth century, had become almost the only way to create new resources. The Wu prefectural school (in present Chekiang) in 1273 had a total of 2,207.3 *mou* of land (roughly 333 acres), of which more than 1,073 *mou* was land confiscated by the local government from commoners for various reasons;[117] schools obviously benefited from this sometimes arbitary official action.[118]

[114] *SS*, 422:13618; Liu Tsai, *Man-t'ang chi*, *SKCS* ed., 21/3b–5b; *SHY*, cj, 2/39b; Hsü Shuo, *Chih-yüan chia-ho chih*, 1288 MS (quoted from John Chaffee, "Education and Examinations in Sung Society," 121), 16/13a–14a; Fan Ch'eng-ta, *Wu-chün chih*, *TSCC* ed., 4:24–25, etc.

[115] To give just one simple example, towards the end of the Sung, between 1227 and 1298, the Buddhist lands in Ch'ang-kuo county (present Ting-hai, Chekiang) made up 20.71% of the entire arable land of the county, while the Buddhist households made up less than 2% of the total number of households. See Huang Min-chih, "Sung-tai liang-Che lu te ssu-yüan yü she-hui," in *Kuo-li Ch'eng-kung ta-hsüeh li-shih hsi li-shih hsüeh-pao*, No. 5 (1978), 349. For systematic studies on the holding of lands by Buddhist temples and monasteries, see, among others, idem, "Sung-tai ssu-yüan yü chuang-yüan chih yen-chiu," in *Ta-lu tsa-chih*, 46/4 (1972), 26–37; Chikusa Gashō, "Fukuken no shakai to jiin," in *Tōyōshi kenkyū*, 15/2 (1965), 1–27, and Aoyama Sadao: "Sō Gen no chihōshi ni mieru shakai keizai shiryō," in *Tōyō gakuhō*, 25/2 (1938), 281–297. Aoyama shows that 21.9% of the total arable land of Fu-chou prefecture was controlled by Buddhist temples.

[116] Hsin-ch'ang County School received construction materials from four local Buddhist temples when the school was founded in 1144. Tu Ch'un-sheng, *Yüeh-chung chin-shih chi*, 4/17a.

[117] Anonymous author, *Chiang-su chin-shih chih*, 20/5b–17a. Based on Fukuzawa Yokurō's calculation. See note 98 above.

[118] See note 98 above.

Before turning to the expenses of schools, let me cite a record to show that such arbitrariness was not necessarily the norm when efforts were made by local officials to raise money and support for schools. Sometimes, as the following quotation shall show, the work involved in financing local schools could really be painstaking:[119]

> After the wars in Hu-pei (of the early 1120s), there was no more fertile land left and the supply of manpower also declined. . . .
> Schools have been revived in these recent years, and local governments were instructed to appropriate confiscated lands for them. Most of these lands did not have tenants, so officials quickly ordered local farmers to assume the responsibility of cultivating them. They are asked to pay rent in kind for their designated lots. . . . [However], most of the lands are not adjacent to the tenants' own lands and it is extremely inconvenient for them to take care of their designated lots. The result is that school lands are often left uncultivated, while tenants continue to have to pay for the rents.
> I have looked into the records of Ch'ang-lin County and found that, in An-hsi Village alone, out of the 123 households paying for renting the school land, only one actually has privately owned land. (Others presumably were tenant-households.) In total, in the nine villages of Ch'ang-lin County, there are 223 households required to pay the crop-rents for the school lands, and of them only 35 actually possess privately owned land. If I decide to consider the hardship of these landless households and release them from assuming the payment for school land rental, then there will be no more income to support students. If I choose to follow the established practice and demand that they continue paying the rents, then there will be no end to the hardship of the poor farmers.
> There is no file or record kept in this military prefectural office, and I have no way to find out how previous governors financed the schools. Moreover, there are no neirless temples or lands which could be used to generate revenue for schools.
> My humble opinion is as follows: the total rent collected to meet the needs of the Ch'ang-lin schools is slightly more than 200 *tan* of rice or wheat. Now the public granary (*ch'ang-ping ts'ang*) of the county could collect [yearly?] about 800 *tan* of crops; in addition, over the years, there has accumulated more than 12,000 strings of cash which now still is in the possession of the granary. Also, the crop revenue now controlled by the granary, excluding the payments made each year at the turn between summer and autumn [just before harvest time], amounts to more than 11,000 *tan* of rice. These do not even include what is still being controlled by the relief granary. Now that this military prefecture is sparsely populated, the expenses for drought and flood relief do not use up a large sum. There are not too many old, sick, poor, or blind people to take care of. I therefore request that your majesty permit this office to allocate [each year] 100 *tan* of wheat from the regular land rents (taxes) to finance

---

[119]Hung Kua, *P'an-chou chi, SPTK* ed., 49:330–331. For a similar kind of experience, see *CYYL*, 109/14b.

the schools so as to release those landless households from paying rents for school land [which they anyway do not till]. . . .

This rather long quotation shows what it was like in Sung times, especially in the mid-twelfth century right after the loss of north China to the Jurchens, for a local official to plan for the finance of schools. It can be said that all the main elements of school financing as disussed above are found in this detailed memorial submitted to Emperor Kao-tsung in 1133. The memorial therefore is significant not merely because of the details; it is also valuable because of the human quality revealed.

Meal provision to students was the major item of expenditure in local schools. There is very little information on the size of the allowance for each student, but the little we do know suggests that the allowance was at best merely adequate to buy a couple of *sheng* of rice. For example, in the period between 1056 and 1063, the Hu-chou school students were given a monthly allowance of 250 cash, which was just enough to purchase about 7.13 *tou* of rice, meaning that each student was receiving about 2.38 *sheng* of rice each day, which, according to the estimate of Kinugawa, did not quite meet the daily minimum of an adult man in Sung times.[120] This is in contrast to the allowance of 300 cash per month then given to University students.[121] The amount of the allowance might have increased in the early twelfth century during the massive educational reforms, but we unfortunately lack evidence of this. During the Southern Sung, the support generally remained at the bare subsistence level; Chu Hsi reported that, around 1190, a prefectural school student received 1.4 *sheng* of rice plus sixty cash per day, which at the time was adequate to purchase about another 0.6 *sheng* of rice, making the total daily allowance a meager 2.0 *sheng*.[122] This was obviously not enough for support, although one can say that at least local government seemed as a rule to have consciously made this minimal allowance constantly available.

Other items of expenditure in local schools consisted of money for ceremonies, and various expenses of a miscellaneous nature. But for lack of evidence, I shall not dwell on these matters any further.

One final point has to be mentioned. Many schools were also fortunate enough to have an additional estate, which could be used to support all kinds of extra or emergent needs, including, as mentioned above, special grants for funerals, fees to cover the travel expenses of students taking

[120] For the figure of the Hu-chou allowance, see note 97 above. For the price of rice, see my *San-lun*, 80–82.
[121] See my *San-lun*, 80–84.
[122] Chu Hsi, *Wen-chi*, 100:1785.

civil service examinations and the like. Income from a separate estate of course was not to be confused with regular revenue generated from official school lands or the outright appropriation of official revenue to support regular educational needs discussed in this section.[123] One clearly sees in this institution some kind of communal effort to achieve equitable educational opportunities for local young men, a practice which became widespread in the thirteenth century after the idea of clan or community school was conceived and promoted by Chu Hsu.[124]

F. Recapitulation

Local education always played an important part in China's statecraft, and activities ranged from actual instruction on the classics and basic primers, to making sacrifices to Confucius, and to sponsoring all kinds of literary meetings. Local education in the Sung was no exception, but the Sung made a few important innovations: the creation of the school estate system, the appointment of special teaching officials, the eventual evolution of the permanent post of educational intendant, and above all, the success in founding at least one school in virtually every Chinese local administrative district. Government schools thus became a permanent feature after the Sung. Structurally, Sung education at the local level no doubt laid the foundation for Chinese local education for several hundred years to come.

The development of Sung local schools reached its height during the early twelfth century when the government sought to recruit distinguished local school graduates for the University, from whence the best would be admitted into service directly. As a result, the government found itself educating and supporting more than 200,000 students. This record was unprecedented. The size of the reform and massive expansion in local schools declined in the Southern Sung, but the idea and practice of admitting local school graduates directly to the University continued. As a result, especially during the Mongol Yüan period, the qualification of local school status eventually developed into a part of the overall qualification hierarchy of the civil service examinations. Thus, in terms of the development of formal education as an integrated part of the civil service examinations, the Sung practices made some rather critical contributions.

As for the evaluation of Sung local education, for all of its achievements,

[123] For a very detailed regulation on the management of this kind of special estate, see Anonymous author, *Chiang-su chin-shih chih*, 15/41b–46a.

[124] Clan schools and community schools during the Sung are immensely important topics for research. Unfortunately, very little has been done.

Sung local schools eventually were overshadowed by academies. This is especially apparent in the Southern Sung. The chief reason for this came, as in the case of higher education, from the creativity exhibited in Neo-Confucian pedagogy.[125] However, State local education during the Sung remained a successful experiment, and the significant increase in the number of local government schools led to the spread of education to a much larger population than at any period before the Sung. On this account alone, the Sung government made a unique contribution.

Most local schools in the Sung times also ran technical (such as medical) schools or elementary schools. As these schools are not directly related to my main concern here, I have left them out in this book.[126]

[125] See Ch. 7, section A.
[126] See note 28 above.

CHAPTER 6

The Civil Service Examinations

The Buddhist temple in the Shen-li mountain, near present Fu-chou, was auspicious; many examination candidates went to pray there. Ch'en Yao-tzu, a young man from Fukien, was no exception. It was sometime just before A.D. 1000. The candidate went to the temple and spent the night there. In the midst of his dreams, he saw a single-legged ghost dancing towards him. The ghost chanted: "If a person becomes an official, then he will have a wife; if he has a wife, then he will have concubines; and if he has money, then he will have land."[1] The young man could not be happier about the dream, and indeed he turned out to be none other than the "first palace graduate" in the *chih-shih* test in A.D. 1000.

This interesting anecdote illustrates the psychological attitude of examination candidates in Sung China. The successful completion of the civil service examinations, perfected during the Sung, became the major object of aspiration for people going to school. To understand the significance of Sung education properly, it is necessary to better understand the nature of the civil service examination system.

A. Historical Background

Systematic written tests, conducted carefully to safeguard impartiality, as a means of recruiting potential civil officials, started only towards the end of the sixth century, during the Sui. It is quite reasonable to say that the civil service examinations as an institution really began in the Sui, although there is no doubt that the institution became socially and politically significant only towards the end of the T'ang, or more specifically, during the Sung.[2] In other words, the open written examination system was but

---

[1] Hung Mai, *I-chien chih*, Han-fen lou ed. (1915), chih-chih, ting, 8/3b.

[2] The recruitment of capable or virtuous persons, commoners and nobles alike, went back all the way to the Han. The practice was generally called "*hsüan-chü*," translatable into examinations, but really means "selection." Systematic examinations based on written tests to find out capable persons specializing in particular subjects were instituted first during the Sui. For a careful study on the distinction of these terms,

one of the several means by which the Chinese government recruited people for the civil service. During the Sui and the T'ang, central government schools, including those directly and indirectly under the Directorate of Education, were as important as places where potential candidates were trained and promoted to officialdom as were the civil service examinations which produced only a very small number of officials. A rough calculation shows that only about 15% of the bureaucracy was made up of officials recruited from the civil service examinations. This changed during the Sung dynasty.[3]

The civil service examinations included, during the T'ang, a great number of subjects,[4] ranging from classical learning, poetry and essay composition to law, mathematics and history. Two subjects were especially prominent in the T'ang examinations: the *belles lettres* (*chin-shih*) and classical knowledge (*ming-ching*). Of these the *chin-shih* subject which tested candidates on policy discussion questions (*ts'e*), memory questions on the classics (*t'ieh-ching*),[5] *fu* prose, and, occasionally, also the *Lao-tzu* and the *Classic of Filial Piety* (*Hsiao-ching*) and various other texts,[6] was the most prestigeous and most coveted, and candidate successful in this subject were sure

---

see Sogabe Sizuo, "Chugoku no senkyo, kokyo to kakyo," in *Shirin*, 53/4 (1970), 42–66. See also Ch'u T'ung-tsu, *Han Social Structure*, ed. by Jack Dull (Seattle: University of Washington Press, 1972), 342–343. See also my "K'o-chü: Sui T'ang chih Ming Ch'ing te k'ao-shih chih-tu," in Cheng Ch'in-jen (ed.), *Li-kuo te hung-kuei* (Taipei: Lien-ching, 1982), 259–315.

[3] This is based on a conversation with Denis Twitchett. The information will be published in his (editor) *Cambridge History of China*, Vol. 4.

[4] For a discussion on the T'ang civil service examination system, see Hou Shao-wen, *T'ang Sung k'ao-shih chih-tu shih* (Taipei: Shang-wu, 1973), 31–81; Yang Shu-fan, *Chung-kuo wen-kuan chih-tu shih* (*Wen-kuan chih-tu* hereafter) (Taipei: Sanmin, 1976), 191–229, Teng Ssu-yü, *Chung-kuo k'ao-shih chih-tu shih* (Taipei: Hsüeh-sheng, 1967), 77–84.

[5] Mostly from the so-called "major classics." During the T'ang, the so-called major classics (*ta-ching*) included the *Record of Rites* (*Li-chi*) and *The Tso Commentary on the Spring and Autumn Annuals* (*Tso-chuan*). The middle classics included the *Book of Poetry* (*Shih-ching*), the *Rites of the Chou* (*Chou-li*) and the *Book of Rites* (*I-li*). The minor classics included the *Book of Changes* (*I-ching*), the *Book of Documents* (*Shang-shu*), the *Spring and Autumn Annals* (*Ch'un-ch'iu*), the *Kung-yang Commentary on the Ch'un-ch'iu* (*Kung-yang chuan*) and the *Ku-liang Commentary on the Ch'un-ch'iu* (*Ku-liang chuan*). The division of classics was revised in the Sung and simplified to consist of only two categories: the major and the minor. For the Sung division, see note 147 of Ch. 4.

[6] Such as a *Rules for Officials* (*Ch'en-kuei*) written by the Empress Wu (r. 684–704), the *Erh-ya* dictionary and the *Analects*, etc. It is to be noted that poetic writing so popular in the T'ang society was not tested in the *chin-shih* subject until 754. See Ch'en Ch'ing-chih, *Chung-kuo chiao-yu shih* (*Chiao-yu shih* hereafter), 176–179.

of brighter careers than those successful in other subjects. Degree-holders in the *chin-shih* and *ming-ching* subjects made up the majority of those recruited via the civil service examinations to officialdom, and although holders of the *chin-shih* graduate degree were much fewer than those of the *ming-ching* degree, the former nonetheless were more powerful and more respected in the T'ang court. This was the case because the government quite arbitrarily limited the qualification of candidates and the chances of entrance through this channel.[7] By the mid-ninth century, the *chin-shih* subject had firmly established itself as the most reliable route to upward mobility within the Chinese government.

Although the examinations as an institution were yet to become perfect, and although the number of qualified students receiving adequate education and support so as to be able to take the examinations were still few, the competition, at least in the *chin-shih* subject, was quickly intensifying. Stories about the onerous preparations, the hardship in the examination hall, as well as the glory that accompanied the success were accordingly plentiful. This is not the place to reproduce these tales, but it suffices to say that the examination system as a visible way for social ascendency had become firmly established, even if the actual opportunities it opened up for commoners were still very limited, assuming that there were possibilities for social restructuring of any magnitude. As for the material and spiritual rewards, it was obvious that they were there to be enjoyed:

> Of the wretchedness of my former years I have no need to brag: Today's gaiety has freed my mind to wander without bounds. Lighthearted in the spring breeze, my horse' hoofs run fast; In a single day I have seen all the girls of Ch'ang-an.[8]

In general, it is incorrect to assert that the civil service examinations were systematically implemented to recruit commoners with the purpose of circumscribing the power and prestige of the traditional aristocratic families. This was not the policy of any T'ang monarch.[9] But there is no question that in a time when traditional landed aristocratic families declined, and their influence in court politics subsided, it was natural that bureaucrats from the civil service examination system were on hand to make up for

[7]The false impression that the subjects tested in the *chin-shih* examination were more difficult than other examinations stemmed from the fact that only the *chin-shih* tests included poetic writing, but, as pointed out in note 6 above, this was hardly a reason why the *chin-shih* graduates should therefore be honored so exceptionally. See also Yang Shu-fan, *Wen-kuan chih-tu*, 204–205.

[8]Meng Chiao, "After Passing the Examination," translated by Irving Y. Lo (with my alteration), in Wu-chi Liu and Irving Y. Lo (eds.), *Sunflower Splendor* (New York: Doubleday, 1975), 164.

[9]Denis Twitchett, "The Composition of the T'ang Ruling Class."

them. After the mid-T'ang, it had become evident that successful *chin-shih* candidates were emerging as a visible political force, capable of exerting a power disproportionate to their numbers in the official bureaucracy. When that power was formally recognized in the Sung, there was no point of return, and subsequent social transformation necessarily followed.

There is one final point to be made about the background to the Sung examination system. This concerns the significance of the number of Candidates. According to the study by Otagi Hajime,[10] the candidates qualifying for the examination administered by the Board of Rites (*Li-pu*) ranged normally between one and three thousand. In theory, these candidates had first been screened at the local level. In other words, there were many more candidates who did not even qualify to take the Board of Rites examinations in the capital. But we know that examinations in local districts were often mere formalities and that the number of candidates who actually sat for the examinations was probably quite small, if formal tests took place regularly.[11] The rather small number of candidates reflected the underdeveloped situation of education as a whole during a time when printing technology was not yet systematically used. It also signified the general lack of importance of the examination system as a social institution. These factors of course changed during Sung times.

B. The Procedure and Content of the Civil Service Examinations

From the discussion above, it is clear that the civil service examinations did not have a significant social role in T'ang China, and were not even the most conspicuous means for upward social mobility. Towards the latter half of the T'ang, however, the system started to acquire an increasingly prominent role in government's selection of potential officials. The government found it useful to rely more on the civil service examinations, because, in this way, the selected bureaucrats could come from a somewhat wider social base. New people started to overshadow the traditional aristocrats. The result was that the Sung decided to endow the examination system with absolute authority and to rely on it almost exclusively as a method of promoting potentially competent officials. This became especially true after the nation was unified in 979. One fourth to one third of the regular

[10] Otagi Hajime, "Todai no kyoko shinshi to kyoko meikei," in *Tōhō gakuhō*, No. 45 (1973), 169–194. T'ang *Li-pu* is generally translated into Board of Rites.

[11] Based on a conversation with Professor Yen Keng-wang. In 621, a total of only 218 were sent to take the Board of Rites (then actually administered by the Department of State Affairs, the *Shang-shu sheng*) tests. See Wang Ting-pao, *T'ang chih-yen* (Shanghai: Ku-chi, 1978), 15:159.

civil officials were recruited from regular civil service examinations (*ch'ang-kung*).[12] In addition to regular degrees, the government also conferred special facilitated degrees (*t'e-tsou ming*) for those who had tried, but failed, in the examinations more than a certain number of times.[13] All included, about one third of the bureaucrats in regular service were degree-holders.[14] The striking contrast to the T'ang situation makes it all the more significant to look into the civil service examination system both as a political and a social institution. At the same time, the Ministry of Personnel promptly appointed most successful candidates to offices. This again is in evident contrast to the T'ang practice which normally kept successful candidates from being actually placed in a position for a few years.[15] Early Sung monarchs repeatedly emphasized the policy of giving special treatment to bureaucrats rising through the route of the examinations, so much so that the Sung probably was unique in China's history in that civil bureaucrats with degrees enjoyed the greatest power and influence in the Court, and in many areas of decision making. The examinations were thus a central feature of Sung political life.[16]

The Chinese governments and historians defined the recruitment of officials as "*hsüan-chü*" or "*ch'a-chü*," and these terms covered a much greater spectrum of acitivities than the term civil service examination system suggests (see Table 12). The part of the recruitment process that directly affected education, especially for the commoners, was the regular examinations. What follows is a discussion of these examination subjects that have significance for education. A summary of these various examinations is on Table 8.

Regular examinations at first were held almost annually, testing nine different subjects, which were then divided into two main categories: the *chin-shih* (the subject of *belles lettres*) and the *chu-k'o* (various [other] subjects). The various subjects then included the Nine Classics (*chiu-ching*), the Five Classics (*wu-ching*), the Code of K'ai-pao Rituals (*K'ai-pao li*), the Three Standard Histories (*san-Shih*), the Three Classics on Rites (*san-Li*), the *Three Commentaries on the Ch'un-ch'iu* (*san-Chuan*), specialization [in one or two classics] (*hsüeh-chiu*) and law (*ming-fa*).[17] Successful candidates in each subject were awarded a degree named after the subject.

---

[12] Lists of the total numbers of successful candidates recruited in Sung China are in Appendices A and B. For the table of the percentages of the bureaucratic force coming from degree-holders, see Table 16.

[13] Edward A. Kracke, *Civil Service*, 58.

[14] See Table 16. Degree-holders made up about half of the civil service manpower.

[15] Teng Ssu-yü, *Chung-kuo k'ao-shih chih-tu shih*, 77–134.

[16] See note 2 above.

[17] Kracke, *Civil Service*, 63.

CHART 3: A Diagram of the Sung Civil Service Examination System

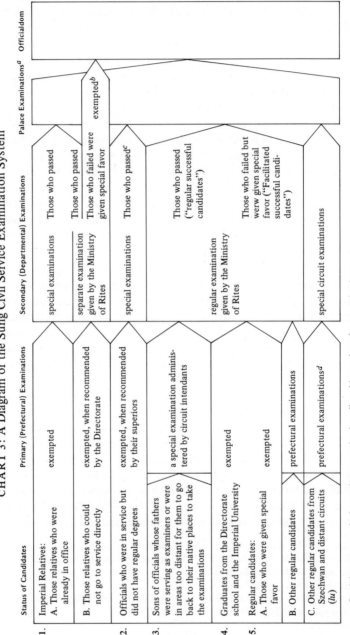

Status of Candidates	Primary (Prefectural) Examinations	Secondary (Departmental) Examinations	Palace Examinations[a]	Officialdom
1. Imperial Relatives: A. Those relatives who were already in office	exempted	special examinations	Those who passed	
B. Those relatives who could not go to service directly	exempted, when recommended by the Directorate	separate examination given by the Ministry of Rites	Those who passed Those who failed were given special favor	exempted[b]
2. Officials who were in service but did not have regular degrees	exempted, when recommended by their superiors	special examinations	Those who passed[c]	
3. Sons of officials whose fathers were serving as examiners or were in areas too distant for them to go back to their native places to take the examinations	a special examination administered by circuit intendants			
4. Graduates from the Directorate school and the Imperial University	exempted	regular examination given by the Ministry of Rites	Those who passed ("regular successful candidates")	
5. Regular candidates: A. Those who were given special favor	exempted		Those who failed but werw given special favor ("Facilitated successful candidates")	
B. Other regular candidates	prefectural examinations			
C. Other regular candidates from Szechwan and distant circuits (lu)	prefectural examinations[d]	special circuit examinations		

a. Candidates were ranked according to grades, but all could pass the palace examinations.

b. These relatives could thereafter go to serve in officialdom without regular degrees.

c. Those who failed in the secondary examinations could go back to serve without regular degrees.

d. Usually held in an earlier date.

TABLE 8   Subjects in the Civil Service Examinations[a]

Subjects	Contents of the tests[b]
Chin-shih (belles lettres)	To compose one shih poem, one fu rhyme-prose, one policy essay (lun); To answer five policy discussion questions (ts'e); To answer ten "written elucidation" (mo-i) questions on either the Ch'un-ch'iu or Li-chi classic.
Chiu-ching (The Nine Classics)[c]	120 memory questions (t'ieh-ching), 60 written elucidation on the Nine Classics.
Wu-ching (The Five Classics)[d]	80 memory questions, 50 written elucidations on the Five Classics.
San-Li (The Three Classics of the Rites)	110 written elucidations on the Rites on the Chou, the Record of Rites and the Book of Rites.
K'ai-pao li (The Code of K'ai-pao Rituals)	300 written elucidations on the Code and its commentary.
Hsüeh-chiu (Specialization in one or two Classics)	70 written elucidations, of them 25 on the Book of Changes, 25 on the Book of Documents, 10 on the Analects, and 10 on the Erh-ya and the Classic of Filial Piety. or, in case the specialization is in the Mao Commentary of the Book of Poetry: Same as above, except that the 50 questions on the Book of Changes and on the Book of Documents be replaced by questions on the Mao Commentary.
San-Chuan (The Three Commentaries on the Ch'un-chiu Classic)	110 written elucidations on the Three Commentaries.
San-Shih (The Three Histories)	300 written elucidation on the three standard histories: The Records of the Historian (Shih-chi), The History of the Former Han Dynasty (Han-shu) and The History of the Later Han Dynasty (Hou-Han shu).
Ming-fa (Law)[e]	40 questions on legal codes (lü) and statutes (ling); 10 written elucidation questions on the Analects; and 10 on the Erh-ya and the Classic of Filial Piety.

a. See Chin Chung-shu, "Pei-Sung k'o-chü chih-tu yen-chiu," in Hsin-ya hsüeh-pao, Vol. 6, No. 1 (1964), 205–281. See especially, 212–216. For an even more detailed discussion on the change of contents and ways of examinations throughout the Sung, see the same author, "Pei-Sung k'o-chü chih-tu yen-chiu hsü," in Kuo-li Ch'eng-kung ta-hsüeh li-shih hsüeh-pao, No. 5 (1978), 134–243. See, especially, 174–190. See also Table 10.

b. Various forms of questions such as mo-i, etc., were employed. See c.

c. The Nine Classics were: the Book of Changes (I-ching), the Book of Documents (Shang-shu), the Book of Poetry (Shih-ching), the Record of Rites (Li-chi), the Book of Rites (I-li), the Rites of the Chou (Chou-li), the Kung-yang Commentary to the Ch'un-ch'iu, the Ku-liang Commentary to the Ch'un-ch'iu, and the Tso Commentary to the Ch'un-ch'iu.

d. The Five Classics were: Changes, Documents, Poetry, Record of Rites and the Kung-yang Commentary.

e. For more information on this subject, see Hsü Tao-lin, "Sung-tai te fa-lü k'ao-shih," in his Chung-kuo fa-chih shih lun-chi, 188–229.

The degree in *chin-shih* enjoyed the highest esteem during the Sung and eventually became the only subject matter tested in the civil service examinations, though other degrees were still awarded for a short time after 1069, when technically the *chin-shih* subject became the only subject used.[18]

Candidates taking the regular examinations were first tested in prefectural seats, where they were tested according to the subjects they had studied and registered to take. This prefectural test, called the *chieh-shih* (lit. "release" examination), was normally given in the early autumn. Successful candidates from the primary prefectural tests were then sent ("released" or "dispatched") by the prefectural government to take the advanced examination in the nation's capital administered by the Ministry of Rites in the spring of the following year. This secondary test in the capital was generally called the departmental examination (*sheng-shih*).[19] The departmental examination was then followed by one last test in the presence of the emperor at the palace. This last examination, the palace examination, was a Sung innovation. Emperor T'ai-tsu (r. 960–975) instituted this final test, reportedly because he personally wished to exercise more care and control over the recruitment to make it more impartial and effective in the promotion of the socially and geographically disadvantaged candidates. The innovation was introduced in 975.[20]

The competition on the prefectural level varied according to time and place. In 1066, Ou-yang Hsiu pointed out that in the southeast, the competition was so intense that only one in every hundred passed, whereas in the northwest, it was very easy to pass the first test, and one in every ten was recruited to take the departmental test.[21] In the beginning, an overall elimination rate of fifty to eighty per cent was set for all prefectures; about twenty to fifty per cent of candidates thus passed the primary, prefectural tests. Then in the early 1020s, the government started to use a quota system so that underdeveloped areas could send more successful candidates, percentagewise, to take the secondary, departmental examination.[22] The creation of a quota system is a significant invention in the Sung examina-

---

[18] See Chin Chung-shu, "Pei-Sung k'o-chü," No. 1, 211–227.

[19] According to the *WHTK*, 30:284, the primary prefectural tests were given in the fall, and those who passed were then sent to the capital in that winter and took the departmental test in the next spring. In 1189, the departmental examination was postponed to the second month and this delay became a precedent. Toward the end of the Southern Sung, the departmental examinations were even occasionally given as late as the third month. See Araki, *Kakyo*, 223.

[20] See Araki, *Kakyo*, 267–288, for a detailed discussion.

[21] Ou-yang Hsiu, *Ch'üan-chi*, Pt. XIII, 14–15.

[22] See detailed study by Araki in his *Kakyo*, 102–127.

tion system (see next section). The system, in effect, gave candidates from the northwest a better chance to take the departmental tests, where competition was a little less intense, so that the government could achieve and maintain a more or less equitable regional representation of successful candidates. To give an example of the intensity of competition in the rich and populous southeast, let me cite the figures reported in 1186. According to the report of the assistant circuit intendant of Fukien, the candidates in Fu-chou for the prefectural tests each time numbered fourteen to fifteen thousand.[23] We know that the quota for Fu-chou in the early 1190s was 100 for each test.[24] The rate of elimination was therefore extremely high, and only about one in every 140 to 150 candidates passed the first test and became eligible to take the departmental examination.

The rate of elimination in the departmental examination was also high, although not as high as that in prefectural tests in the southeast. According to Araki's research, on the average, one-tenth to one-fourteenth of the candidates passed this examination.[25] My opinion is that the competition was slightly more intense than this. Let us first examine Table 9.

From the table one sees that the ratio, except for the year 1034, was close to one-fifteenth to one-seventeenth. But of course, we know that this was pretty much what the actual ratios decreed throughout the Southern Sung. If, however, facilitated degree-holders were included, then actual successful candidates recruited in the departmental tests could well amount to more than 10% each examination year.

As for the palace examination, except for the first few years, there was no elimination, although competition for ranking was intense. The palace examination was thus, in effect, a test of relative achievement rather than another process of selection. The successful candidates who participated in this final examination were placed in exact order of achievement, and further divided into five groups (chia). Those in the first two groups were considered to have "passed with distinction" (chi-ti). Those in the third were "formally qualified" (ch'u-shen). Those in the fourth and fifth groups were simply "passed" (t'ung ch'u-shen). To be listed as the first man in the first group, or as the "first palace graduate" (chuang-yüan) was an achievement eagerly sought and highly honored.[26] A contemporary source says: "if one participates in the civil service examination and does not seek

---

[23] *SHY*, hc, 22/6b.

[24] See the information recorded in the *Yü-ti t'u* compiled by Huang Shang, now in the possession of Rikkokuan in Japan. Reproduced by Aoyama Sadao in his *To Sō jidai no kotsu to chishi chizu no kenkyū* (Tokyo: Yoshikawa kobunkan, 1963).

[25] Araki, *Kakyo*, 223–235.

[26] For a brief account, see Kracke, *Civil Service*, 66–67.

TABLE 9

Percentage of Successful Candidates in the Departmental Examinations[a]

Year	Number of candidates	Number of successful candidates[b]	Percentage[c]	Source
977	5,300+	316 (500)	6.0% (9.4%)	HCP, 18/2a.
983	10,260	691	6.7%	HCP, 24/1a, 4a.
985	10,000+	875	8.8%	HCP, 26/1a, 2a.
992	17,300	1,086 (1,317)	6.3% (7.6%)	HCP, 33/1a, 2ab.
1002	14,562	219 (219)	1.5% (1.5%)	HCP, 51/12b–13a.
1005	13,000+	816 (1,009)	6.3% (7.8%)	HCP, 59/13ab.
1034			20.0%	SHY, hc, 3/17a.
1088	4,732	500 (508)	10.6% (10.7%)	See d.
1109	7,000+	731	10.0%	See e.
1124	15,000+	805	5.4%	SHY, hc, 4/14a, 7/37b.
1128			7.1%	SHY, hc, 4/17b.
1131			7.1%	SHY, hc, 4/24a.
1163			6.4%	WHTK, 32:300.
1169			6.5%	SHY, hc, 4/39b.
1175			6.6%	SHY, hc, 5/3a.
1208			6.4%	SHY, hc, 6/9b.

a. Regular examinations. Other special examinations had special ratios.

b. Bracketed numbers were the total of regular degree and facilitated degree graduates. Numbers of regular degree graduates are listed in the unbracketed column.

c. Unbracketed percentages are for regular degree graduates.

d. For chin-shih degree candidates only. Source is from Hung Mai, Jung-chai ssu-pi, in his Jung-chai sui-pi, Vol. II, 8:704. Bracketed number is from HCP, 409/6b and was for regular degree graduates only.

e. Beginning with 1103, only the chin-shih degree was awarded. Sources are from SHY, hc, 4/6b, 7/32b. The number of facilitated degree receipients was not recorded for that year.

the chuang-yüan title, or if one goes into officialdom and does not strive to become a chief councilor, then one has wasted one's life."[27] The struggle for the highest place in the palace examinations became even more intense after the 1020s, and the first three graduates in the first group in the chin-shih degree were most highly thought of as potential officials. Acccording to the Sung-shih, among the thirty-nine palace examination graduates who passed as the first three in the first group during Jen-tsung's reign (1023–

[27] Wang P'i-chih, Min-shui yen-t'an lu, Chih-pu-tsu chai ts'ung-shu ed. (1921), 4/7b.

1063) (thirteen palace examinations were held during the period), only five did not eventually go up to the position of the councilorship.[28]

The section on the examinations in the *Sung hui-yao* has a detailed record of the posts assigned to the first five palace graduates, others of the first group, and the other four groups given the *chin-shih* degree. It appears that the executive assistantship of the Directorate of Construction (rank 8B), judicial investigator of the High Court of Justice (8A), or *Hsüan-i lang, Hsüan-chiao lang* or *Ch'eng-shih lang* (8B) were the most common titles assigned to the three best graduates.[29] The posts to which they were most commonly actually dispatched appear to have been those of prefectural vice-administrator, circuit supervising official, primary civil aide, or occasionally subprefect. Thus, the official rankings and actual posts assigned to a new graduate varied greatly, although there was a tendency to send new graduates to local posts for administrative apprenticeship.[30] The career of the distinguished graduates, however, was by and large safeguarded, and the importance the government attached to graduates of the regular palace tests was always evident.

Although the content of the civil service examinations varied according to each subject, the emphasis, except for the tests in the *chin-shih* subject, was placed on memory—recitations of the officially decreed classics and their commentaries. In the early Sung, the "written elucidation" (*mo-i*) was the most common test question. The following are a couple of examples of "written elucidations":

Question: "It is said that there were seven authors, who are they?"

Answer: "The seven authors are: so and so, answered respectfully."

Question: "Confucius said of Tzu-ch'an that in him were to be found four virtues that belong to the Way of the gentleman, what are these virtues?"

Answer: "In his private conduct he was courteous, in serving his master he was punctilious, in providing for the needs of the people he gave them even more than their due; in exacting service from the people, he was just. I answer this question with respect."[31]

Candidates for the degree of the *chin-shih* subject (in both the prefectural and departmental examinations) had to take ten "written elucidations"

[28] *SS*, 155:3615–3616.

[29] *SHY*, hc, 2.

[30] Brian McKnight, "Administrators of Hangchow under the Northern Sung," 201.

[31] *WHTK*, 30:283. This is a question asked in the prefectural test. See also Wang Yung, *Yen-i i-mou lu, TSCC* ed., 2:9.

from the *Spring and Autumn Annals* or the *Record of Rites*. Other candidates took even more, depending on the fields they were in.[32]

Another form of test questions was a simple memory test, called "filling out brackets" (memory questions, *t'ieh-ching*). A passage from one of the classics was given with several words as clues, and then candidates were required to complete the whole passage, demonstrating their knowledge of the classic. There is no substantial difference between the two forms of tests mentioned above; they all placed emphasis on the ability of candidates to remember *verbatim* passages of the classics.

Candidates in the *chu-k'o* tests were examined by these two kinds of question, but students taking the exminations in the *chin-shih* subject had to demonstrate their ability, not only to memorize, but also to write poetry in various styles, plus composition of rhyme prose, policy essays (*lun*) and discussions (*ts'e*) (see Table 8). The following is an example of a topic for a policy essay: "Compare the policies of Emperor Wen (r. 179–157 B.C.) and Emperor Hsüan (r. 73–49 B.C.) of the Han dynasty." This topic was given by Emperor Chen-tsung in 1005.[33]

Discussion questions on policy were not greatly different from the policy essays, except that they were designed to test more specifically candidates' ability to reconcile two apparently contradictory interpretations on policy issues found in history. Candidates were therefore to answer these questions to demonstrate their potential ability in policy debates. For example:[34]

> It is stated in the *Book of Kuan-tzu:* "the method by which a sage rules the world is this: he does not let the four classes of people live together. Therefore, there are no complaints, and things run smoothly. As a result, scholars know how to spend their leisure, laborers abide with the orders of officials, merchants go to the marketplaces and farmers go to the fields. Everyone goes to his appropriate place and lives there satisfactorily. Young children are sent to study; their wills are satisfied and they do not change their minds when they see strange things." The *Kuan-tzu* Book further states: "Children of scholars and farmers must always be scholars and farmers and children of merchants and laborers must also always be merchants and laborers, so that a scholar can give instructions and take care of his proper status, and a farmer can work attentively in cultivating his crops to feed the people. Every one is satisfied with his occupation and does not seek to change. This is truly good! Otherwise, hundreds of laborers might all go to the marketplaces and ten thousand merchants might all try to work in the same [most profitable] business; they would all become cunning,

---

[32] For the detailed description of test questions of various subjects, see *WHTK*, 30:283; *SS*, 155:3604–3623.

[33] *SHY*, hc, 7/9a.

[34] Ou-yang Hsiu, *Ch'üan-chi*, Pt. IV, 40–41. Discussion questions of the palace examinations during the Sung are preserved in the section on the civil service examinations in the *SHY*, hc, 7.

deceitful, eager to play tricks, and they would also become capricious, greedy and seek only profits."

Now, to fit people in their occupations is not to improve morals. To see something better and change—what harm is there in this? Take the example of Tuan-mu who became a merchant [after being a disciple of Confucius], Chiao Li who became a fisherman [after being an important official] and Wang Meng who went to sell dust-baskets [after being a prime minister]; these man responded to their times and changed in a myriad ways, why should they have been restricted to their fixed occupations? Similarly, Huang Hsien was originally a lowly veterinarian, Sang Hung-yang a merchant, Sun Shu-ao a wood-cutter, and yet they all were able to preserve their intelligence and help strengthen their states. How can we accuse them of responding to their times and of going to take up responsibilities other than their own occupations! We now have a regulation keeping the descendants of those in despised occupations from taking the civil service examinations. Although this rule has been in force for some time, I consider that it still is a good time to examine this regulation. You candidates have excelled yourselves in knowledge of the past, and in debating various problems; I would like you to spend time considering the issue I have just outlined above.

The most important change in Sung civil service examinations as briefly mentioned above was the abolition in 1069, at the initiative of Wang An-shih, of all the *chu-k'o* subjects. In theory, beginning with this year, there remained only one field and hence one degree in the examinations. Wang's personal concern with the examinations went beyond simply abolishing the various subjects other than the *chin-shih* subject, he also proposed changing the content of the *chin-shih* examination. A new form of test was devised. This is the *ching-i* ("exposition on the classics") style. The idea was to test the ability of candidates in putting classical knowledge into effective use in argumentation. Candidates were required to compose, by juxtaposing direct quotations from the classics, or sentences similar in meaning to certain passages of the classics, into a logically constructed argumentative essay.[35]

The *ching-i* style of questioning in the examinations did not acquire its secure position until the Southern Sung, but even then, it only gradually overshadowed poetic writing and was reluctantly made a compulsory part of the examinations. The process of its eventually becoming the most popular form of writing is too complicated to be discussed here. What is important is that widespread use of this style probably accounted for the ultimate decline of traditional poetic (both *shih* and *fu*) writings in the Sung. The stress this style laid on familiarity with the Confucian classics and more or less imaginative reading of these texts contributed in a certain unmistakable way to the rise of the so-called "Sung School" of classical learning, which was part of the Neo-Confucian movement. The *ching-i* style in its

---

[35] See an example cited in Ch'en Tung-yüan, *Chiao-yü shih*, 249–250.

TABLE 10

Changes in the Contents of Examinations in the *Chin-shih* Subject, 1071–1121

Year	Prefectural examinations	Departmental examinations	Sources
1071	Four tests: (1) 5 exposition (*Ching-i*) questions on the candidate's specialized classic (from 1 of the five classics: *Shih, Shu, I, Chou-li* or *Li-chi*). (2) 10 exposition questions on the *Analects* and *Mencius*. (3) 1 discussion essay. (4) 3 policy discussion questions.	Same as left, except that in the fourth test, candidates were to answer 5, instead of 3, policy discussion questions.	*HCP*, 220/1ab.
1072	Same as above, except that in the second test, candidates were to answer 3 exposition questions each on the *Analects* and *Mencius*.	Same as left.	*HCP*, 234/6b.
1081	One question on legal knowledge added.	2 questions on legal knowledge added.	*HCP*, 311/7b.
1086	Legal knowledge question abolished.	Same as left.	*YH*, 116/13a.
1087	Four tests: (1) 2 exposition questions on the candidate's specialized classic; one exposition question on either the *Analects* or *Mencius*. (2) Composition of one *fu* rhyme-prose and one *shih* poem. (3) 1 discussion essay. (4) 3 policy discussion questions.	Same as left.	*HCP*, 407/5b.
1089[a]	Four tests (candidates were divided into 2 categories: A: "classics" and B: "both in classics and in poetry"; classics were divided into 2 kinds: major and minor): (1) A: 3 exposition questions on the candidate's first specialized classic and 1 exposition question on the *Analects*.	Same as left.	*HCP*, 425/13ab.

	B: 2 exposition questions on the candidate's only specialized classic, 1 exposition question each on the *Analects* and *Mencius*.	
	(2) A: 3 exposition questions on the candidate's second specialized classic and 1 on *Mencius*.	
	B: Composition of 1 *fu* rhyme-prose and 1 *shih* poem.	
	(3) For both A and B: 1 discussion essay.	
	(4) For both A and B: 2 policy discussion questions.	Same as left.
1094[b]	Four tests (candidates were to be examined in classical knowledge only; classics were again divided into 2 kinds: major and minor and candidates were to specialize in one of each or in 2 of the major classics):	HCPSP, 10/4ab.
	(1) 3 exposition questions on the candidate's specialized major classic and 1 on the *Analects*.	
	(2) 3 exposition questions on the candidate's specialized minor classic and 1 on *Mencius*.	
	(3) 1 discussion essay.	
	(4) 2 policy discussion questions.	
1096[c]	Candidates were to specialize in only one classic.	*SHY*, hc, 3/56b–57a.
1097	1 more policy discussion question added; the *Ch'un-ch'iu* classic withdrawn from the examinations.	Same as left
1102	Same as 1081.	*SHY*, hc, 4/3a.
		Same as left

a. For the definition of the major and minor classics, see note 147 of Ch. 4.

b. The division of the classics remained the same. The method of combining major and minor classics was now regulated.

c. This is a return to the 1071 method.

extreme form, however, was the ancestor of the later eight-legged (*pa-ku*) essays commonly tested in Ming and Ch'ing civil service examinations.[36]

The setting and taking of the civil service examinations were one of the most important parts of Sung politics. First of all, the nature of Sung society, in that it was based on a very limited living space, and that it was extremely competitive, probably affected the way the rulers and the people looked at the examination system. The competitiveness of this society made it particularly urgent for the government to act always in accordance with the principle of fairness, or at least, of appearing to be as impartial as possible. The need for an impartial procedure to recruit civil officials became so critical that the examination system had to be relied upon more than ever, and this accounted for T'ai-tsu's belief that the system could abate corruption. The systematization of the prefectural examinations and the uniform quota system for all districts used in the early years of the Sung reflected the pressing need for conducting the examinations strictly and impartially. We therefore turn to the quota system.

C. Anonymity, Recopying and the Quota System

Procedural changes in the examinations were not the central feature of Sung innovations. What actually affected the design and practice of the examination system the most was its stress on impartiality. This was partially a reflection of the rising social significance of the civil service examination system: when the system became a dominant form of social ascendency, demands for increased openness naturally rose in direct response to its importance.

As has already been suggested above, the early Sung emperors appeared to be particularly concerned with how to use the civil service examinations to pass out the rewards of official positions to the socially deprived, so as, in their words, to "curtail favoritism," to "promote the talented poor" or "to be absolutely impartial."[37] It is not clear what their motives were, but there were specific consequences, which included the enacting of primary measures to prevent cheating during the examinations:[38]

---

[36] There is discussion as to whether the *ching-i* style was the precursor of the *pa-ku* (eight-legged) style, commonly used in Ming and Ch'ing examinations. See Ch'in Hui-t'ien, *Wu-li t'ung-k'ao*, 174/14ab, 18a.

[37] *SHY*, hc, 19/2b; *HCP*, 26/2b, 67/15b, 17b; *SHY*, hc, 3/8b. This concern for "*chih-kung*" (absolute impartiality) was still echoed as late as 1128. See *CYYL*, 17/18b.

[38] Araki, *Kakyo*, 243–264; *HCP*, 133/3a; *SHY*, hc, 3/10b, 5/26a. See also section E.

1. In 992, the anonymity principle was established in palace examinations by covering candidates' names.
2. In 1004, officials were formally appointed to be in charge of covering candidates' names and stamping seal marks over the covering papers.
3. In 1012, revised regulations concerning the searching of candidates' bodies and belongings were issued.
4. In 1015, recopying of candidates' scripts by clerks (before being formally marked) was introduced in departmental examinations.
5. In 1033, the anonymity measure was introduced in prefectural examinations.
6. In 1037, recopying was introduced in prefectural examinations.
7. In 1041, the custom, called *kung-chüan*, of submitting one's writings to chief examiners before one sat in the examinations, was outlawed.

The last point needs some explanation. There was a custom during the T'ang dynasty for candidates to visit their examiners as soon as they arrived at the capital and make acquaintance with them by presenting them with their own poetry and other works. The idea was of course for candidates to make headway in the high society of the capital, so that their literary and scholarly achievements could be appreciated and evaluated even before they actually took the civil service examinations.[39] This was the so-called "*kung-chüan*" custom. However, this was feasible only in society where competition for office was largely limited to a select group of the socially esteemed, and where, as a result, fame in the sense of peer concensus, was used to judge whether a candidate could be initiated to the more or less self-perpetuating upper class. With the issuance during the early Sung of numerous measures for the safeguarding of impartiality during the examinations, the value of a custom like that of the *kung-chüan* quickly diminished. By the early eleventh century, it had indeed seemed totally irrelevant as to how good or how respected one was as an accomplished poet. The only important thing was for one to do well in the actual examinations.

This of course is an exaggeration, for we shall soon see that corruption in the examination hall was very common. But it is sufficient now to point out that there was no doubt a heightened sense of the need to maintain open competition in the civil service examinations. A direct consequence of the stress on impartiality was the creation of the quota system, a system that was to help shape Chinese political and scholarly geography for several hundred years to come.

It is by now clear that the number of candidates to be recruited from

[39] For an interesting account of this, see Arthur Waley, *The Life and Times of Po Chü-i* (London: Allen & Unwin, 1949), 18–19, 23.

the departmental examinations depended upon the needs of the government. However, the numbers of candidates to be recommended to take the departmental examinations by each prefecture varied. A so-called "*chieh-o*" (lit. quota [of those to be] released or dispatched) system was accordingly established to decide the numbers of candidates to be recommended by each prefecture. This meant that the government did not feel that there should be a nationally uniform ratio.[40]

The first known discussion about the ratio between successful candidates and failed candidates occurred as late as 997, when the Chief Councilor, Sung Pai (936–1012), recommended a nationally uniform ratio of 20% for both the *chin-shih* and *chu-k'o* candidates.[41] This was followed by an increase to 40% in 1005.[42]

The decision in 1009 to calculate the number of successful prefectural candidates in proportion to the largest number of candidates sitting in the examinations in the previous two examinations (held during the previous five years), and not according to the number of candidates sitting for the examination concerned, probably was the first significant step in the direction of devising quotas for different districts. According to the 1009 method, no matter how many candidates there were in the current test, the proportion was to be 30% of the larger number of candidates sitting for the previous two prefectural examinations.[43] The method, though not complicated, was peculiar and awkward.

A separate development helped to shape the quota system. This was the administering of special examinations held to recruit poets (*tz'u-k'o*) or morally superior classical scholars (*ching-ming hsing-hsiu*). In these examinations, a quota system was used. For example, in the 1008 special examination, the government ordered that certain numbers of candidates be recruited from prefectural tests held in specially appointed areas. But the method for deciding their numbers was based on officially assessed quotas. The list of that year's quotas for the specially appointed areas was simple:[44]

---

[40] Interestingly, a quota system appears to have existed in the late T'ang. In 845, the T'ang government issued a list of quotas of local *chin-shih* candidates to be recommended to the capital. The list shows that an evident bias against the *chin-shih* candidates in general, and those from the south in particular, existed. Professor Yen Keng-wang of Academia Sinica, Taiwan, in commenting on this list, says that it was obviously compiled under Li Te-yü's direction with the overt purpose of cutting down the numbers of *chin-shih* candidates. See my "Quota System," 287–318.

[41] *SHY*, hc, 14/16ab.

[42] *Ibid.*

[43] *SHY*, hc, 14/16b, 17b.

[44] *SHY*, hc, 14/19ab.

K'ai-feng (superior prefecture): 50
Yen-chou (prefecture):   50
Yun-chou (prefecture):   48
T'an-chou (prefecture):   30
P'u-chou (prefecture):   30

From the way quotas were assigned, it is evident that the same could easily have been used in the civil service examinations.

Another factor that made the quota system useful was the wish on the part of the government deliberately to increase the chances of candidates from backward areas. The first instance that I have found occurred in 1011, when Emperor Chen-tsung ordered that candidates from the Ho-pei area be given special favor and be encouraged to take the departmental examinations. Ho-pei was then close to the border and was constantly subject to Khitan threats.[45] Generally speaking, it was a policy of the Sung to give special favors to border and comparatively backward areas.[46] But the clearest pronouncement of official policy on this matter was made in 1041, when the Shan-hsi (Shensi) border suffered a devastating attack by the Tangut Hsi-Hsia. A relief edict was issued:[47] "People on the border who were looted by invaders, their relatives, widowers and widows who are related to them should be given relief. Corvee labor service should be dropped, whenever possible. Officials who are over zealous in demanding that people fulfill their official obligations or are too strict and ruthless will be heavily punished. *Chin-shih* candidates who have already taken the prefectural tests twice, *chu-k'o* candidates who have already taken them thrice, and any candidate who has made the departmental tests (but failed) will be exempted from taking the prefectural tests again. (In addition), those prefectures with an examination quotas of less than ten will be given an additional three." Thus, geography was a factor in the system's operation.

A corollary to the newly established quota system was the enforcement of the regulation that candidates be registered in their native districts and be examined there.[48] The practice obviously implied that the geographical factor in determining who could sit for the departmental examinations was being taken into consideration. And on one occasion, the government even specifically commanded that when two prefectures shared one examination site (because of the small number of candidates), candidates should

---

[45]*SHY*, hc, 14/22b–23a.
[46]Sources on exceptional quotas are found in *SHY*, hc, passim.
[47]*HCP*, 131/21ab.
[48]*SHY*, hc, 14/27b, 15/3ab, etc. For a study of this problem in K'ai-feng, see Araki, *Kakyo*, 151–161; Chin Chung-shu, "Pei-Sung k'o-chü," No. 2, 212–225.

be recruited according to the quota of their own prefectures.[49] Thus, it is obvious that by the early eleventh century, the government had realized that the increased importance of the civil service examinations would make it imperative to take the grographical distribution of candidates into consideration.

Thereafter, repeated revisions were made to accommodate the changing needs of the government, but the government also received occasional individual requests to increase quotas for particular prefectures. The requests generally were made in either of the two forms: a prefect might request that the quota be increased outright, as in the case of Ying-t'ien prefecture which requested in 1025 an increase of three.[50] Or it might bargain for an increase in the quota of *chin-shih* candidates by offering to trade a similar or even larger number of the *chu-k'o* quota.[51] In short, quotas were subject to frequent if minor changes, but the system as such by 1045 had been firmly established and there were only inconsequential complaints about it. In 1045, another adjustment was made to increase quotas and the result was an addition of 359 candidates throughout the empire.[52]

On the whole, it can be shown that the concern on the part of the government about geographical equity (in terms of numbers of candidates allowed to be recommended) superseded the concern for normative impartiality. These two goals could easily come into conflict, as illustrated by a case in 1063 when Ssu-ma Kuang sent a memorial to Emperor Jen-tsung.[53]

Ssu-ma did not directly challenge the quota system on prefectural levels; instead, he suggested that further quotas be instituted in the departmental test. In the memorial, one also sees that the K'ai-feng district was accorded a disproportionately generous prefectural quota with a result that a good number of graduates of departmental tests came from there. This fact had been noted by different officials and it was clear that not only K'ai-feng but northern prefectures in general enjoyed quotas which were much more generous than those in the south.[54] These facts notwithstanding, Ssu-ma nevertheless recommended that a quota system be imposed on the departmental test, apparently believing that the large number of northern candi-

[49]*WHTK*, 31:294.

[50]*SHY*, hc, 15/5a.

[51]*SHY*, hc, 15/7ab. This is about the case of Hsü-chou. The prefecture asked to be allowed to give up a thirty *chu-k'o* quota in exchange for an additional fifteen *chin-shih* quota. The government turned down the request, and gave an outright increase of eight in the quota.

[52]*HCP*, 155/4ab; *SHY*, hc, 15/13ab.

[53]Ssu-ma Kuang, *Wen-kuo kung Ssu-ma Wen-cheng chi* (*Wen-chi* hereafter), *SPTK* ed., 30:262.

[54]See, for examples, Chin Chün-ch'ing, *Chin-shih wen-chi*, *SKCS* ed, 2/3a–7b; Su Sung, *Su Wei-kung wen-chi*, *SKCS* ed., 5/14b–20b.

dates still did not make up a satisfactory ratio of graduates from departmental examinations. The recommendation was opposed by the famous southerner, Ou-yang Hsiu, who asserted that a further quota system would only destory the impartiality principle. Ou-yang bitterly pointed out that successful candidates from the south went through much more difficult prefectural selections than their northern counterparts and that this accounted for the greater proportion of southern *chin-shih* graduates coming from the departmental screening.[55] The result of the debate was that the recommendation by Ssu-ma was turned down, but the debate as such did serve to highlight the tension that existed then between southerners and northerners and the possible biases that could surface in the quota system.[56]

The uneven distribution of quotas that favored the northern districts (especially the so-called "five circuits"[57]), and the capital K'ai-feng as well as backward areas, could jeopardize the spirit of impartiality the government worked so hard to uphold. According to one estimate, roughly five or six candidates in the five circuits competed for one position as successful prefectural candidates, while in other circuits, especially those in the southeast, the ratio could run as high as one in every fifty or sixty.[58]

In general, studies do show that the Northern Sung official stance was to maintain differential treatment for different prefectures in assigning their quotas for successful prefectural candidates, and that the quotas were carefully determined, causing relatively mild and ineffective protests.[59]

The quota system continued to operate in the Southern Sung prefectural examinations. Two major problems seem to have constantly caused concern to the authorities. The first involved candidates originally registered in the north. After the loss of the north, candidates who fled to the south had to take the examinations in the prefectures where they resided and thus competed with the native candidates. Controversies quickly arose and the government consequently devised independent quotas for northern candidates. Eventually, however, the problem was solved by gradually admitting immigrants into the category of locals. Once one had resided in a district (normally, prefecture) for more than seven years, he could register in his new home and be tested there as a native.[60]

---

[55] Ou-yang Hsiu, *Ch'üan-chi*, Pt. IV, 265–266.

[56] See my *San-lun*, 44–45.

[57] See note 52 of Ch. 5. These are the same circuits to receive officially appointed "teaching officials" in 1071 during Wang An-shih's reform. What made these five circuits so much more important than other circuits is not clear. For the present purpose, it is necessary only to point out that the majority of early Sung officials were drawn from these areas. See also note 67 of Ch. 5.

[58] Lu Tien, *T'ao-shan chi*, *SKCS* ed., 4/1a–2a.

[59] See note 40.　　　　[60] *SHY*, hc, 16/22a.

The second problem was even more serious, dealing with candidates who flocked to areas with generous quotas. This had already been common in the Northern Sung and K'ai-feng was clearly the most attractive place.[61] In the Southern Sung, the problem grew to an alarming extent and measures had to be taken, on the one hand, to warn candidates to return to their native prefectures, and on the other hand, to create exceptional quotas for these "wandering candidates" (yu-shih).[62] The quotas set up for them were, without an exception, extremely small.[63] Lin-an, during the Southern Sung, was already losing the generous treatment it was supposed to receive as a national capital. Eventually, because quotas set aside for outside candidates were often so exceptionally small, the scheme therefore did not amount to much. It was in fact abolished towards the end of the dynasty. In any case, both issues complicated the problems hidden by the quota system concerning the ambiguously defined impartiality principle and caused persistent misgivings.

From the discussion above, one sees that the quota system reflected the mechanism of imperial control as exercised through the examination system. The system was above all designed to foster a conviction on the part of the candidates that the government had as much a responsibility to maintain order and to prevent cheating in the examinations, as to maintain equal opportunities for candidates coming from greatly diversified geographical backgrounds. Both concerns were legitimate, arising from the practice of the impartial examinations. There was indeed a feeling that a "fair" process which would select the best for service was necessary, but as the number of candidates increased, this need was perceived to be increasingly urgent, with the measures discussed in this section largely resulting from that perception. Nonetheless, as measures became sophisticated, problems also became complicated. In Chapter 9, by studying the very nature of the examination system as a means of imperial control, we shall see how a simple notion such as that of impartiality could serve to impart legitimacy to a social institution that also carried out carefully designed political functions.

D. Privileges and Appointments after the Examinations

In theory, only those who had passed the final palace examination were eligible for official appointment. Since the palace examination was largely

---

[61] See notes 50 and 51. See also Araki, Kakyo, 174–179.

[62] SHY, hc, 16/7ab, 11a, 19ab, etc.

[63] See my "Quota system."

a formality and only ranking was affected,[64] all graduates of departmental examinations could be regarded as having achieved the goal of entry into officialdom. Candidates who had made the prefectural tests but did not pass the departmental examinations were called *"te-chieh jen"* (lit. persons "released" [to take the departmental examinations]) and were in theory not eligible for any position in the regular civil service. However, *te-chieh jen*, probably because of the fact that they were educated and thus respected, could participate informally in local affairs with some degree of influence. This became increasingly the case during the Southern Sung. The means by which they exercised their influence included their being appointed as officials holding irregular or temporary posts, and being accorded privileges by the government.

The appointment of *te-chieh jen* to local posts can be considered to have been normal, as local governors needed their assistance in various positions which could not be handled by clerks (*li*). Because the *te-chieh* status was not a formal degree, references to appointing successful prefectural candidates to offices are rare; nonetheless, many of them conceivably had accepted teaching posts in local schools.[65] Through participation in local governmental affairs, they could exercise a certain measure of influence with respect to the decision-making process. But even more important was the degree to which their prestige and influence was felt through informal and indirect channels. These included becoming involved with poetry clubs, organized and sponsored by local wealthy elite and the educated, community schools, which were also administered by very much the same people, and many other informal organizations through which the government, along with the powerful landlords, managed to maintain peace and order.[66]

The social or financial privileges awarded the *te-chieh jen* were minimal, although once a privilege was granted, the connected prestige quickly followed. This occurred in 1133 when the government, acting on the recommendation of Yen Wei, decreed that the *te-chieh jen*, including those who had passed the prefectural examination and those who did not have to take it, could be exempted from both the *ting* (adult male) tax and services of both bureaucratic and corvee natures (*chih-i* and *yao-i*).[67] The provision

---

[64] If a candidate committed serious mistakes in the palace examination, he could not be failed, but might be awarded a degree in less respected subjects. For example, Yuan Chiang was given a *hsüeh-chiu* (specialization in one or two classics) and not *chin-shih* degree because he made mistake in poetic rhymes. *SS*, 343:10905.

[65] See note 48 of Ch. 5.

[66] Some preliminary discussion on the lives of the social elite and their role in imperial control is found in Ch. 8, section C.

[67] *CYYL*, 64/3b and *SHY*, sh, 12/8a. The texts say that they were exempted from

was revised in 1137 when it was decreed that they should continue to be exempted from the *ting* tax but could hire replacements for other services so th✻t they did not have to show up in person.[68] In case that the *te-chieh jen* was the only male adult in the household and that his family was truly poor, he might be allowed a total exemption.[69]

However, by 1149, it was found that *te-chieh jen* and University students were being called for service in person and therefore at the suggestion of Wang Pao, a further modification was ordered. The new measure included two parts: for those who had passed the prefectural test and had actually attempted the departmental tests and those who were currently registered University students, if they were the only male adults in the family, they could be exempted from labor services or, otherwise, they could hire replacements; for those whose *te-chih jen* qualification was not earned in the examinations but was awarded,[70] they would only be exempted from service in person and a substitute had to be hired. No mention of the *ting* tax is found in the sources, but presumably, both kinds of *te-chieh jen* continued to be exempted from the tax burden.[71]

There is no evidence indicating any further change in these rules during the rest of the dynasty and it therefore seems probable that, from the mid-twelfth century on, all examination candidates with a regularly earned *te-chieh* (lit. "released" status obtained) qualification were as a rule awarded with some privilege; while this privilege was not particularly significant, it remained a standard practice in later dynasties, and resulted in their rise (called *chü-jen* in Ming and Ch'ing China) as a distinct group within the elite class.

---

ting-i, which should be interpreted as meaning both *ting* and *i*, namely, *ting* taxation and *i* services. This is confirmed by a phrase found in *SHY*, sh, 12/18b, "*ting* tax and *shen* (in person) services" and another in *SHY*, sh, 12/27b, where the distinction between *ting* tax and service in person is clearly made. See also McKnight's study in his *Village and Bureaucracy in Southern Sung China*, 106.

[68] *SHY*, sh, 14/27ab. Wang Pao reported in 1149 that the government ordered the revision because of the abuse of the privilege of exemption. The actual order covered, in addition to *te-chieh jen*, university students, and households headed by woman or by single adult. I take this revision to have been issued around 1137. Wang Pao's memorial is in *CYYL*, 160/3b–4b and *SHY*, sh, 14/30b–31b.

[69] *SHY*, sh, 14/31ab.

[70] Awarded because of "special imperial order" (*t'e-ch'ih*) or of "imperial grace" (*en-shang*). See next note.

[71] *SHY*, sh, 14/30ab; *CYYL*, 160/3b–4b. See also a careful discussion on this in McKnight, *Village and Bureaucracy*, 106–107, and his "Fiscal Privilege and Social Order in Sung China," in John W. Haeger (ed.), *Crisis and Prosperity in Sung China* (Tucson: University of Arizona Press, 1975), 92.

The *te-chieh* people therefore had little legally sanctioned privilege and could not normally be appointed to regular offices. But once a candidate had passed the departmental examination, or for that matter the palace examination, he became an entirely different person in legal terms. Although in theory he had yet to pass another scrutiny (the *ch'üan-shih* appointment selection test) before the government could decide which post to assign him, this scrutiny was often a formality. Indeed, the better graduates from the palace examinations, namely the first few graduates, could be appointed to offices directly.[72] Those who had to take that *ch'üan-shih* also often found it easy to pass and could be appointed quickly. If no suitable posts were available, a graduate could nonetheless be given a titular position so that he could start to receive a salary. He received a further allowance for the actual responsibility taken up when he was assigned to an official post. The treatment the Sung government gave to the successful candidates of the civil service examinations therefore compared very favorably to that of the T'ang.[73]

E. Ambivalence and Abuses

Most of the students who were enrolled in various public and private schools during the Sung shared a feeling not dissimilar to that of Ch'en Yao-tzu, the young worshipper, who dreamed of the dancing ghost; after all, most were preparing for the examinations. As the number of students increased, the candidates also increased; the competition in the examinations became keener, and the preparation for the examinations also became even more onerous. It was natural for candidates to anticipate the receipt of material rewards commensurate to the time and energy they had invested in long and tedious studies. It was also natural for them to always make it clear that these rewards were to help them to live righteously and to fend off corruption; after all, the Chinese governments had always considered that rewards of offices were to "cultivate [officials in] righteousness" (*yang-lien*).

Honors accorded the newly successful candidates were at once colorful

---

[72] This is based on Hsü Tao-lin, "Fa-lü k'ao-shih," 221. Hsü does not cite any source to support his statement, and I have been able neither to substantiate nor refute it. The most comprehensive treatment of Sung bureaucracy I have seen remains Yang Shu-fan's *Wen-kuan chih-tu*, but its treatment of the issue we are concerned here is at best ambiguous and is not as good as that in Hsü's article.

[73] I have left out a discussion of the content of the *ch'üan-shih*. Interested readers should consult Hsü Tao-lin's article cited in note 72. The commonest assignments a new successful candidate received are mentioned in section B of this chapter.

and sumptuous. As soon as the result of the palace examinations were announced, the emperor treated the successful candidates to the so-called *Ch'iung-lin yen* (Banquet in the Garden of the Beautiful Jade Grove).[74] All successful candidates were given a flower to wear, took turns to compose poems and sang them. They also received special imperial presents which as a rule included green robes, boots and a *hu* tablet, the last being a symbol of official status.[75] After the Court moved to Lin-an, the banquet took place in the examination hall, but the moment of glory remained equally lustrous.[76] Successful candidates had their own way of celebration, too, in that a dinner organized by the graduates was normally held and named the "Feast of hearing happy news" (*Wen-hsi yen*).[77] These occasions are often depicted in beautiful poems. The following is by Su Shun-ch'in (1008–1048):[78]

> The minister gave a banquet, and we indulged in happy words
>   and laugher.
> The wine bottles were empty, and our faces flushed.
> We sang like crazy, and shouted loudly at each other;
>   We danced, and fell on the door-steps.
> There was not much thinking at the time;
>   All we did was to enjoy the moment.
> We shall soon go on to the road of officialdom;
>   Pray for us that we do not take our responsibility lightly.

Successful graduates were often in their late twenties or early thirties. They have left us with reminiscences depicting the moments of farewell from their parents and, not infrequently, their beloved ones. "Now we hold hands; now we go for a walk. The mountain and the river make the separation ever more heartbreaking. The green robe is indeed worthwhile, but will our love sustain the hardship? Snow has by now covered the village shop, its wine flag lowered. Should I go? Should I stay? How sorrowful it is for me, as much as it is for you!"[79] Still, the gleeful joy of success could prove to be overwhelming. The T'ang graduates had taken pride in seeing all the "flowers" in Ch'ang-an and so his Sung counterpart had taken time to show off in the P'ing-k'ang Ward where, among others, the renowned

---

[74] Located right outside of Sun-t'ien Gate in southwestern corner of K'ai-feng's outer wall. Araki Toshikazu, "Hoku-Sō jidai ni okeru kakyo no *bunkiken*," in *Kyōto Kyōiku Daigaku kiyō*, Ser. A, No. 47 (1975), 91–108.

[75] *HCP*, 18/2a.

[76] Chao Sheng, *Ch'ao-yeh lei-yao*, 1:9.

[77] See Araki's "Hoku-Sō jidai ni okeru kakyo no *bunkiken*," 102–104.

[78] Su Shun-ch'in, *Su Shun-ch'in chi* (Shanghai: Ku-chi, 1981), 1:3–4.

[79] Liu Kuo, *Lung-chou chi* (Shanghai: Ku-chi, 1979), 11:109.

singing girl, Li Shih-shih, once entertained Emperor Hui-tsung.[80] However, on average, Sung graduates were much older than their T'ang predecessors, and so it is not entirely unexpected that some, probably the seasoned candidates, lamented that their trip to the singing girls after the imperial feast was not quite up to their expectations:[81]

> White horse, green robe, I have achieved the official status
>   in my old age;
> After the dinner at the Garden of the Beautiful Jade Grove, I still
>   was wanting more to drink.
> I strolled through the P'ing-kang Ward, but was not invited [by
>   any girl]
> Carrying back the palace flower (given by the Emperor), I shall
>   therefore see it again when I wake up [in the morn].

The poem reflects the short moment of melancholy after the success. Rewards that were awaiting them far surpassed the transitory solitude. Soon they were to be faced with more sober and more down-to-earth challenges.

In short, to seek to serve in the government by taking the civil service examinations was perfectly legitimate, and since rewards for loyal service were so gratifying, a psychological tension must have necessarily arisen— one that existed between the moralistic ideal of service and the reality that rewards for success could mean potential for moral corruption.[82]

The tension is most clearly seen in the alarms Sung political critics raised about the practicality of administering an examination system that supposedly could also judge the moral performance of candidates. If the government was to be a good one, it had to recruit morally upright officials. To too many people, however, the content of the examinations could neither realistically nor fairly evaluate the ability and virtue of the participants. Criticism abounded to such an extent that one is impressed by the anxiety over the moral perfectibility of their society. It is then small wonder that Chinese historians should traditionally categorize the Sung as an outstanding period of intense moral concern and rectification[83]—after all, it was during this period that the civil service examination system, and its usefulness in

---

[80] For a brief account of Li Shih-shih, see Teng Chih-ch'eng, *Tung-ching meng-hua lu chu* (Hong Kong: Shang-wu, 1961), 137–140.

[81] Ting Ch'uan-ching, *Sung-jen i-shih hui-pien* (Taipei: Shang-wu, 1966), 10:435–436.

[82] David S. Nivison, "Protest Against Conventions and Conventions of Protest," in A. F. Wright (ed.), *The Confucian Persuasion* (Stanford: Stanford University Press, 1960), 177–201.

[83] Miyazaki Ichisada, "Sōdai no shidaifu," in his *Ajia shi kenkyū*, Vol. 4 (Tokyo: Tōyōshi Kenkyū Kai, 1964), 130–169.

investigating the moral performance of candidates, was scrutinized most extensively.

And yet, one suspects that, moral concern notwithstanding, the pressure to succeed probably was more important in the mind of a candidate. Cheating became less an evil when one thought of the possible service which could ensue to the "Chinese people." On the other hand, many viewed the system as an unrealiable means for evaluating candidates' potential, especially their potential for moral performance. They condemned the system for upholding impartiality at the expense of careful observation of candidates' moral aptitude. There thus remained for many sincere candidates two alternatives: to choose to take the examinations, and hence condone the evil therein, or to choose not to take them at all, but then also to renounce all that followed from one's success. This complicated psychological dilemma perhaps best demonstrates the ambivalence of the examination candidates during the Sung, and some serious Sung thinkers pointed out the paradox created by both equally unsatisfactory alternatives. The following is what Yeh Meng-te (1077–1148), an eminent Southern Sung bibliophile and official, had to say about the dilemma:[84]

> If a man chooses not to take the examinations and remains a student, it is surely all right for him to do so. If, however, he chooses to study for the examinations, then, as long as he does not violate justice and moral principles, there is nothing wrong in his seeking to succeed, to be appointed to an office and to seek for promotion. But today there is a kind of people who have been serving as officials and have received their remuneration and yet are making complaints all the time, saying that it is morally more appropriate not to go into officialdom. I wonder if they would indeed choose not to. Often it is they who are the ones to work harder than others to keep their offices. If they cannot find a way to get into service, they often find fault with our system and claim that they could not tolerate these faults and would have to leave. They consequently earn a dubious reputation because of their proclaimed hesitation to serve, and obtain a higher office. Unfortunately, the common people do not usually understand this fact.

Thus, for Yeh, those who protested against a system that was built upon the ostensible desire for impartial assessment of talent were less worthy than the conscientious members of the establishment.

One result of the government's concern with impartiality was that the examinations could be like a contest not only among the candidates who strove to defeat others, but also between the examination officers and the examiners. In the examination hall, the examiners did everything possible to prevent misconduct among the candidates, while, on their own part, many candidates also did everything possible to defeat their examiners—

---

[84]Yeh Meng-te, *Pi-shu lu-hua*, *Hsüeh-chin t'ao-yüan* ed. (1922), 2/65ab.

after years of hard preparation and drilling, now they felt the temptation
to try fraud and cheating.

Preventive measures were noticeably extreme. Li Kou once depicted in
a lively manner how it was in the examination hall:[85]

> I have waited for the examination until mid-autumn, and
>   it is now finally ordered by the emperor.
> The lofty nine portals are opened;
>   the secrecy of the three academies are seemingly revealed.
> The chief-examiner sits behind his curtain;
>   not to be reached, although he is seen.
> The eunuchs stand right in the front entrance;
>   they search every candidates from top to toe.
> Then the names are called;
>   everyone sits on a broken mat, placed on the cold ground.
> Fierce guards stand directly facing me;
>   equipped with arms, they are alert.
> A man may be known since his youth to be good in learning;
>   and that he has learned how to behave himself.
> When he is in the prison of the examination hall,
>   he is wide-eyed and speechless.

A student was required first to submit his family certificate indicating that
he was from a respectable family and that his family, in the case of the
prefectural examinations, had been residing in the district long enough
to be recognized as locals. He also had to submit a written paper which
would then be used to compare his signature and penmanship with those
on his examination papers. Then the candidate was searched thoroughly,
sometimes so strictly so as to make one feel that it was dangerous even
to use colored handkerchiefs to wrap ink-stones and brushes, for fear that
colored cloths might be mistaken for cloths covered with words of classical
texts.[86]

Inside the examination hall, candidates were naturally forbidden to
talk to each other, nor were they permitted to have water or food delivered
to them.[87] If a candidate was thirsty, he might have to drink from the
water provided for his ink-stone—we have reports saying that candidates
emerged from the examination hall with blackened lips.[88] In the case of
the departmental examinations, candles were not permitted, even if the

[85] Li Kou, *Wen-chi*, 35:249.
[86] The measure of checking candidates' bodies was abandoned in 1012, although
regular checking was retained; see *SHY*, hc, 3/10b. See also *SHY*, hc, 5/26a.
[87] There were attempts to smuggle in paper sheets by stuffing them in fishball soup.
See *SHY*, hc, 6/35a.
[88] Shen Kua, *Meng-hsi pi-t'an*, *TSCC* ed., 1:5.

day had turned dark.[89]

After the examinations, the papers were collected and candidates' names and addresses attached to these papers were torn off. Only specially marked symbols were left on the papers and these marks were folded and sealed. The papers were then copied by clerks before they were read and graded. The graders were divided into two groups, the primary graders and the re-graders. After the papers had been so carefully graded, the seals were then opened, and the final results announced.[90]

This whole process, so carefully and strictly regulated, was aimed at preventing misconduct so as to ensure absolute impartiality. But as the measures became more and more strict, the efforts to break the law also increased.

The most common form of examination cheating was the smuggling of a specially printed or written small booklet into. the examination halls. The *Sung hui-yao* is full of records of rules and reminders banning the smuggling of these booklets, but it is also reported that after the examinations, the hall often was full of them. Other wrongdoings included bribing examination officials or hiring someone to sit beside a candidate to help him or actually take the examination for him. Sometimes, a candidate paid up to two thousand strings of cash to clerks to have an examination paper replaced after the examination was over.[91] A narrative of various ways and anecdotes of cheating in the examination system could easily constitute a colorful and amusing essay.

In an examination system so permeated by abuses and misbehavior, scandals were inevitable. Many eminent officials were at one time or other involved in them, particularly while they served as examination officers. Most of the corruption cases resulted from favoritism. Some names which appeared particularly prominently in the scandals were Li Fang (925—

---

[89]Fire was forbidden in central government buildings. In early spring, when the day became dark very quickly, many candidates felt it necessary to use candles. The government insisted that no candles be used. In addition to the possible fire hazard, if candles were permitted, then those who had finished their answers could proceed to help others, presumably friends, so reasoned the government. This seems unlikely, but a reading of *SHY* indicates that candidates seemed to find it difficult to resist others' requests for help. See *SHY*, hc, 3/9b, 5/33b—34a; *WHTK*, 32:301.

[90]See a brief but comprehensive account in *HCP*, 93/5ab.

[91]*SHY*, hc, 4/7b. It is reported that it cost about twenty to thirty strings to hire someone to write a small booklet. See *SHY*, hc, 6/50b; Ou-yang Hsiu, *Ch'üan-chi*, Pt. XIII, 14. See also *SHY*, hc, 6/29a.

996),[92] Ts'ao Chiung,[93] Wang Ch'in-jo (962–1025),[94] Ch'en Yao-tzu,[95] Ou-yang Hsiu and Han Ch'i (both in favor of Su Shih and Su Ch'e, 1039–1112),[96] Sung Min-ch'iu (1019–1097),[97] Lü Tsu-ch'ien (in favor of Lu Chiu-yüan and Ch'en Fu-liang respectively),[98] Ch'in K'uei (1090–1155),[99] and Hsieh Shen-fu.[100]

Very few sources exist which enable us to say with certainty whether any famous official did pass the examinations with some form of fraud. Su Shih and his brother, Su Ch'e, were known to have helped each other in the 1061 decree examination (*chih-k'o*).[101] They were apparently not indicted, because this anecdote has been transmitted to us as a good, amusing story. The Southern Sung scholar Ch'en Fu-liang (1137–1203) was also known to have helped his cousin, Ch'en Fan-sou, during the departmental examination.[102]

Corruption was clearly rampant. And since the civil service examinations were given so much importance, the pressure of the temptation to cheat was tremendous. Also, because one's school performance was not used to evaluate a candidate's ability, institutional education became almost irrelevant; and teachers were respected in a very different sense. It can be argued that the long years spent in drilling in schools were after all necessary, for it is not likely that one could pass the examination without properly preparing himself in some kind of study. Yet in comparison to the grave importance attached to that single contest in the examination hall, education within the school was of little relevance.

The fact that the examination dominated the minds of the candidates and that the school curriculum was exclusively designed to prepare students

---

[92] *WHTK*, 30:284. This happened in 984, when Li Fang was a Han-lin academician.

[93] *SHY*, hc, 19/15b–16a. This happened in 1021, when Ts'ao was a Han-lin academician.

[94] *SS*, 283:9560. This happened in 1000. Wang was then a senior academician of the Tzu-cheng Hall. For more detail, see Chao I, *Nien-erh shih cha-chi*, 25:337–338. See also Araki, *Kakyo*, 258–261, although Araki wrongly puts the time of the scandal as during T'ai-tsung's reign (976–997).

[95] *SS*, 284:9588. This happended in 1005, when Ch'en was a special drafting official of the Secretariat. Ch'en was the "dreamer" referred to at the beginning of this chapter.

[96] Liu Yüan-ch'ing, *Hsien-i pien*, *TSCC* ed., 3/7b. This happened in 1057, a very important year in the history of Sung civil service examinations. See below.

[97] *SHY*, hc, 8/35b. This happened in 1076, when Sung was an academician of the Lung-t'u Hall.

[98] *SS*, 434:12873; Wu Tzu-liang, *Lin-hsia ou-t'an*, *TSCC* ed., 4:41–42.

[99] *SS*, 156:3630; *SHY*, hc, 4/6a.

[100] *SHY*, hc, 5/32ab. Hsieh was then a Chief Councilor of State.

[101] Yü Wen-pao, *Ch'ui-chien lu* (Taipei: Shih-chieh, 1968), 4:93–94.

[102] Wu Tzu-liang, *Lin-hsia ou-t'an*, 4:41–42.

for the examinations can be seen in the experience of Ou-yang Hsiu who served as an examiner in 1057. He made it known that he was in favor of the *ku-wen* style, and was going to use it in the examination that year.[103] The news caused great consternation among the candidates—the *ku-wen* style had not been tested for a long time, and very few candidates ever learned how to write it. Ou-yang Hsiu was only barely able to ride the storm with his fame intact.

The examination system was the only reliable way by which a commoner could hope to move up the social ladder; it was also the only reliable route for him to serve his government. To take the examination thus meant seeking material rewards to pursue the only effective way of serving the state. There was hardly a clear-cut division between the practical expectations and the Confucian ideal of service. The ambivalent attitude of a candidate—undecided between whether to take the examinations or not—is a part of this unhappy dilemma.

For those who actually chose to take the examinations, and were fortunate enough to succeed in moving into officialdom, there was an apt term to describe them, the *"tu-shu jen,"* the "people who read books."[104] Araki Toshikazu suggests that this term probably first became widely used in the Sung, and could be used to describe the new breed of people whose life was planned in such a way as to become centered around the classics. These were the ones who with acute singlemindedness prepared for the examinations, and were intensely keen about the lofty ideals set forth in the very conception of the examination system. A *tu-shu jen* meant one who brought on himself the burden of transmitting the great Chinese tradition, and this every word could indeed strike a resonance in many a person's mind, commanding immediate respect when hearing that some *tu-shu jen* was around. On the other hand, in a more mundane sense, the term also carried a strong connotation of innocence or ignorance. In purely Confucian terms, a *tu-shu jen* embodied the very ideal of not being "an implement"[105] and was thus not a specialist. In both senses, one finds an interesting characteristic that was acquired by the degree-holders who now made up the majority of Chinese upper echelon: a certain sense of aloofness, being remote from the reality of life, but with a paradoxical confidence that their existence was necessary for a good society and for the government. Whether they were the embodiment of "harmless" ignorance or the incarnation of the most perfect Confucian ideal of an "intellectual" remained to be seen.[106]

[103] *HCP*, 185/1a.
[104] See Ch. 1 note 2.
[105] *Analects*, II, 12.
[106] As so vividly depicted in Wu Ching-tzu's *Ju-lin wai-shih* (Scholars).

In any case, it was a paradox and it is hence not ironic to say that if one was sincere in wanting to become a *true* "man who reads classics," then abuses in the examinations should be tolerated, if not necessarily justified, since the ideal was morally correct.

The result was then a perennial protest and complaint against the examination system without being able to create a better alternative. This was the great dilemma in Sung education, and it helped to create a new kind of people, the *tu-shu jen*—the kind of people who protested against the institution, but nevertheless willingly took part in it.

CHAPTER 7

Life in the Government Schools

The profound impact of the civil service examinations upon students' lives marks one of the most important developments in Sung education. During the Sung, the whole process of education gradually became related to the purpose and demands of the examinations.

But Sung people did not simply perceive education as a means towards being appointed to government serivce. For them, it was also a program for promoting the proper moral training of individual students and of the population at large. The main component of Sung education thus consisted of both the further development of the examination system (which caused the decline of the government educational institutions) and a broader vision of education in Neo-Confucian terms (which meant increasing the emphasis upon utilizing all available social channels for the moral cultivation of the subjects). In the following, however, I shall concentrate only on life in government schools and leave out that of other private educational institutions.

A. Students and Teachers in Local Government Schools

While it has been suggested by traditional writers that powerful or wealthy families often sent their sons to government schools to evade labor duties,[1] government schools more typically attracted average and perhaps even poor students. We shall soon see that educational opportunities were so much widened that those who could afford it in any way chose not to attend government schools, despite the fact that the majority of government school students were given subsidies.[2] Local government schools continued to flourish during the Southern Sung, and were by no means completely overshadowed by the academy movement; this was due to the fact that the number of students was also rising.

[1] See Ch. 5, section D above.
[2] The academies no doubt provided an increasingly important alternative to government schools.

Government schools provided only a part of the prerequisite education to those who sought a place in officialdom, and thus educational training in the wider sense was not limited to the narrow curriculum which government schools provided.[3] As a result, we know next to nothing about the actual life of students in Sung local official schools. The little information we do have is so much tinged with morally stereotyped connotations that only an imaginative reading of these materials could help us glimpse into the world of Sung schools. For example, we are told that a certain hardworking and serious student who later became a leading Neo-Confucian thinker, tearfully tore and burned his clothes after he realized that he had been tricked by his classmates into going with them to a wineshop where prostitutes joined them in drinking.[4] But this anecdote is hardly informative and except for telling us that probably local school students were by and large in their late teens,[5] we cannot infer much from it. After all, fun involving wine and girls is only to be expected of students in any schools.

One has to admit that the competition for places in local official schools was not severe. Chu Hsi's decision to establish an academy was made with the full realization that a government school was already in existence at Nan-k'ang where Chu was serving as a prefect. It appears that Chu Hsi was convinced that he would be able to provide a better education than what the existing official school was offering. Lu Chiu-ling's (1132–1180) experience with the local official school was so unsatisfactory that he decided "to retire to his village hut, where he studied with his father and brothers (notably Lu Chiu-yüan), in pursuit of antiquity."[6] Attacks on the govern-

---

[3] A study of the lives of 318 persons who were formally "educated" (fulfilling one or more of the following four criteria: attendance in local government schools, service through *yin* protection, at least one try in the civil service examinations or attendance at the Directorate school or the University), only 15 definitely went to local government schools. Many of them (44 in total) entered service by the *yin* protection method, but a greater number attempted the civil service examinations (103 in total). Others either went into office by graduating with distinction from the University or did not go into service despite their education. The small number of local government school students reflects more the fact that these schools were considered insignificant than that there were indeed so few students who attended them. For example, among the 126 men for whom Yeh Shih wrote tomb inscriptions, only one attended a county school. This shows that in Yeh Shih's mind, and probably also in the minds of many of Yeh Shih's contemporaries, local government education was hardly a meaningful part of one's life. Biographies of the people in this study are from the tomb inscriptions composed by Chu Hsi, Lu Chiu-yüan, Lu Yu, Ch'en Liang and Yeh Shih, and are found in their respective collected works.

[4] *SS*, 447:13196.

[5] See Ch. 5, section D above.

[6] Lu Chiu-yüan, *Lu Chiu-yüan chi* (Peking: Chung-hua, 1980), 27:312.

ment's local educational facilities ran throughout the Southern Sung, and without concurring with a certain Neo-Confucian prejudice that underlay the attacks, we can at least imagine that as long as each county or each prefecture maintained just one official school, with requests for enrollment mounting in the wake of the increasingly literate population, it was only very natural that people believed that these official schools could not accommodate, and hence, educate, the enlarged number of students preparing for the examinations. The attacks probably resulted in the conspicuous silence concerning the life and education in local official schools during the Sung.

It appears that, in terms of the size of local schools during the Northern Sung, the number 200 had a special appeal. The mass establishment of local schools in the 1040s, in response to the reform introduced by Fan Chung-yen, possibly resulted in an overzealous building of schools and the government subsequently ordered that on county level, only those counties with more than two hundred potential students would be allowed to established county schools.[7] This would be the same as saying that at least in the years that followed 1044, schools in theory should have had more than 200 registered students. There are indications that prefectural schools indeed had an average of three to five hundred students.[8] However, this was not what happened at the county level. On the eve of Wang An-shih's reform, many counties had started their own schools apparently without registering as many students as was required by the government. The trend became evident in the early years of the twelfth century. It appears that most schools at the county level had only a few tens of students,[9] while prefectural schools were required to have at least 100 (reduced to 80 in 1111) to qualify for a Court-appointed preceptor.[10] Some larger prefectural schools had as many as several hundred students,[11]

[7]HCP, 120/19a; see also Wang An-shih, Lin-ch'uan chi, 82:523, 528.

[8]Ou-yang Hsiu, Ch'üan-chi, Pt. II, 109 (more than three hundred students in the Chi-chou prefectural school); Su Shih, Su Tung-p'o chi, hou chi, 15, 9:16 (several hundred students in the Nan-an military prefectural school); SHY, cj, 2/2a (several hundred students in Yen-chou prefecture's Confucian temple school); Wang Ch'ang, Chin-shih ts'ui-pien, 132/6a (one hundred and twenty-seven) and many other sources. Of course, schools built before this date did not have this regulation and therefore we are told that the Yü-hang county school had about twenty students when Fan Chung-yen was a subprefect there in 1049–1050. See Fan Chung-yen, Wen-cheng chi, 15:126.

[9]"It was decreed (in 1104) that large counties should support fifty students, middle-sized counties should support forty and small counties thirty." HCPSP, 23/1a. See also HCPSP, 21/13a.

[10]HCPSP, 21/5b–6a, 30/1a.

[11]"Schools with more than five hundred students will have two preceptors." SHY, cj.

and in one exceptional case, the number reached 1,328. The school consequently applied for the appointment of three preceptors.[12] But in general, one would visualize the size of local government schools as having had between several tens and several hundred students.

The trend remained very much the same throughout the Southern Sung. County schools generally continued to have a few scores of students, and some of them had even fewer. Prefectural schools had better facilities and, in average, attracted a couple of hundred students, possibly slightly fewer than their Northern Sung counterparts. For example, Fu-chou prefectural school, which, according to Chu Hsi, ranked as one of the largest schools in the nation during the Southern Sung, did increase from 200 in 1122 to 240 in 1140 and eventually to 300 in 1165. But at the height of the Northern Sung educational reform, the school once had as many as 1,200 students.[13]

From the discussion above, it is evident that local school facilities provided a very limited base for the education of an ever increasing student population. Let us take Fu-chou as an example again. While its prefectural school was giving instruction to 300 students (in 1165), the candidates taking the triannual prefectural qualifying examinations numbered as many as 17,000 (in 1165) and 20,000 (in 1174), requiring as many as 300 copyists to recopy their scripts.[14] From these facts, it is reasonable to conclude that the majority of the candidates were educated in places other than the official prefectural school.

Still, local officials during the Southern Sung continued to build, maintain and repair government schools within their administrative district, and there are stories telling us how devoted prefects or subprefects, many of them under Neo-Confucian influence, paid special attention to seeing that their schools were well managed and instruction therein well conducted. Fan Chung-yen, as early as in the 1030s, already set the example. Serving

---

2/15a; *HCPSP*, 29/18b. Fu-chou prefectural school, for example, had 500 students in 1093. See Liang K'o-chia, *San-shan chih*, *SKCS* ed., 8/5b.

[12] *SHY*, cj, 2/24b–25a. The same source (2/14b) also records that Chi-chou school had 634 students in 1114, this is a 200% increase over 1044 (see note 8 above).

[13] Liang K'o-chia, *San-shan chih*, 12. The numbers cited are for formally registered students. It was common for local schools to accept auditors whose number could nearly double the original number. The Fu-chou prefectural school we are dealing with here also took in 200 auditing students, in addition to the 300 formal students. Lu Chiu-yüan reports that the I-chang county school normally took in a couple of scores of auditors in addition to its 50 formally registered students. See Lu, *Lu Chiu-yüan chi*, 19:230. Chu Hsi's comment is in his *Wen-chi*, 80:1462.

[14] Liang K'o-chia, *San-shan chih*, 7/passim. May we assume that the 300 copyists came primarily from the prefectural school?

as a prefect in Su-chou, he engaged the famous Hu Yüan to become its preceptor,[15] thus beginning the famous and significant relationship between the two educators, a relationship which eventually resulted in the appointment of Hu Yüan to the University in a time when the University was going through its most difficult period and was in urgent need of the leadership of a great teacher.[16] During the Southern Sung, an increased number of local officials took a personal interest in local education, as this was one of the most important part of Neo-Confucian ideology, which then was growing in influence, and their attention ranged from raising more money to support students, such as setting up an estate,[17] or putting aside a special fund for school ceremonies,[18] or replenishing book collections,[19] to actually going to schools to take up teaching duties[20] and the like.

If officials appear to have become even more attentive to the educational programs of local government schools, one might guess that preceptors or other teachers would be even more serious about their teaching tasks.[21] Now that the size of the schools was generally small, and there was a heightened sense of educational responsibility among teachers, one probably would think that a very intimate relationship must have developed between teachers and their students or among the students themselves. Unfortunately, we know very little of this kind of relationship. Let me call attention to a couple of extraordinary facts which should hold the key to the total lack of information about close relationship between local school teachers and their students. The silence concerning this issue is so conspicuous that there must be some reason for it. Wang Ch'uan-shan, the great seventeenth-century interpreter of Sung history stated:[22]

It is often said: "Those who have [the support of] the scholars will prosper." The "have" here does not mean that the rulers should take the scholars as his personal possession. The scholars recommended by the officials to the ruler

---

[15] Huang Tsung-hsi, *Sung Yüan hsüeh-an*, *SPPY* ed., 1/1a–5a.

[16] More on Hu Yüan in the next section.

[17] *SS*, 405:12249; Liu Fu built a *Chi-min chuang* (Estate to Subsidize People) "to provide urgent needs to the commoners, support to candidates taking the departmental examinations and money to school students and elders."

[18] Chu Hsi, *Wen-chi*, 92:1623.

[19] *Ibid.*, 77:1415.

[20] See note 18. See also Lu Chiu-yüan, *Lu Chiu-yüan chi*, 27:315–316; and *SS*, passim. Chu Hsi, on arrival at Nan-k'ang, also made a point of going to lecture in the local prefectural school. See my "Chu Hsi, Academies and the Tradition of Private *Chiang-hsüeh*."

[21] For a discussion on the teachers' life, see my "Life in the Schools of Sung China," 57–59. See also Ch. 5, section C.

[22] Wang Ch'uan-shan, *Sung-lun* (Peking: Chung-hua, 1965), 1:7–9.

are of course to be "had" by the ruler, but if the officials have [the support of] scholars and they use these scholars in the service of the nation, we should then consider that these scholars are indeed also possessed by the ruler. There is no trouble greater than for a ruler to compete for the possession of scholars with his officials. Once a ruler competes with his officials over the possession of scholars, then his officials will compete against him. When officials struggle for the control of scholars, then there will also be struggles among the officials themselves. This could only result in the breaking down of the government's credibility and disturbances will ensure. . . . When high officials cease to consider the recommendation of scholars as a virtue, then scholars will be at a loss. When Confucian teachers do not think that giving instruction to scholars is a meaningful thing, then the scholars will be even more at a loss. If local officials do not consider it a glorious thing to recommend scholars, then all scholars will lose [their chances of service]. How then is it right to claim: "It is illegal to pay visits to the houses of high public officials or to accept private favors from individuals.". . . [If the government was so keen on preventing those deemed illegal], then the result would only be that high officials are no longer confident of themselves, that Confucian teachers are no longer on terms of friendship [with their students], and that local officials are no longer capable of governance. Accordingly, the connection between them will cease to exist, and the potential for the rise of a despot begins to emerge. . . . All of them will only say: "I know only the son of heaven!" What do they know about the son of heaven other than only office and rewards!

This quotation was directed against the order of T'ai-tsu, the founder of the dynasty, who commanded that candidates were to give up the custom of paying visits, after they succeeded in the examinations, to the homes of their examiners and calling them teachers.[23] Although this stricture was intended for civil service examination candidates, as a principle it could be applied in any institution that administered some form of examination. We therefore see that, in 1079, in response to an accusation that University professors did not conduct impartial examinations within the school, the Directorate recommended a practice which was accepted by the government that the University professors were not to administer the internal examinations and that they indeed should avoid meeting students except in classrooms, and that should they decide to meet them, the meeting should only be for discussions on scholarly matters.[24] This recommendation was most unfortunate, because it led to a forced alienation between teachers and their students. Once the internal examinations in the schools were affected by that zeal for fairness, it was only natural that the government would

[23] The decree was ordered in 962. See *SHY*, hc, 3/2a; *HCP*, 3/10a. For a Sung discussion of this matter, see Wang Yung, *Yen-i i-mou lu*, 1:2.

[24] For a detailed discussion which examines nearly all available evidences on this matter, see my *San-lun*, 145–148. See also *SS*, 459:13468 for how a professor dared to break the rule to meet with students.

accept the recommendation that a personal relationship not be allowed to develop between teachers and their students. Monthly examinations within government's local schools existed as early as the mid-eleventh century and became an established practice in 1103 when the government ordered that these monthly examinations be held even in county schools. The first month was designed for students to take the tests in the classics. The second month was for the tests in composing policy essays and the third month for policy discussion questions. These tests would be given again at the beginning of a new season.[25] When this examination method was adopted, Ts'ai Ching was just starting the comprehensive national school system in which better graduates would be recommended to study in the University; it is thus conceivable that certain precautionary measures might have been taken to accompany this examination scheme so that reliable tests could be made within schools. Actually, this came about in 1118 when someone recommended that registered students in local schools should be ordered not to associate themselves with the officials of the districts of their schools.[26] Preceptors in prefectural schools and even instructors in county schools were often paid officials and were thus in theory included in the group with which students had to take care not to be closely associated.

From the discussion above, it is clear that there was a certain dilemma in being a student in government schools. The dilemma is very well diagnosed by Wang Ch'uan-shan, and it is in this light that we see why scarcely anyone in Sung China ever openly claimed that they benefitted in local government schools from intimate association with their mentors. On the other hand, we can also imagine that the teachers who were occasionally mentioned in the biographies of official Sung history might well be teachers in the official schools, even though the biographies do not make that fact explicit.

The brief discussion above suggests that more students in the Sung times attended non-government schools and because of the policy adopted by the government, intimate teacher-student relations could not easily develop on government school premises. This was particularly true after the end of the Northern Sung. Earlier, we do know a little more about the stories of conscientious teachers and how they associated themselves with students. With the influence of Neo-Confucianism, in the thirteenth century, we again hear about the involvement of local officials in government school in their administrative districts. Generally speaking, however, we know next to nothing about the life, intellectual and extracurricular, in local government

---

[25] *HCPSP*, 22/7a.
[26] *SHY*, cj, 2/29b.

schools, and people, especially those under the influence of Neo-Confucian educational ideas, seemed to hold a rather low esteem for the quality of these institutions.

Finally, the Metropolitan Prefectural School in Hangchow, as well as that in the Northern Sung K'ai-feng, has left us with somewhat more information about the life of students there. Often the students from this prefectural school would participate in the activities led by students of the Imperial University. A lot of the political activities of the University students during the Southern Sung had the participation also of the Hangchow Prefectural School. I will discuss this special aspect of local school life in the next section.

B. Life in the University and in the Directorate School

Although it was said that many University students enjoyed life in the University and often stayed there for as long as ten years,[27] it appears that a larger number of students were not enthusiastic: the turnover rate at the University was very high, and the average length of time students spent there did not exceed a few years. The structure of the University indicates that the government expected students to stay in the school for about five to seven years.[28] Yang Chien (1140–1225) went to the University in 1161 when he was twenty years old, and spent a total of seven years studying there, making a few lifelong friends; he graduated in 1168 and took the civil service examinations the following year, when he was twenty-eight years old.[29]

The famous poet Chou Pang-yen (1057–1122) spent five years in the University, where he was made a rector in his last year because of his outstanding *fu* rhyme-prose, the "*Fu* on the Capital Pien (K'ai-feng)" (*Pien-tu fu*).[30]

Since neither the University nor the school of the Directorate of Education actually enforced a residency requirement, it is conceivable that many students spent fewer years than was expected at these institutions.[31] Ch'en Yü-i (1090–1138) went to the University in 1111, at a time when the

[27]Li Hsien-min, *Yün-chai kuang-lu, Shuo-fu tsa-chu, Lung-wei mi-shu* ed. (1794), 24/1a.

[28]See my "Education in Northern Sung China," 103–113.

[29]Feng K'o-yung and Yeh I-shan (eds.), "Tz'u-hu hsien-sheng nien-p'u," in Yang Chien, *Tz'u-hu i-shu, Ssu-ming ts'ung-shu* ed. (1932), 1/3a.

[30]*SS*, 444:13126.

[31]On the relationship between the Imperial University (*T'ai-hsüeh*) and the Directorate of Education (*Kuo-tzu chien*), see Ch. 1, section D.

University was near the height of its development and prestige. He was promoted to the upper-hall and graduated from the University in 1113, having spent only a little more than two years there. He was then appointed to a minor position, because of his status as a University graduate.[32] This was when Ts'ai Ching was in power, and distinguished University graduates were appointed to offices directly. Similarly, Chao Ming-ch'eng, husband of the famous *tz'u* poet Li Ch'ing-chao, was a University student when he was married in 1101. After the marriage, he remained at the University for two more years before he was appointed to office.[33] These examples show that some students obviously spent fewer years than required, yet still profitted from the University course of study.

Others were less diligent in their University work. As mentioned above, University students were frequently exempted from the prefectural tests, and many people registered in the University only to acquire this privilege. For example, Ch'en Liang went to the University in Hangchow in 1168. He failed to pass the departmental examination the following year, and decided to quit the University that winter and went home. One of the reasons he did so, aside from his failure in the civil service examination, was perhaps because his old friend Lü Tsu-ch'ien was already a University professor. Ch'en did not go back while Lü remained in the University; instead, he stayed home for seven years and taught in various private schools, and took time to write many of his important essays which established his fame as a thinker; he then went back to the University in 1176, but apparently failed to pass the entrance examination, as he does not seem to have stayed there long.[34] Ch'en Liang's contemporary, Ch'en Fu-liang, also went to the University about 1176 and stayed for a very short period. These Ch'ens were known by their fellow students collectively as the "two Ch'ens" of the University.[35] These and many other cases indicate that students frequently remained in the University for only a short time, but returned periodically—particularly during an examination year.

The fact that University registration was used to obtain exemption from the prefectural examinations was most evident before the 1044 educational reform. Ou-yang Hsiu was a good example. He first took the civil service examinations in 1027 and failed; he then registered in the Directorate two

---

[32]Cheng Ch'ien, "Ch'en Chien-chai nien-p'u," in *Yu-shih hsüeh-pao*, Vol. II, No. 2 (1960), 1–64.

[33]Li Ch'ing-chao, *Li Ch'ing-chao chi*, ed. by Huang Sheng-chang (Shanghai: Chung-hua, 1962), 162–167.

[34]Yen Hsü-hsin, *Ch'en Lung-ch'uan nien-p'u* (Ch'ang-sha: Shang-wu, 1940), 14–20.

[35]Sun Ch'iang-ming, *Ch'en Wen-chieh kung nien-p'u*, *Ching-hsiang lou ts'ung-shu* ed. (1929), 6ab.

years later, just before another examination year, and passed the *chin-shih* test the following year.[36] Because practices like this were common, in 1044 a regulation concerning the period of residence was recommended.[37] However, the residency requirement was abandoned immediately after the failure of the 1044 reform; and registration only to avoid the prefectural examinations resumed.[38] A reading of Tseng Kung's biography shows that he also pursued a course similar to Ou-yang's, except that he was less lucky.[39]

It is clear that during most of the Sung, students often registered in the University more for convenience than for serious study. Naturally, there were those who valued a governmental higher education, even if it served only as a mark of prestige. Some people enjoyed the *yin* privilege and could enter officialdom directly, but still chose to register in the Directorate school; Li Kang, an early Southern Sung general, is an example.[40] Similarly, the case of Wang Ying-lin shows that while the available education was irrelevant to his success in the civil service examinations, he nonetheless sought a place in the Directorate school; since he achieved his *chin-shih* degree less than one year after he entered the Directorate, that school evidently had not conferred on him any practical or educational help.[41]

Thus, one may say that the higher educational institutions were serving as much a decorative as an educational function and this naturally provoked complaints. Chu Hsi had observed that "the University is worse than prefectural schools, and prefectural schools are worse than county schools, and county schools are still worse than village schools," and dared to suggest that the University be closed down.[42] In reality, of course, people continued to flock to the University, and it took a man like Lu Hsiu-fu to resist the temptation. The famous patriot had passed the entrance examination to go to the University but decided not to register on the ground that University education could not possibly provide him with the education he desired. He returned to his hometown for another four years before he passed the

---

[36] Ou-yang Hsiu, *Ch'üan-chi*, "Nien-p'u," 1–25.

[37] *SHY*, cj, 2/1a.

[38] *HCP*, 153/1ab.

[39] Yang Hsi-min, *Tseng Wen-ting kung nien-p'u*, *Shih-wu chia nien-p'u* ed. (1857–1907), 2ab. Tseng Kung went to the University in 1038, at the age of nineteen, and failed in that year's examination. In 1041, he went back to the University and stayed for a few months, but still could not pass the examination. He eventually made it in 1057.

[40] Chao Hsiao-hsüan, *Li Kang nien-p'u ch'ang-pien* (Hong Kong: New Asia Institute, 1968), 12.

[41] Chang Ta-ch'ing, "Wang Shen-ning nien-p'u," in Wang Ying-lin, *Ssu-ming wen-hsien chi, Ssu-ming ts'ung-shu* ed., 4a.

[42] Chu Hsi, *Chu-tzu yü-lei*, 109/11a–12a.

examination in 1256.[43]

In any case, the institutions continued to attract students. This was particularly the case because the University evidently was becoming a place where wealthy youngsters gathered for the enjoyment of the pursuits of youth. Although there is no solid evidence showing that University students were allowed to live "off-campus," there is plenty of evidence indicating that students went around freely. Many students were married, as in the case of Chao Ming-ch'eng, husband of the great woman-poet, Li Ch'ing-chao. Both his and Li's families were in the capital.[44] It is hard to imagine that he could be separated from his wife for as long as the ten days of each school week. Indeed, most of the students of the University, and particularly of the Directorate school, were wealthy enough to live a happily life. This was so even during the Southern Sung; Lin-an, the capital city, was a prosperous commercial center—and perhaps the largest city in the world at the time. Records of the happy life of students there are plentiful;[45] I shall refer to only a few of them.

One example is a story told by Chou Mi:[46]

During the Ch'un-hsi era (1174–1189), the emperor visited the West Lake. His Royal Barge passed the "Broken Bridge" and stopped at a small but tidy wineshop. The shop was divided by a screen on which a *tz'u* poem was written. The emperor read the poem and liked it. He was then told that the poem and its calligraphy were both written by Yü Kuo-pao, a University student.

When spring arrives, I spend all my money buying flowers.
Day after day, I stay drunk on the banks of the lake.
My jade horse is familiar with the Road of Western Coolness; he proudly whinnies and stops at the shop where I buy my wine.
There are flutes and drums amid the fragrance of red almond, and rope swings under the shadow of green willows.
The warm breeze is everywhere under a sky made for beauties.
Their heads are covered with flowers which spread over their temples.
The painted boat carried away the spring, leaving my memory behind with the water and the mist on the lake.
Tomorrow, let me bring back what's left of today's wine, and come back to look for flowery hairpins on the garden path.

After reading the poem, the emperor smiled and said: "The poem is very good, except that the second last line is too weak and shows that the poet is a poor scholar." He therefore changed it to "Tomorrow, let me come back still drunk, . . ." This change makes the *tz'u* poem totally different.

---

[43] Chiang I-hsüeh, *Lu Hsiu-fu nien-p'u* (Shanghai: Shang-wu, 1936).

[44] See note 35 above.

[45] For more detailed writing on life in the Sung University, see Miyazaki Ichisada, "Sōdai no daigakusei seikatsu," in his *Ajia shi kenkyū*, Vol. 1, 365–401.

[46] Chou Mi, *Wu-lin chiu-shih* (Shanghai: Ku-tien wen-hsüeh, 1957), 3:375–376.

It is said that each dormitory of the University had its own singing girls, and students from different dormitories might engage in occasional skirmishes over some particularly attractive prostitute.[47]

A gathering of such a large number of wealthy young men in the capital area must have caused problems for local authorities. We have read about a memorial submitted by Ch'eng I in 1086 on the organization of the University. In it, Ch'eng I touched upon the problem of how to punish University students who violated local orders.[48] This indicates that as early as the late Northern Sung, the problem of "town versus gown" already existed. It became intense as the position of the University students grew in importance. In the Southern Sung, the University students quarrelled with the Metropolitan Prefect of Hangchow over all kinds of issues. To give one example, in 1210, four students from different schools of the Directorate became involved in a serious conflict with the Hangchow authorities: having illegally purchased a piece of land in the city, they were planning to lease it out for profit. When the Metropolitan Prefect heard of it, he arrested them and confiscated their money. The news was immediately transmitted to the Directorate, and many students went to see the directors to protest; they argued that since these students had been given proper punishment under a fairly strict system of penalties within the Directorate, the Hangchow authorities had no right to arrest them a second time. Particularly protesting the decision of the Prefect to expel the defendants from the Prefecture, the students went so far as to demand the dismissal of the Metropolitan Prefect and other related officials. Many students left their classes and joined in the demonstrations, and somehow the faculty and staff members were convinced of the students' cause and became sympathetic with their position. A group of staff members—including the secretary, two professors, one rector, and a few lower-ranked officials—joined the students in petitioning on the defendants' behalf; they even threatened to resign, claiming that the Hangchow authority was meddling with the internal affairs of the Directorate. The uproar grew so serious that finally the Emperor Ning-tsung became alarmed. He subsequently decreed that the Prefect be removed, and ordered that whenever the local authority decided to arrest any University student, it ought to notify the Directorate first.[49]

[47]For more information about extracurricular activities, see Wang Chien-ch'iu, *Sung-tai t'ai-hsüeh*, 232–242. See also note 45 above and Jacques Gernet (tr. by Hope Wright), *Daily Life in China on the Eve of the Mongol Invasion* (Stanford: Stanford University Press, 1965).

[48]See note 38 above; see also Ch. 4, note 40.

[49]Yü Wen-pao, *Ch'ui-chien lu*, 4:92.

This event reveals how powerful University students had become in the Southern Sung capital. They enjoyed an extremely privileged and influential position in Sung local politics, and that power was also extended to the political arena of national affairs. During the Southern Sung, a few ministers were thrown out of office because of the complaints of University students.[50] It is said that, in order to keep University students quiet, Chia Ssu-tao, the powerful minister in the late Southern Sung, had to bribe student leaders and at the same time plant student-informers to gather information for him. One source even claims that Chia Ssu-tao was able to recite graffiti that appeared in a washroom of the University—to the amazement and great dismay of the Director of the school.[51]

All of these examples portray a University style of life that was, in large measure, easy and relaxed. Instruction was carried on in a loose manner, even though regulations appeared to be strict. In 1077, a University student charged that University lecturers spent only two hours each day in school and usually were absent in the afternoons;[52] this charge was one of the factors leading to the reorganization of the University that year. One might have supposed that, after this reorganization, the University lecturers kept longer hours. However, this was not the case. Li Ko-fei (father of Li Ch'ing-chao) was a rector at the University in 1089. According to one of his friends: "He named his study 'Bamboo Resort' and spent afternoons in that study after he went home from the University. He would sweep his room, prepare brushes and ink-stones, and compose twenty or thirty poems and essays."[53] It seems that teachers enjoyed as much leisure as their students.

One of the other primary attractions of the University was its proximity to the center of power; it was a good place from which to approach political and social dignitaries. The University could help one become acquainted with the life-style of an official. This helps to account for the eagerness of poor students to attend the University. Many encountered great frustrations, as did Ch'en Liang. On the other hand, one might be fortunate enough to meet a patron and work one's way through. For example, we are told that Tung Tun-i hired a University student to be his son's private tutor. The student, from the same native area as Tung, came to teach Tung's son on holidays, and thus was able to go through the University.[54]

---

[50] See next section.
[51] Chou Mi, *Kuei-hsin tsa-chih*, *Hsüeh-chin t'ao-yüan* ed. (1805), pieh-chi, shang, 26b.
[52] *HCP*, 295/4a.
[53] Ts'ao Yüeh-chih, *Chi-pei Ts'ao hsien-sheng chi-lo chi*, *SPTK* ed., 30:198–199.
[54] Tseng Min-hsing, *Tu-hsing tsa-chih*, *TSCC* ed., 57.

In general, however, the University was hardly a place for the poor. Yang Wan-li (1124—1206), a Southern Sung poet, in a letter to one of his disciples, made this point:[55]

> The Imperial University is truly the center for elite young men; however, its life may not be suitable for scholars. If one is not talented, one will not feel easy anywhere. If one's home is not close to the Capital, one will not feel easy there. Above all, if one is not wealthy, then he will not do well in the University. I do not mean that wealth is particularly important, but if one has to leave home and stay in the University for a long period of time, how can he do so without some money?

The picture is clear: the University and the Directorate school were places whose importance lay more in the area of social connections than in formal education. In fact, as stated before, for many young men, socialization in the sense of emulating official life-styles and patterns of thinking was more valuable than actual formal training. This conclusion holds true for education in the University schools. For the students, contacts with high officials and imitating their way of behavior (as well as their mode of thinking) were most instructive; through this type of learning process, students identified themselves with officialdom. In short, the Directorate school and the University institutions were significant less because they helped to develop scholarship than because they helped to fostor among the students the sense of being leaders of Chinese society.

C. Political Activities of University Students

An important part of the life of Sung University students was their involvement in the nation's politics. As there are already a number of articles and even books dealing with this subject, I will therefore offer a rather brief and slightly revisionist summary of the topic. Obviously, the gathering of a group of elite students in the capital, receiving training to become the leaders of the government, could be potentially explosive. Young students could easily entangle themselves in all types of political controversies and the results might not be always what they had intended. Sung University students have left the Chinese people with a respected legacy that was still very much cherished and still alive as late as the 1960s.[56] How the rather complex series of political events came down in historical records as a positive and respectable precedent is worth careful study and attention.

---

[55] Yang Wan-li, *Ch'eng-chai chi, SPTK* ed., 64/9b—10a.

[56] Chow Tse-tsung, *The May Fourth Movement* (Stanford: Stanford University Press, 1960), 11—18.

What accounted for the rise of feeling among University students for imperative involvement in the nation's politics? First of all, intellectuals, the so-called *tu-shu jen*, enjoyed a much more elevated position than ever before in Chinese history.[57] The civil service examinations helped to foster a feeling among the Chinese people that intellectuals were the natural leaders of society. Second, the heightened sense of national urgency in the wake of incessant foreign encroachments no doubt served as another important incentive to the University students to demand a more responsive or aggressive government. The Sung people had by the twelfth century cultivated within themselves enough nationalistic feeling. This newly acquired nationalism started to receive philosophical elaboration during the Southern Sung so that involvement in political criticism was gradually regarded as a morally justifiable action. Southern Sung Neo-Confucian thinkers had come to the conclusion that it was a supreme Confucian responsibility for intellectuals to be the moral critics of their government. As a result, students were eager to be useful when the nation was in crisis, and to choose to respond to the crisis naturally won the approval of contemporary thinkers.[58]

There was yet another element which accounted for the heightened political awareness of University students. This had to do with the nature of Sung politics. Ever since the first political crisis of the early 1040s, Sung officials had found that politicizing students and using them for political struggles was a sure way for the gaining of advantage in the Court. Shih Chieh may be considered to be the first person to employ this tactic. As director of the *Kuo-tzu chien* in 1040, Shih Chieh was well known as a strong opponent of the *p'ien* style of writing. He failed and expelled several tens of Directorate students for their use of the style in composing rhyme-proses *(fu)*. This caused some uproar, but he continued his attacks on the style anyway, and seized the chance of Fan Chung-yen's rise to power to recommend a fellow radical, Sun Fu, a classical scholar, to a professorship

---

[57] One "myth" about a so-called "ancestral instruction" engraved on one of the walls in the imperial palace forbidding later emperors to kill *shih tai-fu* (gentleman-scholars) has been constantly cited as an evidence of the special position intellectuals had in Sung government and society. Although there is only scanty evidence for it, this episode nevertheless was popularized by Wang Ch'uan-shan whose *Sung-lun* (On the Sung) has been widely read in the past two hundred years and has been the most important single source of the Chinese way of interpreting the Sung until recently. The so-called "ancestral instruction" is mentioned in *Sung-lun*, 1:4. See Chang Yin-lin, "Sung T'ai-tsu shih-pei chi Cheng-shih T'ang k'o-shih k'ao," first published in *Wen-shih tsa-chih*, Vol. 1, No. 7 (1941), now in Han-hsüeh yen-chiu shih (ed.), *Sung, Liao, Chin, Yüan shih lun-chi* (Taipei: Han-sheng, 1977), 1–5.

[58] For a discussion of Neo-Confucian nationalism, see Hoyt C. Tillman, "Proto-Nationalism in Twelfth-century China?", in *HJAS*, Vol. 39, No. 2 (1979), 403–428.

at the newly independent University. Both of them utilized their positions at the University to launch a series of attacks on some prominent officials, managing to alienate enough of them to provoke severe revenge which not only cost Fan his reforms, but also brought the downfall of Sun Fu. Shih Chieh escaped abuse because of his sudden death in 1045, but even so, he did not completely avoid his enemies' condemnation, including an accusation that he had escaped to the Tangut Hsi-Hsia by feigning death.[59]

While still a director, Shih also showed special favor to a student named Ho Ch'ün and instigated him to send a memorial to the throne arguing the necessity of abolishing the test in poetic writing in the civil service examinations. The Emperor rejected Ho's suggestion and ordered him to quit the University, but the incident marked the beginning of the direct involvement of University students in political debates, and resulted in all kinds of unforeseeable consequences.[60]

In order that Shih Chieh's involvement of University students in political activities be made into a respectable precedent, there needed a positive and sympathetic interpretation of the incident in relation to Fan Chung-yen's reform movement. Generally speaking, Fan's reform, even though it fell through in less than one year, eventually entered the memory of his contemporaries as being not an entirely bad attempt, and actually became increasingly respected in the 1060s and 1070s as a good model for social transformation in contrast to Wang An-shih's rush for change which was then viewed with suspicion. Shih Chieh's action received much harsher criticism at the beginning. Indeed, a respectable and eminent official, speaking probably for a majority of his contemporaries, gave the following indictment in the wake of the failure of the 1044 reform: "[Shih Chieh] espoused strange and outlandish ideas, and possessed unorthodox and opaque ways of thinking."[61] He even bitterly made the accusation that Shih Chieh "went beyond the limit of standards, and misled students."[62] But, in the late eleventh century, thanks to the new way of looking at the 1044 reform, Shih Chieh's reputation was retrieved, and in 1089, he was lauded as "the good man of the Sage Dynasty" and his known descendents were found and "recruited [to serve in the government]."[63] All these factors paved the way for a positive interpretation of his involving University students

---

[59] Hsü Yü-feng, "Shih Chieh nien-p'u," in *Tse-shan pan-yüeh k'an*, Vol. 2, No. 20 (1942), 58–77.

[60] For Ho Ch'ün, see *SS*, 457:13435–13436. See also Wang Chien-ch'iu, *Sung-tai t'ai-hsüeh*, 150, 210 and 226.

[61] *HCP*, 158/4b–5a.

[62] *Ibid.*

[63] *HCP*, 436/6b–7a.

in political struggles.

In short, one has to bear in mind the special nature of Sung intellectuals' manner of conducting political debates or, for that matter, power struggles, to understand the incident which involved Shih Chieh and his students and which, by the time of Wang An-shih's reform, had become a respectable precedent that could encourage further and unabated participation of young students in the complicated and ruthless political arena. The overall sense of Sung national crisis provided a background that would justify University students' political activism.

The next time that University students involved themselves in political affairs occurred during Wang An-shih's reform. A professor of the University who was not happy with the reforms awarded an excellent grade to a student who, in an examination within the University, alluded unfavorably to Wang Mang's reforms in the first century A.D. This event greatly displeased the reformers who consequently demanded that all professors then teaching at the University be purged.[64] In retrospect, one can see that the incident was but a pretext used by the reformers to seize full control of the University which they viewed as an important center for the propagation of reform ideas in particular and their own political philosophy in general. The purge succeeded, but the struggle to control the University continued and went on in such a fierce manner that eventually it resulted in an even more severe scandal involving a number of prominent officials as well as the faculty of the University. This is the famous Yü Fan incident which I referred to in the previous section. In the twelfth month of 1077, Yü Fan wrote to the emperor complaining that University professors not only were negligent in teaching, but were also currying private favors in the examinations within the school. This complaint received a great deal of attention and resulted in the dismissal of more than fifteen officials directly and indirectly related to the scandal. The magnitude of its seriousness is reflected in the fact that professors were henceforth asked neither to meet with students on private occasions nor to socialize with each other, save for scholarly discussions.[65]

Other ideological struggles surrounding the content of the civil service examinations and the controversies over the new commentaries being prepared by reformers only added to the polarization or politicization of the University students who were constantly shoved around, and were at a great loss as to what constituted the sure way for a move into officialdom.[66]

[64]*HCP*, 228/6b—7a. See also my *San-lun*, 138—139.

[65]For a detailed discussion of this incident, see my *San-lun*, 145—148. See also notes 23 and 52 above.

[66]For a general discussion on classical education during the Northern Sung, see P'i Hsi-jui, *Ching-hsüeh li-shih*.

At the same time, lingering party struggles on all fronts only added fuel to their frustrations, and University students as a consequence became even more restless, resorting eventually to all-out attacks on any one they regarded as a bad element, creating malaise and courting foreign invasions. The attacks came during the last two years of the Northern Sung when it appeared to any sensible person that the Sung government was not going to be able to keep its grip on north China. The leader of the attacks, as mentioned above, was a University student called Ch'en Tung, but Yang Shih (1053—1135), then a professor in the University, was probably equally important in helping to shape the mood for open criticism.

Yang Shih was an outstanding student of Ch'eng I, the famous Neo-Confucian scholar who was deeply involved in the party struggles opposing Wang An-shih's reform.[67] Unfortunately for Yang Shih, the master-disciple relationship created suspicion among the reformers who, then still dominating the Imperial University, considered Yang's ideological stance unacceptable. Yang Shih made every effort, not without success, to keep a low profile by frequently visiting Buddhist temples or monasteries to show his distaste for political controversy. In the meantime, however, he managed to maintain some relationship with one of Ts'ai Ching's sons, in order to continue a degree of communication with the reform faction.[68] Unfortunatly again for Yang Shih, all of his careful designs did not hold things together; the situation within and without the capital had deteriorated to such an extent that even he could not contain the students. A total of ten memorials were drafted by Ch'en Tung and sent to Hui-tsung, Ch'in-tsung (r. 1126) and Kao-tsung between mid-1125 and mid-1127 to criticize, above all, the moral defects of the Court which they interpreted as the prime cause for the foreign invasion. In the process, Yang Shih secretly supported the University students, while at the same time keeping himself ostensibly clear of accusations or implications of his involvement in the students' recalcitrant criticism of the nation's affairs.

The behavoir of Yang Shih fell into exactly the same pattern as Shih Chieh's, except that the University students were now definitely more vociferous and blatant.[69] Their demands included the purging of six power-

---

[67]Ch'eng I had never come close to the core of the anti-reform faction, but was in general agreement with them in opposing Wang's policies. For his involvement in the reorganization of the University, see Ch. 4, section C.

[68]Anonymous author, *Ching-k'ang yao-lu* (Taipei: Wen-hai, 1967), 8:475—478. See also Wang Chien-ch'iu, *Sung-tai t'ai-hsüeh*, 249—250.

[69]For Yang Shih's involvement, see *HCPSP*, passim. My basis for arguing that Yang played an important role in instigating University student protests is based on his vehement opposition to reform ideas. He was appointed in 1125 to head the Directorate

ful officials in the Hui-tsung and Ch'in-tsung government, and later, the further purging of a couple of moderate officials advocating peaceful measures in dealing with the Jurchens; they also made forceful demands advocating stronger military operations against the invading enemy. At one point, as mentioned before, they were so powerful as to be capable of mobilizing tens of thousands of people to follow them in an appeal in front of the palace.[70] This was a rather trying moment for the nation's leaders, as the Jurchens were holding the capital in seige, and the activities of students only helped to deepen the crisis, widening the cleavage between the opposing cliques, long at each other's throats.

In the first month of 1126 the government for the first time issued an order forbidding the students of the capital schools to make political demands. Though it also saw to it that anti-reformers were restored of their reputations posthumously, the measures did not contain the students for long. They returned again and again throughout the last days of the Northern Sung government and indeed even after the government fled to the south. The first couple of years of the new government's rule were no less chaotic and confusing, riven with charges and plots, resulting from both the history of cliquish conflict and the loss of the northern Chinese territory. During the early months of the new regime, the University students found in a nationalistic and militant general, Li Kang (1083–1140), the embodiment

---

(and hence the University), arousing strong suspicion among the pro-reform students who physically attacked him. But his appointment, interestingly, was recommended by Wu Min who was then an object of anti-reform students' criticism. Moreover, Yang, apparently in order to cool down the heat among students, took pains to organize picnics at and visits to monasteries or temples. He then associated himself with Ts'ai Hsiu, the eldest son of Ts'ai Ching. All these conflicting actions can only be understood as indicative of some calculation on Yang's part and his association with University students was thus not as simple and straightforward as his compatriots, Ch'en Huan and Tsou Hao, who, openly claiming that they were followers of Yang, had earlier been exiled because of their support of University students. Hu Hung, in commenting on whether Tsou and Ch'en were Yang's students, made a rather intriguing observation that they could not be considered as his students, despite their admiration of Yang. Thus, one feels that there must be some rather significant information missing concerning Yang's role in the University in the final years of the Northern Sung. See Wang Chien-ch'iu, *Sung-tai t'ai-hsüeh*, 249–251; Chu Hsi, *I-Lo yüan-yüan lu*, Ming ed. (Taipei: Wen-hai, 1968), 10/9b–10b.

[70] The first comprehensive study of Ch'en Tung's activities is by Ch'e, Yi, a Sung author whose *Sung ta'i-hsüeh-sheng Ch'en Tung chin-chung lu* preserves a good deal of the primary sources. Wang Shih-han's *Han-men chui-hsüeh, Shang-hu i-chi* ed., compiled in the seventeenth century is a more recent and systematic collection of the relevant sources. I have relied almost exclusively on Wang Chien-ch'iu's *Sung-tai t'ai-hsüeh*, 264–289.

of their ideals and rallied behind him.[71] But Li Kang did not have the support of the civil bureaucracy, and his reputation therefore only created difficulties for him, although he might have also utilized the hopes that rested on him to move up in the Court. Under such circumstances, it is probably not far from truth to say that the students were not much more than pawns in the hands of scheming politicians; some of whom were glad to see that the more outspoken ones be removed from the scene. The situation must have been frightening for anyone seeking self-advancement. Eventually, a certain trend of rationalism, emphasizing moderation and civil bureaucratic control won the day, but even this was achieved with a heavy toll; a couple of the most adamant University students, including Ch'en Tung himself, lost their lives. At the suggestion of the powerful officials under attack, the newly enthroned emperor ordered the execution of these students, and Li Kang was temporarily removed from his post. This occurred in the seventh month of 1127.[72]

Thus, the tradition of political involvement on the part of Sung University students had by the mid-twelfth century became truly alarming, with young students now used as political pawns. Nonetheless, it appears that these students were not just innocent participants in a game they were not sufficiently experienced to play. To exploit their feelings could be equally risky, and as time went on, very few politicians could afford not to pay attention to students' demands. We have mentioned one story about Chia Ssu-tao's use of student-informers to spy on University students.[73] Ts'ai Ching reportedly would also make frequent visits to the University to eat *man-t'ou* (that is, to share regular meals) with them, in the hope that he would impress the University students that he had care and concern for them, by demonstrating that he too, could take simple food.[74]

Thus, one may safely say that University students were playing an increasingly important role in Sung politics, and that the role became even more visible as time went on. This situation did not escape the observation of keen writers. The most famous of them, Chou Mi (1232–1308), reported in the late thirteenth century that since the Ch'un-hsi era (1174–1189), nearly all the metropolitan prefects of the capital Lin-an who left in disgrace were causalities of University student complaints.[75] Amongst the prefects,

[71] On Li Kang, see note 40 above, and John W. Haeger, "1126–27: Political Crisis and the Integrity of Culture," in idem (ed.), *Crisis and Prosperity in Sung China*, 143–162.
[72] *CYYL*, 7/6a.
[73] See note 51 above.
[74] Chu Hsi, *Chu-tzu yü-lei*, 130/17a.
[75] Chou Mi, *Kuei-hsin tsa-chih*, pieh-chi, hsia.

the most famous probably was Chao Shih-i, who served as a metropolitan prefect when Han T'e-chou (1151–1202) was in power.[76] A scion of the powerful Han family, and an imperial relative by marriage, Han T'e-chou had contributed to the ascendance of Emperor Ning-tsung (r. 1195–1224) who rewarded him with so much power as to give him virtual control over the Court.[77] Among the number of incidents which involved Han T'e-chou, the most famous was his order banning the Neo-Confucian school of thinking, which was then growing in influence.[78] Han was a widower, but reportedly had fourteen mistresses. It happened that, in 1197, he was given four beautiful pearls, which he then gave to the four mistresses he was especially fond of, unwittingly causing jealousy among the other ten women. Chao Shih-i was able to learn of the incident and quickly borrowed enough money to purchase another ten pearls to give to the neglected ladies. Chao's promotion soon after this event was interpreted as a return of favor from Han T'e-chou and accordingly viewed with great contempt, especially by the University students.[79]

Nortorious for his sychophancy and scandalous relations with Han T'e-chou, Chao nevertheless managed to survive the purge after Han died in disgrace, and continued to be the metropolitan prefect of Lin-an until the students succeeded in getting rid of him finally in 1210.[80] The events surrounding Chao Shih-i show that student meddling in national politics had by this time escalated to a critical degree. As a result another prefect of Lin-an, Chao Yü-ch'ou, was forced to resort to expelling students not formally registered in the University (the yu-shih, "wandering scholars"). But his intimate relationship with Shih Sung-chih (d. 1256), then the most powerful minister, again caused him trouble and a few years after the fall of Shih (1252), Chao was also forced out by pressure from students.[81]

The case of the restoration of Shih Sung-chih to the position of prime minister provided another opportunity for University students to exercise their pressure.[82] A total of 144 students from the University, 67 students from the Military School, 94 students from the Metropolitan Prefectural School and 34 students from the School of Imperial Relatives took part

---

[76] Another incident involving Chao is mentioned in the previous section, note 49.

[77] See note 66 of Ch. 4.

[78] For a recent and excellent study of this event, see Conrad Schirokauer, "Neo-Confucians Under Attack: The Condemnation of Wei-hsüeh," in John W. Haeger (ed.), Crisis and Prosperity in Sung China, 163–198.

[79] Liu Shih-chü, Hsü Sung chung-hsing pien-nien Tzu-chih t'ung-chien, TSCC ed., 12:153–154.

[80] See note 75 above.

[81] Wang Chien-ch'iu, Sung-tai t'ai-hsüeh, 307–308.

[82] SS, 416:12484–12485, 425:12678; Chou Mi, Kuei-hsin tsa-chih, pieh-chi, hsia.

in petitioning against the appointment, on the ground that Shih did not properly observe the mourning period required for the death of his father.[83] The event shows that the University students were meddling in politics even at the highest level in the government. Their involvement occurred not only once. The decision by Emperor Ning-tsung to remove Chao Ju-yü (1140–1196), then immensely popular in and out of the government, also created uproar among University students. Although Han T'e-chou threatened to punish those who petitioned, the students remained adamant for quite a while.[84]

In general, University students could not actually affect the politics at the highest level; but their courage in addressing themselves to issues so highly sensitive was therefore a sign of their idealism. Indeed, we lack evidence about the people behind the students. It is conceivable that by the Southern Sung, the trend of events was already strong enough for students to play a positive, but equally risky, role in the nation's politics. Results of their interference, however, were not always positive or useful.[85]

Finally, traditional accounts never fail to mention the brave deeds of University students—accompanying the captured emperors to the enemy's Court, killing themselves rather than giving in to the enemy, raising money to pay for the futile release of captured emperors or memorializing emperors about military strategies, and the like.[86] Many of these deeds no doubt were idealistic, voluntary actions; without them, the meddling in politics might not receive such laudable recognition.

There is no need to describe all of the political activities in which University students were involved.[87] Naturally, as time went on, students must have done as much harm as good to normal political processes, and not everybody was sympathetic towards them. For example, Chou Mi, the important informant on the Imperial University whom we already mentioned before, was quite to the point when he accused the University students of succumbing to Chia Ssu-tao's bribery.[88] He also pointed out that the University students were less than attentive to the necessity of maintaining good "town versus gown" relations: "merchants in the city suffered all

[83] *SS*, 414:12425–12426.
[84] *SS*, 392:11988–11989, 474:13772–13773.
[85] Wang Chien-ch'iu, *Sung-tai t'ai-hsüeh*, 264–319.
[86] *Ibid.*, 350–378.
[87] The most comprehensive study of Sung University students' political activities remains Wang Chien-ch'iu's *Sung-tai t'ai-hsüeh*. See especially, 256–387. A comprehensive table listing the names of student leaders and their political activities is found on 378–387.
[88] Chou Mi, *Kuei-hsin tsa-chih*, cited from Sheng Lang-hsi, "Sung-tai chih t'ai-hsüeh chiao-yü," in *Min-to tsa-chih*, 7/3 (1927), 19.

kinds of damages [inflicted by the University students], and they had no authority to complain to," so he charged.[89] In general, nevertheless, we come to view students' political activism in a more or less favorable light, a perspective I find to come very close to that of the Neo-Confucian's. We indeed owe a lot of our understanding of Sung political history in general, and of the students' role in it in particular, to Neo-Confucian interpretations.

Let me now summarize the political activism of Sung University students by pointing out a few characteristics. First of all, most of the powerful prime ministers condemned by Neo-Confucians had during the Sung period come under fierce attacks by the students. They were Ts'ai Ching, Ch'in K'uai, Han T'e-chou, Shih Mi-yüan, Shih Sung-chih, Chia Ssu-tao and the less known Ting Ta-ch'üan. Their adversaries, such as the anti-reformers (in the case of Ts'ai Ching), Lü I-hao (1071—1139) and Yüeh Fei (in the case of Ch'in K'uei), Chao Ju-yü and a number of eminent Neo-Confucian thinkers (in the case of Han T'e-chou), Chen Te-hsiu (1178—1235) and Wei Liao-weng (1178—1237) (in the case of Shih Mi-yüan), Hsü Yüan-chieh (1194—1245) and Liu Han-pi (in the case of Shih Sung-chih),[90] Tung Huai, Liu Fu (1217—1276) and Ch'en I-chung (in the case of Ting Ta-ch'üan) and so on, on the other hand, earned historical reputation as good officials and during their life time, had had the support of the University students.

Secondly, except for the isolated incident in 1126 when University students mobilized tens of thousands of commoners to take part in their demonstration against the powerful high officials, the activities in the capital schools had very little, if any, involvement at local levels. There was neither experience in, nor a mechanism for organizing the masses in national politics. But even so, the government dealt with political activism with the greatest care and suspicion, and its impact was quite impressive.

Thirdy, there was clearly a very strong Neo-Confucian dimension in the rhetoric and practice of student activism. Many students shared the ideo-logical convictions of Neo-Confucians. There is no question that Neo-Confuciansim was on the rise; but in its growth, while groping for forms to consolidate its influence, it certainly found in the activities of the students an excellent forum for its propagation; after all, the mainbody of Neo-Confucian concepts consisted of mostly philosophical statements, and Neo-Confucian thinkers were only barely starting to seek ways of practicing them. Shih Chieh and Yang Shih were prominent examples; they were out-siders. By the Southern Sung, a large number of civil bureaucrats must

---

[89] *Ibid.*
[90] Shih had fared less badly than his uncle Mi-yüan, but somehow because of this relationship, the University students persistently opposed his prime ministership.

have become increasingly sympathetic to the Neo-Confucian cause, and were willing to sponsor its experimentation, but Neo-Confucianism was still far removed from becoming the dominant ideological force. Its anti-reform background and its political philosophy bestowed upon Neo-Confucians a characteristically critical role, and in that peculiar role, the Neo-Confucians had to struggle for greater attention from the government by acting as morally and conscientiously independent critics, representing intellectuals at large. This paradoxical position was indeed difficult to maintain and due to their success in mobilizing University students, Neo-Confucians were able to accomplish their political mission. After all, University students were not bureaucrats, but their influence had grown so disproportionately enormous, that it became possible for the rhetoric to supersede the action, and for outsiders to overwhelm the insiders. In short, there were, in the writings of contemporaries and later historians, close relations in terms of political beliefs between the students and the Neo-Confucians seeking to magnify their political and intellectual influence.[91]

One final point is that the students' political activities partook of the most important feature of any student movement in world history in that students were themselves ultimately victims of their involvements. I have already made this point in the beginning of this section and wish to point out that one of the main reasons that these students generally won the sympathy of their contemporaries was precisely because self advancement figured very little in their search for involvement. Except probably for one occasion, that of Liu Fu who memorialized Emperor Li-tsung, criticizing a couple of the latter's favorite officials, resulting in his appointment to office,[92] most University students who meddled in Court politics, ended up being reprimanded, jailed, exiled or put to death.[93] It is perhaps here that we see the fundamental reason for the glorious recognition which their activism eventually acquired.

---

[91] A very detailed discussion on the struggle for acceptance and indeed dominance of Neo-Confucianism is found in Anonymous author, *Ch'ing-yüan tang-chin*, *SKCS* ed.

[92] *SS*, 405:12242–12249.

[93] For a useful, if less detailed discussion on the issues covered here, see Miyazaki Ichisada, "Sōdai no daigakusei seikatsu," 386–394.

Part III
The Nature and Significance of the Examinations for Sung Education

The purpose of Sung official education was to prepare an adequate number of people to serve in the government. The development of this government education, however, was significantly shaped by repeated attempts to coordinate it with the civil service examinations.

It is generally agreed that the Sung, and especially the Northern Sung, underwent some important changes including the rise in importance of civil bureaucrats, many of whom were successful candidates from the civil service examinations. Following the decline of traditional aristocratic families during the eighth and ninth centuries,[1] warlords and wealthy mercenary generals dominated tenth-century China.[2] But by the eleventh century, China started to see the emergence of *tu-shu jen* who now overshadowed the soldiers of fortune.[3] This change, among others, marked one of the most significant developments of late medieval Chinese history and had a tremendous impact on China's educational ideals and institutions. Of course, some policies adopted by early Sung rulers helped to strengthen the impact. The most conspicuous one was T'ai-tsu's decision to bring down the influence of military men;[4] subsequent measures taken by T'ai-tsung and, especially, Chen-tsung also contributed to enhance the esteemed position of civil service examination degree-holders.[5] In addition, because of the increase in the educated population seeking advancement into officialdom, the civil service examination system became an institution larger than a simple mechanism for producing useful officials to serve the monarch. It took on a social dimension which inevitably encroached on

---

[1] Denis Twitchett, "The Composition of the T'ang Ruling Class." See also note 6 for more information. In using the term, "family," I have by and large followed the traditional Chinese practice to include, conveniently, all members of one kinship group definable by genealogical ties. The cohesiveness and strength of identity were often dependent of how powerful the "family" was.

[2] Thomas H. C. Lee, "Quota system."

[3] Sun Kuo-tung, "T'ang Sung chih-chi she-hui men-ti chih hsiao-jung" ("Men-ti hsiao-jung" hereafter), in his *T'ang Sung shih lun-ts'ung* (Hong Kong: Lung-men, 1980), 201–308.

[4] The policy adopted by T'ai-tsu to reduce the power of military generals in the Court was accompanied by his another decision to station the best troops in the capital area. These measures, according to the interpretation of Chiang Fu-ts'ung, created a situation in which military men were constantly thrown into fierce competition for imperial favor, while civil officials received persistent protection for their activities. See his "Sung-tai i-ko kuo-ts'e te chien-t'ao," in his *Sung-shih hsin-t'an* (Taipei: Cheng-chung, 1970), 1–52.

[5] Beginning with T'ai-tsung's reign, the number of successful candidates from the examinations was suddenly increased by six times. For more information about this see my "Quota System." See also note 37 of Ch. 6.

the development of education. Thus, while the government continued to see to it that schools were built, the civil service examinations were relied upon to such an unprecedented extent as to undermine the effectiveness of official education. It is therefore necessary to study the system thoroughly, considering its social and political nature in order to understand the achievement and problems of Sung education.

CHAPTER 8

The Social Significance: Impartiality, Equality and Social Mobility

The most obvious goal of the civil service examination system unfortunately overlapped with that of education in state schools: both sought to provide the government with sufficiently prepared personnel for service. The history of the civil service examination system since its inception in the late sixth century shows that the system was designed with a specifically defined purpose: it was to be used to curtail the influence of the hereditary aristocratic families.[6] But with the increase in the number of degreed civil bureaucrats, the system quickly became a center of controversy. One hardly needs to be remined of the series of factional struggles between the descendents of noble families and the newly risen degree-holders in mid-T'ang.[7] The picture in the late tenth century was, however, different from that of the mid-T'ang, in that the collapse of the T'ang order had created opportunities for professional bandits and their official counterparts to rise in the arena of nation's power struggle. Sheer use of force became the mark of the north China plain. Tenth-century China was thus characterized by the dominance of military men abusing their power for personal profiteering. A civil service examination degree was almost meaningless in such an environment, unless the degree-holder was able to find a strong man to protect him. As a whole, the period was a rapidly changing one, with the phenomenal rise of powerful

---

[6] See Twitchett's article cited in note 1. See also David Johnson, *The Medieval Chinese Oligarchy.* It is necessary to point out here that the examination system was perhaps employed to combat the aristocratic dominance of the medieval Chinese government, but the decline of the traditional aristocratic families was not merely a result of the rise of the examination system. See Ch. 1, section C and Ch. 6, section A.

[7] This statement is based on the classicial study by Ch'en Yin-k'o in his *T'ang-tai cheng-chih shih shu-lun kao* (Hong Kong: Chung-hua, 1974). It is now being challenged by David Johnson, who points out that statistically commoners rising through the examinations seldom reached high posts traditionally occupied by aristocrats, and therefore did not actually become a challenge to the latter's power. See his *Medieval Chinese Oligarchy,* 121–137. While admitting that new people did not actually over-whelm the traditional nobles, I do think that they were vociferous enough to leave their mark in historical records. In other words, they struggled fiercely, though success only came after the dynastic demise.

generals accumulating tremendous wealth only to be destroyed in one or two generations. I shall give just a couple of examples: Sang Wei-han (d. 946), who happened to have risen to officialdom by acquiring a *chin-shih* degree, was able to accumulate an impressive fortune. Yet his wealth did not even pass to his son. Instead, his property was forcibly taken over by Chang Yen-tse, a military adventurer who, in turn, lost it to the Khitans.[8] Another case is Li Ssu-chao (d. 922), the adopted son of Li K'o-jou who was the brother of the late T'ang dynasty (923–936) founder. Li's wife, nee Yang, was an exceptionally enterprising woman who built up a family fortune, apparently by using the influence of her husband, a military man. But the wealth and achievement did not last. Li's seven sons vied fiercely with one another over the property, and the struggle which ensued ultimately claimed the lives of six of the brothers. The last son inherited the fortune, only to see the energy of the family dwindle and its fame disintegrate in just another generation.[9] This unstable situation provided enough incentive for the ultimate victor to be immediately suspicious of even his closest military subordinates. He took steps to reduce their power and systematically retired them, so that a new power configuration could take shape. The examination system answered to the needs of such a policy.[10] In the first place, the abuse of power by military men was curbed; this was done in the first few years of the dynasty by abolishing the feudalistic *fan-chen* system. The result was the quick decline of professional soldiers in the government and in society at large.[11] Since traditional hereditary families of national prominence had all but disappeared, it then seemed only natural for the government to rely on another method for the recruitment of qualified people for service. Thus, the civil service examinations as a recruiting mechanism were enthusiastically adopted, or rather, revived. In this chapter, I shall discuss the three important issues related to the examination system as a reliable social institution and how this social institution affected Sung society in such matters as mobility and the emergence of an elite social class.

[8] Hsüeh Chü-cheng, *Chiu Wu-tai shih* (Peking: Chung-hua, 1976), 89:1161–1169.
[9] *Ibid.*, 52:701–708.
[10] See my "Quota System."
[11] A statistical study shows that, from 889 to 997, as many as 32.4% of prominent people were of military background. This is in drastic contrast to the previous period from 756 to 888 when the same group made up only 9% of the elite officials, and to the following period from 998 to 1126 when the military accounted only for 8.7%. See Sun Kuo-tung's "Men-ti hsiao-jung." See also Table 11, which is adapted from Sun's original tables.

A. Impartial Recruitment

There were as many advantages in the employment of the examination method as there were defects. First of all, the examination system had a distinct strength as a political and social institution.[12] It seemingly embodied the very ideal of social justice. The Sung government adopted and invented a number of measures to safeguard impartiality in the examinations, and we know that these measures helped to enhance the respectability of the institution. Secondly, the examination system was regarded as also an embodiment of the ancient ideal of meritocratic government. One may even argue that the institution derived more respectability from its being a realization of an ancient ideal than from its being capable of safeguarding impartial selection. In reality, these two are the same, except that Confucian thinkers had always insisted on defining the ideal of meritocracy in terms of selecting the morally qualified candidate. Without going into this fine distinction between a great tradition and a meritocratic principle, I shall only take up the question as to whether the system did operate as a truly impartial institution.

There was no doubt in the mind of Sung policy-makers that the examination system should play a larger role than serving merely as an impartial institution for recruiting qualified candidates for office. But it was clear to them that the system relied heavily on its impartiality for success. The government adopted various measures to insure that the system was respectable. But abuse and corruption were also abundant, as students of the Sung have shown.[13] It is therefore important to discover how Sung people in general viewed the institution itself. First of all, for contemporaries, the problem of the system lay not in its lack of impartiality; instead, it lay somewhere else: the system could not be reasonably relied on for the recruitment of morally upright candidates. Indeed, at least during the early years of the dynasty, there was little concern over whether the system was doing enough to maintain fairness. Chao I, writing in the eighteenth century, concluded that the measures taken to prevent abuses were very relaxed, as compared to those employed during the Ming and Ch'ing.[14] In other words, most people felt that the system as such was to be trusted as basically impartial and was adequate to achieve some kind of social justice. To illustrate this, I would like to cite Hsia Sung's comment:[15]

---

[12] See later.
[13] For the measures adopted, see my *San-lun,* 39. See also Ch. 6, sections D and E.
[14] Chao I, *Nien-erh shih cha-chi,* 25:337–338.
[15] Hsia Sung, *Wen-chuang chi,* 15/6a–8a.

The examination on the *chin-shih* subject was established in the Sui, and was given special stress during the T'ang. Each year, not more than thirty successful candidates passed the examinations. They believed that the most useful officials and the ablest generals and ministers were all recruited through this channel. I believe that this is true. However, even though officials administered the examinations very carefully, they could not prevent sneaky tricks and the influence of powerful politicians. This resulted in much controversy. If we want to promote those who are poor, and we are right in doing so, then we will be blamed [by powerful politicians for not giving them special favors]. On the other hand, if we want rather to recruit only the wealthy and the powerful, then we will not be blamed, but then we are not right to do so. . . .

For Hsia Sung, who was persistently suspicious that the T'ang administration of the examination system catered too much to the "wealthy and the powerful," the system nevertheless should be trusted as being capable of redressing social injustice in the form of providing an opportunity for the poor to move up. To him, it must have been the impartial quality that made it possible to achieve its goal. Hsia's belief was also essentially what Sung people regarded as the rationale for the examinations. They appeared to believe that the impartial outlook was adequate, because it could create a just distribution of opportunities among the candidates. For the government, which administered the examinations, however, the system also had to achieve other, and perhaps greater, goals. The system had to respond to requests for social, geographical and above all, moral justice.

It is necessary to stop here to ponder the very idea of impartiality and how it was related to social justice. There is evidently a clear distinction between "impartiality" and "justice." Impartiality is merely a means toward establishing justice, which is more complicated and has to be placed in proper social, political or economical context, depending on its overall concern.[16] Modern interpreters of the traditional Chinese examination system appear not to have been sanguine about this distinction. They usually consider the rate of social mobility generated by the examinations as the most reliable criterion for assessing the system. For them, open competition for entrance to service was by and large fulfilled during late imperial China.[17]

---

[16] In other words, one may say that "impartiality" is only a procedural or formal justice, and is different from substative justice. That this type of justice (defined by John Rawls as "justice as regularity" in his *A Theory of Justice* [Cambridge: Harvard University Press, 1971], 235) cannot be automatically regarded as substantive justice needs no explanation.

[17] The most famous interpreter is of course Ping-ti Ho. It is to be cautioned that Ho never tried in his book to relate "justice" to "equal opportunity." But the implication is there. Francis Hsu, an anthropologist, approaching the same issue with another methodology, arrived at the same conclusion. See his "Social Mobility in China," in

The problems in such interpretations are two fold. First, openness within the system, which created equal possibilities for all candidates, is not similar to openness in society at large. A just social institution must be open to society as a whole. Second, it is misleading to say that people in the Sung ever felt it necessary to design an examination system which would achieve the ideal of an open society as we understand it today. What, then, did Sung people mean by the impartial nature of the system? What did the policy-makers aim at?

Obviously, the Sung people must have believed that the examination system should satisfy a larger goal than maintaining an impartial or open competition. Shen Kou (1028–1067) articulated this belief:[18]

> [The present system of the examination] in fact is not the ancient way of a government's recruiting able men and making them officials. The reason why this is so is because the people who first proposed this system concentrated only on laying down detailed regulations, trying merely to satisfy their contemporaries. They therefore did not know what the "great fairness" (ta-kung) in the world is, and ignored the fundamentals of governing a state.

For Shen Kou, the examination system ought to be designed to achieve a "great fairness." He dismissed technical impartiality as inadequate. Similarly, Su Sung (1020–1101) made this observation in 1069: "Anonymity and recopying measures were originally intended to insure ultimate impartiality (chih-kung), but to suspect the candidates is actually not the way to accomplish it."[19] Su Sung even proposed that candidates be required to submit a piece of their own writing to examiners before they took the examinations. This was a practice widely used in the T'ang and had only been abolished as recently as 1043.[20]

One part of their concern about the "fairness," or impartiality, was seen in the chronic debates over how quotas should be assigned. The famous quarrel between Ssu-ma Kuang and Ou-yang Hsiu, already noted by various scholars, immediately comes to mind. The discussion there, including the practice of the quota system, leaves us the impression that the government had a desire to strike some kind of regional balance, at the obvious expense of guaranteeing an absolutely fair opportunity to individual candi-

---

American Sociological Review, XIV (1949), 764–771. See Johanna M. Menzel (ed.), *The Chinese Civil Service* (Lexington, Mass.: D. C. Heath and Co., 1963).

[18] Shen Kou, *Hsi-hsi chi*, in *Shen-shih san hsien-sheng chi*, *SPTK* ed. (1936), 2(7)/67b–69a.

[19] Su Sung, *Su Wei-kung wen-chi*, 1831 lithographic ed., 15/6a–8a.

[20] See *HCP*, 133/3a. See also an interesting account of this so-called "kung-chüan" system in Arthur Waley, *The Life and Times of Po Chü-i*, 18–19, 23.

dates. The significance of the quota system has never been carefully studied before. It is therefore necessary to remind readers of the pioneer work of Kracke, who proposed a highly respectable interpretation of the quota system.[21] For him, the quota system was devised so that it could respond to different political needs of the government; among these needs, regional balance in terms of the production of successful candidates from the examinations was among the foremost.

The quota system had evidently been set up to fulfill a greater political purpose than that of technical impartiality. Regional power realignment was no doubt in the minds of early policy-makers. Gradually the examinations became more competitive for candidates from the lower Yangtze valley and the southeast coast which were then the most developed regions in the nation.[22] The purpose of this geographical consideration therefore was more than maintaining some degree of impartiality, but was related to what Sung policy-makers thought of as political and, possibly, social justice. The impact was enormous. The quota system created a situation in that candidates from the same prefecture were made to compete among themselves. By the end of the Southern Sung, quotas were even assigned on subprefectural (county) level. This is to say that candidates were competing in prefectural tests with other candidates from the same county. The result was, of course, for some prominent families to become interested in manipulating the results of the local examinations. Two things can be discussed in connection with this hypothetical development.

First, the tenth-century society, in which military power and exploitation were the surest guarantees to wealth and social prominence, had quickly made way for a more or less civil society, in which successful candidates were awarded the best opportunities for honor and privilege. As a result, many people started to send their sons to take the examinations. This

---

[21] Edward A. Kracke, Jr., "Region, Family and Individual in the Chinese Examination System," in John K. Fairbank (ed.), *Chinese Thought and Institutions* (Chicago: University of Chicago Press, 1957), 251–268.

[22] A few words must be said concerning what I mean by "regions" here. I have found G. William Skinner's scheme very useful, and have by and large adopted it here. It is nevertheless necessary also to point to the fact that Skinner's definition of "regions," which are based on nineteenth-century material and defined according to functional criteria, is not necessarily correct for the Sung period. I have thus modified his scheme by defining the lower Yangtze valley region to include the tributory area of the Huai River and the Grand Canal which was during the Sung times a major economic and transportation link, making present Ho-nan (including K'ai-feng) a part of the lower Yangtze region. For Skinner's definition, see his "Rural Urbanization in Nineteenth-Century China," in his (ed.), *The City in Late Imperial China* (Stanford: Stanford University Press, 1977), 211–249.

development was accompanied by the decline of the aristocrats and nationally prominent clans. In the early Sung, many wealthy or powerful clans were systematically destroyed by the government; it was common for them to become dispersed after their branches moved away from the native town. One example illustrates the fate of a big family in the tenth and eleventh centuries. The Ma branch of Lin-tzu (of present Shan-tung) rose in prominence by engaging in commercial activities during the late Five Dynasties period. It produced as many as twenty *chin-shih* degree-holders in the 970s. What is intriguing is that in Pei-hai (present Wei-hsien, Shan-tung), a town not more than fifty miles from Lin-tzu, there was also a Ma family. According to a meticulous study by Otagi Hajime, the Ma's of Lin-tzu were related genealogically to the Pei-hai Ma's.[23] However, it appears to us that very little communication occurred between these two branches. This situation would be completely unimaginable in the eighth or even ninth century.[24] The power and influence of kinship organizations was thus severely reduced and localized. At the same time, new conceptions of kinship organization started to emerge, centered in the activities of corporated lineages; to assert the influence of a lineage, it became increasingly clear that a degree in the examinations was important. With the county now becoming an arena for competition, locally powerful families quickly organized themselves into lineages with corporate properties so as to manipulate that competition.

Secondly, the history of Sung local administration seems to suggest that subprefectural seats were where the direct central power ceased to extend, and where local prominent families took over the continum of the exercise of central authority. The subprefectural seat, as a result, became only one of the several economic centers in the area, and urban development made it impossible for government officials to be as involved directly in local affairs as before. In G. William Skinner's words.[25]

> My point is that this area (county), which was by no means limited to commercial matters, grew increasingly restricted in subsequent dynastic eras. That is, I see a long-term secular trend beginning in the T'ang whereby the degree of official involvement in local affairs—not only in marketing and commerce but also in social regulation (e.g., dispute resolution) and administration itself—steadily declined, a retrenchment forced by the growing scale of empire.

This development created a possibility for locally prominent lineages to exercise their economic and social influence within the counties where

---

[23] Otagi Hajime, "Godai Sō jō no shinkō kanryō," in *Shirin*, Vol. 57, No. 4 (1974), 57–96.

[24] Thomas H. C. Lee, "Quota System."

[25] G. William Skinner, *The City in Late Imperial China*, 25.

they resided, effecting a certain degree of political control.

The two phenomena developed side by side to provide a context within which a new social and economic "class" started to emerge.[26] During the Southern Sung, because the government awarded special privileges to all candidates passing the prefectural (primary) examinations, it was natural for prominent local families to seek to monopolize at least this chance of tax and/or labor exemption.[27] It was they who organized requests for more generous quotas. But they also sought to monopolize the chances for upward social mobility in their own districts. The result was the steady increase of their dominance over community affairs. By the same token, we also see that they were seeking to perpetuate their power over a series of generations.[28] The development in later dynasties bore witness to this trend.

It is thus useful to reiterate the obvious political overtone of the quota system. There is no doubt that respectability in the sense of technical impartially had been only a minor factor in the decision to use the examinations as the most trusted method to recruit people for service. The method was meant to fulfill some greater purposes: in the case of the quota system, one sees geo-political considerations behind the design of the mechanism. The result, coupled with the development in Sung local administration, was to stimulate the rise of a new socioeconomic "class" whose power base was confined in the counties, but whose influence within those areas became increasingly important. They took up the government's authority at the

---

[26]Wealth continued to play a very important role in deciding the social status of a local elite, but it was also becoming evident that a degree from the civil service examinations was the most effective means to keep wealth, especially to keep it over generations. For the importance of wealth, see Brian E. McKnight, *Village and Bureaucracy in Southern Sung China*, 178–185.

[27]Special privileges were given to the *te-chieh jen* during the Southern Sung. Information can be found in *SHY*, sh, 12/8a, 14/27ab, 30a–31b, 64/3b, 160/3b–4b. See also McKnight, *Village and Bureaucracy in Southern Sung China*, 106–107. A detailed discussion of this issue is in Ch. 6, section D.

[28]See this quotation from Aoyama Sadao:

"In the Sung period, passing the state examinations, especially the *chin-shih* examinations, meant a great deal for the purpose of bringing a family to prosperity; for once a man rose to a fairly good post, his descendents, even his family members in a broader sense, could easily become officials by means of the appointment on account of ancestors or others. If we count in collateral lines, the family status would quite often extend for more than two generations. A study of the successful examinees from Fu-chou will show that such men reached about 50%; and . . . it seems that their family status even more often lasted much longer. . . ."

Aoyama Sadao, "The Newly-Risen Bureaucrats in Fukien at the Five-Dynasty-Sung Period," in *Memoire of the Research Department of the Tōyō Bunko*, 21 (1962), 1–48.

point where it started to dissipate and were responsible for social, economic and political control in their own counties. The question of impartiality as past and present interpreters of the examination system saw it thus conceals much greater political consideration, which, if left unnoticed, could lead to misunderstanding the whole spectrum of the significance of the examination system.

B. Social Mobility

Social mobility is a modern concept and carries implications not necessarily accepted in the past. It is very easy to equate impartiality with equal opportunity and, thus, with potential for high social mobility. Many studies of traditional Chinese examinations have used the concept of social mobility to evaluate the success of the examinations as a social institution. However, it seems self-evident that creating a high degree of social mobility was never a primary concern of the Sung government.

The apparent high degree of possibility for examination candidates of poor background to succeed does not mean that the institution had the effect of creating a high rate of general social mobility. Whether there was much mobility in Sung society as a whole, vertical and horizontal, is entirely a different issue.[29] Since the Sung government had so few positions, the rewards the examinations extended to the commoners were nelgligible and affected only an extremely small range of people.[30]

It is impossible to deny that the examination system was open to virtually all people aspiring after a position in officialdom. It was a great virtue to make the competition open, since the social and financial significance of entrance to officialdom was so tremendous. There is, therefore, the argument that by keeping the competition open and impartial, the examination was safeguarding the ideal of "equal opportunity." In simplistic socio-

[29]I have profited from discussing this point with Professor Shiba Yoshinobu who, citing G. William Skinner, points out to me that the current state of scholarship supports the argument that there was a high degree of social mobility in late Imperial China, possibly including the Sung, and that commercial and other occupational activities were mainly responsible for precipitating the mobility. See G. William Skinner, "Mobility Strategies in Late Imperial China: A Regional Systems Analysis," in Carol A. Smith (ed.), *Regional Analysis* (New York: Academic Press, 1976), Vol. 1, 327–364. See also note 68.

[30]John Chaffee, in his Ph.D. thesis, estimates that about 3.2% of Sung adult males were involved in an average prefectural examination. The estimate is based on the assumption that male adults made up 20% of Sung population. This would mean that in a typical prefectural test, about 0.64% of the Sung population were sitting in the examination halls. See Chaffee, "Education and Examination in Sung Society," 61.

logical terms, this meant guaranteeing a degree of social justice.[31] It appears, however, that the system was kept open because of two main reasons. First, especially in the early years of the Sung, the government under Emperor Chen-tsung had used the examination system to redress the social injustices which afflicted the poor. I have, however, pointed out that this act of Chen-tsung was essentially calculated to cut down the influence of military men and hereditary high officials who still dominated his Court. The appearance of social justice was designed to achieve a political purpose.[32] Secondly, by the mid-eleventh century the institution had become a major political and social institution affecting a large number of qualified scholars seeking positions in the government which otherwise would be almost completely denied to them. The government had to act responsibly by safeguarding the institution's openness or impartiality. It is obvious that any government would have at least the sense of protecting the accountability of an institution as important as the civil service examinations by maintaining its essential incorruptibility.

Accountability and calculated political goals, nonetheless, do not amount to safeguarding the ideal of social justice.[33] Therefore, even if we define social justice as equal opportunity, a definition already subject to scrutiny, the civil service examination system could hardly qualify as a system that

---

[31] It is difficult to deny that ever since Pitrim Sorokin formulated the concept of social mobility, the concensus among sociologists has been that a high rate of social mobility is one denominator of "modernity" (one that was accepted by Ping-ti Ho in his article: "Aspects of Social Mobility in Imperial China," in *Comparative Studies in Society and History*, Vol. 1 [1959], 330–359), with modernity defined as "openness," or for that matter, "equal opportunity." Indeed, "social mobility and social equality should not be kept as separate discussions" (S. M. Miller and P. Roby, "Strategies for Social Mobility: A Policy Framework," in *American Sociologist*, Vol. 6 [1971], 22). A study of the mobility phenomenon, in the hope of deciding whether a certain social institution was created or managed under a sound policy, inevitably leads to debates as to the definition of social justice. As already mentioned in note 16, for the purpose of this book, I have adopted the most usually accepted definition of "justice" as "equality" in the sense of "equal opportunity" for social rewards. It is defined as a substantive justice, not a formal justice which Aristotle called "impartiality." See Felix E. Oppenheim, "Equality: The Concept of Equality," in *The International Encyclopedia of Social Sciences* (New York: MacMillan & The Free Press, 1968). See also Frederick A. Olafson, "Introduction," in his *Justice and Social Policy* (Englewood Cliffs, N. J.: Prentice-Hall, 1961), vi–viii. See note 15 of Ch. 1.

[32] See note 4 above.

[33] I may be accused of anachronism by using a *non-Chinese* concept of "justice" to explain the examination system. It indeed is interesting to see that neither of the two most important anthologies of Chinese philosophy and thought, namely, Wm. Theodore de Bary (ed.), *Sources of Chinese Tradition* and Wing-tsit Chan (ed.), *A Source Book in Chinese Philosophy*, has an entry for "justice" in their indices.

was designed to achieve it. First, the examination system with its tremendous potential for shaping the practice of education often became an instrument for ideological purification and control rather than for equality of opportunities; second, the high turnover rate within the bureaucracy served to enhance the control of the monarch over it; and, third, the institution, by awarding a great portion of wealth and social prestige to a handful of successful candidates, in effect, could not uphold the very essence of what we today would justly call as "fair."[34]

Having said this much negatively about the examination system, let me now examine the following two issues concerning social mobility in the most commonly accepted sense. First, were new people being recruited into officialdom *en masse*? Secondly, if so, then what were the social and political consequences of this phenomenon? There have been some statistical studies on the issue of social mobility during the Sung, caused either by the examinations or by other social factors.[35] A study of the family backgrounds of prominent officials from the mid-eighth century to the end of the Northern Sung, by Sun Kuo-tung (see Table 11), shows that there was a steady rise in the number of prominent officials who rose through the channel of the civil service examinations. By the eleventh century, nearly 40% of prominent officials were degree-holders of poor family background (see note *f* of Table 11). In other words, people coming from non-distinguished families but holding degrees made up more than one third of the prominent officials in early Sung. Sun's article clearly documents the change in this aspect over nearly four centuries of Chinese history.

A second study is by Ch'en I-yen, who made a statistical analysis of the family background of 1,953 Northern Sung people who had biographies in the standard *Sung History* (*Sung-shih*). Ch'en concluded that more than 55% of them came from families without previous service records. Taken as such, this would be quite remarkable. Ch'en's conclusion, however, was based on an assumption that any one who failed to have the names of his immediate ancestors recorded in his official biography came *ipso facto* from a non-official family. This interpretation has a certain degree of danger. After some recalculation, I found that even if we exclude from our totals those people whose biographies do not have information on their immediate

---

[34]I have used "fairness" in the most usual sense, fully aware of the definition based on "social contract" theories adopted by John Rawls, in his famous *A Theory of Justice,* which would make the examination system look very malicious.

[35]Sun Kuo-tung, "Men-ti hsiao-jung"; Ch'en I-yen, "Ts'ung pu-i ju-shih, lun Pei-Sung pu-i chieh-ts'eng te she-hui liu-tung," in *Ssu yü yen,* Vol. 9, No. 4 (1972), 244– 253; Edward A. Kracke, Jr., "Family vs. Merit in Chinese Civil Service Examinations Under the Empire," in *HJAS,* Vol. 10 (1947), 103–123.

TABLE 11

Family Background of Prominent Chinese Officials, 756–1126

Categories	Periods									
	A:756–888		B:889–906		C:907–959		D:960–997		E:998–1126	
Big clans or high officials	464	69.0%	28	60.9%	101	21.0%	123	32.8%	156	19.0%
Lowly ranked officials or locally powerful families	100	14.9%	9	19.6%	127	26.3%^{a}	91	24.3%^{c}	252	30.8%^{e}
Poor families	90	13.4%	7	15.2%	239	49.6%^{b}	156	41.6%^{d}	387	47.3%^{f}
Unknown	18	2.7%	2	4.3%	15	3.1%	5	1.3%	24	2.9%

Explanations: Based on Sun Kuo-tung, "Men-ti hsiao-jung," 279, 283. Note that the figure 98 for the "han-tsu" category ("Poor families" in this table) for period 756–906 in Sun's table (1) on p. 279 should be 97.

a. Of the 127 people belonging to this category, 46 rose through military channels, to make up 9.5% of the total prominent officials. This is in contrast to the 2.5% of the previous periods A and B (756–906).

b. Among them, 145 rose through military channels, making up 30.1%, in contrast to the previous 7.1% during periods A and B (756–906).

c. Among the 91, 16 rose through military channels, making up 4.3% of the total number of prominent officials.

d. Among the 156 , 78 rose through military channels, making up 20.8% of the total prominent officials.

e. 33 out of the 252 rose through military channels, making up 4.0% of the total number of prominent officials.

f. Only 37 of the 387 rose through military channels, accounting for 4.5% of the total number of prominent officials; this is in stark contrast to the 20.8% of the previous period and in even stronger contrast to the 39.9% of people who rose through taking the civil service examinations in the same period.

forebears, a total of 32.5% of Northern Sung people who have biographies in the *Sung History* still came from non-official families. This figure is smaller than Sun Kuo-tung's, because they are of a different nature, but both serve to pin-point the high percentage of prominent Sung people of commoner origin.

A third study is provided by the late Edward A. Kracke. Kracke found that 57.3% of successful candidates from two examinations (1148 and 1256) during the Southern Sung came from commoner families without forebears in government service. This percentage was even higher than for the Northern Sung. Although the trend in Sung bureaucracy was a steady erosion in the percentage of degree-holders occupying the entire bureaucratic work-force, the number of them coming from non-official backgrounds seems to have been steadily increasing.

In short, the three studies now available to us all indicate that there was a steady increase in the percentage of prominent people (notably, officials) who came from families claiming no service records for their fathers, grandfathers and great-grandfathers in the examinations, as well as an increase in the percentage of those who were successful candidates from the civil service examinations. This brings me back to my earlier contention that there was indeed a high rate of turn-over within officialdom. But this could hardly be interpreted as a high rate of social mobility. To begin with, since the system recruited so few people, there were plenty of commoners from non-official backgrounds to be recruited from.[36] Secondly, and more importantly, we hardly know anything about downward mobility. I previously pointed out that there was a tendency during the Sung for locally powerful families to seek perpetuation of their power over generations. In other words, downward social mobility was becoming unlikely for these families. There are a few examples to illustrate this point (see Appendix F): many elite families (lineages) in the Sung were able to maintain their prominence for about five generations on the average. In other words, many of them were able to produce at least one degree-holder in every generation for five consecutive generations. We shall find that they were in no way comparable to their Ming and Ch'ing counterparts which, according to Ping-ti Ho, generally lasted for eight generations, which, according to him, was not a remarkable feat.[37] However, since my records are based on an extremely selective group of materials (see explanation accompanying the genealogical charts), I believe that it was rather remarkable for a family to be able to continue to prosper for such a long time.[38] The conclusion from

[36] See note 30 above.
[37] Ping-ti Ho, *The Ladder*, 166.
[38] If we possessed as complete a record as that used by Hilary J. Beattie, we might

these two points is that while the examination system did recruit in large
numbers from the commoners, it did not successfully prevent powerful
local families from maintaining their prominence by producing officials
over long periods of time. How they managed to do this is a separate issue.[39]

I have repeatedly suggested that political factors were always the central
influence in the practice of the examinations. I shall demonstrate this point
by referring to some of the prominent families. The Ssu-ma's acquired its
prominence in Kuang's time. The fortune of this family lasted for a couple
of generations, but because of Kuang's heavy involvement in the party
struggles of the late eleventh century, his son, K'ang, was never able to
move up to true prominence. The family disappeared from the political
scene in another two generations, obviously because of unfavorable political
fortune. Similary, the Sung Ch'i branch of the Sung family from K'ai-feng
had less success than the Sung Hsiang branch, despite the fact that Ch'i
achieved a higher office than Hsiang. The reason was because Pao-kuo,
son of Ch'i, was too closely associated with Ts'ai Ching, whose downfall
in the early twelfth century also brought the fortune of this Sung branch
to a rather abrupt end. It took some generations before it reemerged towards
the end of the dynasty. The Sung Hsiang branch had been luckier, but even
so, it ceased to produce any more officials in the sixth generation. Very
much the same occurred in the Shih family, which produced two chief
councillors, namely, Shi Mi-yüan (1164–1233) and Shih Sung-chih.[40]
Shih Mi-yüan had been powerful and exploitative but, luckily, successful,
so much so that the fortune of his branch was not affected at least immediately after his death. Sung-chih, however, was less lucky and within a few
years of his death was posthumously disgraced. As a result, the fortune
of not only his branch, but also the entire family was abruptly brought
to an end. But the most illustrative case certainly belongs to the Han family

_____

find the estimates here too modest. See Beattie, *Land and Lineage in China*. Also,
as Patricia Ebrey argued, the Sung conception of kinship was anything but partilineal,
and therefore, if this concept had been actually in force, then a Sung person might
be broadly related, in kinship terms, to a far greater group than a patrilineal lineage.
This would then mean that probably a far greater proportion of successful candidates
came from elite "families." I doubt if cohesiveness could be extended to such an
extent as to incorporate all members definable in Sung kinship terms as found by Ebrey.
For the purpose of this book, I feel that patrilineal lineage (as defined in note 69 below)
should remain the basic kinship group that was actually operational. For Ebrey's discussions, see her "Women in Kinship System of the Southern Sung Upper Class," in Richard
Guisso (ed.), *Woman in China* (Toronto: University of Toronto Press, 1982), pp. 113–129.

[39]See section C.

[40]Shih Mi-yüan for the period from 1209 to 1233 and Shih Sung-chih for 1239
to 1246.

of An-yang. The family had produced as many as four chief councillors during the Sung dynasty and was married into the imperial house by the mid-twelfth century, about one century after the first Han, namely, Han Ch'i, made the name famous. However, the family's fortune came to an equally unhappy end when Han T'e-chou was charged with sedition and posthumously disgraced. The later Hans were converted to Neo-Confucianism and moved to K'uai-chi (present Shao-hsing) where some of them served as minor officials, while others became Neo-Confucian teachers. These cases show that political vissicitudes were always behind the prosperity and prominence of families of national fame.[41] The political nature of the civil service examinations is therefore very clear.

The trend of downward mobility shows that during the Sung, political factors were practically the decisive ones in the fortune of many prominent official families. The situation of downward mobility being so, it is conceivable that the entire mobility phenomenon in relation to the examinations was heavily constrained politically and socially. To have about 7,905 (47.3% of a bureaucracy of about 15,000 civil bureaucrats) prominent officials coming from commoner backgrounds in a nation of about one hundred million people is not a specially remarkable achievement.[42] Moreover, not all of the Sung bureaucrats of commoner background rose through the civil service examinations.[43]

From the discussion above, it seems that the apparent high degree of mobility rate among the successful candidates of the civil service examinations during the Sung should be understood more as an indication of the instability of officialdom than of the mobility of Chinese society. A study of the downward mobility further suggests that political conditions had a significant role in the careers of many prominent officials and the fate of their families. The examination system thus should be looked upon as a political institution more than anything else. The political dimension of the system will receive a more detailed analysis in the next section.

C. Political Consideration and the Means for Political Power

It is said that Emperor T'ai-tsung was so fond of meeting with the newly admitted candidates that he composed poems while holding reception ban-

---

[41] One hardly needs to be reminded of the fate of Wang An-shih's family. We know next to nothing about his son and virtually nothing about his decendants.

[42] For the numbers of Sung bureaucrats, see Table 15. The population figure is based on the household figure for the early twelfth century (1110, see SS, 85:2095). The average number of people in a family is estimated to be five.

[43] My estimate shows that any time during the Sung, there were about 8,038 degree-

quets for them, and this practice had, as a result, become standard during the Sung dynasty.[44] The monarchs must certainly have taken great delight in meeting the fledgling officials who would, in Wen Yen-po's famous dictum, "share the ruling of all under heaven (*t'ien-hsia*)."[45] There were debates throughout the Sung on whether the civil service examinations could actually select the most morally qualified candidates. Some argued for residence in schools as a more reliable criterion.[46] But there had never been any doubt about the need to have a group of chosen elite to help the ruler in his government. Education and examination alike shared the purpose of "cultivating bureaucrats" (*yang-shih*).[47] It is then perfectly understandable that the Sung ruler derived satisfaction from the knowledge that "the best and the brightest" were at his side in his exercise of statecraft.

To understand the full political dimension of what Chinese governments and historians defined as *hsüan-chü*, it is probably most convenient to refer to historical encyclopedias which almost invariably have a section on the examinations. The following are tables of contents from two important encyclopedic works dating from Sung times. One is the *Sung hui-yao,* which I have repeatedly cited. Another is *Wen-hsien t'ung-k'ao,* edited by the famous institutional historian, Ma Tuan-lin, also cited frequently as an authority.

From Tables 12 and 13 one sees how comprehensively a Sung Chinese referred to the examinations. Some of the items included in *hsüan-chü* had little to do with education. But for the Sung ruler, admission into service by examinations had a much more comprehensive meaning than what we have so far discussed and defined as the civil service examinations. Still, the regular civil service examinations were definitely the most important part of the *hsüan-chü*, and should be understood in *hsüan-chü* terms.

What was the essential nature of *hsüan-chü*? In the simplest terms, it was a system by which the Chinese government recruited those it wanted for service and by which it also rated their merit and judged their performance. The English term, civil service examination system, does not imply this merit-rating function. But the system certainly was a part of what we may label as control of all bureaucrats, both in service and on the waiting

---

holders serving in the government or waiting for appointment. Of them, about 4,606 (using the 57.3% of Kracke's estimate) were of commoner background. See Appendix C for the figure 8,038. See also Table 16.

[44] Liu Pan, *Kung-fu shih-hua, Pai-ch'uan hsüeh-hai* ed. (reprint of Sung edition), now included in *Pai-pu ts'ung-shu* (Taipei: I-wen, 1967), la.

[45] *WHTK*, 12:130.

[46] See Chin Chung-shu, "Pei-Sung k'o-chü."

[47] Ch'en Tung-yüan, *Chiao-yü shih*, 2–4.

TABLE 12

Table of Contents of the *Hsüan-chü* Section in the *Sung hui-yao*

kung-chü	Selection by contributing [talented persons] (regular examinations).
kung-chü yin	Seals used in the regular examinations.
ch'in-shih (tien-shih)	Imperial (palace) examinations.
tz'u chi-ti	Pass with distinction [in the palace examinations].
tz'u ch'u-shen	Formally qualified [in the palace examinations].
t'ung-tzu ch'u-shen	Success in the children's examinations.
shih p'an	Examination in person-speech-writing-decision [for admission to lowly-ranked offices, after one passed the civil serive examinations].
chih-k'o	Decree examinations.
ching-ming hsing-hsiu k'o	Examinations for recruiting those "well versed in classicial learning and morally outstanding."
chih-k'o, hung-tz'u k'o	Decree examinations; Examinations in *tz'u* poetry.
ming-ching k'o	Examinations in classical knowledge.
pa-hsing k'o	Examinations in eight virtues.
t'ung-tzu k'o	Children's examinations.
ch'ang-ming	Formal announcement of examination results.
en-k'o (t'e-tsou ming)	Facilitated degrees.
shih-fa	Legal examinations.
hsin-k'o ming-fa	New legal examinations.
ts'ao-t'ing	Special examinations [held for candidates already in service].
fa-chieh	Dispatching [successful candidates from prefectural examinations to sit in the departmental examinations].
chiao-shou	[Appointment of] preceptors.
wu-chü	Military examinations.
tsung-shih ying-chü	Imperial relatives taking the examinations.
hsiao-shih	[Rewarding] loyalists.
pai-p'ien	Examination in composing one hundred pieces of poems.
shih-kuan	[Appointment of] examiners.
hsüan-shih	Selection of *shih* (examinations).
k'ao-k'o	Merit rating.
ch'üan-hsüan	Selection for appointment.
ch'üan-shih	Examinations for appointment.
chü-kuan	Sponsorship in office appointment.
p'i-chü	Special imperial appointment.
chao-shih	Special imperial examinations [of individual candidates].
min-hsü chiu-tsu	Imperial gifts for old prominent clans.
t'e-en ch'u-chih	Special appointment by imperial favor.
chü i-i	Election of recluses and hermits.
li-ch'ien	Special awards to recluses without actual appointment to offices.

TABLE 13

Table of Contents of the *Hsüan-chü* Section in the
Wen-hsien t'ung-k'ao

chü-shih	Election of *shih* (scholars, students, candidates).
hsien-liang fang-cheng	[Selection of those who are] virtuous, kind, righteous and straight in behavior.
hsiao-lien	[Selection of those who are] filially pious and incorruptible.
wu-chü	Military examinations.
jen-tzu	Appointment to office of high officials' sons.
t'ung-k'o	Children's examinations.
li-tao	The way of an official (merit rating).
tzu-hsüan chin-na	Buying of official posts.
fang-chi	Astronomer-astrologists, physicians, etc.
chü-kuan	Sponsorship in office appointment.
p'i-chü	Special imperial appointment.
k'ao-k'o	Merit rating.

list. In short, the civil service examination system, being a part of Chinese *hsüan-chü*, was an instrument for political control.

Three points support this contention. First of all, the extremely satisfying rewards Chinese officials derived from their office, status and prestige, account for the desire of virtually *all* officials to stay in office. As a result, behavior in the examination hall and in service shared one fundamentally similar trait: avoidance of minor mistakes and errors. This is what Li Ch'ing-ch'en (1032–1102) had to say in the late eleventh century:[48]

> Nowadays, officials are judged by their small faults and not by their important activities, by the irresponsible criticism prevalent in official circles and not by an examination of their actual administration.... Only those who carefully protect their personal career interests by avoiding controversies and following the prevailing trend can go on safely without blame. Consequently, only mediocre officials will rise steadily by promotion.

While this type of bureaucratic behavior is considered universal, one may say that the civil service examinations produced even more bureaucrats of this behavior type than other institutions.

[48] Quoted by James T. C. Liu, in his "Some Classifications of Bureaucrats in Chinese Historiography," in David S. Nivison and Arthur F. Wright (eds.), *Confucianism in Action* (Stanford: Stanford University Press, 1959), 169. Criticisms of this type of behavior trait are plentiful in the writings of Ming loyalists.

Secondly, the system helped to formulate and perpetuate a social class which was to take up the duty of government on a local level. During the Sung, the average number of graduates of the civil service examinations (including *chin-shih* and *chu-k'o* examinations, regular and facilitated) over any thirty-year period was 8,038.[49] Since the average entrance age of *chin-shih* degree-holders was about thirty, and successful candidates could expect to serve for about thirty years,[50] the average number of bureaucrats who were degree-holders would then be about eight thousand. At the same time, this also means that, on the average, there could have been about thirty-two thousand candidates who tried but failed in each departmental examination.[51] Naturally, since many candidates took the departmental examinations repeatedly, the actual number of these unsuccessful candidates from departmental examinations was probably smaller than this; for convenience, let us assume that 25,000 was the figure.[52] This number is of some practical value: the unsuccessful candidates of departmental examinations started to receive some privileges beginning with the Southern Sung, and consequently were closer than their counterpart in

----

[49] See note 43 above.

[50] The mean ages in the examinations of 1148 and 1256 were 35.64 and 35.66 respectively. See Edward A. Kracke, Jr., *Civil Service*, 60. But the average age of the entrance for *chin-shih* degree-holders found in Weng T'ung-wen's *Réportoire des dates hommes célèbre des Song* (Paris: Mouton & Co., 1962) is 29.9 years. The average age of this same group of people is about 63.5 years (based on a random sampling of 120 among 465 known cases). This would mean that the life expectancy of a thirty years old Sung degree-holder was about thirty-three years. For convenience, it is reasonable to assume that the average length of service for Sung degree-holders was about thirty years.

[51] An average of about 20% of candidates taking the departmental examinations were recruited. This would mean that about four in every five candidates failed to actually gain the degree. Thus, about 32,000 people at any time during the dynasty were successful candidates of the prefectural examinations who failed in the departmental tests. For a detailed discussion on the figure of 20%, see Ch. 6, section D.

[52] John Chaffee, in his Ph.D. thesis, using another method of calculation has arrived at an estimate of the *chü-jen* (*te-chieh jen*) population as being "in the range of fifteen to fifty thousand, or fifteen to thirty thousand after the early Sung." His estimates very much confirm mine. I have chosen to take the figure 25,000 as the most reliable estimate, because I feel Chaffee's estimates, useful as they are in arriving at an estimate of the percentage the *chü-jen* constituted in the male population (0.15%–0.25%), are of too wide a range for practical purposes here. Meanwhile, since it is reasonable to assume that the life expectancy of a 30-year old *chü-jen* probably was shorter than that of a *chin-shih* of the same age (33 years, as mentioned in note 50), then the number of existing *chü-jen* should be fewer than the 32,000 which is based on the life expectancy of *chin-shih* degree-holders. Taking the fact that some *chü-jen* repeatedly sat in the examinations, one may then safely conclude that 25,000, instead of 32,000 is a more realistic estimate. For Chaffee's estimates, see his "Education and Examinations in Sung Society," 50–51.

the Northern Sung to the non-office-holding *chü-jen* we find in the Ming and Ch'ing. Therefore, during the Northern Sung, the percentage of privileged people (consisting *mainly* of all officials, and University students) in the nation's population was only 0.036%, a percentage very close to that of the "upper gentry" in the Ch'ing national population (see Table 14). For the Southern Sung, because of the awarding of tax and/or labor exemption status to the *chü-jen*, the privileged people quickly swelled to more than 0.1% of the nation's population. This development is both interesting and significant. First of all, the history of the examination system shows that it was for the imperial Chinese government to recruit more candidates than it actually needed, so that those privileged people who nonetheless did not obtain the highest degree could still supplement the government's administration at the local level.

This point, already touched upon in the preceding section, is best illustrated if we relate it to the mechanism of the quota system. The use of the quota system was such that in those areas which were more advanced economically or culturally, the percentage of *te-chieh jen* (referred to as *chü-jen* hereafter for convenience of comparison) in the county's population would be smaller than those in the less developed areas, because quotas assigned for less developed areas were usually more generous. Now, while there is no study of area power configuration during the Sung, an article by James B. Parsons on that of the Ming shows that advanced areas such as Pei Chih-li (present Hopei), Chekiang and Chiang-hsi often possessed more provincial, prefectural and county officials.[53] If Parson's findings are applicable to the Sung, and I believe they are,[54] then we may find that in those areas where the central government assigned a greater number of officials, the number of *chü-jen* in percentage terms tended to be smaller. I think this fact is extremely illuminating, because it shows that *chü-jen*, by viture of their education, were trusted by the government to supplement its bureaucracy in local administration.

Having discussed the second essential nature of the examination system, let me now turn to some examples, before moving on to further arguments.

---

[53] James B. Parsons, "The Ming Dynasty Bureaucracy: Aspects of Background Forces," in Charles O. Hucker (ed.), *Chinese Government in Ming Times*, 175–227.

[54] Less developed areas were chronically in need of more central government appointed officials. For some useful examples, see *SHY*, hc, 23/9ab, passim. Robert Hymes, in his recent dissertation, "Prominence and Power in Sung China" (Ph.D. dissertation, University of Pennsylvania, 1979), suggests that a "lower degree" without official appointment could also be a route to social prominence. This confirms my argument and I am sure that the Sung government was fully aware of the social significance of a non-official (and actually non-degreed) "*chü-jen*" status in local communities.

TABLE 14

Changing Sizes of the "Gentry" in the Sung and the Ch'ing

	Sung		Ch'ing	
	c. 1100 Entire bureaucratic force, without *chü-jen*, plus Univ. students	c. 1200 Entire bureaucratic force, plus Univ. students and *chü-jen*	Pre-Taiping period Upper gentry	Post-Taiping period Upper gentry
No. of counties[a]	1,162	703	1,514	1,523
National population[b]	100,000,000	63,360,000	430,000,000	440,000,000
Average county population	86,059	90,128	284,015	288,903
Gentry population	37,800[c]	64,516[d]	125,000[e]	204,000[e]
Gentry population in each county	33	92	83	134
Percentage	0.038%	0.102%	0.029%	0.046%

Explanation: The term, "gentry," is used in a narrowly defined sense in that it included primarily those who acquired special privileges from the civil service examinations. Their family members, as well as those who enjoyed elite status in Chinese society through other means, are not included.

a. The figure for c. 1100 Sung is from *SS*, 85:2095. That for c. 1200 Sung is from Ku Tsu-yü's *Tu-shih fang-yü chi-yao*, 1901 Tu-shu chi-ch'eng chü ed., 8/50a; those for the Ch'ing are from T'ung-tsu Ch'ü, *Local Government in China under the Ch'ing* (Cambridge, Mass.: Harvard University Press, 1962), 2.

b. Those for the Sung are from Ping-ti Ho, "An Estimate of the Total Population of Sung-Chin China," in Francois Aubin (ed.), *Études Song*, series I, no. 1 (Paris: Mouton & Co., 1971), 33–53. Those for the Ch'ing are from Ping-ti Ho, *Studies on the Population of China, 1368–1953* (Cambridge, Mass: Harvard University Press, 1959), 264 and from Ito Takeo, "Chung-kuo te jen-k'ou t'ung-chi," tr. by Hsi-po, in Hsiang-kang Ya-tung hsüeh-she (ed.), *Chung-kuo li-tai jen-k'ou wen-t'i lun-chi* (Hong Kong: Lung-men, 1965), 260.

c. For the total of the bureaucratic force (estimated at 34,000), see Table 15; the number of University students for 1104 was 3,800. See Table 3.

d. See Table 15 for the number of the entire bureaucratic force (37,800 in 1201). The number of University students for c. 1205 was 1,716. See Table 3.

e. From Chung-li Chang, *The Chinese Gentry*, 132.

The first one concerns the frequency of occurrence of the term, *hsiang-kung chin-shih*, which meant a successful candidate in the subject of *chin-shih* from the primary prefectural examinations and hence, *chü-jen*. The term is often found in stone inscriptions describing the title of the person who either wrote or composed the inscription, notably that of tombstones.[55] A *hsiang-kung chin-shih* was not an official title, but obviously signified a definite social status in local communities. Secondly, *chü-jen* took part in all kinds of community affairs. In his fine study of Fu-chien local theater, Tanaka points out that local elite, such as merchants, landlords, and above all, heads of powerful families often actively involved themselves in promoting dramas and plays.[56] Organization of local education, community schools, granaries and the maintenance of local temples were also under the leadership of these local *chü-jen* and their family members. On the more leisurely side, it was also these "scholars" who, in club meetings where they composed poems, provided towns and villages with some degree of cultural sophistication: "literary people organized poetic clubs. Officials and respectable scholars, along with Confucian students residing in the Capital (Hangchow) organized them. They would take pleasure in following their mood to compose poems. These poems are read and appreciated by others, widely recited in all places and are not to be equalled by those of other clubs."[57]

I shall now move on to the third point concerning the nature of the civil service examinations. This has to do with education directly. We are fortunate to have two sets of educational statistics each for 1104 and 1109. These statistics, reproduced in Table 7, belonged to the period when late Northern Sung educational reform reached its zenith. However, when one compares them, one instantly finds that within five years, the number of students registered in government schools dwindled by about one fourth. This is a very sharp decline. But more importantly, the entire reform effort fell through after Ts'ai Ching's demise. Among Ts'ai Ching's ideas, abolition of the examination system and replacing it with a comprehensive educational program ranked foremost. The result was for an unprecedented number of children to register in schools, and to learn the subjects traditionally taught only to those preparing to go into service. However, there were not enough positions in the government to accomodate such a large number of people now forced to accept the kind of education only useful in the civil service. Ts'ai Ching was caught in a dilemma: to carry out a compre-

---

[55] Based on my impression derived from reading stone inscriptions.

[56] Tanaka Issei, "Chūgoku chihōgeki no hatten kōzō," in *Tōyō bunka*, 58 (1977), 1—42.

[57] Wu Tzu-mu, *Meng-liang lu*, 19:299.

hensive, semi-compulsory educational program, he had to offer enough official posts to take in those otherwise "useless" students. The secret of Chinese bureaucracy, however, lay in its exclusiveness and in its awarding tremendous social rewards, including wealth, prestige and privilege, to a rather selected group of social elite, so as to demand their allegiance in return. This would mean a constant effort to check the growth of bureaucratic manpower, even at the expense of administrative efficiency.[58] In view of this circumstance, it was natural that the reform should fail completely. The constraining force of the size of bureaucracy defined the civil service examination's political nature once and for all.

The conclusion from the points above must be that the civil service examinations were but one part of official control including both recruitment and merit rating in traditional Chinese government; in creating a local elite, using them to supplement the central government, and in purposefully rewarding the bureaucrats with disproportionately large rewards, the Sung government sought to create and manipulate a group of social elite whose qualification for reward was a very special kind of education, and whose power they closely watched and defined.

It is nevertheless also true that Chinese government was less than impartial in that it also often rewarded those who were wealthy and powerful enough to circumvent the mechanism to become a part of the establishment. In other words, the civil service examinations were not the only means to rise into prominence. The size of Sung bureaucracy ranged from about ten thousand to about fifty thousand (see Table 16), and since the average total number of degree-holders at any time in the Sung was around eight

---

[58] One widely held view about Sung bureaucracy has been that the Sung government made too many awards of otherwise unneeded posts to rather unqualified people, resulting in constraints on the government's budget. Whether the Sung government during Ts'ai Ching's reform period was indeed not able to absorb so many graduates from schools because there were not enough jobs to assign to them, or whether it was to the benefit of the officials and the government to see to it that the bureaucracy did not expand too fast, remains to be explored. In any case, it is a fact that people during Sung times and afterwards made constant complaints about the excessive expansion of the Sung bureaucracy. See Yang Shu-fan, *Wen-kuan chih-tu*, 408, for more information about the size of the Sung bureaucracy, and its constraints on the government's revenue. Incidentally, one should also take note of the argument put forth by G. William Skinner that at the local level, late imperial China did not seem to be interested in seeing its administrative efficacy improved. See note 25 above. See also Edmund H. Worthy, "Regional Control in the Southern Sung Salt Administration," in John Winthrop Haeger (ed.), *Crisis and Prosperity in Sung China*, 101–142, for Worthy's interesting observation on how some degree of tolerance for the illicit sale of salt was necessary to prevent the unnecessary expansion of managerial personnel or, for that matter, the number of officials.

thousand, they therefore made up only about one fifth to at most half of the entire bureaucratic manpower, with the exception of the first eighty years of the dynasty. This means that the importance of the civil service examination degrees eroded throughout the dynasty and that other channels of upward mobility, which were less open, were available to those with special relations in terms of being the descendents of high officials[59] or scions of wealthy families. The chance of buying into officialdom has, however, so far not been carefully studied, and we are unsure of its significance.[60] From what little we know, it appears that the possibility for a merchant—who was usually banned from taking the civil service exminations—to buy his way into officialdom outright was nearly impossible. On the other hand, for children of wealthy merchants to have a good education was very easy, and we have plenty of examples to illustrate this fact. The following is one:[61]

> P'eng Tse was a wealthy merchant and amassed quite a lot of property. He was respectful to Confucian scholarship and invited teachers and friends for his son, without worrying how much this would cost him. He once used his savings to buy two sets of the classics printed by the Directorate of Education. He placed one set in the prefectural school, and another in his home. The prefect, Yang Pien, wrote a special essay to commemorate this event. In the essay, however, it was mentioned that [P'eng] Tse was a businessman, and this embarrassed his descendants. When the Junior Lord of the Court of Imperial Family, Hsü Shih-min, served as a prefect at the prefecture, he saw the essay and commented that the work (what P'eng had done) was good, which outshone the fact that P'eng was a merchant. He therefore ordered his subordinate, Yü Hsiang, to copy down the essay and engrave it on a stone tablet. The descendants then began to feel honored.

This story illustrates the importance of wealth in connection with education. At least in the mind of the writer, above, and the descendants of Mr. P'eng, some kind of education for the examinations was very important, much more important than being wealthy.

One may also ask whether wealth played some role in an individual's

---

[59]Kracke, *Civil Service*, passim. The fact that degree-holders were quickly losing their importance was noted as early as the Southern Sung by Hung Mai. See his *Jung-chai sui-pi* (Shanghai: Ku-chi, 1978), Vol. 1, 9:119–120.

[60]The only article I can think of is by Sung Hsi (Sung Shee), "Sung-tai shih-ta-fu tui shang-jen te t'ai-tu" ("Sung-tai shih-ta-fu" hereafter), in *SSYCC*, Vol. 2 (1964), 199–212.

[61]Lo Hsiu-i, *Ch'uan-hsin lu,* in *Shuo-fu,* cited from Sung Hsi, "Sung-tai shih-ta-fu," 212.

TABLE 15

The Varying Sizes of the Sung Bureaucracy

Time	Civil Service		Military Service	Total
	Court and capital rank	Executory rank		
997	800	—	—	—
1004–1007	—	—	—	10,000+
1004–1016	—	—	—	9,785
early Sung	—	—	—	13,000+
1017–1021	—	—	4,200+	—
1023–1031	2,000–	—	—	—
1034–1037	—	—	4,000–	—
1038–1039	—	—	—	15,443
1046	2,700+	10,000+	6,000+	(18,700+)
1047	2,800+	10,000+	6,500+	(19,300+)
1049	—	—	—	17,300+
1049–1053	—	—	—	20,000+
1064–1067	2,800+	—	—	24,000+
c. 1078	10,193 (total)		12,826	24,549
1079			11,690	—
1085	2,800–3,000+	4,000+	11,930+	(18,730+)
1086	2,800+	10,000+	15,500+	(28,300+)
1088	—	—	—	34,000+
1111	4,000+	—	23,000+	—
1113	—	—	27,967	—
1119	(4,000+)[a]	16,512	30,691+	(51,203+)
1120	—	—	23,000+	—
1122	—	—	31,082	—
1165–1173	3,000–4,000	7,000–8,000	—	—
1191	4,159	12,869	16,488	33,516
1196	4,159	13,670	25,230	(43,059)
1201	3,133	15,204	19,470	(37,808)
1213	2,392	17,006	19,472	(38,870)
1256	—	—	—	24,000+

Explanations: This table is based on my "Sung-tai kuan-yüan shu te t'ung-chi," in *Shih-huo*, Vol. 14, Nos. 5–6 (1984), 17–29.

Except for *a*, which is an estimate based on the information of 1111, all other bracketed figures are actual totals derivable from Sung sources, though not directly included therein.

TABLE 16

The Size of the Sung Bureaucracy Contrasted with That
of Degree-holders

Time	Size of bureaucracy	Total of degree-holders of the previous 30 years		Percentage
997–1022	9,785	992–1021	8,653	88.43
early Sung	13,000	1001–1030	7,685	59.12
1038–1039	15,443	1008–1037	6,955	45.04
1046	18,700	1016–1045	7,085	37.89
1047	19,300	1017–1046	8,963	46,44
1049	17,300	1019–1048	8,963	51.81
1049–1053	20,000	1019–1048	8,963	44.82
1064–1067	24,000	1035–1064	9,549	39.79
1078	24,549	1047–1076	9,139	37.23
1085	18,730	1055–1084	9,218	50.82
1086	28,300	1056–1085	10,640	37.60
1088	34,000	1058–1087	9,639	28.35
1119	51,203	1089–1118	7,060	13.79
1191	33,516	1161–1190	5,764	17.20
1196	43,059	1166–1195	6,034	14.01
1201	37,808	1171–1200	6,164	16.30
1213	38,870	1183–1212	8,264	21.26
1256	24,000			
Average	26,198		8,038*	30.68

Explanation:　It is assumed that the degree-holders of the previous 30 years would still have been in service when the size of the bureaucracy of that year was recorded. *For this figure, see Appendix C.

opportunity for examination success.[62] Recent studies on Ming, and particularly, Ch'ing, social history have indicated that wealth in the form of land-owning and lineage organization were two important factors behind the success of individual candidates,[63] to such an extent that the local elite was able to monopolize the outcome of the examination results, or at least, dominate the source from which successful candidates were drawn. I have previously shown that the examination system by its nature had created a power elite to help supplement local administration which the

[62] Miyazaki Ichisada strongly advocates this view, which has subsequently influenced a number of interpreters of the Chinese examination system and social mobility. For Miyazaki's view, see his *China's Examination Hell,* tr. by Conrad Schirokauer (New York: Weatherhill, 1976), 118–121.

[63] Beattie, *Land and Lineage in China,* 127–132.

government was not able to assume adequately. It is now worthwhile to consider the methods by which local powerful families sought to amass wealth and influence, and whether the examination degree status helped to perpetuate their family fortunes. In order to arrive at reliable answers, I refer to the following interconnected facts.

First, in his important study on the local bureaucracy of the Sung, Brian McKnight has concluded that, at least during the early part of the Sung, wealth *per se* was critical in determining "the distribution of responsibilities and influence in rural areas."[64]

Secondly, a number of studies, notably by Sung Hsi (Sung Shee) and Ch'üan Han-sheng, have pointed out that government officials were chronically involved in commercial activities. Some of them were in the business of what their contemporaries in Europe would call "usury."[65] An "educated" person obviously had a very ambivalent attitude towards commercial profit-taking, and land-owning activities certainly were also part of the general effort to become rich. This was especially so in the Southern Sung, when purchase of land became easier.

Thirdly, the Sung was a wealthy society. During the later half of the dynasty, despite its narrowed *Lebensraum,* it had experienced one of the rare moments in Chinese history during which maritime commerce created an unprecedented prosperity.[66] It is conceivable that a high degree of horizontal mobility existed, although we lack studies in this aspect of Sung society.[67] It is also conceivable that, as a result, there were probably more people who could afford to have education, but were not able to get a footing in the bureaucracy. Indeed, it is well known that many Neo-Confucian scholars working in the academies often had impressive family wealth behind them.[68] Societal prosperity therefore helped the progress of education, but it could at the same time make the examinations more competitive, and preparations for them more expensive.

Finally, it has now become clear that during the Sung, Chinese conception and practice of clan or lineage organization underwent some significant

---

[64] McKnight, *Village and Bureaucracy in Southern Sung China,* 182.

[65] Sung Hsi, "Sung-tai shih-ta-fu"; Aoyama Sadao, "Hoku-Sō o chushin to suru shitaifu no chike to seikatsu rinri," in *Tōyō gakuhō,* 57 (1976), Nos. 1 & 2, 35–63.

[66] Jung-pang Lo, "The Rise of China as a Sea Power," in *Far Eastern Quarterly,* 14 (1955), 489–503.

[67] See note 29 above. Some evidence of this can be seen in such facts as Wei-chou (in present Hopei) being known for famous physicians, Ching-te chen rising to become the center of pottery manufacturing and Mei-chou (in present Szechwan) being noted for its people's knowledge of litigation, etc.

[68] Enough evidences can be found in *SS,* passim.

change;[69] narrower but better organized families emerged to replace the aristocratic clans of national prestige of medieval China.[70] New and wealthy families had a more precisely defined structure and coordination than before, but had to rely more on government power for the perpetuation of their influence. Consequently, taking part in the preparations of members for the examinations became increasingly an important family activity.[71]

Taken together, these facts present a clear conclusion that there was a wide spectrum of power elite composed not merely of degree-holders but also of others who, by virtue of their wealth, were influential at the local level. The power and influence of these people were consolidated by the strength of lineage oragnizations. However, with the conception of lineage now defined more narrowly, and its sphere of influence circumscribed, it was necessary for them to seek to produce as many officials as possible, preferably those holding a degree in the examinations, over a number of generations. Many factors, indeed, affected the fortunes of such families.[72]

[69] Throughout this book, I have by and large followed the definitions on the "clan" and "lineage" by Maurice Freedman (*Lineage Organization in Southeastern China*, London: University of London Press, 1958). In my reading of sources on medieval Chinese families, I have come to believe that the medieval Chinese conception of *tsu* is very close to what Freedman would consider as clan, which, although lacking communal estates and by no means localized, could in those days still command a certain degree of solidarity as long as genealogical ties could be established. The situation had by the Sung changed so that only clans with definite genealogical ties and clearly defined according to locality could actually function—as seen in the cases referred to in section A of this chapter. Corporate estates gradually started to appear after the mid-eleventh century, with the notable case of the Fan "clan" as a very famous example. But the transitional nature remained, so that what Freedman called "higher-order lineages" continued to have a certain attraction. The entire process of evolution in the changing attitudes towards genealogical connections was obviously intertwined with the development of the civil service examinations. See also works by Aoyama Sadao cited in note 65; his "Sōdai ni okeru Shisen kanryō keifu ni tsuite no ichi kōsatsu," in *Wada Hakushi koki kinen Tōyōshi ronso* (Tokyo: Kodansha, 1960), 37–48 and "Godai Sō ni okeru Kōsei no shinkō kanryō," in *Wada Hakushi kanreki kinen Tōyōshi ronsō* (Tokyo: Kōdansha, 1951), 19–37. Another important article is by Chikusa Gashō, "Hoku-Sō shitaifu no shikyo to baiden," in *Shirin*, Vol. 54, No. 2 (1971), 28–53. Articles cited by Ihara Hiroshi in his "Nan-Sō no Shisen ni okeru teikyo shijin," in *Tōhōgaku*, 54 (1977), 46–62, are also useful.

[70] Capably studied by Patricia B. Ebrey, *The Aristocratic Families of Early Imperial China* (Cambridge: Cambridge University Press, 1978) and by David G. Johnson, *The Medieval Chinese Oligarchy*. It is interesting to find that early Sung genealogical compilers arbitrarily limited themselves to include only direct descent lines up to five generations, a practice later abandoned. See Morita Ken, "Sō Gen jidai ni okeru shūfu," in *Tōyōshi kenkyū*, No. 37 (1979), 27–53.

[71] Evident in some of the famous "family instructions" (*chia-hsün*).

[72] Speaking of the "death" of lineages, Maurice Freedman pointed out: "The climate

But in terms of the perpetuation of lineage strength and prosperity, constant success in the civil service examinations was evidently the most important.[73] In short, the answer to the question as to how local powerful families sought to amass wealth and perpetuate their fortunes was that the degree indeed helped to strengthen the prestige and influence of the families, as evidenced by so many instances of bureaucrats engaging conveniently in commercial profit-taking and land-owning activities.[74]

D. Recapitulation

The examination system had the important function of recruiting from among the Chinese people a group of well-educated students to serve in officialdom. The strength of the institution relied heavily on impartiality in that the competition among candidates was open and equal.[75] The nature

hazards of the area of China we are concerned with—typhoons, floods, and drought—must certainly have borne *more* (my italics) heavily on those with fewer accumulated resources and have led to their being the first to give up the struggle. . . ." See his *Chinese Lineage and Society: Fukien and Kwangtung* (London: University of London Press, 1966), 8.

Denis C. Twitchett, in his study on the Fan Clan's chartiable estate, on the other hand, assigned the "economic problem posed by the Chinese inheritance system, which led to the continual fragmentation and diminution of family holdings" as the most important factor leading to the decline of a clan. See his "Fan Clan's Charitable Estate," in Nivison and Wright (eds.), *Confucianism in Action,* 97–133. See also a recent study by John C. H. Fei and Ts'ui-jung Liu, "The Growth and Decline of Chinese Family Clans," in *Journal of Interdisciplinary History,* XII:3 (1982), 375–408.

[73] See Patricia Ebrey's review on Beattie's *Land and Lineage in China* in *American Historical Review,* Vol. 85 (1980), 961–962; a similar concern is also expressed by Jerry Dennerline in his review of the same book in *HJAS,* Vol. 40 (1980), 549–555.

[74] The problems of whether the civil service examinations were basically responsible for creating the Chinese social elite class in the Sung or whether there was a basically self perpetuating elite class which constantly tried to manipulate the results of the examinations has been studied in a number of excellent monographs and dissertations, many of which came to my attention too late to be included here. Let me reiterate that the rise of the Sung social elite was more a result of political evolution than of the examinations. This is why I argue that the elite class consisted of more than bureaucrats and *chu-jen* and their families. On the other hand, the evolution of the Chinese social structure was also heavily affected by the practice of the examinations. I emphasize that ultimately it was political force exercised through the examinations which had the decisive influence on the fortune of many *elite* lineages, even if the government might not always wish to exercise that particular form of power.

In short, I consider that while the growth and appearance of lineages could take many forms, its perpetuation hinged heavily on success in the examinations—more than on anything else.

[75] Clearly seen in Ping-ti Ho's *Ladder.*

of the system, however, was to create or maintain an elite class by awarding its members with tremendous social honor, prestige and privilege. This limited the route of upward social mobility to almost one way only and, thus, maintained the allegiance of successful candidates to the monarch. The system also had to bring about a degree of regional power balance by creating a quota system, which, along with the tax and labor exemptions given to successful candidates from prefectural tests (the *chü-jen*), helped the perpetuation of the elite. The government in later dynasties relied on their cooperation to supplement administering local affairs.

The number of people directly affected by the civil service examinations was very small indeed, and therefore the system did not help to create much significant mobility. On the contrary, by creating or perpetuating the powerful local elite families, the system had the potential of further blocking the chances of upward mobility for commoners without a strong family background.

During the Sung, a large stratum of socially powerful and influential people, a good number of them degree-holders, made up the elite class. For this class, which was most visible in lineage forms, to self-perpetuate, it had to produce as many successful candidates as possible. Degree-holding was obviously the most important means for the maintenance and perpetuation of family fortunes.[76]

---

[76] See notes 73 and 74 above. See also David Johnson, *The Medieval Chinese Oligarchy*. I would hasten to say that the social phenomena discussed above did not constitute the center of Neo-Confucian, and consequently, late Chinese concerns with and criticisms of the examination system.

CHAPTER 9

The Moral Purposes

The Sung people continued to accept the premise that the primary function of the civil service examinations was to recruit officials. The ideal Confucian society was necessarily hierarchical, with the people on the uppermost echelon enjoying the greatest proportion of social rewards. However, it was the supreme Confucian belief that moral performance should be the only criterion in the process of selection.[1] How this could actually be implemented, and whether the civil service examination system, with its emphasis on impartiality (*kung*), could indeed carry out the ideal of electing the morally qualified are questions subject to intense debates. The heat of such debates during the Sung reached such an unprecedented degree that at one point the government even considered suspending or even abolishing the examination system. The crux of the issue lay in the feasibility of the examination system to fulfill that ancient Confucian ideal. Nearly every one agreed that the system could not actually select the most morally upright persons for service, but they failed to discover an appropriate alternative to achieve that goal. Ultimately, it was left to Neo-Confucians under the leadership of Chu Hsi to provide yet another answer, that of the *shu-yüan* education.

The famous memorial written by Chu Hsi in 1187, though never formally submitted, has been known to generations of Chinese students as having made the most searching criticism of the examination system. It questioned the very nature of the system as such and examined the root of its problems. While one may not agree with Chu Hsi's diagnosis, the memorial did sufficiently summarize basic issues thought to be real and important during the Sung.[2]

---

[1] See Ch. 1, section A.

[2] Chu Hsi, *Wen-chi,* 69:1273–1277. This memorial got to be reproduced in abridged form in the *SS* "Treatise on the Examinations" (156:3633–3634), in the famous encyclopaedia compiled in the eighteenth century, the *Ku-chin t'u-shu chi-ch'eng* (Taipei: Wen-hsing photoreprinted ed., 1964), 661/28a, and in *WHTK,* 42:339–340, etc.

In ancient times, school education and the examinations began by sending students to village and county schools and from there to the capital. Students learned how to behave righteously; they also learned the *tao* and other skills. The intelligent and upright ones were then elected [into officialdom]. The ideal was to see to it that those who wished to stay in schools would have schools to attend, those who were elected into officialdom would not have to rely on other skills [for living], and those who entered officialdom would not have been chosen by other routes than the examinations. The result was that scholars could be secure in their pursuits and did not have to worry about other enviable enterprises. All they had to worry about was how they could live up to the demanded standard of moral perfection; they did not have to worry about whether office and fortune would be bestowed on them. Confucius said: "If a person does not say things that contain errors and does not behave in such a way as to cause remorse, then fortune is with him." Mencius said: "When one succeeds in cultivating heavenly endowments, then earthly rewards (endowments) will follow." . . .

Education during the [ancient] Three Dynasties was such that the acquisition of skills occupied the lowest priority, though the skills were practical and indispensible. The system of election was so well legislated that it could help the cultivation of the mind and the material force of an individual, and could assist in his moral attainments. The methods of the ancients could create a moral person, upgrade good social customs, smooth out worldly affairs and bring about ultimate harmony. The current method, on the other hand, is different: its prefectural tests could recruit people, but the recruitment was not impartial; it opened up various routes for entry [to officialdom], including the University, the Directorate, and others, outside that of the regular examinations, and created a situation where people shamelessly competed for offices; also, teachers in the system did not relate their teaching to the practice of moral discipline, and even the so-called "skills" were but empty words without pragmatic advantage. . . .

Now those who are enthusiastic about the examination system complain that its problems lie in candidates' lack of knowledge of style and in their simple-minded attitude in abiding by the form of the tests. The so-called *hun-pu* ("mixed admission method") was accordingly proposed.[3] But this could only add to the defects of the examination system. Some are aware of these problems and have proposed that we go back to the Three-Hall method of directly promoting students from local prefectural and county schools [to the University] as was practiced during the Ch'ung-ning era,[4] by which we send selected students to the Imperial University. This method seems better than that of *hun-pu*, but if we should indeed implement it, then there would be too large a number of students. I am afraid that we do not have enough money and crops to put them up in prefectures and counties. If we take in all of them, we will have a shortage of food; if we continue the old policy, the result is that we continue to have great difficulties in selection and that the chance for them to move up will be even more limited. . . .

I have given much thought to this problem and found that if we want to

---

[3] See Ch. 4, section E and Table 4.
[4] See Ch. 4, section E and Ch. 5, section D.

carry out an overall transformation so as to revive the old method as practiced by ancient kings, and to rectify the current social customs, then the only way is to follow what Master [Ch'eng] Ming-tao proposed during the Hsi-ning era.[5] [After we have done what Ming-tao suggested], then we shall have reached the root of the problem, corrected it, and removed all the defects. . . .

This quotation, though lengthy, pinpoints the basic dilemma about the theoretically "impartial" examinations that Sung policy-makers and thinkers encountered. It is clear that there was a need to make the examination very fair, but to do so would be at the obvious expense of that ancient Chinese conviction: the need for the morally qualified to take up office. Throughout the Sung, the issue was never satisfactorily solved. From the viewpoint of the government, impartiality could not be abandoned. Bitter about the difficulty in actually examining the moral performance of individual candidates, Neo-Confucians resorted to condemning the system as such, to establishing academies as a way of protest, and to eventually turning academies into better places for preparing examination candidates. Let us study the development of how the examination system was maintained to no one's satisfaction.

A. The 1044 Reform in Education and in the Examinations

The famous "Ten-point Memorial" submitted by Han Ch'i and Fan Chung-yen in 1043 set the train of reforms into motion.[6] Of the ten proposals for change,[7] one was concerned exclusively with changes in education and

[5] What Ch'eng Ming-tao (Hao) proposed in essence was to practice what later was actually implemented by Ts'ai Ching, namely, the local san-she method, though Ch'eng Hao did not use this term. For a discussion of Ch'eng's ideas in connection to the problem Chu Hsi outlined here, see my San-lun, 61–62.

[6] See James T. C. Liu, Ou-yang Hsiu, 40–51 and passim. See also Peter Buriks, "Fan Chung-yens Versuch einer Reform des chinesischen Beamterstaats, 1043–1044," in Oriens Extremus, No. 3 (1956), 57–80; No. 4 (1957), 153–184.

[7] Namely, (1) strictness in evaluating the bureaucrats' performance, for the purpose of eliminating entrenched incompetents; (2) vigilance against favoritism, to begin with a reduction of the number of privileged appointments in yin forms; (3) a reform of the examination standards, de-empasizing poetic writings and stressing essays and discussion questions; (4) careful choice of regional officials, who would be charged with recommending and sponsoring their subordinates; (5) an increase in the land attached to local posts, to ensure a sufficient income for the officeholders and to minimize the temptations of bribery and embezzlement; (6) promotion of land reclamation and dike repairs, and implementation of measures to facilitate an efficient grain transport system; (7) creation of local militias among the peasants, to strengthen internal order and external defense; (8) full implementation of amnesty and reduction of

the civil service examinations. It is necessary to summarize the main points here.[8]

The memorial begins with an argument for the importance of education defined as the instruction of students in the classics, because it was held that this kind of knowledge was useful for "managing the nation and the world."[9] It then points out that the examinations had placed too much emphasis on poetic writing and the evaluation of a candidate's performance often hinged on his correct use of rhymes and meters. Han and Fan proposed that policy essay and discussion essay questions be tested in the *chin-shih* examinations. The memorial then details some of the technical measures to ensure that older candidates who were never trained to answer such essay questions be allowed some degree of leniency in the marking. The memorial then touches on the examination of chu-k'o candidates and suggests that they be tested not only on memorial questions, but also on questions on the meaning of the classics. It then suggests that candidates taking the primary, prefectural examinations be examined on their moral performance— "only those whose behavior is spotless and whose scholarly achievement is qualified should be sent to take the departmental examinations."[10] As a collorary to this, it is suggested that the anonymity measures at least in the prefectural examinations be eliminated. The memorial ends with a reiteration that *chin-shih* candidates doing well in the essay questions be given priority in the appointment to offices over those doing well in poetic writing.

From this memorial one sees that the reformers were above all concerned with how the government could actually carry out the investigation of the moral performance of candidates without sacrificing the principle of impartiality. Reformers, striving to maintain a degree of fairness, believed that some technical changes should be adequate to achieve the fundamental goal of recruiting morally qualified persons. The formula was a simple one: those who showed a greater ability in writing policy and discussion essays,[11]

---

criminal senstences, if ordered, so as to ensure the feeling among those pardoned of gratefulness; (9) elimination of contradictions, loopholes and inequities in the codes and government regulations, and insistence thereafter on strict law enforcement; (10) reduction of the corvee, including a measure to reduce the need for it by consolidating several prefectures or subprefectures into one. See James T. C. Liu, *Ou-yang Hsiu*, 43–44.

[8]*HCP*, 143/5b–7b. For a German translation, see Peter Buriks, *op. cit.*

[9]*HCP*, 143/5b–6a.

[10]*Ibid.*, 143/7a.

[11]The distinction between a *lun* (policy essay) and *ts'e* (policy discussion question) is so slight that I, for narrative convenience, shall not make an effort to always distinguish them, except where necessary.

or in interpreting classical passages were believed to have a better potential to become upright officials.

Another memorial drafted by Fan himself, but endorsed by Ou-yang Hsiu, Sung Ch'i (998–1061) and other reformers soon followed. It specifically spelled out that residence in school, which could ideally provide opportunities to conduct long-term observation of the moral performance of students, was the most reliable criterion for selection. It also concurred with the previous point that knowledge of the classics and expertise in policy matters as reflected in their *lun* and *ts'e* essays were more impoitant than excellence in *belles lettres* or familiarity with texts such as the classics.[12] Obviously, those advocating the recruitment of morally qualified people for service prevailed, as an imperial edict was issued immediately after the second memorial. The decree took pains to define what kind of candidates could be allowed to take the prefectural examinations:[13]

> Students should have registered and studied at schools for at least three hundred days before they can sit in the prefectural examinations held normally in the autumn; those who have taken previous tests are required to study for only one hundred days. Students who have to take care of their parents because no one else can do it for them can secure permission to study at home. Candidates in the prefectural tests should guarantee that they do not have records in one of the following seven moral defects: concealing the fact that they are in a mourning period; a record of criminal offense; obvious defects in practicing filial piety and brotherly love which constitute an offense against the law and that they have been fined in copper (payment in lieu of punishment) [more than] twice, or those which, though not legally an offensive, nonetheless constitute an offense against one's community; the counterfeiting of one's registered native locality; having a father or a grandfather who had committed the most serious four among the ten seditious crimes; and, finally, belonging to lowly occupations such as traders or laborers, or having previously been Buddhist or Taoist monks. Those who have such defects in moral behavior should be banned from taking the examinations.

The same edict also ordered that *chin-shih* candidates take three parts in the examinations, two of them dealing with *ts'e* and *lun* respectively; poetic writing now constituted only one third of every examination.[14] Classical learning in terms of comprehension of the meaning of the texts was given recognition in the examinations, a principle also applied in other *chu-k'o* subjects so that, for example, tests on the subject of the *Three Histories*

---

[12] The memorial was submitted in the third month of 1044. See *HCP*, 147/9a–10a.

[13] *HCP*, 147/10a–11a.

[14] *Ibid.;* note that *ts'e* and *lun* together made up only one third of the *chin-shih* test previously (see note 9 above).

(*san-Shih*) should emphasize candidates' understanding of, say, the significance, not merely the content, of historical events. These modifications, combined with the regulations on school residence and the qualifications of prefectural examination candidates, demonstrate the reformers' committment to ensuring the selection of morally respectable persons. In any case, there was at the time no lack of intellectual radicalism.[15] These reforms had *radical* moral overtones and resulted in the conviction that seriousness in classical studies was the basis for moral success, which could then be easily converted into political aptitude.

The University, as mentioned before, was made independent in 1040 and grew into a center for reform ideas. At the instigation of reformers, the University was ordered to require students to study for at least five hundred days before they could sit for the departmental examinations (University graduates were exempted from taking the prefectural tests). The reformers also touched on various areas of education at the local level and the civil service examinations. They endeavored to establish local schools and allocated official land as well as endowments of books to them. They drew up new regulations on the qualifications of local school teachers who were now to be appointed by circuit intendants for three-year terms. They also promulgated the measure that candidates for prefectural examinations should produce a warranty of their moral uprightness from two qualified candidates of departmental examinations. All of these changes reflect a basic concern for careful observation of, or investigation into, the behavior of students or candidates. The leaders of the reforms included Fan Chung-yen, Chang Fang-p'ing, Han Ch'i and Ou-yang Hsiu. In the University, Sun Fu and the maverick Shih Chieh also played active roles.

Critics of the reformers' belief that investigation of the moral performance of candidates would not undercut the quest for impartial examinations, lost no time in fighting back. The residence regulation was abolished as early as the winter of 1044,[16] only about half a year after the educational reform edict was promulgated. Anti-reformers such as Yang Ch'a attacked the stress on policy essay questions, which they considered "incomprehensible speculations."[17] Ultimately, the anonymity measure was restored in the perfectural examinations.[18] This was ordered in the fifth month of 1045, and it was also decreed that "the content of the examinations for the *chin-*

---

[15] Briefly mentioned in Ch. 4, section C.

[16] *HCP*, 153/1ab. The reason given is that the residence requirement was "inconvenient."

[17] *HCP*, 155/4b. See Chin Chung-shu, "Pei-Sung k'o-chü," No. 1, 257.

[18] *HCP*, 153/1ab, 164/3b–5a.

shih and various other subjects should follow the old system."[19] The reason given for this reversal was that the discussion and policy essay questions were very hard to grade, and that they would only promote "too much speculation and unrealistic talk."[20] Thus, the reformers' work on a new examination system that was more related to the ideal of recruiting morally qualified candidates had to be abandoned. The desire to grade impartially returned as the basic concern of the Sung government.

The downfall of Fan and his cohorts had tremendous implications for education and the examinations. For example, in higher education, the Imperial University again became part of the Directorate [School], its property was confiscated, and its budget sharply reduced.[21] Indeed, the period after the 1044 Reform was the most difficult for the University, during which Hu Yüan and Li Kou managed to maintain some continuity within the University, which at one time had as few as twenty or thirty students.[22] Another example touches the local schools which were continued, but with less visible activism. Without due recognition from the central government and without a proper link between education and the examinations, local schools found it difficult to provide students with appropriate incentive and necessary justification for studying there. In 1047, when Li Kou wrote the "Note on the Endowment of Land for the School in Shao-wu Military Prefecture," he had this to say:[23] "I have traveled many a day south of the Yangtse and the Huai Rivers, and many places have schools. If I visited a place and asked: 'Are the rooms in good order?' I often got the answer: 'They are used for dwellings for retired officials,' 'Are there enough food and equipment here?' Answer: 'They fill the kitchen of the prefectural office.'"

The inherent problem in the examination system was not solved, and continued to be hotly debated. On top of the doubts about how the examination system could reliably be used to measure the moral performance of individual candidates, the debates about the merit of the quota system also drew the attention of people as important as Ssu-ma Kuang and Ou-yang Hsiu, whose famous clash over how the quota system should be devised has been discussed before.[24] A debate of similar nature occurred at about the same time. This was the one between Liu Ch'ang and Cheng Hsün. Cheng Hsün, according to Liu Ch'ang, recommended that in the primary prefectural

[19] *Ibid.*, 155/4b.
[20] *Ibid.*, 164/3b–4b.
[21] See Ch. 4, section C. See also note 105 of Ch. 4.
[22] See note 21.
[23] Li Kou, *Wen-chi*, 23:173.
[24] See Ch. 6, section C, especially, notes 53 and 55.

tests there should be just one successful candidate in every ten. In other words, Cheng Hsün was suggesting the abolition of the quota system in prefectural tests. Liu Ch'ang was opposed to Cheng's recommendation. In his memorial, Liu warned of the possibility that most of the candidates in the departmental tests would as a result come form Fu-chien, Chiang-nan, Szechwan, and Kuang-tung, should Cheng Hsün's recommendation be accepted. These areas were more advanced than others during the Sung.[25] In any case, the debates over the merit of the quota system only served to demonstrate how the examination as a whole was viewed during this post-1044 reform era.

By the 1060s, it again began to trouble many that the examination system was not recruiting morally qualified candidates. Many pointed to the need for a clear policy to govern the practice of the civil service examinations which had serious defects in not being able to give substance to the Confucian ideal of selecting only the virtuous. Where school education should stand in the nation's *hsüan-chü* became problematic. This is exemplified by one memorial submitted by Pao Cheng (999–1062).[26]

> Therefore, the causes for prosperity or anarchy lie in the ways in which virtuous officials are recruited. It is important to have the right persons. *The History of the Former Han* says: "The virtue of a ruler is in essence to discover the right people." It is natural that man seeks high office. To do that, a man often tries to make himself look righteous and hide the evil part of his own self. Where the distinction between the righteous and the evil lies is exceedingly hard to detect. . . . Therefore a ruler should be very careful in the selection of officials. The method of electing a good official during the Three Dynasties is not clear to us and I hesitate to discuss it. As for those methods employed in the times after the Han, then I would say that the policy adopted during the T'ien-pao era (742–755) is unparalleled. There were schools in every prefecture and every county. In early winter, the schools would hold examinations. Distinguished graduates would then be sent, along with those elected outside of the schools, to the capital. These were the *hsiang-kung*. The government required local governors to make it clear to the candidates that those who passed should consider the failure a disgrace. The students who were truly righteous would be promoted, but those who were not would be dismissed. There was not one who was not impartial in conducting the selections. . . . In short, they had carefully designed their methods of distinguishing the talented and the righteous. This accounts for their unprecedented prosperity and cultural sophistication. . . .
>
> The present method of selecting officials is different from that of the T'ang. In villages and hamlets (*hsiang-li*), people do not examine the moral performance of candidates; the Ministry of Rites also does not take up that responsibility. All we do is to seal off the names of the candidates, and recopy their scripts. We employ complicated measures to regulate their conduct [in the examination

---

[25] Liu Ch'ang, *Kung-shih chi*, TSCC ed., 33:403–405.
[26] Pao Cheng, *Hsiao-su Pao-kung tsou-i*, TSCC ed., 2:25–26.

halls]. Furthermore, Your Majesty has to involve your own self in holding palace examinations to test them, during which they are to answer three questions (one *fu* rhyme-prose, one *shih* poem and one discussion question) or to compose as many as one hundred poems. The decision on who should pass and who should fail is made in three or four days. The examinations are truly elaborated, but I am afraid that this entire scheme is not the ideal method for advancing the virtuous and dismissing morally disqualified candidates. . . .

This memorial by Pao Cheng was clearly radical; he called into doubt nearly all the measures adopted by the Sung government to prevent corruption in the examinations: the measures of anonymity, recopying after the examinations, and the new palace examination. On the other hand, he openly advocated the alleged T'ang practice of recommending graduates from local schools and singled it out as the basis of the cultural success of the T'ang. Radical as he was, Pao, however, was representative of many of his contemporaries.

B. Educational Reforms: 1069–1126

Emperor Shen-tsung's call for a comprehensive reevaluation of the examination system in 1069 was a culmination of the debates of the previous decades.[27] Among the seven momorials answering to the order still extant, we find that, with the sole exception of Su Shih, all were in favor of making the examination system more responsive to the need to investigate the moral performance of candidates. The ideas of Ch'eng Ming-tao concerning education and the examinations, cited as the "only way. . . to follow" by Chu Hsi in his famous essay quoted at the beginning of this chapter, are found in Ch'eng's memorial submitted on this occasion.[28] Ch'eng Hao (Ming-tao) unequivocally spoke in favor of promoting students directly from local and central government schools. His ideas found an echo in 1080 when Li Ting and others decided to directly recommend distinguished graduates from the Imperial University to service,[29] and in Tseng Kung's memorial submitted the same year (1080).[30]

It is therefore clear that there was great dissatisfaction towards the current examination system in the second half of the eleventh century, and school education was looked upon as a necessary part of the selection process. Recommendations came in daily, and the reforms carried on by Wang An-shih and his followers were to take up the challenge. They had to devise something

[27] Already mentioned in Ch. 4, section B.
[28] See note 5 of this chapter.
[29] See Ch. 4, section C.
[30] *HCP*, 310/4ab.

to satisfactorily solve the problem of coordinating the two parts of the selection institution. Presumably, advancement of graducates from schools could be based on actual observation of the moral performance of candidates over a sufficient length of time.

First of all, Wang An-shih was certainly concerned with how the moral performance of individual candidates could be measured, or more precisely, how morally trustworthy candidates could actually be recruited. He wrote a couple of essays entitled "On Talent," to discuss the theoretical aspect of these concerns.[31] But these essays do not clearly show how he would actually propose to reform the examination system. Rather it was in his famous memorial of 1068, "A Memorial Requesting That the Regulations [for the Examinations] be Changed," that his whole spectrum of thinking on the subject was spelled out unmistakably.[32] The memorial suggested that the *ming-ching* (subjects on the classics, i.e., *chu-k'o*) subjects be abolished altogether,[33] and that teaching officials be appointed to the five major circuits.[34] The interesting point about this memorial, and thus Wang's thinking on education, is that he began the memorial with a statement relating to what we may render as "moral uniformity" (*i tao-te*). "The ancient method of selecting officials depended essentially on the establishment of schools. For this tended to produce uniform thinking amongst the officials on ethical matters. . . ," pronounced Wang.[35] The phrase, "moral uniformity," quickly became widely circulated, creating uneasiness among those not in agreement with his reform ideas.[36] And indeed, what Wang advocated was more than objectivity in evaluating the moral quality of an individual candidate. He was essentially aiming at bringing about a unified interpretation of ethical teaching as found in the classics. This is most evident in his pressure to make standard the new commentaries under his sponsorship or editorship as the absolute basis for marking examination scripts.[37] Criticisms are reflected in what eventually appeared in Li

---

[31] Wang An-shih, *Lin-ch'uan hsien-sheng wen-chi* (*Lin-ch'uan chi* hereafter), 64:680–682, 69:734–735. These essays are discussed in H. R. Williamson, *Wang An Shih, Chinese Statesman and Educationalist of the Sung Dynasty* (London: Arthur Probsthain, 1935), Vol. 1, 330–336, with the second essay translated in full in 330–333.

[32] Wang An-shih, *Lin-ch'uan chi*, 42:450; Williamson, op. cit., Vol. 2, 337 and passim.

[33] *Ibid.*

[34] *Ibid.* See also Ch'i Hsia, *Wang An-shih pien-fa* (Shanghai: Jen-min, 1979), 105–106.

[35] See note 32 above.

[36] The phrase reappeared in Shen-tsung's order to compile the new commentaries on the classics. See *HCP*, 229/5a. It also appeared in many contemporary writings. See Chin Chung-shu, "Pei-Sung k'o-chü," No. 1, 273.

[37] Liang Ch'i-ch'ao, *Wang Ching-kung* (Taipei: Chung-hua, 1956), 113–114. See also Ch'i Hsia, *Wang An-shih pien-fa*, 109–110.

T'ao's drafted chronicle of the Northern Sung: "This was done with a view to unifying the method of interpretation of the classics, and also with the idea of unifying men's thinking on moral and philosophical subjects. The students of the time were compelled to study these new books, as the chief examiners required candidates to use, in their answers, the interpretations they contained. In this way the old commentator's on the classics were ignored, being supplanted by these *New Commentaries*."[38]

The excessive zeal in trying to absolutize one school of interpretation must have been one of the reasons eventually leading to the fall of Wang An-shih.[39] This is most evident in the uproar that occurred in the Imperial University when the new commentaries were introduced.[40] It was obviously Wang's conviction that once the examinations were replaced by a system of government school education, and that once his own school of interpreting the classics was accepted, then he could achieve "uniformity of ethical behavior," as well as recruiting morally qualified people.

Wang An-shih was soon forced to leave the Court, but Shen-tsung continued to believe in reform. So did Wang's followers, whose policies on the examinations were less consistent than those of Wang An-shih, perhaps because the followers were primarily concerned with developing higher education. However, there was at least one important measure that resulted from Wang's followers' ideas and legislation on the examinations. The measure shows that they had a rather realistic view of the purpose of the examinations. This was the enactment in early 1081, at the instigation of Chang Tun (then the head of the Secretariat-chancellery), of the regulations requiring the *chin-shih* degree candidates to answer questions on legal knowlegde.[41] According to this plan, candidates were to answer one question on legal knowledge in the prefectural tests and two in the departmental tests. This matter shows that reformers were as much concerned with the purpose as with the procedure of the examinations.[42] Generally speaking, however, throughout the reform period from 1068 to 1085, concern

---

[38]*HCP*, 265/24b–25a; Williamson, *Wang An Shih*, Vol. 1, 341.

[39]The most comprehensive study on Wang An-shih to date is by Higashi Ichio, but Higashi in this monumental work appears to have failed to appreciate this part of Wang An-shih's dogmatic personality which traditionally has been held responsible for his failure to attract people to work with him. Liang Ch'i-ch'ao, in his *Wang Ching-kung* agreed that Wang had intended to ban all existing commentaries. See note 37 above.

[40]See my *San-lun*, 138.

[41]*HCP*, 311/7b.

[42]The decision to recruit more students specializing in the *Chou-li* and the *Li-chi* was another indication. See *HCP*, 229/22b.

remained over how the examination system could better fulfill the ancient goal of admitting only those who were distinguished for moral uprightness. This concern played a central role in debates over issue related to education and examinations.

The more adamant opponents of Wang's reforms probably disliked all the measures enacted, but except for a notable few, such as Su Shih and Liu Pan,[43] the majority of them seemed to agree with Wang that the examinations were in real need of change. Anti-reformers, however, obviously did not have confidence in either the sincerity or capability of the Wang An-shih group and doubted whether the educational system adopted by Wang An-shih and his associates could indeed replace the examination system satisfactorily. The leader of the anti-reformers was Ssu-ma Kuang whose attitudes were critical throughout the reaction period (1086–1094).

As early as 1069, in his response to Emperor Shen-tsung's order to submit recommendations on how to reform the examinations, Ssu-ma had made the following suggestions: first, since a righteous person was not always readily known to the government, it was necessary that "intelligent and impartial officials find out and elect" these people. Ssu-ma went as far as to suggest how this sponsorship should be enacted, suggesting the number of candidates a ranking official should recommend each year. According to his plan, those who recommended the most reliable and trustworthy people should be rewarded. The people recommended by officials should proceed directly to take the departmental examinations which, consisting at the time of conventional subjects, should be changed to examine more questions related to classical knowledge. Ssu-ma's second recommendation was that the government should pay greater attention than it did at the time to local schools, which he sarcastically described as places where "retired officials or officials in a mourning period meet wealthy town people to have fun; they consume food without actually conducting any study." He wished to see that rigorous teaching be conducted and that newly admitted students not be provided with room and board. Graduates from these schools, he believed, would then have been sufficiently trained to be exempted from the prefectural tests. They should make up at least half of the prefectural quota of successful candidates to take the departmental examinations.[44]

The second recommendation obviously was in line with the contemporary idea of how school education could at least partially correct the

---

[43] Liu Pan, *P'eng-ch'eng chi*, *TSCC* ed., 24:337–339. Su Shih, *Su Tung-p'o chi*, *KHTS* ed., Vol. 14, 39–41. Su's opinion in this memorial is partially translated in Williamson, *Wang An Shih*, Vol. 1, 337–338.

[44] Ssu-ma Kuang, *Wen-chi*, 39:319–322.

inadequacy of the examination system in terms of recruiting morally upright candidates. Ssu-ma was unwilling to go as far as condemning the system as a whole,[45] but was prepared to argue that the system could be improved to respond to the needs then thought not to have been properly filled. At the same time, Ssu-ma was also greatly concerned with how classical knowledge could be made the center of the examinations.[46] All of these reflected the fact that at least in the area of policies concerning education and the examinations, Ssu-ma had subscribed to the views current in the late 1060s.

Subsequent developments created a situation that forced Ssu-ma to reevaluate his own position in the area of education. The first reaction was directed against Wang An-shih's attempt to dogmatize his own interpretation of the classics. In the early 1070s, Ssu-ma obliquely referred to the tendency in the examinations to adopt new, "speculative and absurd arguments" and requested that the emperor ban them.[47] But in general, Ssu-ma's displeasure with the reform was directed against its financial measures.[48] Ssu-ma Kuang soon left Kai-feng for Lo-yang and was so preoccupied with his compilation of the monumental work, the *Tzu-chih t'ung-chien*, that he did not make any more comments on education until he returned to Court in 1086. Among the first memorials he submitted after his return was one dealing with the examinations.[49] This was a quite lengthy discussion on the issues he saw as related to the examinations in general and to Wang's policy in particular. He agreed with Wang's criticism of the system which gave priority to skills in composing poems over capability in understanding the classics, "resulting in candidates valuing flowery writings at the expense of going to the roots of moral commitment." But he was even more unhappy with Wang An-shih's attempt at standardizing the interpretation of the classics. "Wang An-shih should not have tried to use his own private scholarship to overshadow that of the ancient writers," he complained.[50]

In practical terms, Ssu-ma Kuang offered very much what he had already

---

[45] The memorial's tone implies that he did not personally wish to find fault with the system, but would go along with those who were dissatisfied with it.

[46] In a memorial submitted after the one just discussed, Ssu-ma urged that even those who were entering service by the *yin* protection method be examined on their classical knowledge. See Ssu-ma Kuang, *Wen-chi*, 41:329.

[47] *Ibid.*, 45:351–352.

[48] Most of the educational reforms were actually carried out not by Wang himself, but by his followers. See my *San-lun*, 129–157.

[49] Ssu-ma Kuang, *Wen-chi*, 52:389–391.

[50] *Ibid.*, 52:389.

offered nearly twenty years before.[51] He made two suggestions. One was to continue to place emphasis on the importance of classical learning, demanding that the actual tests center on the classics. The other was that the examination of "people well versed in classical learning and morally outstanding" (*ching-ming hsing-hsiu*) be given a more important place in the examinations, and that ranking officials in the government should recommend appropriate persons to take these places. Ssu-ma also recommended the abolition of the new test on legal knowledge, suggesting that *chin-shih* candidates should not be required to answer such questions. Not long afterwards, Ssu-ma even recommended instituting an examination called "Ten Categories" (*shih-k'o*),[52] which would examine nearly exclusively only the moral performance of candidates. The recommendation, however, was apparently not enacted.

Within the anti-reform camp there were other opinions as to how the examinations could be improved. The following four measures were the most important ones that were enacted during the period when anti-reformers returned to power:

1. The *Spring and Autumn Annals* was restored as a subject in the examinations. The subject was also reincluded in the University curriculum at about the same time.[53]
2. The *ching-ming hsing-hsiu* examination along with the sponsorship method as recommended by Ssu-ma was formally decreed for adoption in the fourth month of 1086 (the memorial itself was submitted in the third month).[54]
3. Stress on poetry was revived (not without causing scruples on the part of some less adamant anti-reformers). Equal numbers of successful candidates were to be admitted to the examinations in poetry and in classics.[55]
4. The degree in law was to be maintained, but candidates examined in the subject should answer questions on the *Analects* and the *Classic of Filial Piety*.[56]

[51] The entire memorial is in *ibid.*, 52:389–391.
[52] *Ibid.*, 53:400; *HCP*, 382/3a–5a.
[53] *SHY*, hc, 3/49ab.
[54] *HCP*, 371/5b–7a.
[55] The measure was most controversial. Sources concerning the quarrels over this particular decision are to be found in *HCP*, 425/4a, 13ab; *SHY*, hc, 3/50b–51a; and other private works.
[56] *HCP*, 407/5ab. It is interesting to note that *Mencius* was now replaced by the *Hsiao-ching*. This reflects the personal predilection of Ssu-ma Kuang who disliked *Mencius* and thought highly of the *Hsiao-ching*. See Chün-chieh Huang, "The Rise of

The significance of Ssu-ma's opinions and the anti-reform measures during the reaction (1086–1094) lay in the interesting development of perspectives on the examinations. Apparently, people continued to be dissatisfied with the examination system, but the specific reasons why it could not be used to actually carry out the commonly held ideal had now become blurred. Ssu-ma Kuang no longer questioned the validity or at least the need to have anonymous examinations, quite unlike the reformers of the 1040s whom he and other anti-reformers so respected. Some other anti-reformers, probably under the influence of Su Shih, now even demanded that poetic writing, which had previously been vehemently condemned by nearly every one, be restored to the examinations. The sponsorship method, which Ssu-ma had persistently wanted to institute, was indeed adopted, but watered down so much that it became insignificant.[57]

One therefore sees in this reaction that any suggestion on how to change the examination system would encounter opposition from some part of the government. Moreover, it appeared that the earlier concensus on the problems with the examinations had, by the 1080s, completely disappeared. Poetry was not regarded as "sick" (*ping*) any more, and anonymity measures designed primarily to maintain the ideal of impartial examinations were restored. Nonetheless, the legacy of reform efforts continued well into the final years of the Northern Sung.

Generally speaking, the majority of Sung people seemed to have subscribed to at least the rhetoric of the moral significance of the examinations. But among them, many had come to the conclusion that the system as such had little to do with how the moral ideal of recruitment could be actually practiced. Some would even go as far as to question the thesis that the best possible method to recruit the potential officials was to do it through school education, by observation over a long period of time. Pi Chung-yu (1040–1082), who was at some point sympathetic to the reform cause, would have the following to say, suggesting that both school education and examinations had respective reasons for existence:[58]

---

the *Mencius:* Historical Interpretations of Mencian Morality," Ph.D. thesis, University of Washington, 1980. See also Teraji Jun, "Tenjin sōkan setsu yori mitaru Shiba Kō to Ō Anseki," in *Shigaku zasshi,* Vol. 76, No. 10 (1967), 34–62. For Ssu-ma's own statements about his attitude towards *Mencius,* see his *Wen-chi,* 73:520–533.

[57] Ssu-ma's original proposal in 1069 would have officials recommend between one to three persons depending on the ranks of the officials themselves. In the 1086 memorial Ssu-ma changed his mind to suggest that only capital officials (*ching-kuan*) and above could sponsor three each year. See Ssu-ma Kuang, *Wen-chi,* 53:400–401, 39:320.

[58] Pi Chung-yu, *Hsi-t'ai chi, TSCC* ed., 5:59–60.

The method of "presenting the best from the villages and selecting the most useful from the hamlets" which was practiced in the age of the Three Dynasties may not be so easy to practice now, but we should indeed institute the more important parts of it, so that students and officials may acquire self-cultivation. We can then send for teachers and scholars and [ask them to teach students how] to perfect the proper relationship between a ruler and his officials, the piety between fathers and sons, the hierarchy between older and younger brothers, so that they all know how to tell right from wrong and can accept correct moral discipline and moral knowledge. As for skills in poetry or in classical learning, we have to imitate the ancient way of testing the candidates and we will then be able to grade them according to their ability. This is to say that we ought to continue a separate civil service examination system so that candidates may continue to take it; we ought to preserve this system, even if we do not care too much about it.

This interesting argument in favor of a separate examination system, so as to satisfy those who would like to go into service reflects a keen awareness of the rising concern about the validity of the examination system then facing a mounting challenge from the reformers determined to abolish it. Another memorial, submitted by Huang Shang (1043–1129), possibly during the reform of Ts'ai Ching, also reflected a similar dilemma:[59]

There are two ways [of teaching and learning]. One is to give examples to instruct students. This could be practiced in schools. . . . However, instruction given in schools may not necessarily cultivate the talent and moral character of students. Schools could indoctrinate, but an individual student is not likely to abide by this kind of teaching. Moreover, it is doubtful if any individual can actually absorb the instruction he receives in schools. Therefore, the ancients practiced at once the cultivation of talents and the recruitment of them, and let them supplement each other. It was Emperor Shen-tsung who decided to use schools as a place to cultivate talented people, and launched a program which had never been dreamed of before. He tried to enlist and encourage Confucian scholars. . . . and tried simultaneously to revive the method of "presenting the best from villages and selecting the useful from the hamlets." . . .

Obviously Huang Shang was attempting to give justification to the comprehensive educational program launched by the reformers, but secretly he was also hoping that people would not forget that there was yet another traditional system of examinations. And indeed, as if he felt that he had not made the point clear enough, he went so far as to distinguish between two types of education and argued that both would be needed in order to accomplish the ideal of schools and examinations:[60]

[59] Huang Shang, *Yen-shan chi, SKCS* ed., 18/6ab.

[60] *Ibid.,* 18/11b–12a. For a preliminary analysis of the use of the vocabulary of this article, see my *San-lun*, 70.

> The way of establishing local schools ought to be like this: in villages (*tang*), there should be schools (*hsiang*) and these *hsiang* schools are to cultivate the talents of students. Their chief function is thus the prefecting of a gentleman. In hamlets (*sui*), there should also be schools (*hsü*). These *hsü* schools are places where students shoot at targets. The chielf function of these schools is the selection of gentlemen. Only when these two functions are accomplished can we say that the ideal of schools has been achieved.

Opinions like these dominated the thinking on education in the first couple of decades of the twelfth century. It goes without saying that under these circumstances, attempts to enforce the measures aimed at replacing the examinations by a comprehensive government school system must necessarily have encountered tremendous opposition. By the time that Ts'ai Ching sought to institute a comprehensive national school system, most people had become skeptical of its chance for success. Still, Ts'ai Ching and his faction perpetuated the difficult ideal, hoping to select morally upright people for service. They thought that this would be more effective than the conventional method of the civil service examinations. The great irony was that they were consequently accused of moral irresponsibility, and of scheming to debase the nation's moral standards.

The most important innovation of Ts'ai Ching's educational program was naturally the practice of universal education, in the hope that selection within schools could ultimately replace the examination system. In reality, he faced tremendous oppositions, so much so that he never actually succeeded in suspending one single examination.[61] Seeing that he was not going to succeed in abolishing the examination system entirely, he recommended, in 1107, a new examination system called "method of selecting people outstanding in eight kinds of moral achievements" (*pa-hsing hsüan-kuan fa*).[62] I have briefly mentioned this method,[63] and pointed out that *pa-hsing* candidates were allowed to enter the University without taking any entrance examination.

To insure the respectability of this *pa-hsing* system, Ts'ai Ching persuaded Emperor Hui-tsung to write out the decree in his famous writing style and have rubbings of the decree sent to all local schools, where it was engraved on stone.[64] Ts'ai Ching also recommended, in the eleventh month of 1111, that students recruited from the *pa-hsing* system be provided with board in local schools, in 1113, that graduates of *pa-hsing* examinations be allowed

---

[61] For a detailed discussion on this matter, see Chin Chung-shu, "Pei-Sung k'o-chü," No. 2, 217–230.

[62] Yang Chung-liang, *Chi-shih pen-mo,* 126/1a–4b.

[63] Ch. 4, section E.

[64] *Chi-shih pen-mo,* 126/3ab. The inscription is still available in many works.

to teach in prefectural schools, and that those *pa-hsing* candidates attending the upper-hall of the University be given official status with their families classed as official households.[65]

The *pa-hsing* system obviously represented the final stage in the Sung effort to create an alternative to the current system of formal, impartial and anonymous examinations. Developments like this, which could not replace the conventional tripartite examinations, show that by the last two decades of the Northern Sung, the search for change had exhausted its own cause and energy, and sheer perpetuation of reform conviction as such only served to highlight the obstinacy of those who clung to some lofty ideal which by then had proved to be impossible to institute.

By the second decade of the twelfth century, despite the fact that it was generally agreed that examinations as such were not satisfactory, the failure to find a concensus on how to reform them had become evident. As a result, Ts'ai Ching's entire program failed. I have elsewhere attributed the failure to the limitation of available bureaucratic positions; the tenacity of Ts'ai Ching's faction, insisting on their own version of reforming program, also accounted for the ultimate failure.[66] The moral inadequacy found in Ts'ai Ching and his associates became evident in their inexplicable determination to enact and restore certain symbolic measures at whatever cost. To give just one example, the professional schools were always restored and placed under the Directorate of Education whenever Ts'ai Ching was in power, despite the fact that they were well managed under other government agencies.[67] As such, any particular suggestion on any policy change reflected not so much a sincere commitment to national or educational needs as a mere symbol of the ideology of the political factions. One can scarcely read much significance into the series of changes, abolitions, restorations and suspensions during the twenty years when Ts'ai Ching and his opponents took turns controlling the Chinese government. Meanwhile, the Chinese dynasty was left to erode, decline and eventually be conquered.

Three important concepts that emerged during the reforms continued to be debated and served as point of departure in Southern Sung educational policies. First, the promotion of outstanding graduates directly from local schools to the University or the exemption of them from primary prefectural tests continued to be regarded as a possible alternative to the examination

---

[65] *Ibid.,* 126.

[66] For some careful study of Ts'ai Ching and his image in Chinese history, see R. Trauzettel, *Ts'ai Ching als Typus des illegitimen Ministers* (Berlin: K. Urlaub, 1964).

[67] See Chart 2 on p. 102; see also Chart 4 for the various policy controversies and changes from 1070 to 1122.

system. Secondly, knowledge of the classics was considered essential to a candidate's potential as an official in the government. Thirdly, the emphasis on such impartial measures as recopying continued to make some people uneasy, with the result that the search for a more responsible sponsorship system continued to play an important role in the thinking on education and the examinations. We shall see these three components of thinking on the examination system and their defects reappear in the Southern Sung. By and large, however, the main trend of thinking during the Southern Sung about the moral purpose of examinations and how education could be related to the system was that the examinations as an institution could not possibly be transformed into one that could realistically recruit only the morally qualified. Instead, it was in education that one could hope to train enough good and morally upright people for the service of the government. Changes in institutional terms could not solve the dilemma that existed for the examinations; only a change in mind could. Education that came increasingly under Neo-Confucian influence during the Southern Sung was a consequence of this realization.[68]

C. Policy and Purpose of Education and the Examinations, 1127–1279

It seems that by the end of the Northern Sung the whole spectrum of possible changes with regards to the civil service examinations had all been proposed and tried, and with the endless controversies, most people had grown tired and skeptical of institutional reforms. The basic components of the reform ideas concerning how best to recruit morally qualified candidates continued to be tested but few new ideas developed, and even attempts to restore a certain measure originally proposed by the reform faction would cause barely a ripple within and without the Court. Attention indeed had shifted to the Neo-Confucian philosophy and the academies. It seems that more and more people had become disillusioned, not only with the examination system as such, but even with the government schools.

To properly understand this trend of thinking, however, one has to study first what the Southern Sung government, and intellectuals as a whole, thought of as the purpose of education and the examinations. No doubt, moral concern was always there, even when most people were convinced that few official institutions could be trusted to carry out the concern. This is evident in Chu Hsi's memorial cited at the beginning of this chapter.

[68] For a comprehensive collection of memorials dealing with policies of the examinations, see Chao Ju-yü, *Sung ming-ch'en tsou-i, SKCS* ed., 80, 81 and 82/1a–14a.

Criticisms of the examinations and the vicious results of preparing for the examinations abound in the writings of Neo-Confucians and need not be discussed here. It is important to remember that most people had abandoned the simplistic belief that examinations could realistically measure both the moral and intellectual achievements of candidates. Yeh Meng-te's comment comes to mind again immediately: "If a man chooses not to take the examinations and remains a student, it is surely all right for him to do so. If, however, he chooses to study for the examinations, then, in so far as he does not violate justice and moral principles, there is nothing wrong in his seeking to succeed, to be appointed to an office and to seek for promotion. . . ."[69] Yeh seems to see no reason to find fault with a person who "sought to succeed, to be appointed and to seek for promotion," but one feels that Yeh was categorizing this kind of person as different from those who chose to remain students. It is then understandable that Chu Hsi would make such a comment: "a gentleman (shih) should be able to distinguish between the examinations and education."[70]

The loss of interest in the examinations served to account for the fact that very little was written during the Southern Sung concerning how to improve them. Three issues, nonetheless, continued to be important, and the following is a brief summary of the debates and policy changes related to them.

The first issue concerned whether poetic writing in the forms of shih (poem) and fu (rhyme-prose) should be examined. We have already seen in the previous section that Northern Sung reformers distrusted these skills, regarding them as being of little value in the training of a person to become a useful bureaucrat. They also did not think that accomplishment in poetic writing had anything to do with one's moral performance. The reformers therefore recommended abolishing the tests on poetic composition. As a result, throughout the Northern Sung, the wisdom of the abolition of the poetry tests became a point of contention, marking the difference in policy matters between reformers and their opponents.

The first years of the Southern Sung, however, saw the restoration of poetic composition in the examinations. Candidates were to answer questions on both types of questions, namely, poetic composition and classical knowledge.[71] The method was changed again in 1137, when the new system

---

[69] Cited in Ch. 6, note 84.

[70] Chu Hsi, Chu-tzu yü-lei chi-lüeh, TSCC ed., 3:81.

[71] No direct evidence proves this, but from the later development one can see that this was what occurred. Also, in 1128, in legislating on the examination for teaching officials, the government decreed that poetic composition should *also* be examined,

was to examine those who specialized only in classical knowledge and those who specialized only in poetic writings as two different categories of candidates.[72] Apparently, the new method did not stipulate that each category of candidates should be given a separate quota, and as a result, those in poetic writing were making up a disproportionate majority of the successful candidates. Complaints were plentiful, pointing out that candidates might as a result abandon the learning of the classics.[73] So the government decided in 1157 that all candidates should be examined in both the classics and poetic writing.[74] But then it rescinded this order in 1161,[75] the reason given being that few candidates could be well versed in both arts, and that the inclusion of poetic composition, moreover, resulted in a reduction of chances to examine the candidates' ability in answering essay questions.[76] This new decision was accompanied by the regulation that only one third of the successful candidates from prefectural tests should be students of poetic writing.[77] This is the final decision on this matter as far as the source goes.

In general, then it is evident that the official position throughout the Southern Sung was in favor of examining candidates' classical knowledge, as well as their ability to compose essays discussing policy matters. This naturally affected the practice of education, then and later.

The second issue concerning the relationship between education and the examinations was sponsorship. The desire to have a reliable method for observing the moral performance of candidates continued to be strong in the Southern Sung, and sponsorship therefore remained attractive. But it was the method of "Ten Categories" proposed by Ssu-ma Kuang which was most often referred to when new methods of sponsorship were presented to the Court. The first imperial decree ordering officials to recommend people for service came in 1131. This was a result of Emperor Kao-tsung's reading of memorials by Ssu-ma Kuang and thirty-two, possibly, anti-reform officials. These memorials were selected and presented to the emperor by

---

indicating that the decision was following, possibly, that of the civil service examinations. See Tables 6 and 10.

[72] *CYYL*, 113/10ab.

[73] *Ibid.*, 115/19b–20a.

[74] *Ibid.*, 176/3a.

[75] *Ibid.*, 188/14b–15a. This shows that the combined examination method probably was practiced only once, that is, in the prefectural and departmental examinations of 1159 and 1160.

[76] See *HTC*, 134:3542. See also Huang Wei and Yang Shih-ch'i, *Li-tai ming-ch'en tsou-i*, 1416 ed. (Taipei: Hsüeh-sheng, 1964), 169/2b.

[77] *CYYL*, 188/15a.

Ch'en Hsiang (1017–1080), although Kao-tsung was prudent enough to order that no prejudice should be shown against those who had been previously associated with Ts'ai Ching and Wang Fu. The latter was also a condemned minister, though opposed to Ts'ai Ching.[78] This order was followed by another one in 1133 which formally restored the method of "Ten Categories" proposed by Ssu-ma Kuang.[79] Similarly, the order in 1156 that a new "Six Categories" sponsorship system should be instituted also referred to Ssu-ma's original recommendation. The so-called "Six-Categories" included: being polished in writing, capable of serving in posts requiring the preparation of official documents; being virtuous and fair, capable of serving in posts related to policy criticism; being familiar with legal codes and theories, capable of serving in legal appointments; being frugal and careful, capable of serving in posts connected with financial matters; being righteous, kind and compassionate, and renowned for merits, capable of serving in such posts as director, commissioner or prefect; being clever and shrewd, and distinguished in both intelligence and courage, capable of serving in the military posts of general or commander.[80] The reason that Ssu-ma's name should be invoked shows how Southern Sung policy-makers continued to share the concerns Ssu-ma had had more than seventy years before. The order stipulated that the method for recommendation should be similar to what Ssu-ma originally suggested, namely, capital officials should recommend three persons each year.[81]

The method of sponsorship continued to be debated through out the dynasty.[82] But as time went on, it became increasingly evident that the sponsorship method had as many problems as any other examination method, and fewer and fewer, if indeed any, memorials related the sponsorship method to the examination system. The usefulness of the latter was not questioned any further. As regards to the sponsorship method, the following ideas were discussed. First, how to make the system more directly responsive in terms of the recruitment of recluses who deliberately avoided taking examinations. One official recommended that, in each season, one recluse should be recommended by each circuit.[83] Second, with increased suspicion that the system might give rise to corruption, more and more

[78] Ibid., 49/9ab.

[79] HTC, 113:2995.

[80] CYYL, 172/13ab.

[81] Ssu-ma Kuang, Wen-chi, 53:401. See also note 57.

[82] See the convenient collection of memorials dealing with this subject in Huang Wei and Yang Shih-ch'i, Li-tai ming-ch'en tsou-i, 169/1a–170/25b.

[83] Recommended by Yen Shuo-yu, see ibid., 169/19ab. The recommendation does not seem to have been accepted.

people advocated limiting the number of people recommended. Suggestions were also made to limit the qualification of patrons so that fewer officials could recommend candidates.[84] But it was definitely the issue about how sponsorship could be made to work impartially which attracted the most attention. For example, Li Ch'un's recommendation in Emperor Hsiao-tsung's time would forbid what he called "[getting through] joints and knots" (*kuan-chieh*) by making the patron receive the same punishment the sponsored person would receive in case the latter violated the law.[85] Others advocated that the selection from schools be restored.[86] Still others suggested that the qualifications of people to be sponsored be clearly defined so that it would be easier for officials to decide whom to recommend.[87] In general, however, there was no serious suggestion that sponsorship should be abolished.[88] Thirdly, the method of directly promoting outstanding graduates from schools to service continued to have its advocates. First of all, local school graduates during the Southern Sung continued to enjoy intermittent opportunities to have a special quota in the entrance examination for the University.[89] Upon the recommendation of Lo Ts'ung-yen (1072–1135), the government decided in 1144 that, of the prefectural examination quotas, one third should be reserved for graduates of local schools.[90]

It is thus obvious that reformers' beliefs about school education and its reliability in achieving the ideal of selecting only the most potentially qualified people continued to have appeal. Indeed, this ideal was also shared by Neo-Confucians,[91] as witnessed in the famous memorial of Chu Hsi cited at the beginning of this chapter. Similarly, Chao Ju-yü, as late as 1194,

---

[84] *Ibid.*, 170/11b–12a, 19b–20b.

[85] *Ibid.*, 170/11b.

[86] See later.

[87] Huang Wei and Yang Shih-ch'i, *Li-tai ming-ch'en tsou-i*, 169/19b.

[88] It is necessary to point out that I have limited myself to the sponsorship of non-official candidates, and have left out the sponsorship within the bureaucracy. The latter during the early Northern Sung is the subject of Edward A. Kracke's *Civil Service*.

[89] See Ch. 4, section E and Table 4.

[90] See note 85 of Ch. 5; *CYYL*, 152/11b–12a; *HTC*, 126:3349.

[91] Neo-Confucians saw in education an end in itself, and believed that it was the only way to ensure the moral rectitude of students. The best of them should then be selected for service. This attitude was slightly different from that of Wang An-shih and his followers, who, while sharing the view that long-term observation of students' performance in schools was the most reliable base for selection, nevertheless did not quite see that moral training was the center of education. Some Neo-Confucians apparently felt that it would be simply too costly if schools were set up merely for the preparation of students to become officials. In general, on the surface, both felt strongly the need for school education.

would have the following to say.[92]

> In this country, there are schools in the capital as well as in all prefectures and counties. As a result, the intellectual atmosphere has been auspicious since the Ch'ing-li times; in fairness it could be compared to that of the Three Dynasties. The [Three-] Hall system was then introduced in the Ch'ung-ning and Ta-kuan eras, and scholars were cultivated in every place. The achievement has more or less measured up to the ancient ideal of "selecting from townships, villages, hamlets, and boroughs." The result was that, for a while, students were specially careful about their behavior: they would not walk in the streets without properly dressing themselves and would humble themselves and yield the way to elders in town or to teachers of their school. This was a respectable custom. The only fault then was in students' being forced to study only the *New Commentaries,* and studying the *Lao-tzu* and the *Chuang-tzu* at the expense of the *Spring and Autumn Annals.* History as a discipline was completely abandoned. On top of this, they (reformers) also abolished the civil service examinations, so that poor students aspiring to move up were forced to study [only what the reformers prescribed]. Things like these were doing violence to the principle of nature, and therefore could not succeed and had to be abandoned. But one should by no means blame the failure on the [Three-] Hall system itself. The failure stemmed from the evils of the time.
>
> Since the government moved [to the South], we have stopped fighting and concentrated on promoting cultural excellence. We have restored the Imperial University in the temporary capital and started civil service examinations in every prefecture. A scholar should congratulate himself that he has been born in such a time. However, we see more superficiality and pretentiousness than faithfulness and loyalty. The government has demurred at this. The reason why this is so is because the rise and fall of scholars has nothing to do with schools. We have to use measures like pasting over the names of candidates to examine how morally they behave. They have polished themselves in writing flowery essays without having the determination to actually learn anything. They regard schools as no more than boarding houses and treat their teachers as any common folk walking on the street. Monthly quizzes and seasonal tests are mere formalities. Any ideal of government education and cultivation of the people is totally missed. . . .

Chao then went ahead to suggest that the Three-Hall system on a local level, that is, the progressive promotion system in both local and higher educational institutions, be restored.[93]

It does not appear that Chao's recommendation was adopted. However, as discussed before, we do know that the special quotas set up for local school graduates in the entrance examination for the University was used for quite a large part of Southern Sung period. All of these show that at

---

[92] Huang Wei and Yang Shih-ch'i, *Li-tai ming-ch'en tsou-i,* 170/16b–17a. The dating is based on the fact that Chao was appointed chief examiner in 1194. See *SS,* 392: 11983.

[93] *Ibid.*

least one trend of the reformers' legacy had become deeply rooted in the educational thinking of Southern Sung officials: the direct promotion method as practiced by Ts'ai Ching was never restored in its entirety, but some part of it, and certainly the idea itself, remained important throughout the Southern Sung. But people had few illusions that the method could fulfill satisfactorily the ideal of recruiting only morally qualified candidates.

The discussion above does not include special references to contributions by Neo-Confucians who obviously had even stronger opinions about education and the examinations. But our discussion centering on policy debates serves adequately to show that the concern about the ancient ideal of selecting only the morally qualified candidates, though continuing to preoccupy the thinkers, had become obviously impractical and could never be carried out in a manner that would be satisfactory to everyone.

The last time that some active efforts to regenerate government education in terms of moral selection can be seen was during the reign of Emperor Li-tsung (r. 1225–1264). This was a time when Neo-Confucians came back to power and exerted some influence.[94] In terms of policy, however, the period was not very innovative.

Emperor Li-tsung took a personal interest in education, especially higher education. After all, he was enthroned during the height of student activism, at a time when Neo-Confucians had more or less succeeded in their struggle for political influence. He paid at least one visit to the University;[95] ordered that the three capital schools (the University, the Military School and the School for Imperial Relatives) select morally upright students for prizes;[96] took a personal interest in the palace's primary school;[97] awarded his own calligraphic pieces to schools and examiners in examination years;[98] intervened in the management of the University;[99] ordered the wandering scholars to return to their hometown for registration for the examinations;[100] and, above all, decreed in 1250 that the quotas in the University's

[94] The *i-li* scholarship, that is, Neo-Confucian ideas, were formally admitted into the civil service examination syllabus in 1229. See *HTC*, 165:4484.

[95] In 1241. See *HTC*, 170:4630. Twenty years later, in 1261, he sent his son to pay sacrifice to Confucius in the University. See *SS*, 45:876.

[96] Students "well versed in classical learning (*ching-ming*), morally outstanding (*hsing-hsiu*), and upright in determination (*ch'i-chieh*)," were ordered to be given prizes. See *HTC*, 171:4676 and 172:4681.

[97] Established to educate children of imperial relatives. See *HTC*, 171:4677.

[98] *HTC*, 163:4446, 171:4676.

[99] For example, in 1248, when a University student got into trouble because of excessive drinking, the Emperor intervened to keep the Director of the University who asked to resign because of the incident. See *HTC*, 172:4694.

[100] *HTC*, 173:4712. The affairs of the wandering scholars caused some uproar in

entrance examination set for local candidates be divided equally between school graduates and other candidates.[101] Finally, in 1252, the Emperor even decreed that the government reserve ten to twenty positions in the departmental examinations for those candidates well known for their moral excellence.[102] This was a time when the Sung dynasty was rapidly declining, but this was also a time when the government gave education its final attention. There was nothing significantly new. One senses that while the moral purpose of education should be the same as that of the examinations, that they be related to each other and that both should receive equal attention, the government had ceased to think that it could promulgate any meaningful policy to achieve that ideal.

It is no wonder that there was not much significant development in government education and in the civil service examinations in the Southern Sung. The situation had largely settled into normalcy after the uproars and disturbances in the early twelfth century. The prevalent thinking that school education could not, and perhaps should not, be reduced to simply preparing students for the examinations seems to have taken hold among policy-makers in the Southern Sung. Ch'eng Pi, writing in the final years of the dynasty, would have the following to say which, in a very important way, echoed what early twelfth-century thinkers had pronounced:[103]

> In the Former Han, there was a *T'ai-ch'ang* School, and there was also a *T'ai-hsüeh*, but we do not know where students were actually taught. In the Later Han, there was a *Pi-yung* and a *Hung-tu* School, but we also do not know their curriculum or how students were recruited. During the T'ang, besides the *Kuo-tzu* School and the *T'ai-hsüeh*, there were also the School of Four Gates, and the *Hung-wen* School. [For all of these schools], however, those who stayed in their native places were selected and presented [to the government] by local governors, and those who traveled and were away from home were then presented [to the government] by government school. [It is therefore obvious that] recruitment from villages and hamlets had always been different from the recruitment from schools.

If Ch'eng Pi was any indication, and I believe he was,[104] then we can very safely conclude by saying that by the Southern Sung, it had become evident that the moral ideal of the examinations believed by the Sung people to

---

the Court, and the government never actually succeeded in disbanding them. See *ibid.*, 173:4714. See also Ch. 10, section A.

[101] *HTC*, 173:4707.

[102] *Ibid.*, 173:4726.

[103] Ch'eng Pi, *Lo-shui chi, SKCS* ed., 5/16a–18b.

[104] For his life, see *SS*, 422:12616–12617; Huang K'uan-ch'ung, "Ch'eng Pi nien-p'u," in *Shih-yüan*, Vol. 5 (1974), 115–162.

have been actually practiced in antiquity had become merely a hollow dream. While most of them continued to be concerned with the important function of the examination system in recruiting above all the virtuous, they had become realistic enough to cease thinking that they could actually evaluate the moral performance of candidates.

D. Recapitulation

The Sung people concerned with the use of the examinations certainly were aware that the system had become an important social as well as political institution unprecedented in Chinese history. One reason why they were so anxious to make the system good enough to carry out the ancient ideal of selecting only morally meritorious people for service stemmed from precisely this awareness. In their mind, this was the essence of meritocracy so long advocated by generations of Confucian followers. In the previous chapter, we examined the idea of impartiality as a way to achieve fair selection of candidates, and found that the principle did not always help to make examinations an effective machinery for political control. From the government's viewpoint, impartial selection was not entirely desirable, because the government had a greater responsibility for equality beyond simply choosing the best.

The basic concern was, of course, how to select only morally meritorious people for service. The moral ideal was lofty, and we see that all factions shared this similar conviction that the examinations should be reformed or even transformed to fulfill the ideal. This was so despite the great differences in opinions on how reforms could be implemented. The kernel of the debates was how school education could be administered with an eye to preparing the best of the students for service. Examinations which produced too many unsure factors could be replaced by long-term observation in schools. For various reaons, by the late eleventh century, there were already people defending the impartial examinations as no less useful than selection through schools. The debate culminated in the early twelfth century, when Ts'ai Ching went ahead with his massive reform program. By then, many peoole had become convinced that the examination system was merely a scapegoat, and that the state school system did not have the social structure to sustain it. This realization was best expressed by Chu Hsi who quoted Ch'eng Hao's plan with approval, but questioned how the nation was going to pay for such a massive educational system.[105]

---

[105]See the quotation at the beginning of this chapter; see also Chu Hsi and Lu Tsu-ch'ien, *Reflections on Things at Hand,* 264–265, quoted in p. 272.

Thus, by the Southern Sung, very few officials continued to talk about how to improve examinations or how to relate government schools to the selection of potential officials. Even though the concern that the government should only examine the moral performance of candidates continued to reappear in the Southern Sung, and sponsorship, the direct promotion method and reserving special quotas for school graduates were prosposed now and then, Southern Sung policy-makers seem to have generally resigned themselves from espousing any significant change. Even towards the end of the dynasty, when attempts were made to restore the dignity of government schools and the examinations, there was very little innovation.

The discussion above provides a good background for us to understand yet another vision which also stemmed from concerns over the moral purpose of education. Obviously, one could not simply hope that a sound institution could fulfill all the moral requirements of a nation. Now, if there simply was not a school in the nation that could train students according to the best standards of moral education, then what good were the examinations? This is a forceful question, posed by Neo-Confucians, who courageously took it upon themsevles to answer it.

Part IV
A Concluding Evaluation

CHAPTER 10

The Significance and Strength of
Sung Government Education

In the previous chapters, I argued that the examination system was primarily designed for political control. I also pointed out that, despite many people's hope of making the system more responsive to recruiting only morally qualified candidates, they found it incapable of achieving that hope. As a result, school education, which at one point was about to be trusted to correct the deficiency of the examinations in this aspect, became ultimately separated from any effective part of the selection process. Or one may say that the examinations were kept intact so much so that they over- shadowed the educational effectiveness of governmental schools. Unless a school was officially recognized as a candidate-producing institution having a share in the quota of local successful candidates, nobody would consider it as an effective educational institution. The development in later dynasties bore this out clearly, and government schools were either absorbed into the examination system, or faced with fierce competition from other private, community or clan schools which were also producing candidates of equal capability.[1]

But why was this so? Why could government schools not be relied on as the best possible instructional institutions? First, one may question the nature of Sung higher education and ask how effective the education of the Imperial University was. One way of answering this would be to explore the image of the University in the minds of Sung intellectuals. But the most significant development of Sung higher education actually was its evolution into an institution that was open to commoners. By the Southern Sung, it had become obvious that the school relied primarily on entrance examina- tions to recruit students, and successful candidates (or sometimes unsuccess- ful ones) or distinguished graduates of local schools were making up the basic student population of the University, whose graduates would then be permitted to take the departmental examinations with more generous quotas.[2] Studying the composition of University graduates could help us

---

[1] These institutions will be studied in a book being edited by Wm. Theodore de Bary.
[2] One technical point related to qualification of University graduates has to be

to understand not only many of the significant developments in higher education in later dynasties, but also the role of the Sung Imperial University in government education as a whole.

Secondly, it has been repeatedly pointed out in Part II that we possess very little information about the students and their life in local prefectural or county schools. This has to be placed in the context of the government's regulations on the relationship between students and their teachers. However, we do know that most schools had rather good financial arrangements. It appears that in most of the Sung period, the government paid quite enough attention in financial terms to schools, and the support that schools managed to give to students was not insignificant. Did local schools succeed in being the most attractive place for education? Within the context of finance and preparation for the civil service examinations, I shall attempt an answer to this question also in this chapter.

A. The Educational Significance of the Imperial University

The long chapter on Sung higher education and the parts on the life in the University should suffice to show that the Imperial University students obviously played a rather important role in Sung politics. It is now necessary to discuss the following questions concerning the significance of Sung University students' education, how the Sung government viewed the educational achievement of the University and, above all, how the Sung University affected the development of higher education in later dynasties.

Obviously, Sung higher educational institutions were gradually opened to commoners and during the height of the Northern Sung reforms, an additional *Pi-yung* school was even founded specially to admit students recommended from local schools. Evidence shows that the majority of *Pi-yung* students were also of commoner background. During the Southern Sung, because of the entrance method, the University was actually admitting only those who had already attempted the civil service examinations, and hence was accepting essentially from the same pool of candidates as the civil service examinations. It is therefore likely that the composition of University students in terms of social background was rather similar to that of the candidates for the civil service examinations.

---

made clear here; they were exempted from taking the primary, first level tests in the civil service examinations. Other privileges, such as exemptions from labor services etc. applied equally to University students and the *te-chieh jen*. Therefore, those *te-chieh jen* taking an examination to enter the University must have been those who failed in the departmental examinations.

A preliminary check on the standard *Sung-shih* biographies (from Chapters 244 to 474) shows that at least 125 had received some form of University education. Of those 125, however, we only know for sure the family background of 46. As to the remaining 79, we unfortunately possess no direct information about whether they came from families with members previously in service or not.[3] Among the 46 family backgrounds we do know, it is interesting to note that those who came from families without any previous record of service numbered 22, and those having forebears with official titles numbered 24. This suggests that the Imperial University indeed was pretty open to a rather wide spectrum of people, more so than the civil service examinations.

It is important, however, to note that this information is biased. First of all, the nature of the *Sung-shih* biographies almost entirely dictated the way information about University education was recorded. Among the 125 whom we know to have received some form of University education, at least 56 were students during Hui-tsung's reign, meaning that they were recruited to the University (possibly from local schools) during the time when Ts'ai Ching undertook his mass educational reform. Some of these students eventually were permitted to enter officialdom without taking the examinations. Since Chinese official biographies had the tendency of recording only the method by which a person entered into service, it is no wonder that we possess better information about the University education of people during Hui-tsung's reign when University graduates were eligible for direct appointment to office.[4] Since it is also true that, generally speaking, very few Chinese biographies include information about the schooling of individuals, the lack of that information is therefore not necessarily a reflection of the relative unimportance of education received at schools. Furthermore, one feature about the information found in the *Sung-shih* biographies does stand out clearly: nearly all of those 125 people were obscure or politically unimportant. In the case of nearly all the more famous University students with biographies in the *Sung-shih*, who eventually rose to high offices or became famous scholars, there is no mention of their experiences in the University.[5] The conclusion must therefore be that from the official view point, a University education was not considered to be either

---

[3] As mentioned above, this is only a preliminary survey, and the information has come exclusively from the *SS* biographies.

[4] For a useful discussion on the problem of Chinese biographies, see Denis C. Twitchett, "Problems of Chinese Biography," in Arthur F. Wright and D. C. Twitchett (eds.), *Confucian Personalities*, 24.

[5] Such as Ou-yang Hsiu, Lü Tsu-ch'ien, Ch'en Liang, Wang Ying-lin and Lu Chiu-yüan.

significant or important in one's life, and that despite the fact that a good many University students now came with commoners' background, a demand for a University education was unnecessary in both political and intellectual arenas.[6]

It is in this light that we should interpret the phenomenon of the wandering scholars. The phenomenon compares interestingly with the similar one in medieval Europe in that these scholars seem to have caused more trouble for authorities than their intellectual contributions would warrant.[7] Candidates during the Northern Sung preferred to take the examinations in the Capital. Because of the admission methods adopted by the University during the Southern Sung, which paved the way for a rise in the number of wandering scholars, many of them obviously unsuccessful applicants who chose to stay in Hangchow to continue to prepare for the civil service as well as for the University's entrance examinations, the University became very attractive in this peculiar sense. Under the circumstances, however, the gathering of a great number of young students only helped to worsen the situation and complicate the political activities of the regular University students.[8] To illustrate this point further, the government appeared to be totally at a loss as to how to deal with the *yu-shih* problems; after all, it was rather difficult to control them because they were not officially registered students. Repeated efforts to disperse them failed, and Emperor Li-tsung had to resort to reserving a special quota for them in the Metropolitan Prefectural School of Hangchow.[9] He soon reversed himself and ordered a tightening of the control.[10] He even had his order engraved on stone and erected on the campus.[11] All of these conflicting measures seem

[6]No matter how open the Imperial University now was to commoners, people of commoner's background made up only a small portion of the Sung bureaucracy and hence the Sung upper class. See Ch. 8.

[7]I am making a brave statement here, fully aware that modern interpreters on medieval European education, notably Charles Haskins, were not altogether negative about wandering scholars. Could what Peter Abelard did, when he was a "wandering scholar," have happened in Sung China? I hope so. He referred to "travelling through various places in search of discussion. . . ." This sort of thing seemed to have been also cherished as part of China's private *chiang-hsüeh* tradition. Incidentally, it may not be irrelevant to know that, in today's Japan, a "Wanderer" (*ron-jin*) means one who has failed university admission examinations and is still preparing for them.

[8]Wang Chien-ch'iu, *Sung-tai t'ai-hsüeh*, 309–312. For Chia Ssu-tao's confrontation with the *yu-shih*, see Chou Mi, *Ch'i-tung yeh-yü*, Han-fen lou ed. (1915), 17/10a and *SS*, 474:13873.

[9]*HTC*, 173:4712, 4716. A special quota for them was also created in the prefectural examinations in the capital area. See note 62 of Ch. 6.

[10]*HTC*, 173:4762.

[11]*Ibid.*, 175:4764.

to show that wandering scholars, while being attracted to the University, were perhaps not engaging in much more serious preparations than joining their University compatriots in all kinds of frivolous activities. It was only when the Mongols were approaching Hangchow that University students, with wandering scholars perhaps joining them, suddenly shifted their attention.

In short, the University evidently developed into an institution, during the Southern Sung, which served students more socially than academically. I have already argued this in discussing life within the University. Nonetheless, the convergence, at least in institutional terms, of the Directorate School and the University, as well as the University's increased openness, also characterized Sung higher education. This development means that the University was admitting more students of commoner background. But it is more accurate to interpret the development as meaning that the educational quality of the T'ang, which strongly reflected aristocratic ideals and concerns, had given way to reflecting the influence of those advocating the need to recruit capable bureaucrats.[12] In other words, the higher educational institutions had evolved into a kind of "way station" of the civil service examinations. The University admitted examination candidates who, through the University, went into service. Since the chance for making it into officialdom was largely guaranteed when students entered the University, it was very natural that the University became more like a large social gathering than a serious academic institution.

The rather flamboyant life of the University students could not continue. When the Mongols decided to make the Directorate of National Youth a part of the civil service examinations, the social nature of the University faced its first major challenge. But when the founder of the Ming dynasty tightened his control of the University by reinstalling the stone-tablet erected by Emperor Li-tsung, the tradition of University students' interference in national politics came to an end.[13]

In institutional terms, on the other hand, the University (or the Directorate, as the two were now inseperable) continued to evolve into a more integrated part of the civil service examinations. By Yüan times, mere registration at the Directorate School was considered adequate for fulfilling the requirements and one could be appointed immediately to office.[14]

---

[12] For a brief discussion of the aristocratic nature of T'ang higher education, see my *San-lun*, 41–42.

[13] Wang Chien-ch'iu, *Sung-tai t'ai-hsüeh*, 389.

[14] Distinguished students were recruited directly into officialdom, called *kung-sheng* (tribute students). The name is reminiscent of the *kung-shih* used during Ts'ai Ching's "Three-Hall" period (see note 85 of Ch. 6).

In this sense, then, the higher educational institution which could claim ancestry at least back to Han times finally became absorbed into the nation's recruiting machinery.

The development had its periods of resistence. During the Sung, the reforms forestalled the tendency of higher educational institutions to degenerate into mere way stations for the examinations. The paradox was that reformers were even keener than their opponents in wanting to make the University more reliable as a recruitment mechanism. They hoped that better education, especially moral training, acquired from lengthy residence at schools and an improved and progressive curriculum, could achieve the purpose. Unfortunately for them, the reform efforts failed.

The failure of reforms also doomed their programs for technical schools. Given their very short periods of existence as part of the educational portfolio, these schools never achieved much. On the other hand, calligraphy, painting and mathematics, under government sponsorship, progressed markedly during the Sung.[15] But government educational agencies, notably the Directorate of Education, played little part in the progress.

All told, then, it is understandable that the Sung government did not provide its people with totally satisfactory higher education. It is true that individual students and events helped to create a certain legacy which continues to be cherished. In general, however, contemporary as well as later interpreters obviously felt less than comfortable when they weighed the performance of Sung higher education.

B. The Significance and Strength of Local Government Education

It has been pointed out that most Sung people were silent about the education they received in government schools, especially at the local level.[16] Aside from the tendency in Chinese biographical writing to leave out such information, I speculate that this was also partly a result of the people's conception of government education. Indeed, with so much Neo-Confucian criticism of Sung education as preparation for the examinations, one might tend to conclude that Sung government education in prefectures and counties during the Southern Sung was of rather poor quality and actual instruction was not systematically carried out. One might even think that government

---

[15] In a wider sense, of course, the cultural brilliance of the Sung was partly accounted for by their success in education. A good history of Sung education should really take up the challenge to explain it.

[16] Ch. 7, section A.

education stagnated and the number of schools ceased to grow. There is some truth in these conclusions. At least in institutional terms, the number of schools founded by the government declined after the capital was moved to the South. One reason for this was that by the end of the Northern Sung, most prefectures and counties already had their own government schools.[17] Therefore, school founding after that occurred mainly when a new administrative district was created and when a new school subsequently had to be established. With the increase in the demand for education, government schools quickly became inadequate to fulfill these needs.

The composition of the student body in local schools will, perhaps, elude us forever. As has been pointed out previously,[18] most people chose to keep silent about their experiences in local schools. Nonetheless, this fact certainly does not mean that locally powerful or wealthy families did not send their children to local schools. We have many references to abuse of school lands and privileges by powerful families from towns or villages, and these examples are indicative that there were perhaps as many children from wealthy backgrounds as there were from poor ones.[19] My impression is that wealthy children made as much use of local government schools as did poor children. This was particularly true in the Northern Sung, when academies were not as yet popular enough to lure away students.

Fan Chung-yen, as well as many famous educationalists including Hu Yüan, Chou Tun-i and Li Kou all spent time at local government schools.[20]

---

[17] A useful survey by John Chaffee has this to show:

Earliest reference to Sung schools (references per decade)

Period	Prefectural schools	County schools	Total
960– 997	1.6	2.6	4.2
998–1021	4.2	9.2	13.4
1022–1064	19.0	21.2	40.2
1064–1085	15.0	16.4	31.4
1086–1100	3.3	21.3	24.6
1101–1126	6.5	19.6	26.1
1127–1162	3.6	13.6	17.2
1163–1189	2.6	8.1	10.7
1190–1224	1.4	8.3	9.7
1225–1264	1.0	6.2	7.2
1265–1279	1.3	3.3	4.6

See his "Education and Examinations in Sung Society," 210 and 212.

[18] Ch. 7, section A.

[19] For references to abuses, see Ch. 5, section E. See also *WHTK*, 46:433.

[20] *SS*, 432:12837. See also useful references in Mai Chung-kui, *Sung Yüan li-hsüeh-chia chu-shu sheng-tsu nien-piao* (Hong Kong: Hsin-ya yen-chiu so, 1968), passim.

Many officials, indeed nearly all the early Northern Sung local officials, participated in one way or another in the founding or repairing of prefectural or county schools. It is conceivable that at least during the 1044 reform and the early twelfth-century reform, local education was rather popular and very well administered.

The situation changed slightly during the Southern Sung. The main problem of education at the time has been mentioned many times: it was too much overshadowed by the interest of the students in their preparation for the examinations. A large number of regular local school students received meal allowances, had funds to cover their emergency needs, and enjoyed special quotas in the entrance examinations for the Imperial University or in the prefectural examinations.[21] If this were not enough to attract students, one would indeed be surprised to know what would, unless of course a private school could offer a better curriculum or teaching that would give its students a better chance to pass the examinations. After all, the prevalent attitude towards education was that it was preparation for the civil service examinations.

In other words, local government education continued to flourish throughout the Southern Sung, and it appears that these schools continued to attract students who were registered to prepare for the examinations. They also attended these schools for the privileges awarded and for the convenience. However, since it was a custom, or perhaps a policy, for the government to set up only one school in each prefecture or county, and the government could only support a certain number of students, it is thus also conceivable that more students were seeking admission to the schools than could actually be admitted. This was one of the basic reasons behind the establishment by Chu Hsi, and later by many local prefects and subprefects, of additional schools, namely, academies, to admit the students not admissable under the governmental framework of education. Advocates of academies had to demonstrate that academies were by no means a worse place to prepare for the examinations. Or better, they had to put forward an educational philosophy demonstrating that education had a wider significance than for entrance to officialdom. In any case, it is through the attacks by Neo-Confucians, who were the mainstay of those advocating academies, that we come to feel that local government education had declined in the Southern Sung.[22]

There were obviously more students in the Southern Sung than government could or would support in the state schools. Who were these people? First of all, children of officials, or those wealthy enough, probably received

[21] See Ch. 5, section D.
[22] A study of the *shu-yüan* should make a useful book.

as much instruction from private tutors as from formal, organized schools.[23] These people often came from families with educational, and most likely, official backgrounds. This situation was less clearly so in the Northern Sung, but it became evident after the twelfth century.[24] Secondly, as the size of the literate population increased, it is equally conceivable that some students would elect or be forced to study in private academies, as suggested above. Academies indeed offered some very distinct curriculum advantages which attracted some people who believed that their children would actually receive better education in *shu-yüan*. The distinguished educational program of the academies did not prevail easily; it had to be adjusted to contemporary needs. But it was in this process of adjustment that it was to grow and mature, intellectually and educationally.[25] Students in academies eventually made up the largest portion of the student population of late Imperial China.[26] From a wider perspective, then, it is not too far from truth to say that government education had indeed been declining since the Southern Sung, overshadowed by what was offered in academies. Nonetheless, in the process of "officialization," we also see mutual adjustments so that academies would involve themselves more systematically in preparing students for the civil serive examinations. Official resentment towards Neo-Confucians also softened, so that government schools eventually incorporated the ideas and curriculum previously only offered in academies. In any case, these two categories of students, along with those officially admitted into government schools, made up the student population in Southern Sung China. It is difficult to estimate the ratio between these different categories of students, but all indications show that the larger portion of them were non-government school students.

In retrospect, it is at once understandable why local government education was overshadowed by private education while it nonetheless continued

---

[23] In my "Life in Sung Schools."

[24] As a result of the response to the social importance of the civil service examinations.

[25] The adjustment process is aptly named "officialization" by Terada Gō in his *Kyōiku shi*, 313–317. See for an example of the development in *SS*, 450:13257, "Scholars in T'an (in present Hu-nan) were keen about studying at schools. The distinguished graduates from prefectural school, who did well in the monthly tests were promoted to study in the Yüeh-lu academy (*shu-yüan*) in Western Hu-nan. If they again performed well, they would then be promoted to study in the Yüeh-lu *ching-she* (*Vihara* academy)."

[26] An estimate of the students registered in government schools in the fifteenth century shows that they did not exceed 32,500. This figure certainly means only those who were admitted to government schools. The total number of students should therefore far exceed this. See Ping-ti Ho, *The Ladder*, 173.

to serve a stratum of the Sung population who needed education. The Sung government eventually lost interest in establishing more than one school in each administrative district perhaps for two reasons. The infamous attempt by Ts'ai Ching must have made it psychologically difficult to reinstitute a similar type of mass education, and, secondly, the financial burden must also have been too obvious to any policy-maker. Chu Hsi had more than once made the second point clear.[27]

> In ancient times, boys entered school at eight and college at fifteen. Those whose talents could be developed were selected and gathered in the college, whereas the inferior ones were returned to the farm, for scholars and farmers did not exchange occupations. Having entered college, one would not work on the farm. Thus scholars and farmers were completely differentiated.
>
> As to support in college, there was no worry about sons of officials. But even sons of commoners, as soon as they entered college, were sure to be supported [by the state]. Scholars in ancient times entered college at fifteen and did not begin to serve in the government until the age of forty. In the intervening twenty-five years, since there was no profit for them to chase after, their purpose was clear. They would necessarily go after the good and in this way their virtue would be perfected. People of later generations would have from childhood the intention of chasing after profit. How could they tend toward the good? Therefore the ancients would not allow people to serve in government until they were forty, for only then were their minds settled. It would do no harm merely to earn a living. But the temptation of wealth from emolument is most harmful.
>
> I do not know on what basis Master Ch'eng said this. In ancient times, in teaching the young, elders in small communities would sit in front of the school and watch them come and leave. They came to school at a definite time. Having finished their lessons, they would withdraw to study at home. When they were promoted [to college], they also went at a definite time. They farmed in the spring and summer and studied the rest of the time. I have never heared that the government had to support them. A family was given a hundred *mou* (of land) in the first place. And now more food had to be provided for students! Where did they get all this food?

As for the first point, the very fact that few, if any, were willing to come out to defend Ts'ai Ching, or even Wang An-shih, was enough to show that their educational policies had come down as some kind of impractical, if not disastrous, experience. Even in the courageous memorial by Chao Ju-yü, cited above, one sees the need to condemn the absolutist tendency of the reform attempts.

Local government education during the Sung had its glorious days, and in its contribution to preparing students for the examinations, it was quite

---

[27]Once in his memorial cited at the beginning of Ch. 9. Another in Chu Hsi and Lu Tzu-ch'ien, *Chin-ssu lu*, tr. by Wing-tsit Chan, *Reflections on Things at Hand*, 264–265, which is quoted here.

successful. But with the increase in student population, and with institutional changes which made local government schools increasingly subservient to the needs of registering students preparing for the examinations, these schools became ever more a part of an educational program which was clearly less than satisfactory to the Neo-Confucian educationalists. This program did not decline, it simply became less responsive to the more demanding educational requirements.

C. A General Conclusion

I set out to study the function and organization of government education, and pointed out that the civil service examinations had a tremendous influence on the development of Sung education in general, and government education in particular. The most important issue in Sung education, therefore, was how it should be related to the civil service examinations. There were at least three serious reform attempts to clarify or to reconsider the relations: the 1044 reform, Wang An-shih's reform and Ts'ai Ching's reform. In general, however, government education was influenced by the students' desire to prepare for the examinations. Eventually, government schools, by virtue of enjoying a high quota for their graduates in the number of candidates recruited to take part in the departmental examinations, became institutionally a part of the civil service examinations. In the previous section, I used this and other facts to argue that government schools were therefore a success during the Sung dynasty.

The success is, however, to be understood only in very narrow sense— if we interpret education as preparation for office. Naturally, I, like the Sung people, cannot accept an approach as limited as this. From the earliest days of the dynasty, there were already constant complaints about the crippling effects preparations for examinations had on the practice of education. The criticisms culminated in the attacks by Neo-Confucians, and the belief that government education substantially declined during the Southern Sung was very much a direct result of this Neo-Confucian interpretation. There is some truth in this; viewed from whatever angle, education should be more than preparation for office. Schools founded and administered by the government had indeed failed to uphold some of the ideals entrusted to them. The value of these schools had declined or at least had not succeeded in impressing people that there was value in their education other than in preparing students for the examinations. Instead, in the course of their development, they had become increasingly subordinate to the functions of the civil service examinations.

Reform attempts did not succeed in changing the situation either. Basic-ally, reforms were comprised of the following ideas and measures:[28]

1. Those who were concerned with the moral ideal of recruitment advocated measures such as residence or sponsorship. In general, they also felt the need to examine candidates on their ability to write policy essays or discussions.
2. Those who were more concerned with institutional changes advocated measures such as a mass national educational system and a built-in promotion scheme so as to replace the examinations. They also felt the need to change the content of the civil service examinations, by laying more emphasis on certain classics and the commentaries, compiled by them, on these classics.

Since these two approaches were essentially similar in their dissatisfaction with the development of education, one may say that reformers initially had the support and understanding of those who eventually turned against them. The failure of reform movements thus cannot be simply attributed to any mistake on the reformers' own part concerning the correct under-standing of the issues involved in the relations between educational practice and the need for a sound examination system.

In this book, I proposed a basic answer based on an analysis of the feasibility for the Sung to abolish the examination system and to replace it with a national educational program. My conclusion is that with the domination of one prominent channel for upward social mobility, any educational project that would educate more students than Chinese official-dom could absorb, definitely could not succeed. This is in addition to the facts that Ts'ai Ching and his followers could not in both their behavior and their practice convince their contemporaries that what they proposed was morally motivated and could indeed provide an answer to the issue. It remained unsolved.

The rise of a Neo-Confucian world view and educational theory would

[28]The division does not correspond exactly with the traditional definition of Sung reforms. I do not always follow the Sung division between reformers and their oppo-nents in the book, because I do not see the need; actually, I even go further to suggest that, in institutional terms, the educational scheme proposed by Ch'eng Hao, an anti-reformers, was essentially similar to that of Ts'ai Ching. The division here is therefore for convenience. Robert Hartwell's theory of "historicists vs. classicials" is good for understanding the different approaches to policy analysis but is not applicable here. Robert Hartwell, "Historical Analogism, Public Policy and Social Science in Eleventh and Twelfth Century China," in *American Historical Review*, Vol. 76, No. 3 (1971), 690–727.

direct people's attention to the education of the mind and the behavior of the individual. They preached the belief that it was in the transformation of the mind of an individual that education could be achieved. The Neo-Confucian educational program included community schools, clan schools and above all, academies.

The background of the rise of academies is complex.[29] Socially, because of the widespread use of printing technology, the number of people seeking education quickly increased. During the height of the early twelfth-century reform, the total number of students supported by the government had reached two hundred thousand. It was an enormous task just to manage the provision of meals, not to mention other necessities, for these students.[30] The government must have found that it was too much of a burden to handle this job, and decided to dismantle the program. But in any case, Ts'ai Ching's project failed, and during the Southern Sung, the government simply ceased to build more than one school in each administrative district. Academies relied on the excess students for survival, but since Neo-Confucians succeeded in devising a better educational curriculum and pedagogy for academies, the academies eventually became even more attractive than government schools. Intellectually, the long tradition of China's private education provided a respectable legacy, and Neo-Confucians found in this tradition a justification and a source of inspiration for their academies. Ultimately, the academies had to rely on the general dissatisfaction towards the changing nature of Sung government education to succeed in demonstrating that they had a better educational program. All of these factors created the new institution which in later periods of Chinese history ironically produced more successful candidates in the civil service examinations than government schools did.

When academies were eventually awarded quotas for the civil service examinations, however, the distinction between them and government schools became completely blurred.[31] The process can be called "officializa-

[29]See my "Chu Hsi, Academies and the Tradition of Private *Chiang-hsüeh*."

[30]The difficulty involved is best reflected in the following quotation: "During the Ch'ung-ning era (1102–1106), schools were built for the first time. All prefectures and counties had to establish schools and prepare provisions for students. There was not a single day when officials were not busy. Students were given coupons (for provisions) as soon as they were admitted to schools. The distribution of coupons could not be delayed. If any official delayed in issuing coupons, he could be charged with obstructing the educational administration and could be punished without immunity." Lu Yu, *Lao-hsüeh an pi-chi, Hsüeh-chin t'ao-yüan* ed. (1805) (Shanghai: Shang-wu, 1922), 2/7a.

[31]See my "Ssu-jen chiang-hsüeh" and Sheng Lang-hsi, *Chung-kuo shu-yüan chih-tu*, 138.

tion" *par excellence.* Obviously, a process as important as this must necessarily reflect the struggle for supremacy by Neo-Confucian thinkers and how Neo-Confucianism as both a world-view and an educational program succeeded in becoming the intellectual orthodoxy of late Imperial China. In this sense, then, the whole story of Sung government education, while interesting in its own light, serves best to illustrate the rise of Neo-Confucian education, which itself is another important chapter in the history of Sung education.

APPENDICES

A. Numbers of *Chin-shih* Degrees Conferred during the Sung Dynasty

B. Numbers of *Chu-k'o* Degrees Conferred during the Sung Dynasty

C. Numbers of Degree-holders Computed on Twenty- and Thirty-year Totals

D. Proposals on Educational Reform by Han Ch'i and Fan Chung-yen in 1043

E. Educational Program Issued by Ts'ai Ching in 1101

F. Genealogical Charts of Eight Prominent Sung Families

APPENDIX A

Numbers of *Chin-shih* Degrees Conferred during
the Sung Dynasty

Year	Sources				Conclusion
	(1) *SHY*	(2) *HCP*	(3) *WHTK*	(4) *Kang-yao*	
960	–	19	19	19	19
961	–	11	11	11	11
962	–	15	15	15	15
963	–	8	8	8	8
964	–	8	8	8	8
965	–	7	7	7	7
966	–	6	6	6	6
967	–	10	10	10	10
968	–	10	11	11	11
969	–	7	7	7	7
970	–	8 (106)	8 (106)	8	8 (106)
971	–	10	10	10	10
972	–	11	11	11	11
973	26	26	26	26	26
975	31	30	31	31	31
977	109	109 (184)*	109 (184)*	109	109 (63)
978	74	74	74	74	74
980	119	119	121	121	119
983	229	175	239	239	239
985	179	179	258	258	179
	76	76	–	–	76
988	54	28	28	28	28
	47	700*	700*	–	47
	31	31	31	–	31
989	186	186	186	186	186
992	353	353	353	353	353
998	–	50	50	353	50
999	–	70	71	71	70
1000	365 (236)	414 (260)	409	409	414 (236)
	13	–	–	13	13
1002	38	38	38	38	38
1005	247 (111)	246 (118)	247	247 (62)	247 (111)
1006	146 (205)	96 (662)*	–	96	96 (81)
1008	370	207	207	207	207
1009	31	31	31	31	31
1011	31	31	31	31	31
1012	126	126	126	126	126
1014	21	21	21	21	21
1015	197 (84)	203 (78)	280	280	203 (78)

Year	Sources				Conclusion
	(1) *SHY*	(2) *HCP*	(3) *WHTK*	(4) *Kang-yao*	
1019	240	162	140	140	162
1020	– (105)	–	–	–	– (105)
1024	207 (43)	206	200	200	207 (43)
1027	377 (109)	379 (242)*	77	377	377 (109)
1030	249	249	249	249	249
1034	715 (857)*	501 (857)*	499	499	501 (440)
1038	310 (26)	310 (165)	310	310	310 (165)
1042	436	432 (364)*	435	435	432 (187)
1046	538 (223)	537	538	538	538 (223)
1049	489	543	498	498	489
1053	520 (166)	520 (75)	520	520	520 (75)
1057	388 (122)	388 (214)*	388	388	388 (122)
1059	163 (29)	163 (65)*	165	165	163 (29)
1061	183 (44)	193 (43)*	183	283	183 (44)
1063	194 (72)	194 (100)*	193	193	193 (72)
1065	–	361*	200	200	200
1067	–	305	250	250	305
1070	355	–	295	295	295
1073	348 (475)	596*(691)*	400	400	348 (475)
1076	426 (477)	596*(593)*	422	422	426 (447)
1079	602*(778)*	602*(778)*	348	348	348 (450)
1082	592*(836)*	593*(836)*	445	445	445 (628)
1085	–	575*(847)*	485	485	485 (714)
1088	523 (533)*	508 (533)*	523	523	523 (531)
1091	602 (323)*	602*(323)*	519	519	519 (278)
1094	513 (346)*	600	512	512	513 (296)
1097	569 (?)	609	564	564	569 (?)
1100	–	–	561	561	561
1103	538	538	538	538	538
1106	671	–	671	671	671
1109	731	–	685	685	685
1112	713	–	713	713	713
1115	670	–	670	670	670
1118	783	–	783	783	783
1121	630	–	630	630	630
1124	705	–	805	805	805
1128	451	–	451	451	451
	103	–	87	103	103
1132	259 (158)	–	259	259	259 (158)
	120	–	120	120	120
1135	220 (272)	–	220	219	220 (272)
	–	–	137	137	137
1138	295 (?)	–	293	293	293 (?)
1142	253 (514)	–	254	254	254 (514)
	–	–	144	144	144

Year	Sources				Conclusion
	(1) *SHY*	(2) *HCP*	(3) *WHTK*	(4) *Kang-yao*	
1145	300 (247)	–	300	300	300 (247)
	–	–	73	73	73
	–	–	–	36	–
1148	331 (457)	–	330	330	330 (457)
	–	–	23	23	23
	–	–	–	75	–
1151	404 (531)	–	404	404	404 (531)
	–	–	18	18	18
	–	–	–	124	–
1154	356 (434)	–	348	348	348 (434)
	–	–	63	63	63
	–	–	–	75	–
1157	426 (392)	–	426	426	426 (392)
	–	–	–	19	19
	–	–	–	129	–
1160	412 (513)	–	412	412	412 (513)
	–	–	16	16	16
	–	–	–	112	–
1163	537 (277)	–	541	–	537 (277)
1166	494 (295)	–	492	–	494 (295)
1169	391 (291)	–	592	–	391 (291)
1172	389 (481)	–	389	–	389 (481)
1175	–	–	426	–	426
1178	–	–	417	–	417
1181	–	–	379	–	379
1185	–	–	395	–	395
1187	–	–	435	–	435
1190	–	–	557	–	557
1193	–	–	386	–	396
1196	506 (578)	–	506	–	506 (578)
1199	412 (789)	–	412	–	412 (789)
	–	–	4	–	4
1202	439 (497)	–	435	–	439 (497)
1205	433 (611)	–	38	–	433 (611)
1208	425 (641)	–	426	–	425 (641)
	–	–	4	–	4
1211	461 (679)	–	465	–	461 (679)
1214	504 (669)	–	502	–	504 (669)
1217	523 (663)	–	523	–	523 (663)
1220	475 (647)	–	475	–	475 (647)
1223	549 (679)	–	550	–	549 (679)
1226	–	–	987	–	987
1226	–	–	557	–	557
1232	–	–	493	–	493
1235	–	–	466	–	466
1238	–	–	422	–	422

Explanations:
1. Numbers in brackets are those of facilitated *chin-shih* degrees (*t'e-tsou-ming chin-shih*).
2. Asterisked numbers are the total numbers of graduates in both *chin-shih* and *chu-k'o*, regular and facilitated.
3. When more than one number is cited in one source in the same year, it means that more than one test was given in that year.
4. Figures included in the "Conclusion" column are derived from comparing the sources and are adopted as the most likely numbers of *chin-shih* graduates recruited in that year. Appendix C is computed on this basis. The detailed process by which the conclusions are arrived is omitted here.

APPENDIX B

Numbers of *Chu-k'o* Degrees Conferred during the Sung Dynasty

Year	Sources			Conclusion
	(1) *SHY*	(2) *HCP*	(3) *WHTK*	
966	–	9	–	9
972	–	17	–	17
973	101	101	96	101
975	34	34	24	34
977	208	207 (X)	207 (X)	207 (121)
978	82	70	82	82
980	534	533	534	534
983	764	516	285	516
985	318	318	699	318
	302	302	–	302
988	–	100	110	100
	621	X	X	621
	89	89	89	89
989	478	523	478	478
992	–	964	774	964
998	–	150	150	150
999	–	174	180	174
1000	432 (697)	432 (697)	1,129	432 (697)
	345	–	–	345
1002	182	181	180	181
1005	570 (75)	570 (75)	570	570 (75)
	698 (997)	698 (X)	–	698 (581)
1008	320	652	320	320
1009	54	54	–	54
1011	50	50	–	50
1012	377	376	377	377
1014	21	–	–	21
1015	65 (72)	373	65	65 (72)
1019	154	154	154	154
1024	354	277	354	354
1027	894 (234)	698 (X)	894	894 (234)
1030	573	573	573	573
1034	481 (X)	282 (X)	481	481 (417)
1038	617 (587)	414 (984)	617	617 (587)
1042	332	407 (X)	407	407 (177)
1046	455 (1,655)	415 (702)	415	415 (702)
1049	550	550	550	550
1053	526 (430)	522 (430)	522	522 (430)
1057	389 (102)	389 (X)	389	389 (102)

Year	Sources			Conclusion
	(1) *SHY*	(2) *HCP*	(3) *WHTK*	
1059	184 (16)	176 (X)	184	184 (16)
1061	102 (41)	102 (X)	102	102 (41)
1063	147 (28)	147 (X)	11	147 (28)
1065	–	X	18	161
1067	–	211	36	211
1070	474	–	472	474
1073	– (217)	X (X)	40	248 (217)
1076	194	X (X)	194	194 (146)
1079	X (X)	–	–	254 (328)
1082	X (X)	X (X)	–	147 (268)
1085	–	X (X)	–	90 (133)
1088	X (X)	73 (X)	–	73 (65)
1091	X (X)	X (X)	–	83 (45)
1094	X (X)	X	–	87 (50)

Explanations:
1. Numbers in brackets are the numbers of the facilitated degree-holders.
2. X means that the source only gives an unspecified total of degree-holders in both the *chin-shih* and *chu-k'o*. These numbers are given in Appendix A.
3. When more than one number is cited in a source in the same year, it means that more than one test was given in that year.
4. Again, numbers adopted as conclusive are derived by comparing the sources. A detailed description as to how they were arrived at is omitted here.

APPENDIX C

Numbers of Degree-holders Computed on Twenty- and Thirty-year Totals

	A	B	C	D	A + C	Total
I. Twenty-year Period:						
960- 979	371	169	451	121	822	1,112
980- 999	1,368	–	4,246	–	5,614	5,614
1000-1019	1,589	611	3,267	1,425	4,856	6,892
1020-1039	1,644	764	2,919	1,231	4,563	6,558
1040-1059	2,529	636	2,467	1,427	4,996	7,059
1060-1079	2,299	1,488	1,791	760	4,090	6,338
1080-1099	2,541	2,447	480	561	3,021	6,029
1100-1119	4,621	–	–	–	–	4,621
1120-1139	2,881	430	–	–	–	3,311
1140-1159	2,402	2,575	–	–	–	4,977
1160-1179	3,082	1,857	–	–	–	4,939
1180-1199	3,084	1,367	–	–	–	4,451
1200-1219	2,789	3,760	–	–	–	6,549
Average:	2,400	1,462	2,232	921	–	5,265
II. Thirty-year Period:						
960- 989	1,266	169	3,409	121	4,675	4,965
990-1019	2,062	611	4,555	1,425	6,617	8,653
1020-1049	3,102	1,174	4,291	2,110	7,393	10,677
1050-1079	3,370	1,714	2,886	1,308	6,256	9,278
1080-1109	4,996	2,447	480	561	5,476	8,484
1110-1139	5,047	430	–	–	–	5,477
1140-1169	4,252	3,951	–	–	–	8,203
1170-1199	4,316	1,848	–	–	–	6,164
1200-1229	5,357	5,086	–	–	–	10,443
Average:	3,752	1,714	3,124	1,105	–	8,038

Explanatory notes:
1. A: Total *chin-shih* degrees conferred over the period.
   B: Total facilitated *chin-shih* degrees conferred.
   C: Total *chu-k'o* degrees conferred.
   D: Total facilitated *chu-k'o* degrees conferred.
2. Because of the incompleteness of information, the total numbers were most likely larger than what are presented here. This is more particularly so for numbers of facilitated degrees, and especially those after 1160.

APPENDIX D

Proposals on Educational Reform by
Han Ch'i and Fan Chung-yen in 1043*

Thirdly, the examinations should be carefully conducted. The responsibilities of the village leaders as defined by the *Rites of the Chou* have been long ignored. Nowadays, in the prefectures, we may still see that there are intelligent school teachers, and thanks to them, these teachers can instruct our students about the *tao* of ruling the nation and the people. But our government has been specially fond of examining *chin-shih* students in the art of poetic composition and *chu-k'o* (various subjects) students in their ability to memorize. Both have abandoned the main ideal of the civil service examinations, and have replaced it with obscure measures. As a result, among the scholars who decorate your Court not more than one or two out of every ten is a man of vision. This is especially dangerous in a time when the nation is in deep crisis and in need of talents. It is therefore necessary to teach students the art of managing the nation and the world, and recruit only those who are trained in these arts. Only then can we hope to remedy the inadequacy. Some may say that curing this hopeless disease is not of the first priority. We would argue that, even a stable nation, to keep it safe, still needs to implement the measure [as suggested above] in the afternoon of the very day when it is first proposed. There is indeed no time to waste before the nation grows into turmoil. We shall therefore recommend that officials of those circuits or prefectures where there are schools enlist scholars well versed in the classics to teach in the schools. The purpose is to instruct students on how to behave themselves.

As for the subjects in the recruitment of candidates, we propose that we adopt the recommendation by Chia Ch'ang-ch'ao and others that *chin-shih* candidates should first answer policy essay and discussion essay questions and then proceed to the second part of the examination to compose poems and *fu* rhyme-prose. They also recommended that *chu-k'o* candidates should not just answer written elucidations, but should also be tested on the meanings of selected passages from the classics. The purpose is to see to it that candidates shall not concentrate only on elegent writing, but shall also comprehend the significance [of their own writings]. We could then hope that scholarship will be promoted and those careless about their moral conduct will be converted. We think these are the most important goals.

*Source: *HCP*, 143/5b–7b. See note 8 of Ch. 9.

[Besides the recommendations of Chia Ch'ang-ch'ao and others], there were also those proposed by Ou-yang Hsiu and Ts'ai Hsiang recommending that candidates be evaluated and screened immediately after each part of the test, so that there would not be too many scripts to mark and that the marking could be more carefully done. We are afraid that if we indeed implement the method of evaluating and screening candidates [after each part], some older ones may feel that they are deliberately excluded as they have not been well trained in writing policy and discussion essays, or in studying the meanings of the classics [they specialize in]. We therefore suggest that those *chin-shih* candidates who have taken the examinations more than three times be allowed to sit for all three parts of the [*chin-shih*] test with policy essays and discussion questions taken before poetic composition. Their scripts [from all three parts] should also be marked together so that they could be evaluated according to their performance in either the essay and discussion questions or poetic composition. Those who have so far taken only two or one examination are still young and can afford to continue their studies. They should be tested, evaluated and screened part by part.

[Similarly], in the *chu-k'o* tests, those who could pass the earlier parts should be questioned on the meaning of ten passages of the classics [they specialize in]. Those who cannot pass the earlier parts should then be required to answer oral questions from the examiners. If a candidate can answer seven questions, then he has passed the test in his subject. Those who have not previously studied the meaning of the classics and have taken the examinations more than three times should be tested only on "written elucidation" questions (*mo-i*) and then their answers would be rated as either "acceptable" (*ch'u*) or "comprehensive" (*t'ung*). As for those who have so far taken the examinations only once or twice, they should have more than eight "comprehensive" answers [to the written elucidation questions] by the last part of the test to qualify for the degree.

Moreover, the *chin-shih* and *chu-k'o* candidates recommended by the local government [to take part in the departmental examinations] should have already been investigated as to their moral conduct in the primary examinations. Only after this procedure should they be examined in writing. The practice now does not require that candidates be examined on their moral conduct; rather, they are examined on skills in flowery writing and memory. The practice, in addition, uses the anonymity method, which ends up testing the candidates only on writing. These methods are not in accord with the [ancient] ideal of selection.

Furthermore, in the *chü-jen* examinations held by the Southern Department [of Rites] (*nan-sheng*), the arrangement was for candidates to take two parts: the first part is poetic composition and the second part the policy essays. All candidates without exception try to do their best and since they all have had enough experience in taking examinations, they seldom make mistakes. They are then sent to sit for the palace examination. This examination covers both poetic composition and essay questions in one test. This creates a situation in that one single mistake in rhyme or in expression can result in the expulsion of the candidate, no matter how hard he has spent his life preparing for the examinations. On the other hand, if a candidate does not make any mistake in the rhymes, then even if he is young and elementary in studies he will quickly move along the road to officialdom. [In short,] there is no investigation of the moral conduct of candidates in local examinations. These candidates are examined only on their ability in not making mistakes in rhymes and meters. It is no wonder that students find that success in the civil service examinations depends more on luck than on moral performance or scholarly achievement. An intelligent ruler should of course see to it that a candidate gets recruited because of his moral and scholarly achievement. It is certainly not a good thing for a nation to see that scholars feel that it is fate that decides their chance for advancement; there is no reason for them to confuse good and evil and to attribute the confusion to the heavens.

Your humble officials therefore ask that the regulations on the prefectural examinations be revised so that only those whose behavior is spotless and who qualify in scholarly achievement are allowed to be sent to take the departmental examinations. [In the prefectural tests,] the anonymity measure of covering the names of candidates on the scripts should be abolished. As for the departmental tests, since the candidates have been previously screened in their native prefectures on their moral conduct, the anonymity measure should continue, so that the scholarly achievement of candidates can be evaluated fairly and responsibly, determining who should pass and how they should be ranked. The candidates are then sent to take the [palace] examination in the presence of the emperor and they are examined by different examiners. A new ranking is then prepared. This will be compared to that of the departmental examination, which is only now announced. If both rankings place the same candidates in the same group (*chia*), but rank them in different order within the group, then there is no need for adjustment [within this group]. Those who are ranked in different groups will be very few. In these cases, their names in the scripts should again be covered, and the scripts would be reevaluated before the final grouping is announced by the emperor. This is the most reliable way for determining the ranking. Should there be more than three candidates who are ranked in different groups, then the emperor should decide how to rank them.

In the scripts of the *chin-shih* subject, those which are distinguished in policy essays and discussion questions, but are only good in poetic works should be graded as distinguished, whereas those which are distinguished in poetic works, but are only good in essays and discussions should be rated as being only good. In the scripts of the *chu-k'o* subjects, those which are distinguished in explaining the meaning of the classics should be awarded a distinguished grade, whereas those which are distinguished in elucidations should be given only good standing. Successful candidates with distinguished grades should be recommended to office right away, while those with only good grades should be ordered to wait for appointment [according to the needs set forth by the Department of Personnel]. It has been an established custom that all successful candidates be kept on a waiting list, but because of the shortage of people to fill the various local posts at the beginning of this dynasty, the government has had to appoint all new successful candidates immediately to offices. Qualified potential officials (*hsüan-jen*) have steadily grown in number so that we now have more than enough of them. It is therefore necessary to carry out some reform, which at the same time could encourage students to pay more attention to their studies, and to know better the way sages cultivated their minds. It is hoped that the reform will result in the government's recruiting the right people, and in the people's securing appropriate rewards.

APPENDIX E

Educational Program Issued by Ts'ai Ching in 1101*

On the second day of the eighth month of the first year in the Ch'ung-ning era, the Right Executive Department of Ministries Ts'ai Ching memorialized that school education at the present time be given the first priority and that schools be established all over China so as to educate students. He recommended that [the following programs] be successively put into practice:

1. Abolish the quota of successful candidates of the K'ai-feng prefecture. With the exception of fifty places for natives of K'ai-feng, the rest of the original quota should be made available for the method of "presenting scholars" (kung-shih). Other areas should take one-third of their assigned quotas for the same purpose.

2. Schools should be established all over China to cultivate scholars. If a prefecture is too small or does not have enough examination candidates, students from two or three different prefectures should gather to attend one prefectural school.

3. Prefectural schools should be established and each school should have two (SHY: one) preceptors. SHY adds: If a school has more than 100 students and if this school asks for one more teacher, it should be permitted. The regulations about the appointment of preceptors published in the Yüan-yu era (1086–1094) are now abolished.

4. School lands should be increased so as to support students. Unoccupied lands (unclaimed lands) should be transferred to the schools. If the amount of land given is not enough for stipends, incomes from official estates and properties should be made available to meet the deficiency.

5. An examination and recruitment regulation will be devised and published. This will recommend that students be presented to the Imperial University. Students recruited to be presented to the University should participate in regular civil service examinations but be tested separately. Those who have passed the primary prefectural examination with marks of the first rank will be admitted to the middle class of the Upper-Hall of the University. Those who pass the examination with seconds are to be admitted to the lower class [of the Upper-Hall]. Those who pass the examination with thirds will be sent to the Inner-Hall. The rest will become students of the Outer-Hall. Those who do not pass or those who fail in

*Sources: HCPSP, 20/6a–7b; SHY, cj, 2/7a–9b.

regular primary examination but whose scholarly achievement and behavior are respected in their villages will also be presented, contingent upon the recommendation of a prefect, a circuit intendant or a prefectural vice-administrator or upon the recommendation of the director of the Directorate of Education, the vice-director, or a professor of the Directorate.

6. Two circuit intendants will be sent to the circuits. They will supervise the prefect and the prefectural vice-administrator or the subprefect and his subordinate. [The latter should] examine schools once every ten days, while the intendant should visit all the schools under his supervision once every year. The students to be presented should be examined and chosen by the instructors who in turn should report to the prefect, the prefectural vice-administrator and the intendants. The circuit intendants will re-examine them and then turn in a list of names of the students to be presented. The list should be put together by the intendants, the prefect, and the prefectural vice-administrator. On the basis of this list, the students will then be sent to the University. If they do not present good students, or if they fail to present students at all, they will all be punished according to regulations. HCP only records the program above in the following summary form: Prefects and circuit intendants will be asked to be in charge of presenting scholars [to the University]. HCP then follows: If the students presented pass the examination with first grades or are promoted quickly within the University, [the intendants et al.] will be awarded accordingly.

7. Subprefectural schools should also be established. HCP then states: The subprefect and his assistant should look into the proper use of school lands and tax funds to subsidize the schools. SHY continues the first sentence by saying: The subprefect and his assistant are to see to it that a master and an instructor are appointed to each school, that they are given due salaries and that persons in charge of guiding schools are conducting their duties properly. . . . The subprefect and his assistant should look into the proper use of school lands and various tax funds for the schools.

8. HCP states: Subprefectural schools' students are to be examined and chosen to attend the prefectural schools. SHY states: Students of subprefectural schools should attend school for at least one year. After that the master and the instructor will examine them and select those whose conduct and scholarly works are good and report the result to the subprefect and his assistant. They should then inspect the report and submit their own inspections to the prefect and the prefectural vice-administrator who should again evaluate the report in consultation with the instructors. After that, the students [nominated and accepted] will be sent to the prefectural schools. This procedure is also to be applied in the prefectures without instructors. Prefectural or subprefectural school students who have attended

school for more than two years and who have violated the regulations more than five times, of which three are violations of the third degree or worse, and students who have failed in school examinations to obtain third grade or better on five occasions and who do not seem to be educatable, should all be dismissed. A regulation on how to dismiss students will be issued. This will ensure that students work hard. Those who are not registered in subprefectural schools can still take the entrance examination to go to prefectural schools whenever there are places. Those who are dismissed from prefectural schools, nonetheless, will be permitted to attend subprefectural schools. If they again violate regulations three times, or if they violate a regulation of the third degree or worse, or if they fail to obtain the third grade for five successive times, they will be dismissed again. Anyone who has committed a crime punishable by flogging or worse should be ashamed of himself and should never be allowed to attend any school.

Following point 8, the *HCP* states: 9. Elementary schools should be built in prefectural and subprefectural schools.

The program recorded in detail in *SHY* cited above (8) is outlined in *HCP* which states simply: 10. Regulations on how students should be examined and promoted.

HCP states: 11. The children of officials who serve out of the capital should be allowed to attend the schools [of the area where their fathers serve and to take the primary civil service examinations there].

SHY states: The children of relatives of officials should be allowed to attend the schools in the areas where their fathers serve, because they are not legally allowed to go back to their native area, [there to take the primary civil service examinations.] They are not allowed, however, to be presented [to the University] by the schools they attend either. Instead, after having attended school for one year and having not committed any crime of the second grade or worse, they will be given certificates and be sent to the Imperial University and there be presented by the Directorate of National Youth.

SHY states: 12. Elementary schools should be established in prefectures and subprefectures along with the prefectural and subprefectural schools. Children of ten years old and up should be permitted to attend these elementary schools. Teachers of these schools will receive due salary and rations.

APPENDIX F

Genealogical Charts of Eight Prominent Sung Families

Explanation:

The following genealogical charts are based on the information found in Wang Te-i, *Sung-jen chuan-chi tzu-liao so-yin* (Taipei: Tien-wen, 1974–1976). The assumption is that persons whose names appear in this index are of some degree of representativeness: a person must have been of some prominence or importance to be recorded in sources that are still extant today. These charts therefore in a way indicate the size and political strength of some representative prominent families in Sung China.

A geographical name next to the name of a person means that beginning with this person, the branch of the family started to call themselves natives of the new place, cutting themselves off, in effect, from their lineage in the old location. Information of this kind, not systematically presented here, serves to illustrate the extent of family cohesiveness.

Abbreviations:

c: *chin-shih* degree
n: no office
of: office, entrance method unknown

ot: office by other entrance methods
r: related
y: *yin* protection

1. Ssu-ma 司馬 family of Hsia-hsien 夏縣

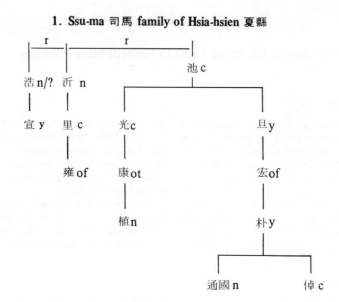

2. Sung 宋 family of K'ai-feng 開封

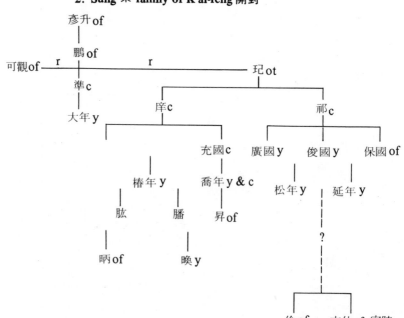

3. Sung 宋 family of Ch'ang-an 長安

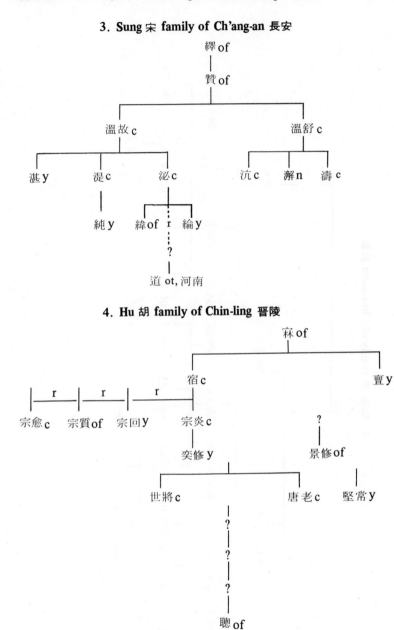

4. Hu 胡 family of Chin-ling 晉陵

5. Shih 史 family of Chin-hsien 鄞縣

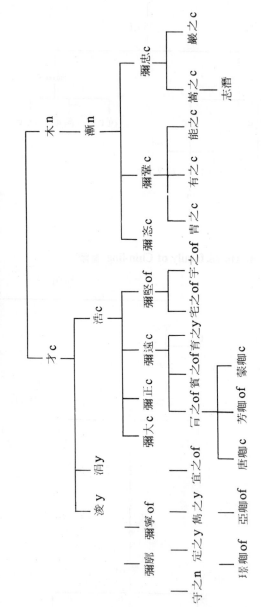

6. Li 李 family of Jao-yang 饒陽

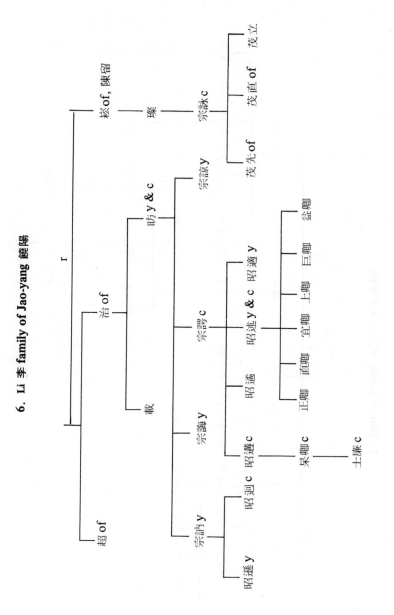

7. Han 韓 family of An-yang 安陽

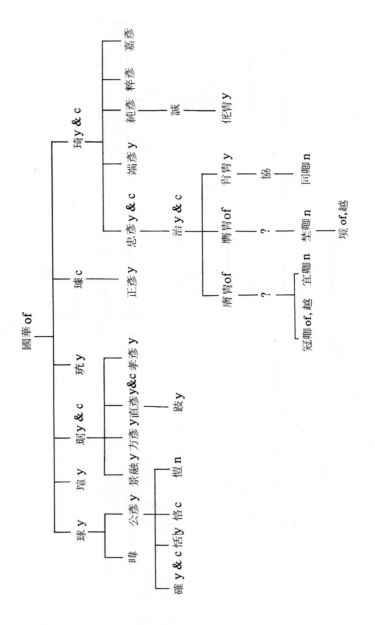

8. Li 李 family of Ching-chao 京兆

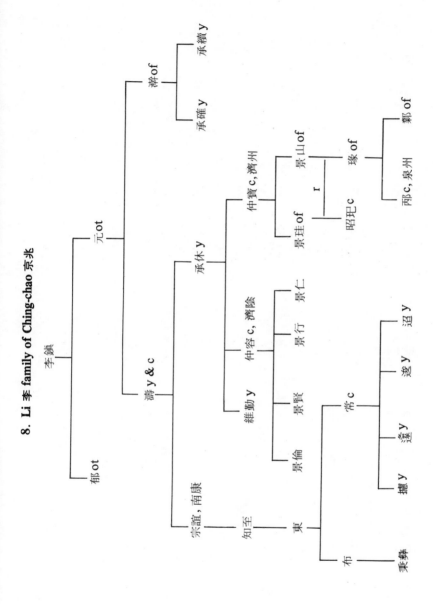

Bibliography

I. Works in Chinese and Japanese

Academia Sinica (Chung-yang yen-chiu yüan 中央研究院). *Bulletin of the Institute of History and Philology* (*Li-shih yü-yen yen-chiu so chi-k'an* 歷史語言研究所集刊). [*AS/BIHP*]

Anonymous author. *Chiang-su chin-shih chih* 江蘇金石志. In Yen Keng-wang (ed.), *Shih-k'o shih-liao ts'ung-shu* (q.v.).

────── . *Ching-k'ang yao-lu* 靖康要錄 (Taipei 台北 : Wen-hai 文海, 1967).

────── . *Ch'ing-yüan tang-chin* 慶元黨禁 , *SKCS* ed.

────── . *Sung-chi san-ch'ao cheng-yao* 宋季三朝政要 , *TSCC* ed.

────── . *Sung ta-chao-ling chi* 宋大詔令集 (Peking 北京 : Chung-hua 中華, 1962).

────── . *T'ai-i chü chu-k'o ch'eng-wen ko* 太醫局諸科程文格 , *SKCS* ed.

Aoyama, Sadao 青山定雄. "Godai Sō ni okeru Kōsei no shinkō kanryō" 五代宋における江西の新興官僚. In *Wada Hakushi kanreki kinen Tōyōshi ronsō* 和田博士還曆紀念東洋史論叢(Tokyo 東京 : Kōdansha 講談社, 1951), 19–37.

────── . "Hoku-Sō o chūshin to suru shitaifu no chike to seikatsu rinri" 北宋を中心とする士大夫の治家と生活倫理. In *Tōyō gakuhō* 東洋學報 , Vol. 57, Nos. 1 & 2 (1976), 35–63.

────── . "Sō Gen no chihōshi ni mieru shakai keizai shiryō" 宋元の地方史にみえる社會經済史料. In *Tōyō gakuhō*, Vol. 25, No. 2 (1938), 281–297.

────── . "Sōdai ni okeru Shisen kanryō keifu ni tsuite no ichi kōsatsu" 宋元における四川官僚系譜についての一考察. In *Wada Hakushi koki kinen Tōyōshi ronsō* 和田博士古稀紀念東洋史論叢 (Tokyo: Kōdansha 講談社 , 1960), 37–48.

────── . *Tō Sō jidai no kōtsū to chishi chizu no kenkyū* 唐宋時代の交通と地誌地圖の研究 (Tokyo: Yoshikawa kōbunkan 吉川弘文館, 1963).

Araki, Toshikazu 荒木敏一. "Hoku Sō jidai ni okeru kakyo no *bunkiken*" 北宋時代における科舉の聞喜宴. In *Kyōtō Kyōiku Daigaku kiyō* 京都教育大學紀要, Series A, No. 47 (1975), 91–108.

────── . *Sōdai kakyo seido kenkyū* 宋代科舉制度研究 (Kyoto 京都： Dōhōsha 同朋社 , 1969). [*Kakyo*]

Chang, Chung-ch'i 張仲炘. *Hu-pei chin-shih chih* 湖北金石志 . In Yen Keng-wang (ed.), *Shih-k'o shih-liao ts'ung-shu* (q.v.).

Chang, Ta-ch'ang 張大昌. "Wang Shen-ning nien-p'u" 王深寧年譜. In Wang Ying-lin 王應麟, *Ssu-ming wen-hsien chi* 四明文獻集 , *Ssu-ming ts'ung-shu* 四明叢書 ed.

Chang, Tsai 張載. *Chang Tsai chi* 張載集 (Peking: Chung-hua, 1978).

Chang, Yin-lin 張蔭麟. "Sung T'ai-tsu shih-pei chi Cheng-shih t'ang k'o-shih k'ao" 宋太祖誓碑及政事堂刻石考. First published in *Wen-shih tsa-chih* 文史雜誌 , Vol. 1, No. 7 (1941), now included in Han-hsüeh yen-chiu shih 漢學研究室 (ed.), *Sung, Liao, Chin, Yüan shih lun-chi* 宋遼金元史論集 (Taipei: Han-sheng 漢聲 , 1977), 1–5.

Chao, Hsiao-hsüan 趙效宣. *Li Kang nien-p'u ch'ang-pien* 李綱年譜長編 (Hong Kong: New Asia Institute, 1968).

Chao, I 趙翼. *Nien-erh shih cha-chi* 廿二史劄記 (Taipei: Shih-chieh 世界, 1958).

Chao, Ju-yü 趙汝愚. *Sung ming-ch'en tsou-i chi* 宋名臣奏議集, *SKCS* ed.

Chao, Sheng 趙昇. *Ch'ao-yeh lei-yao* 朝野類要, *TSCC* ed.

Chao, T'ieh-han 趙鐵寒. "Sung-tai te chou-hsüeh" 宋代的州學. In *SSYCC*, Vol. 2, 343–363.

————. *"Hsü Tzu-chih t'ung-chien ch'ang-pien chi-shih pen-mo* t'i-tuan" 續資治通鑑長編記事本末題端. In Yang Chung-liang, *Chi-shih pen-mo* (q.v.), Vol. I, 1–5.

Ch'en Ch'i-yu 陳奇猷. *Han Fei tzu chi-shih* 韓非子集釋 (Hong Kong: Chung-hua 中華, 1974).

Ch'en, Ch'ing-chih 陳青之. *Chung-kuo chiao-yü shih* 中國教育史 (Shanghai: Shang-wu 商務, 1936). [*Chiao-yü shih*]

Ch'en, I-yen 陳義彥, "Ts'ung pu-i ju-shih, lun Pei-Sung pu-i chieh-ts'eng te she-hui liu-tung" 從布衣入士, 論北宋布衣階層的社會流動. *Ssu yü yen* 思與言, Vol. 9, No. 4 4 (1972), 244–253.

Ch'en, P'an 陳槃. "Ch'un-ch'iu shih-tai te chiao-yü" 春秋時代的教育. *AS/BIHP*, 45 (1974), 731–812.

Ch'en, Shou-ch'i 陳壽祺. *Fu-chien t'ung-chih* 福建通志, 1871 ed. (Taipei: Ch'eng-wen 成文, 1968).

Ch'en, Teng-yüan 陳登原. "Han P'ing-yüan chuan" 韓平原傳. In *Chin-ling hsüeh-pao* 金陵學報, Vol. 4, No. 2 (1934), 89–142.

Ch'en, Tung-yüan 陳東原. "Ch'an-lin te hsüeh-hsiao chih-tu" 禪林的學校制度. In *Min-to tsa-chih* 民鐸雜誌, Vol. 6, No. 3 (1925).

————. *Chung-kuo chiao-yü shih* 中國教育史 (Taipei: Shang-wu, 1976). [*Chiao-yü shih*]

Ch'en, Yin-k'o 陳寅恪. *T'ang-tai cheng-chih shih shu-lun kao* 唐代政治史述論稿 (Hong Kong: Chung-hua, 1974).

Cheng, Ch'ien 鄭騫. "Ch'en Chien-chai nien-p'u" 陳簡齋年譜. *Yu-shih hsüeh-pao* 幼獅學報, Vol. II, No. 2 (1960), 1–64.

Ch'eng, I 程頤. *I-ch'uan i-shu* 伊川遺書. In *Erh-Ch'eng ch'üan-shu* 二程全書, *SPPY* ed.

Ch'eng, Pi 程泌. *Lo-shui chi* 洛水集, *SKCS* ed.

Ch'i, Hsia 漆俠. "Sung-tai hsüeh-t'ien chih chung feng-chien tsu-tien kuan-hsi te fa-chan" 宋代學田制中封建租佃關係的發展. In *She-hui k'o-hsüeh chan-hsien* 社會科學戰線, 1979/3, 147–153.

————. *Wang An-shih pien-fa* 王安石變法 (Shanghai: Jen-min 人民, 1979).

Chiang, Fu-ts'ung 蔣復璁. "Sung-tai i-ko kuo-ts'e te chien-t'ao" 宋代一個國策的檢討. In his *Sung-shih hsin-t'an* 宋史新談 (Taipei: Cheng-chung 正中, 1970), 1–52.

Chiang, I-hsüeh 蔣逸雪. *Lu Hsiu-fu nien-p'u* 陸秀夫年譜 (Shanghai: Shang-wu, 1936).

Chiao, Hung 焦紘. *Ching-hsüeh chih* 京學志, Ming 明 ed. (Taipei: Kuo-feng 國風, 1965).

Ch'ien, Mu 錢穆. *Chu-tzu hsüeh t'i-kang* 朱子學提綱 (Taipei: San-min 三民, 1971).

————. *Kuo-shih ta-kang* 國史大綱 (Taipei: Shang-wu, 1960).

————. "Lüeh-lun Wei, Chin, Nan-pei ch'ao shih-tai hsüeh-shu wen-hua yü tang-shih men-ti chih kuan-hsi" 略論魏晉南北朝時代學術文化與當時門第之關係. In his *Chung-kuo hsüeh-shu ssu-hsiang shih lun-ts'ung* 中國學術思想史論叢, Vol. III (Taipei: Tung-hua 東華, 1977), 134–199.

————. *Sung, Ming li-hsüeh kai-shu* 宋明理學概述 (Taipei: Chung-hua wen-hua shih-yeh ch'u-pan wei-yüan hui, 1956).

Ch'ien, Pao-ts'ung 錢寶琮 (collator). *Suan-ching shih-shu* 算經十書, 2 vols. (Peking: Chung-hua, 1963).

Ch'ien, Ti-chih 錢地之. *Lun-yü Han Sung chi-chieh* 論語漢宋集解 (Taipei: Chung-hua, 1980).

Chikusa, Gashō 竺沙雅章. "Fukuken no shakai to jiin" 福建の社會と寺院. In *Tōyōshi kenkyū* 東洋史研究, Vol. 15, No. 2 (1965), 1–27.

———. "Hoku-Sō shitaifu no shikyo to baiden" 北宋士大夫の徙居と買田. In *Shirin* 史林, Vol. 54, No. 2 (1971), 28–53.

Chin, Chün-ch'ing 金君卿. *Chin-shih wen-chi* 金氏文集, *SKCS* ed.

Chin, Chung-shu 金中樞. "Pei-Sung k'o-chü chih-tu yen-chiu" 北宋科舉制度研究. In *Hsin-ya hsüeh-pao* 新亞學報, Vol. 6 (1964), No. 1, 205–281; No. 2, 163–242. ["Pei-Sung k'o-chü"]

———. "Pei-Sung k'o-chü chih-tu yen-chiu hsü" 北宋科舉制度研究續. In *Kuo-li Ch'eng-kung ta-hsüeh li-shih hsüeh-pao* 國立成功大學歷史學報, No. 5 (1978), 135–243; No. 6 (1979), 87–186. ["Pei-Sung k'o-chü shü"]

Ch'in, Hui-t'ien 秦蕙田. *Wu-li t'ung-k'ao* 五禮通考, 1880 Chiang-su shu-chü 江蘇書局 ed. (Taipei: Hsin-hsing 新興, 1970).

Chin, Yü-fu 金毓黻. *Chung-kuo shih-hsüeh shih* 中國史學史 (Shanghai: Shang-wu, 1957). [*Shih-hsüeh shih*]

Chou, Mi 周密. *Ch'i-tung yeh-yü* 齊東野語, Han-fen lou 涵芬樓 ed. (1915).

———. *Kuei-hsin tsa-chih* 癸辛雜識, *Hsüeh-chin t'ao-yüan* 學津討原 ed. (1805).

———. *Wu-lin chiu-shih* 武林舊事 (Shanghai: Ku-tien 古典, 1957).

Chou, Tun-i 周敦頤. *Chou-tzu ch'üan-shu* 周子全書, *Wan-yu wen-k'u* 萬有文庫 ed. (Shanghai: Shang-wu, 1937).

Chou, Ying-ho 周應和. *Ching-ting Chien-k'ang chih* 景定建康志, *SKCS* ed.

Chu, Hsi. *Hui-an hsien-sheng Chu Wen-kung wen-chi* 晦庵先生朱文公文集, *SPTK* ed. [*Wen-chi*]

———. *I-Lo yüan-yüan lu* 伊洛淵源錄, Ming ed. (Taipei: Wen-hai, 1968).

———. *Chu-tzu yü-lei* 朱子語類, 1473 reprint of 1270 ed. (Taipei: Cheng-chung 正中, 1962 reprint).

———. *Chu-tzu yü-lei chi-lüeh* 朱子語類輯略, *TSCC* ed.

Chu, Hsi 朱熹 and Lü Tsu-ch'ien 呂祖謙 (eds.). *Chin-ssu lu* 近思錄, *SPPY* ed.

Chu, I-tsun 朱彝尊. *Ching-i k'ao* 經義考, 8 vols., *SPPY* ed.

Fan, Ch'eng-ta 范成大. *Wu-chün chih* 吳郡志, *TSCC* ed.

Fan, Chung-yen 范仲淹. *Fan Wen-cheng kung chi* 范文正公集, *TSCC* ed. [*Wen-cheng chi*]

Fan, Yeh 范曄. *Hou-Han shu* 後漢書 (Peking: Chung-hua, 1965).

Fang, Hsüan-ling 房玄齡. *Chin-shu* 晉書 (Peking: Chung-hua, 1974).

Feng, K'o-yung 馮可鏞 and Yeh I-shan 葉奕山 (eds.). "Tz'u-hu hsien-sheng nien-p'u" 慈湖先生年譜. In Yang Chien 楊簡, *Tz'u-hu i-shu* 慈湖遺書, *Ssu-ming ts'ung-shu* ed. (1932).

Fukuzawa, Yokurō 福澤與九郎. "Sō Gen jidai shū ken gakusan kō" 宋元時代州縣學產考. *Fukuoka Gakugei Daigaku kiyō* 福岡學藝大學紀要, No. 8 (1958), 27–42 and No. 9 (1959), 27–36.

Fujiyoshi, Masasumi 藤善眞澄. "Setsuwa yori mita shomin Bukkyō" 說話よりみた庶民佛教. In Makita Tairyō 牧田諦亮 (ed.), *Gōdai shūkyō shi kenkyū* 五代宗教史研究 (Kyoto 京都: Heirakuji 平樂寺, 1972), 199–243.

Fumoto, Yasutaka 麓保孝. *Hoku Sō ni okeru Jugaku no tenkai* 北宋における儒學の展開 (Tokyo: Shoseki Ryūtsūsho 書籍流通處, 1968).

Han, Yuan-chi 韓元吉. *Nan-chien chia-i kao* 南澗甲乙稿, *SKCS* ed.

Higashi, Ichio 東一夫. *Ō Anseki shimpō no kenkyū* 王安石新法の研究 (Tokyo: Kazama shobō 風間書房, 1970).

Ho, Yu-sen 何祐森. "Liang-Sung hsüeh-feng chih ti-li fen-pu" 兩宋學風之地理分佈. In *Hsin-ya hsüeh-pao*, Vol. 1 (1955), 331–379.

————. "Yüan-tai hsüeh-shu chih ti-li fen-pu" 元代學術之地理分佈. In *Hsin-ya hsüeh-pao*, Vol. 2 (1956), 361–408.

Hou, Shao-wen 侯紹文. *T'ang Sung k'ao-shih chih-tu shih* 唐宋考試制度史 (Taipei: Shang-wu, 1973).

Hou, Wai-lu 侯外廬. *Chung-kuo ssu-hsiang t'ung-shih* 中國思想通史, 6 vols. (Peking: Jen-min 人民, 1957).

Hsia, Sung 夏竦. *Wen-chuang chi* 文莊集, *SKCS* ed.

Hsiao, Kung-ch'üan 蕭公權. *Chung-kuo cheng-chih ssu-hsiang shih* 中國政治思想史, 6 vols. (Taipei: Chung-hua wen-hua shih-yeh ch'u-pan wei-yüan hui, 1954).

Hsieh, Shen-fu 謝深甫. *Ch'ing-yüan t'iao-fa shih-li* 慶元條法事例, Sung ed. (Tokyo: Koten kenkyukai 古典研究會, 1968).

Hsü, Meng-hsin 徐夢莘. *San-ch'ao pei-meng hui-pien* 三朝北盟會編 (Taipei: Wen-hai 文海, 1962 reprint).

Hsü, Sung 徐松 (comp.). *Sung hui-yao chi-kao* 宋會要輯稿 (Peking: Chung-hua, 1966, reprint of 1936 Pei-p'ing t'u-shu kuan 北平圖書館 ed.). [*SHY*]

Hsü, Tao-lin 徐道鄰. "Sung-tai te fa-lü k'ao-shih" 宋代的法律考試. In his *Chung-kuo fa-chih shih lun-chi* 中國法制史論集 (Taipei: Chih-wen 智文, 1975), 188–229. ["Fa-lü k'ao-shih"]

Hsü, Yü-feng 徐毓峯. "Shih Chieh nien-p'u" 石介年譜. In *Tse-shan pan-yüeh k'an* 責善半月刊, Vol. 2, No. 20 (1942), 58–77.

Hsüeh, Chü-cheng 薛居正. *Chiu Wu-tai shih* 舊五代史 (Peking: Chung-hua, 1976).

Hu, Mei-ch'i 胡美琦. *Chung-kuo chiao-yü shih* 中國教育史 (Taipei: San-min 三民, 1978). [*Chiao-yü shih*]

Huang, Chün-chieh 黃俊傑. *Ch'un-ch'iu Chan-kuo shih-tai shang-hsien cheng-chih te li-lun yü shih-chi* 春秋戰國時代尚賢政治的理論與實際 (Taipei: Wen-hsüeh 問學, 1977), [*Shang-hsien cheng-chih*]

Huang, I-chou 黃以周 et al. *Hsü Tzu-chih t'ung-chien ch'ang-pien shih-pu* 續資治通鑑長編拾補. Published in 1881 by Chekiang shu-chü, and now included in Li T'ao's *HCP* (q.v.). [*HCPSP*]

Huang, K'uan-ch'ung 黃寬重. "Ch'eng Pi nien-p'u" 程泌年譜. In *Shih-yüan* 史原, Vol. 5 (1974), 115–162.

Huang, Min-chih 黃敏枝. "Sung-tai liang-Che lu te ssu-yüan yü she-hui" 宋代兩浙路的寺院與社會. In *Kuo-li Ch'eng-kung ta-hsüeh li-shih hsi li-shih hsüeh-pao* 國立成功大學歷史系歷史學報, No. 5 (1978), 319–349.

————. "Sung-tai ssu-yüan yü chuang-yüan chih yen-chiu" 宋代寺院與莊園之研究. In *Ta-lu tsa-chih* 大陸雜誌, Vol. 46, No. 4 (1972), 26–37.

Huang, Pen-chi 黃本驥. *Li-tai chih-kuan piao* 歷代職官表 (Shanghai: Chung-hua, 1965).

Huang, Shang 黃裳. *Yen-shan chi* 演山集, *SKCS* ed.

Huang, Tsung-hsi 黃宗羲. *Sung Yüan hsüeh-an* 宋元學案, *SPPY* ed.

Huang, Wei 黃維 and Yang Shih-ch'i 楊士奇. *Li-tai ming-ch'en tsou-i* 歷代名臣奏議, 1416 ed. (Taipei: Hsüeh-sheng 學生, 1964 reprint).

Hui-chiao 惠皎. *Kao-seng chuan* 高僧傳, Hai-shan hsien-kuan 海山仙館 ed. (Taipei: Kuang-wen 廣文, 1971).

Hung Kua 洪适. *P'an-chou chi*, SPTK ed.

Hung, Mai 洪 邁 . *Jung-chai sui-pi* 容齋隨筆 , 2 vols. (Shanghai: Ku-chi, 1978).

————— . *I-chien chih* 夷堅志 , Han-fen lou ed. (1915).

Ihara, Hiroshi 尹原弘 . "Nan-Sō no Shisen ni okeru teikyo shijin" 南宋の四川における定居士人 . In *Tōhōgaku* 東方學 , No. 54 (1977), 46–62.

Juan, Chih-sheng 阮芝生 . "Hsüeh-an t'i-ts'ai yüan-liu ch'u-t'an" 學案體裁源流初探 . In Tu Wei-yün et al. (eds.), *Chung-kuo shih-hsüeh shih lun-wen hsüan-chi* (q.v.), Vol. I, 574–596.

Juan, Yüan 阮元 . *Liang-Che chin-shih chih* 兩浙金石志 . In Yen Keng-wang (ed.), *Shih-k'o shih-liao ts'ung-shu* (q.v.).

Kanaya, Osamu 金谷治 . *Junshi* 荀子 (Tokyo: Iwanami 岩波 , 1962).

Kano, Ryōchi 狩野艮知 . *Shina kyōgaku shi ryaku* 支那教育史略 . Translated into Chinese as *Chih-na chiao-yü shih-lüeh* (Shanghai: Shang-wu, 1889).

Kao, Ming-shih 高明士 . "T'ang-tai hsüeh-chih chih yüan-yüan chi ch'i yen-pien" 唐代學制之淵源及其演變 . In *Kuo-li T'ai-wan ta-hsüeh li-shi hsüeh-shi hsüeh-pao* 國立臺灣大學歷史學系學報 , No. 4 (1977), 195–219. ["T'ang-tai hsüeh-chih"]

————— . "T'ang-tai kung-chü tui ju-hsüeh yen-chiu te ying-hsiang" 唐代貢舉對儒學研究的影響 . In *Kuo-li pien-i kuan kuan-kan* 國立編譯館館刊 , Vol. 2, No. 1 (1973), 61–94.

————— . "T'ang-tai te ssu-hsüeh chiao-yü" 唐代的私學教育 . In *Kuo-li T'ai-wan ta-hsüeh wen shih che hsüeh-pao* 國立臺灣大學文史哲學報 , No. 20 (1971), 219–289. ["Ssu-hsüeh"]

————— . "T'ang-tai te kuan-hsüeh hsing-cheng" 唐代的官學行政 . In *Ta-lu tsa-chih*, Vol. 37, Nos. 11 & 12 (1968), 39–53.

Kao, Ssu-sun 高似孫 . *Shan-lu* 剡錄 , 1870 ed. (Taipei: Ch'eng-wen 成文 , 1970 reprint).

Kinugawa, Tsuyoshi 衣川強 . "Kanryō to kanhō" 官僚と官俸 . In *Tōhō gakuhō* 東方學報 , No. 42 (1973), 177–208.

Ko, Sheng-chung 葛勝仲 . *Tan-yang chi* 澹陽集 , *Ch'ang-chou hsien-che i-shu* 常州先哲遺書 ed. (1896).

Ku, Shu-sen 顧樹森 . *Chung-kuo ku-tai chiao-yü chia yü-lu lei-li* 中國古代教育家語錄類例 (Shanghai: Chiao-yü, 1983).

Kung, Chia 龔甲 (comp.). *Hang-chou fu-chih* 杭州府志 , 1896 ed. (Taipei: Ch'eng-wen, 1974 reprint).

Kuo-hsüeh chi-pen ts'ung-shu 國學基本叢書 (Shanghai: Shang-wu, 1937?). Selected from *Wan-yu wen-k'u* (q.v.). [*KHTS*]

Li, Chia-chü 酈家駒 . "Shih-lun kuan-yü Han T'e-chou p'ing-chia te jo-kan wen-t'i" 試論關於韓侂胄評價的若干問題 . In *Chung-kuo shih yen-chiu* 中國史研究 , 1981/2, 146–161.

Li, Chih 李燾 . *Huang Sung shih-ch'ao kang-yao* 皇宋十朝綱要 (Shanghai: Tung-fang hsüeh-hui 東方學會 , 1927, reprinted by Taipei: Wen-hai, 1967). [*Kang-yao*]

Li, Ch'ing-chao 李清照 . *Li Ch'ing-chao chi* 李清照集 , ed. by Huang Sheng-chang 黃盛璋 (Shanghai: Chung-hua, 1962).

Li, Hsien-min 李獻民 . *Yün-chai kuang-lu* 雲齋廣錄 , *Shuo-fu tsa-chu* 說郛雜著 , *Lung-wei mi-shu* 龍威秘書 ed. (1794).

Li, Hsin-ch'uan 李心傳 . *Chien-yen i-lai ch'ao-yeh lei-yao* 建炎以來朝野類要 . 1901 Kuang-ya shu-chü ed. (Taipei: Wen-hai, 1968 reprint).

————— . *Chien-yen i-lai hsi-nien yao-lu* 建炎以來繫年要錄 , 1901 Kuang-ya shu-chü ed. (Taipei: Wen-hai, 1968 reprint). [*CYYL*]

Li, Hung-ch'i (Thomas H. C. Lee) 李弘祺 . "Chiang-chang i-feng: ssu-jen chiang-hsüeh te ch'uan-t'ung" 絳帳遺風：私人講學的傳統 . In Liu Tai (ed.), *Chung-kuo wen-hua hsin-lun* (q.v.), Vol. II (*Hao-han te hsüeh-hai* 浩瀚的學海 , ed. by Lin Ch'ing-chang 林慶彰), 343–410. ["Ssu-jen chiang-hsüeh"]

——— . "K'o-chu: Sui, T'ang chih Ming, Ch'ing te k'ao-shih chih-tu" 科舉：隋唐至明清的考試制度. In Liu Tai (ed.), *Chung-kuo wen-hua hsin-lun* (q.v.), Vol. IV (*Li-kuo te hung-kuei* 立國的宏規, ed. by Cheng Ch'in-jen 鄭欽仁), 259–315.

——— . *Sung-tai chiao-yü san-lun* 宋代教育散論 (Taipei: Tung-sheng 東昇 , 1979). [*San-lun*]

——— . "Sung-tai kuan-yüan shu te t'ung-chi" 宋代官員數的統計 In *shih-huo* 食貨 , 14/5–6, (1984), 17–29.

——— . "Sung-tai ti-fang hsüeh-hsiao chih-shih k'ao" 宋代地方學校職事考 . *Shih-hsüeh p'ing-lun* 史學評論 , Vol. 8 (1984), 223–241.

Li, Kou 李覯. *Chih-chiang Li hsien-sheng wen-chi* 直講李先生文集, *SPTK* ed. [*Wen-chi*]

Li, Ming-huan 李銘皖 et al. *Su-chou fu-chih* 蘇州府志, 1883 ed. (Taipei: Ch'eng-wen, 1970 reprint).

Li, T'ao 李燾. *Hsü Tzu-chih t'ung-chien ch'ang-pien* 續資治通鑑長編 , 1881 Chekiang shu-chü 浙江書局 ed. Now reprinted by Yang Chia-lo 楊家駱 with fragments found in the Ming encyclopedia *Yung-lo ta-tien* 永樂大典 and Huang I-chou's *HCPSP* (q.v.) inserted between chs. 209 and 210, 484 and 485, and after ch. 520 (Taipei: Shih-chieh, 1965). [*HCP*]

Li, Yen 李儼. "T'ang, Sung, Yüan, Ming shu-hsüeh chiao-yü chih-tu" 唐宋元明數學教育制度. In his *Chung-suan shih lun-ts'ung* 中算史論叢 , Vol. IV (Peking: K'o-hsüeh 科學 , 1955). ["Shu-hsüeh chiao-yü"]

Liang, Ch'i-ch'ao 梁啓超. *Wang Ching-kung* 王荊公 (Taipei: Chung-hua, 1956), (Shanghai: Kuang-chih 廣智 , 1908), or Liang Ch'i-ch'ao et al., *Chung-kuo liu ta cheng-chih chia* 中國六大政治家 (Taipei: Cheng-chung 正中 , 1963), 5/1–208.

Liang, K'o-chia 梁克家. *San-shan chih* 三山志, *SKCS* ed.

Lin, Chi-chung 林季仲 . *Chu-hsüan tsa-chu* 竹軒雜著, *SKCS* ed.

Lin, Tzu-hsün 林子勛. "Sung-tai ti-fang chiao-yü te fa-chan" 宋代地方教育的發展. In *Hua-kang hsüeh-pao* 華岡學報 , No. 2 (1965), 155–176.

Liu, Ch'ang 劉敞. *Kung-shih chi* 公是集 , *TSCC* ed.

Liu, Chen 劉眞. "Sung-tai te hsüeh-kuei han hsiang-yüeh" 宋代的學規和鄉約. In *SSYCC*, Vol. I (1958), 367–392.

Liu, Chih 劉摯. *Chung-su chi* 忠肅集 , *SKCS* ed.

Liu, Hsü 劉昫. *Chiu T'ang-shu* 舊唐書 (Peking: Chung-hua, 1975).

Liu, Kuo 劉過. *Lung-chou chi* 瀧州集 (Shanghai: Ku-chi, 1978).

Liu, Pan 劉攽. *Kung-fu shih-hua* 貢父詩話, *Pai-ch'uan hsüeh-hai* 百川學海 ed. Now included in *Pai-pu ts'ung-shu* 百部叢書 (Taipei: I-wen 藝文 , 1967).

——— . *P'eng-ch'eng chi* 彭城集 , *TSCC* ed.

Liu, Po-chi 劉伯驥 . *Sung-tai cheng-chiao shih* 宋代政教史 , 2 vols. (Taipei: Chung-hua, 1971).

Liu, Shih-chü 劉師舉. *Hsü Sung chung-hsing pien-nien tzu-chih t'ung-chien* 續宋中興編年資治通鑑, *TSCC* ed.

Liu, Tai 劉岱 (ed.). *Chung-kuo wen-hua hsin-lun* 中國文化新論 , 11 vols. (Taipei: Lien-ching 聯經 , 1980–1982).

Liu, Tsai 劉宰. *Man-t'ang chi* 漫塘集, *SKCS* ed.

Liu, Tzu-chien 劉子健 (James T. C. Liu). "Liu Tsai han chen-chi" 劉宰和賑饑. In *Pei-ching ta-hsüeh hsüeh-pao* 北京大學學報 , 1979/3, 53–61 and 1979/4, 41–55.

Liu, Yüan-ch'ing 劉元卿 . *Hsien-i pien* 賢奕編 , *TSCC* ed.

Lo, Hsiu-i 羅綉宜 . *Ch'uan-hsin lu* 傳信錄 .

Lo, Lung-chih 羅龍治. *Chin-shih k'o yü T'ang-tai te wen-hsüeh yü she-hui* 進士科與唐代的文學與社會 (Taipei: Tai-wan ta-hsüeh 台灣大學, 1971).

Lu, Chiu-yüan 陸九淵. *Lu Chiu-yüan chi* 陸九淵集 (Peking: Chung-hua, 1980).

Lü, Ssu-mien 呂思勉. *Yen-shih hsü-cha* 燕石續扎 (Shanghai: Jen-min 人民, 1958).

Lu, Tien 陸佃. *T'ao-shan chi* 陶山集, *SKCS* ed.

Lu, Tseng-hsiang 陸曾祥. *Pa-ch'iung shih chin-shih pu-cheng* 八瓊室金石補正, Wu-hsing Hsi-ku lou 吳興希古樓 ed. (Taipei: Wen-hai, 1967).

Lu, Yu 陸游. *Lao-hsüeh an pi-chi* 老學庵筆記, *Hsüeh-chin t'ao-yüan* 學津討原 ed. (1805) (Shanghai: Shang-wu, 1922).

Ma, Heng 馬衡. *Fan-chiang chai chin-shih ts'ung-kao* 凡將齋金石叢稿 (Peking: Hsin-hua 新華, 1977).

Ma, Tuan-lin 馬端臨. *Wen-hsien t'ung-k'ao* 文獻通考, *Wan-yu wen-k'u* (q.v.) ed. [*WHTK*]

Mai, Chung-kuei 麥仲貴. *Sung Yüan li-hsüeh chia chu-shu sheng-tsu nien-piao* 宋元理學家著述生卒年表 (Hong Kong: Hsin-ya yen-chiu so, 1968).

Mei, Ying-fa 梅應發. *K'ai-ch'ing ssu-Ming hsü-chih* 開慶四明續志, *Sung Yüan ssu-Ming liu-chih* 宋元四明六志 ed.

Meng, Hsien-ch'eng 孟憲承 et al. *Chung-kuo ku-tai chiao-yü shih tzu-liao* 中國古代教育史資料 (Peking: Jen-min, 1982).

Miyazaki, Ichisada 宮崎市定. *Ajia shi kenkyu* アジア史研究, Vol. 1 (Kyoto: Nakamura 中村, 1962); Vol. 4 (Tokyo: Tōyōshi Kenkyū Kai, 1964).

————. *Kyūhin kannin hō no kenkyū* 九品官人法の研究 (Tokyo: Dōhōsha 同朋社, 1977).

————. "Sōdai no daigakusei seikatsu" 宋代の太學生生活. In his *Ajia shi kenkyū* (q.v.), Vol. 1, 365–401.

————. "Sōdai no shidaifu" 宋代の士大夫. In his *Ajia shi kenkyū* (q.v.), Vol. 4, 130–169.

Miyashita, Saburo 宮下三郎. "Sō Gen no iryō" 宋元の醫療. In Yabuuchi Kiyoshi 藪內清 (ed.), *Sō Gen jidai no kagaku gijutsu shi* 宋元時代の科學技術史 (Kyoto: Kyoto Daigaku Jimbun Kagaku Kenkyujō 京都大學人文科學研究所, 1967, 123–170.

Morita, Ken 森田憲. "Sō Gen jidai ni okeru shūfu" 宋元時代における修譜. In *Tōyōshi kenkyū* 東洋史研究, No. 37 (1979), 27–53.

Mou, Jun-sun 牟潤孫. "Liang-Sung Ch'un-ch'iu hsüeh chih chu-liu" 兩宋春秋學之主流. In *SSYCC*, Vol. III (1966), 103–123.

Naba, Toshisada 那波利貞. "Tō shōhon *Zōshō* kō" 唐抄本雜抄考. In his *Tōdai shakai bunka shi kenkyū* 唐代社會文化史研究 (Tokyo: Sōbunka 創文社, 1974), 197–268.

Otagi, Hajime 愛宕元. "Godai Sō jō no shinkō kanryō" 五代宋上の新興官僚. In *Shirin* 史林, Vol. 57, No. 4 (1974), 57–96.

————. "Tōdai no kyōkō shinshi to kyōkō meikai" 唐代の郷貢進士與郷貢明經. In *Tōhō gakuhō* 東方學報, No. 45 (1973), 169–194.

Ou-yang, Hsiu 歐陽修. *Hsin T'ang-shu* 新唐書 (Peking: Chung-hua, 1975). [*HTS*]

Pai, Shou-i 白壽彝. "Ma Tuan-lin te shih-hsüeh ssu-hsiang" 馬端臨的史學思想. In Wu Tse 吳澤 (ed.), *Chung-kuo shih-hsüeh shih lun-chi* 中國史學史論集 (Shanghai: Jen-min, 1980), Vol. II, 353–398.

Pan, Ku 班固. *Han-shu* 漢書 (Peking: Chung-hua, 1962).

Pao, Cheng 包拯. *Hsiao-su Pao-kung tsou-i* 孝肅包公奏議, *TSCC* ed.

P'eng, Hsin-wei 彭信威. *Chung-kuo huo-pi shih* 中國貨幣史 (Shanghai: Jen-min, 1965).

Pi, Chung-yu 畢仲游. *Hsi-t'ai chi* 西臺集, *TSCC* ed.

P'i, Hsi-jui 皮錫瑞. *Ching-hsüeh li-shih* 經學歷史, *KHTS* ed.

Pi, Yüan 畢 沅 . *Hsü Tzu-chih t'ung-chien* 續資治通鑑 (Peking: Chung-hua, 1957). [*HTC*]

Sanaka, Sō 佐中壯 . "Sōgaku ni tsukeru iwayuru hihanteki kenkyū no tansaku ni tsuite" 宋學につける所謂批判てき研究の探索について. In *Shigaku zasshi* 史學雜誌, Vol. 54, No. 14 (1944).

Shen, Kou 沈 遘 . *Hsi-hsi chi* 西溪集 . In *Shen-shih san hsien-sheng chi* 沈氏三先生集, *SPTK* ed.

Shen, Kua 沈 括 . *Meng-hsi pi-t'an* 夢溪筆談 , *TSCC* ed.

Shen, Yüeh 沈 約 . *Sung-shu* 宋 書 (Peking: Chung-hua, 1974).

Sheng, Lang-hsi 盛 朗西. *Chung-kuo shu-yüan chih-tu* 中國書院制度 (Taipei: Hua-shih 華世 , 1977).

————— . "Sung-tai chih t'ai-hsüeh chiao-yü" 宋代之太學教育. In *Min-to tsa-chih* 民鐸 雜誌 , Vol. 7 (1927), No. 2, 1–30; No. 3, 1–22; No. 4, 1–29; No. 5, 1–19.

Shimada, Kenji 島田虔次. *Shushigaku to Yōmeigaku* 朱子學と陽明學 (Tokyo: Iwanami 岩波 , 1967).

Sogabe, Sizuo 曾 我 部 靜 雄. "Chūgoku no senkyo, kōkyo to kakyo" 中國の選擧、貢擧 と科擧. In *Shirin*, Vol. 53, No. 4 (1970), 42–66.

Ssu-k'u ch'üan-shu 四庫全書. The *chen-pen* 珍本 edition by Shang-wu has been used, including the first series (Shanghai, 1934) and the second through tenth series (Taipei, 1971–1979). [*SKCS*]

Ssu-ma, Kuang 司馬光. *Wen-kuo kung Ssu-ma Wen-cheng chi* 溫國公司馬文正集 , *SPTK* ed. [*Wen-chi*]

Ssu-pu pei-yao 四部備要 (Taipei: Chung-hua, 1966). [*SPPY*].

Ssu-pu ts'ung-k'an 四部叢刊 (*so-yin* 縮印 ed.) (Shanghai: Shang-wu, 1936). [*SPTK*]

Su, Ch'e 蘇轍 . *Lung-ch'uan pieh-chih* 龍川別志 , Han-fen lou ed. (Shanghai: Shang-wu, 1933).

Su, Shih 蘇軾 . *Su Tung-p'o chi* 蘇東坡集 , *KHTS* ed.

————— . *Tung-p'o tsou-i* 東坡奏議 . In *Tung-p'o ch'i-chi* 東坡七集 , *SPPY* ed.

Su, Shun-ch'in 蘇舜欽 . *Su Shun-ch'in chi* 蘇舜欽集 (Shanghai: Ku-chi, 1981).

Su, Sung 蘇 頌 . *Su Wei-kung wen-chi* 蘇魏公文集 , *SKCS* ed. or 1831 lithographic ed.

Sudō, Yoshiyuki 周藤吉之. "Nan-Sō no Ri Tō to *Shiji tsugan chōhen* no seiritsu" 南宋 の李燾と資治通鑑長編の成立. In his *Sōdai shi kenkyū* (q.v.), 469–512.

————— . *Sōdaishi kenkyū* 宋代史研究 (Tokyo: Tōyō Bunko 東洋文庫, 1969).

Sun, Ch'iang-ming 孫鏘鳴. *Ch'en Wen-chieh kung nien-p'u* 陳文節公年譜, *Ching-hsiang lou ts'ung-shu* 敬鄉樓叢書 ed. (1929).

Sun, Kuo-tung 孫國棟. "T'ang Sung chih-chi she-hui men-ti chih hsiao-jung" 唐宋之際 社會門第之消融. In his *T'ang Sung shih lun-ts'ung* 唐宋史論叢 (Hong Kong: Lungmen, 1980), 201–308. ["Men-ti hsiao-jung"]

Sung, Hsi (Sung Shee) 宋晞 . "Sung-tai shih-ta-fu tui shang-jen te t'ai-tu" 宋代士大夫對商 人的態度. In *SSYCC*, Vol. II (1964), 199–212. ["Sung-tai shih-ta-fu"]

Sung-shih yen-chiu hui 宋史研究會. *Sung-shih yen-chiu chi* 宋史研究集, Vols. 1–12 (Taipei: Chung-hua ts'ung-shu pien-shen wei-yüan hui 中華叢書編審委員會, 1958–1981). [*SSYCC*]

Suzuki, Kei 鈴木敬 . "Gagaku o chūshin to shita Kisō Gain no kaikaku to intai sansuiga yōshiki no seiritsu" 畫學を中心とした徽宗畫院の改革と院體山水畫樣式の成立 . In *Tōyō Bunka Kenkyūjo shūyō* 東洋文化研究所集要 , No. 38 (1965), 145–184. ["Gagaku o chūshin"]

Taga, Akigoro 多賀秋五郎. *Tōdai kyōiku shi no kenkyū* 唐代教育史の研究 (Tokyo: Fumaidō 不昧堂 , 1953).

Takikawa, Masajirō 瀧川政次郎. "Sōhan *Sangaku genryū* ni tsuite" 宋板算學源流につい

て. In his *Shina hosei shi kenkyū* 支那法制史研究 (Tokyo: Yuhikaku 有斐閣, 1940).

Tanaka, Issei 田仲一成. "Chūgoku chihōgeki no hatten kōzō" 中國地方劇の發展構造. In *Tōyō bunka* 東洋文化, 58 (1977), 1–42.

T'ang, Ch'eng-pin 湯承彬. "Han-tai chiao-yü chih-tu yen-chiu" 漢代教育制度研究. In *Kuo-li Cheng-chih ta-hsüeh hsüeh-pao* 國立政治大學學報, Vol. 20 (1969), 153–176.

T'ang, Chung 湯中. *Sung hui-yao yen-chiu* 宋會要研究 (Shanghai: Shang-wu, 1932).

Teng, Chih-ch'eng 鄧之誠. *Tung-ching meng-hua lu chu* 東京夢華錄注 (Hong Kong: Shang-wu, 1961).

Teng, Kuang-ming 鄧廣銘. *Wang An-shih* 王安石 (Peking: Jen-min, 1975).

Teng, Ssu-yü 鄧嗣禹. *Chung-kuo k'ao-shih chih-tu shih* 中國考試制度史 (Taipei: Hsüeh-sheng 學生, 1967).

Teraji, Jun 寺地遵. "Tenjin sōkan setsu yori mitaru Shiba Kō to Ō Anseki" 天人相關說より見たる司馬光と王安石. In *Shigaku zasshi* 史學雜誌, Vol. 76, No. 10 (1967), 34–62.

Terada, Gō 寺田剛. *Sōdai kyōiku shi gaisetsu* 宋代教育史概說 (Tokyo: Hakubunsha 學文社, 1965). [*Kyōiku shi*]

T'ien, K'uang 田況. *Ju-lin kung-i* 儒林公議, *TSCC* ed.

Ting, Ch'uan-ching 丁傳靖. *Sung-jen i-shih hui-pien* 宋人軼事彙編 (Taipei: Shang-wu, 1966).

T'o-t'o 托托 (ed.). *Sung-shih* 宋史 (Peking: Chung-hua, 1977). [*SS*]

Ts'ai, Shang-hsiang 蔡上翔. *Wang Ching-kung nien-p'u k'ao-lüeh* 王荊公年譜考略 (Shanghai: Jen-min, 1974).

Ts'ao, Tui-chih 曹兌之. *Chi-pei Ts'ao hsien-sheng chi-lo chi* 濟北曹先生雞肋集, *SPTK* ed.

Tseng, Min-hsing 曾敏行. *Tu-hsing tsa-chih* 獨醒雜誌, *TSCC* ed.

Ts'ung-shu chi-ch'eng 叢書集成 (Shanghai: Shang-wu, 1935–1937). [*TSCC*]

Tu, Ch'un-sheng 杜春生. *Yüeh-chung chin-shih chi* 越中金石記. In Yen Keng-wang (ed.), *Shih-k'o shih-liao ts'ung-shu* (q.v.).

Tu, Wei-yün 杜維運 et al. (eds.). *Chung-kuo shih-hsüeh shih lun-wen hsüan-chi* 中國史學史論文選集, 3 vols. (Taipei: Hua-shih 華世, 1976–1980).

Tu, Yu 杜佑. *T'ung-tien* 通典, *Wan-yu wen-k'u* ed. (q.v.).

Wan-yu wen-k'u 萬有文庫 (Shanghai: Shang-wu, 1933).

Wang, An-shih 王安石. *Lin-ch'uan hsien-sheng wen-chi* 臨川先生文集 (Hong Kong: Chung-hua, 1971).

Wang, Ch'ang 王昶. *Chin-shih ts'ui-pien* 金石萃編, Sao-yeh shan-fang 掃葉山房 ed. (Shanghai, 1919).

Wang, Chien-ch'iu 王建秋. *Sung-tai t'ai-hsüeh yü t'ai-hsüeh sheng* 宋代太學與太學生 (Taipei: Chung-kuo hsüeh-shu chu-tso chiang-chu ch'u-pan wei-yüan hui 中國學術著作獎助出版委員會, 1965). [*Sung-tai t'ai-hsüeh*]

Wang, Ch'uan-shan 王船山. *Sung-lun* 宋論 (Peking: Chung-hua, 1965).

Wang, Ch'ung-min 王重民. *Tun-huang ku-chi hsü-lu* 敦煌古籍敍錄 (Peking: Chung-hua, 1979).

Wang, P'i-chih 王闢之. *Min-shui yen-t'an lu* 澠水燕談錄, *Chih-pu-tsu chai ts'ung-shu* 知不足齋叢書 ed. (1921).

Wang, Shih-han 汪師韓. *Han-men chui-hsüeh* 韓門綴學, *Shang-hu i-chi* 上湖遺集 ed.

Wang, Shou-nan 王壽南 (ed.). *Chung-kuo li-tai ssu-hsiang chia* 中國歷代思想家 (Taipei: Shang-wu, 1977).

Wang, Te-i 王德毅. *Sung-jen chuan-chi tzu-liao so-yin* 宋人傳記資料索引 (Taipei: Tien-wen 典文, 1974–1976).

Wang, Ting-pao 王定保. *T'ang chih-yen* 唐摭言 (Shanghai: Ku-chi, 1978).

Wang, Tseng-yü 王曾瑜. "Sung-ch'ao chieh-chi chieh-kou k'ai-shu" 宋朝階級結構概述. In *She-hui k'o-hsüeh chan-hsien* 社會科學戰線, 1979/4, 128–136.

Wang, Ying-lin 王應麟. *Yü-hai* 玉海, Yüan ed. (Taipei: Hua-lien 華聯, 1964 reprint). [*YH*]

Wang, Yün-wu 王雲五. *Sung Yüan chiao-hsüeh ssu-hsiang* 宋元教學思想 (Taipei: Shang-wu, 1971).

Wang, Yung 王栐. *Yen-i i-mou lu* 燕翼貽謀錄, *TSCC* ed.

Wei, Cheng 魏徵 et al. *Sui-shu* 隋書 (Peking: Chung-hua, 1973).

Weng, T'ung-wen 翁同文. "Yin-shua shu tui-yü shu-chi ch'eng-pen te ying-hsiang" 印刷術對於書籍成本的影響. In *Ch'ing-hua hsüeh-pao* 清華學報, Vol. 6, Nos. 1 & 2 (1967), 35–43.

Weng, Yen-chen 翁衍楨. "Ku-tai erh-t'ung tu-wu" 古代兒童讀物. In *T'u-shu-kuan hsüeh chi-k'an* 圖書館學季刊, Vol. 10, No. 1 (1936), 91–146.

Wu, Han 吳晗. "Ming-ch'ao te hsüeh-hsiao" 明朝的學校. In his *Tu-shih cha-chi* 讀史劄記 (Peking: San-lien 三聯, 1961), 317–341.

Wu, Hsiu-chih 吳秀之 et al. *Wu-hsien chih* 吳縣志, 1933 ed. (Taipei: Ch'eng-wen, 1970 reprint).

Wu, Tzu-liang 吳自良. *Lin-hsia ou-t'an* 林下偶談, *TSCC* ed.

Wu, Tzu-mu 吳自牧. *Meng-liang lu* 夢粱錄 (Shanghai: Ku-chi, 1956).

Yang, Chi-jen 楊吉仁. *San-kuo liang-Chin hsüeh-hsiao yü hsüan-shih chih-tu* 三國兩晉學校與選士制度 (Taipei: Cheng-chung 正中, 1968). ["Hsüan-shih chih-tu"]

Yang, Chia-lo 楊家駱. "Hsü Tzu-chih t'ung-chien ch'ang-pien chi-lüeh" 續資治通鑑長編輯略. In *HCP*, Vol. I, 1/1a–2/2b.

——————. "Hsü Tzu-chih t'ung-chien ch'ang-pien hsin-ting-pen hsü" 新定本序. In *HCP*, Vol. I, 1–17.

Yang, Chung-liang 楊仲良. *Hsü Tzu-chih t'ung-chien ch'ang-pien chi-shih pen-mo* 記事本末, 1893 Kuang-ya shu-chü 廣雅書局 *Chi-shih pen-mo hui-k'o* 彙刻 ed. (Taipei: Wen-hai, 1967). [*Chi-shih pen-mo*]

Yang, Hsi-min 楊希憫. *Tseng Wen-ting kung nien-p'u* 曾文定公年譜, *Shih-wu chia nien-p'u* 十五家年譜 ed. (1857–1907).

Yang, K'uan 楊寬. "Wo-kuo ku-tai ta-hsüeh te t'e-tien chi ch'i ch'i-yüan" 我國古代大學的特點及其起源. In his *Ku-shih hsin-t'an* (q.v.), 197–217. ["Ku-tai ta-hsüeh"]

——————. *Ku-shih hsin-t'an* 古史新談 (Peking: Chung-hua, 1965).

Yang, Shu-fan 楊樹藩. "Han Fei" 韓非. In Wang Shou-nan (ed.), *Chung-kuo li-tai ssu-hsiang chia* (q.v.), Vol. II, 721–801.

——————. *Chung-kuo wen-kuan chih-tu shih* 中國文官制度史 (Taipei: San-min 三民, 1976). [*Wen-kuan chih-tu*]

Yang, Tse-ming 楊澤名. "Ming-t'ang chien-chu lüeh-k'ao" 明堂建築略考. In *Chung-kuo chien-chu* 中國建築, Vol. 3, No. 2 (1935), 57–60.

Yang, Wan-li 楊萬里. *Ch'eng-chai chi* 誠齋集, *SPTK* ed.

Yeh, Meng-te 葉夢得. *Pi-shu lu-hua* 避暑錄話, *Hsüeh-chin t'ao-yüan* ed. (1922).

Yeh, Shih 葉適. *Shui-hsin chi* 水心集, *SPPY* ed.

Yeh, Te-hui 葉德輝. *Shu-lin ch'ing-hua* 書林清話.

Yen, Hsü-hsin 顏虛心. *Ch'en Lung-ch'uan nien-p'u* 陳龍川年譜 (Ch'ang-sha 長沙: Shang-wu, 1940).

Yen, Keng-wang 嚴耕望. *Chung-kuo ti-fang hsing-cheng chih-tu shih* 中國地方行政制度史, Part I (Taipei: Chung-yang yen-chiu yüan Li-shih yü-yen yen-chiu so 中央研究院歷史語言研究所, 1961), Part II (same publisher, 1963).

————— . "Hsin-lo liu-T'ang hsüeh-sheng yü seng-t'u" 新羅留唐學生與僧徒 . In his *T'ang-shih yen-chiu lun-ts'ung* (q.v.), 425–481.

————— (ed.). *Shih-k'o shih-liao ts'ung-shu* 石刻史料叢書 (Taipei: I-wen, 1967).

————— . "T'ang-jen hsi-yeh shan-lin ssu-yüan chih feng-shang" 唐人習業山林寺院之風 尚. In his *T'ang-shih yen-chiu lun-ts'ung* (q.v.), 367–424.

————— . *T'ang-shih yen-chiu lun-ts'ung* 唐史研究論叢 (Hong Kong: Hsin-ya yen-chiu so 新亞研究所 , 1969).

Yü, Wen-pao 俞文豹 . *Ch'ui-chien lu* 吹劍錄 (Taipei: Shih-chieh, 1968).

Yü, Ying-shih 余英時 . *Chung-kuo chih-shih chieh-ts'eng shih-lun* 中國知識階層史論 (Taipei: Lien-ching, 1970).

————— . "Chung-kuo shih-hsüeh te hsien chieh-tuan: fan-sheng yü chan-wang" 中國史 學的現階段：反省與展望. In *Shih-hsüeh p'ing-lun* 史學評論 , No. 1 (1979), 1–24.

II. Works in Western Languages

Aoyama, Sadao. "The Newly-Risen Bureaucrats in Fukien at the Five-dynasty–Sung Period." In *Memoire of the Research Department of the Tōyō Bunko*, 21 (1962), 1–48.

Ariès, Philippe. *Centuries of Childhood*. Tr. by Robert Baldick (New York: Alfred A. Knopf, 1962).

de Bary, Wm. Theodore. "A Reappraisal of Neo-Confucianism." In Arthur F. Wright (ed.), *Studies in Chinese Thought* (q.v.).

————— . *The Liberal Tradition in China* (Hong Kong: The Chinese University Press, 1983).

————— (ed.). *Sources of Chinese Tradition* (New York: Columbia University Press, 1960).

Beasley, W. G. and E. G. Pulleyblank (eds.). *Historians of China and Japan* (Oxford: Oxford University Press, 1961).

Beattie, Hilary J. *Land and Lineage in China* (Cambridge: Cambridge University Press, 1979).

Brumbaugh, Robert and Nathaniel M. Lawrence. *Philosophical Themes in Modern Education* (Boston: Houghton Mifflin, 1973).

Buriks, Peter. "Fan Chung-yens Versuch einer Reform des chinesischen beamterstaats, 1043–1044." In *Oriens Extremus*, No. 3 (1956), 57–80; No. 4 (1957), 153–184.

Chaffee, John. "Education and Examinations in Sung Society." Ph.D. thesis, University of Chicago, 1979.

Chan, Hok-lam. " 'Comprehensiveness' (*T'ung*) and 'Change' (*Pien*) in Ma Tuan-lin's Historical Thought." In Hok-lam Chan and Wm. Theodore de Bary (eds.), *Yüan Thought* (New York: Columbia University Press, 1982), 27–88.

Chan, Wing-tsit. *A Source Book in Chinese Philosophy* (Princeton: Princeton University Press, 1963).

Chang, Chung-li. *The Chinese Gentry* (Seattle: University of Washington Press, 1955).

Chen, Kenneth K. S. *The Chinese Transformation of Buddhism* (Princeton: Princeton University Press, 1973).

Chow, Tse-tsung. *The May Fourth Movement* (Stanford: Stanford University Press, 1960).

Chu, Hsi and Lü Tsu-ch'ien (eds.). *Reflections on Things at Hand*. Tr. by Wing-tsit Chan (New York: Columbia University Press, 1967).

Ch'u, T'ung-tsu. *Han Social Structure*. Ed. by Jack Dull (Seattle: University of Washington Press, 1972).

Creel, H. G. *Confucius and the Chinese Way* (New York: Harper & Row, 1960).

————— . *The Origins of Chinese Statecraft* (Chicago and London: University of Chicago Press, 1970).

————— . *Shen Pu-hai* (Chicago: University of Chicago Press, 1974).

Curtis, S. J. *History of Education in Great Britain* (London: University Tutorial Press, 1948).

Dennerline, Jerry. "Book Review: Hilary J. Beattie, *Land and Lineage in China.*" In *HJAS*, Vol. 40 (1980), 549–555.

Eberhard, Wolfram. *Rulers and Conquerors* (Leiden: E. J. Brill, 1965).

Ebrey, Patricia B. *The Aristocratic Families of Early Imperial China* (Cambridge: Cambridge University Press, 1978).

————— . "Women in Kinship System of the Southern Sung Upper Class." In Richard Guisso (ed.), *Woman in China* (Toronto: University of Toronto Press, 1982), 113–129.

Eisenstein, Elizabeth. *The Printing Press as an Agent of Change*, 2 vols. (Cambridge: Cambridge University Press, 1979).

Fairbank, John King (ed.). *Chinese Thought and Institutions* (Chicago: University of Chicago Press, 1957).

Fei, John C. H. and Ts'ui-jung Liu. "The Growth and Decline of Chinese Family Clans." In *Journal of Interdisciplinary History*, Vol. XII, No. 3 (1982), 375–408.

Franke, Herbert. "Chia Ssu-tao (1213–1275): A 'Bad Last Minister'?" In Aurhur F. Wright and Denis C. Twitchett (eds.), *Confucian Personalities* (q.v.), 217–234.

Freedman, Maurice. *Chinese Lineage and Society: Fukien and Kwangtung* (London: University of London Press, 1966).

————— . *Lineage Organization in Southeastern China* (London: University Press, 1958).

Galt, Howard. *A History of Chinese Educational Institutions* (London: A. Probsthain, 1951).

Gernet, Jacques. *Daily Life in China on the Eve of the Mongol Invasion*. Tr. by Hope Wright (Stanford: Stanford University Press, 1965).

Gough, Kathleen. "Implications of Literacy in Traditional China and India." In Jack Goody (ed.), *Literacy in Traditional Societies* (Cambridge: Cambridge University Press, 1968), 69–84.

Graham, A. C. *Two Chinese Philosophers* (London: Lund Humpheries, 1958).

Grimm, Tilemann. "Inauguration of *T'i-chü hsüeh-shih ssu* (Education Intendants) during the Northern Sung Dynasty." In *Études Song*, Vol. 1 (1976), 259–274.

————— . "Ming Educational Intendants." In Charles O. Hucker (ed.), *Chinese Government in Ming Times, Seven Studies* (q.v.), 129–148.

Haeger, John W. (ed.). *Crisis and Prosperity in Sung China* (Tucson: University of Arizona Press, 1975).

————— . "1126–27: Political Crisis and the Integrity of Culture." In John W. Haeger (ed.), *Crisis and Prosperity in Sung China* (q.v.), 143–162.

Hartwell, Robert. "Financial Expertise, Examinations, and the Formulation of Economic Policy in Northern Sung China." In *JAS*, Vol. 30 (1971), 281–314.

————— . "Historical Analogism, Public Policy and Social Science in Eleventh and Twelfth Century China." In *American Historical Review*, Vol. 76, No. 3 (1971), 690–727.

Hervouet, Yves (ed.). *A Sung Bibliography* (Hong Kong: The Chinese University Press, 1979).

Ho, Ping-ti. *The Ladder of Success in Imperial China* (New York: Columbia University Press, 1962). [*The Ladder*]

——— . "Aspects of Social Mobility in Imperial China." In *Comparative Studies in Society and History*, Vol. 1 (1959), 330–359.

Houn, Franklin. "The Civil Recruitment System of the Han Dynasty." In *Ch'ing-hua hsüeh-pao*, Vol. 1 (1956), 138–164.

Hsiao, Kung-chuan. *A History of Chinese Political Thought*. Tr. by F. W. Mote, Vol. I (Princeton: Princeton University Press, 1979).

——— . *Rural China, Imperial Control in the Nineteenth Century* (Seattle: University of Washington Press, 1960).

Hsieh, Shan-yuan. *The Life and Thought of Li Kou, 1009–1059* (San Francisco: Chinese Materials Center, 1979).

Hsu, Francis L. "Social Mobility in China." In *American Sociological Review*, XIV (1949), 764–771.

Huang, Chün-chieh. "The Rise of the *Mencius:* Historical Interpretations of Mencian Morality." Ph.D. thesis, University of Washington, 1980.

Hucker, Charles O. (ed.). *Chinese Government in Ming Times, Seven Studies* (New York: Columbia University Press, 1969).

Johnson, David. *The Medieval Chinese Oligarchy* (Boulder: Westview Press, 1977).

Kracke, Edward A. *Civil Service in Early Sung China, 960–1067* (Cambridge: Harvard University Press, 1953). [*Civil Service*]

——— . "The Expansion of Educational Opportunities in the Reign of Hui-tsung of the Sung and Its Implications." In *Sung Studies Newsletter*, No. 13 (1977), 6–30.

——— . "Family vs. Merit in Chinese Civil Service Examinations under the Empire." In *HJAS*, Vol. 10 (1947), 103–123.

——— . "Region, Family and Individual in the Chinese Examination System." In John K. Fairbank (ed.), *Chinese Thought and Institutions* (q.v.), 251–268.

Lau, D. C. "Theories of Human Nature in *Mencius* and *Shyuntzyy.*" In *Bulletin of School of Oriental and African Studies*, No. 15, Pt. 3 (1953), 541–565.

Lee, Thomas H. C. "Chu Hsi, Academies and the Tradition of Private *Chiang-hsüeh.*" In *Chinese Studies*, Vol. 2, No. 1 (1984), 301–329.

——— . "The Discovery of Childhood: Children and Education in Sung China." In Sigrid Paul (ed.), *Kultur, Begriff und Wort in China und Japan* (Berlin: Dietrich Reimer, 1984), 159–189.

——— . "Education in Northern Sung China." Ph.D. thesis, Yale University, 1974.

——— . "Life in the Schools of Sung China." In *JAS*, Vol. 37 (1977), 45–60. ["Life in Sung Schools"]

——— . "The Social Significance of the Quota System in Sung Civil Service Examinations." *JICS/CUHK*, 13 (1982), 287–318. ["Quota System"]

——— . "Technical Officers, Legal Bureaucrats and Special Training Schools in Sung China." In *Ch'ing-hua hsüeh-pao* (forthcoming). ["Technical Officers"]

Lenski, Gehard. *Power and Privilege* (New York: McGraw-Hill, 1966).

Liu, James T. C. *Ou-yang Hsiu* (Stanford: Stanford University Press, 1967).

——— . "Some Classifications of Bureaucrats in Chinese Historiography." In David S. Nivison and Arthur F. Wright (eds.), *Confucianism in Action* (q.v.), 165–181.

Liu, Wu-chi and Irving Y. Lo (eds.). *Sunflower Splendor* (New York: Doubleday, 1975).

Lo, Jung-pang. "The Rise of China as a Sea Power." In *Far Eastern Quarterly*, 14 (1955), 489–503.

Marx, Karl. *Critique of Hegel's "Philosophy of Right"*. Ed. by Joseph O'Malley (Cambridge: Cambridge University Press, 1970).

Maspero, Henri. "Le *Ming-t'ang* et la crise religieuse chinoise avant les Han." In *Mélanges chinoises et bouddhiques*, No. 8 (1948–51), 1–71.

McKnight, Brian. "Administrators of Hangchow under the Northern Sung." In *HJAS*, Vol. 30 (1970), 185–211.

————. "Fiscal Privilege and Social Order in Sung China." In John W. Haeger (ed.), *Crisis and Prosperity in Sung China* (q.v.), 79–100.

————. *Village and Bureaucracy in Southern Sung China* (Chicago: University of Chicago Press, 1971).

Menzel, Johanna M. (ed.). *The Chinese Civil Service* (Lexington, Mass.: D. C. Health and Co., 1963).

Miller, S. M. and P. Roby. "Strategies for Social Mobility: A Policy Framework." In *American Sociologist*, Vol. 6 (1971), 18–22.

Miyazaki, Ichisada. *China's Examination Hell*. Tr. by Conrad Schirokauer (New York: Weatherhill, 1976).

Munro, Donald. *The Concept of Man in Early China* (Stanford: Stanford University Press, 1969). [*The Concept of Man*]

Needham, Joseph. *Science and Civilisation in China*, several volumes (Cambridge: Cambridge University Press, 1955–   ). [*Science and Civilisation*]

Needham, Joseph and Lu Gwei-djen. "China and the Origin of Qualifying Examinations in Medicine." In idem (eds.), *Clerks and Craftsmen in China and the West* (Cambridge: Cambridge University Press, 1970).

Nivison, David S. "Protest Against Conventions and Conventions of Protest." In A. F. Wright (ed.), *The Confucian Persuasion* (q.v.), 177–201.

Nivison, David S. and Arthur F. Wright (eds.). *Confucianism in Action* (Stanford: Stanford University Press, 1959).

Olafson, Frederick A. *Justice and Social Policy* (Englewood Cliffs, N. J.: Prentice-Hall, 1961).

Oppenheim, Felix E. "Equality: The Concept of Equality." In *The International Encyclopedia of Social Sciences* (New York: MacMillan & The Free Press, 1968).

Parsons, James B. "The Ming Dynasty Bureaucracy: Aspects of Background Forces." In Charles O. Hucker (ed.), *Chinese Government in Ming Times* (q.v.), 175–227.

Rawls, John. *A Theory of Justice* (Cambridge: Harvard University Press, 1971).

Rawski, Evelyn S. *Education and Popular Literacy in Ch'ing China* (Ann Arbor: University of Michigan Press, 1979).

Schirokauer, Conrad. "Neo-Confucians under Attack: The Condemnation of *Wei-hsüeh.*" In John W. Haeger (ed.), *Crisis and Prosperity in Sung China* (q.v.), 163–198.

Schwartz, Benjamin. "Area Studies as a Critical Discipline." In *JAS*, Vol. 40, No. 1 (1981), 15–26.

Sivin, Nathan. "Book Review: Lam Lay Yong, *A Critical Study of the Yang Hui Suan Fa.*" In *Bulletin of Sung-Yüan Studies*, No. 16 (1981), 91–94.

Skinner, G. William (ed.). *The City in Late Imperial China* (Stanford: Stanford University Press, 1977).

————. "Mobility Strategies in Late Imperial China: A Regional System Analysis." In Carol A. Smith (ed.), *Regional Analysis* (New York: Academic Press, 1976), Vol. I, 327–364.

Sutherland, Gillian. "The Study of the History of Education." In *History*, 54 (1969), 49–59.

Talbott, John. "Education in Intellectual and Social History." In Felix Gilbert and

Stephen R. Graubard (eds.), *Historical Studies Today* (New York: W. W. Norton & Co., 1972), 193–201.

Tillman, Hoyt C. "Proto-nationalism in Twelfth-century China?" In *HJAS*, Vol. 39, No. 2 (1979), 403–428.

Trauzettel, R. *Ts'ai Ching als Typus des illegitimen ministers* (Berlin: K. Urlaub, 1964).

Twitchett, Denis C. *Cambridge History of China,* Vol. 3 (1979).

————. "The Composition of the T'ang Ruling Class." In Arthur F. Wright and Denis C. Twitchett (eds.), *Perspectives on the T'ang* (q.v.), 47–86.

————. "A Critique of Some Recent Studies of Modern Chinese Social-Economic History." In *Transactions of the International Conference of Orientalists in Japan,* Vol. X (1965), 28–41.

————. "Fan Clan's Charitable Estate." In David S. Nivison and Arthur F. Wright (eds.), *Confucianism in Action* (q.v.), 97–133.

————. "Problems of Chinese Biographies." In Arthur F. Wright and Denis C. Twitchett (eds.), *Confucian Personalities* (q.v.), 24–39.

Wakeman, Frederick. "The Price of Autonomy: Intellectuals in Ming and Ch'ing China." In *Daedalus* (Spring, 1972), 35–70.

Waley, Arthur. *The Life and Times of Po Chü-i* (London: Allen & Unwin, 1949).

————. *Three Ways of Thought in Ancient China* (Garden City, N.Y.: Doubleday Anchor Books, 1956).

Watt, Ian. *The Rise of the Novel* (Berkeley: University of California Press, 1967).

Wechsler, Howard. "Factionalism in Early T'ang Government." In Arthur F. Wright and Denis Twitchett (eds.), *Perspectives on the T'ang* (q.v.), 87–120.

Weng, T'ung-wen. *Réportorie des dates hommes célèbre des Song* (Paris: Mouton & Co., 1962).

Wenley, A. G. "A Note on the So-called Sung Academy of Painting." In *HJAS*, Vol. 6 (1941), 269–272.

Williamson, H. R. *Wang An Shih, Chinese Statesman and Educationalist of the Sung Dynasty* (London: Arthur Probsthain, 1935), 2 vols. [*Wang An Shih*]

Woodward, William H. (ed.). *Vittorino da Feltre and Other Humanist Educators* (New York: Teachers College, Columbia University Press, 1963).

Worthy, Edmund H. "Regional Control in the Southern Sung Salt Administration." In John W. Haeger (ed.), *Crisis and Prosperity in Sung China* (q.v.), 101–142.

Wright, Arthur F. "Historiography: Chinese." In *International Encyclopedia of Social Sciences* (New York: MacMillan, 1968), Vol. 6, 400–407.

———— (ed.). *The Confucian Persuasion* (Stanford: Stanford University Press, 1960).

———— (ed.). *Studies in Chinese Thought* (Chicago: University of Chicago Press, 1953).

Wright, Arthur F. and Denis C. Twitchett (eds.). *Confucian Personalities* (Stanford: Stanford University Press, 1962).

———— (eds.). *Perspectives on the T'ang* (New Haven: Yale University Press, 1973).

Yü, Ying-shih. "The Study of Chinese History: Retrospect and Prospect." Tr. by Thomas H. C. Lee and Chün-chieh Huang, in *Renditions,* No. 15 (1981), 7–26.

Glossary-Index